D0213078

Piedmont
College Library

Demorest, Ga.

82517

D
111
.M5
v.9

940.5 M468

Medievalia et
humanistica.

MEDIEVALIA ET HUMANISTICA

MEDIEVALIA ET HUMANISTICA

New Series
Edited by Paul Maurice Clogan

MEDIEVALIA ET HUMANISTICA

STUDIES IN MEDIEVAL & RENAISSANCE CULTURE

NEW SERIES: NUMBER 9

EDITED BY

PAUL MAURICE CLOGAN

CAMBRIDGE UNIVERSITY PRESS

CAMBRIDGE

LONDON · NEW YORK · MELBOURNE

Published by the Syndics of the Cambridge University Press
The Pitt Building, Trumpington Street, Cambridge CB2 1RP
Bentley House, 200 Euston Road, London NW1 2DB
32 East 57th Street, New York, NY 10022, USA
296 Beaconsfield Parade, Middle Park, Melbourne 3206, Australia

© The Medieval and Renaissance Society 1979

Library of Congress Catalogue Card Number: 75-32451

ISBN 0 521 22446 2
ISSN 0076 6127

First published 1979

Printed in the United States of America
Typeset, printed, and bound by
Vail-Ballou Press, Inc., Binghamton, New York

5/7/79 Ret. 29 50

Contents

Editorial Note

Since 1970, the new series has sought to promote significant scholarship, criticism, and reviews in the several fields of medieval and Renaissance studies. It has published articles drawn from a wide variety of disciplines and given attention to new directions in humanistic scholarship and to significant topics of general interest. This series has been particularly concerned with exchange between specializations, and scholars of diverse approaches have complemented each other's efforts on questions of common interest.

Medievalia et Humanistica is sponsored by the Modern Language Association of America, and publication in the series is open to contributions from all sources. The Editorial Board welcomes scholarly, critical, or interdisciplinary articles of significant interest on significant material and urges contributors to communicate in a clear and concise style the larger implications in addition to the material of their research. Texts, maps, illustrations, diagrams, and musical examples will be published when they are essential to the argument of the article. In preparing and submitting manuscripts for consideration, potential contributors are advised to follow carefully the instructions given below on page xv. Articles may be submitted to any of the editors. Books for review and inquiries concerning *Fasciculi* I–XVII in the original series should be addressed to the Editor, *Medievalia et Humanistica*, P.O. Box 13348, North Texas Station, Denton, Texas 76203.

Inquiries concerning subscriptions should be addressed to the Publisher, Cambridge University Press, 510 North Avenue, New Rochelle, New York 10801, or at P.O. Box 110, Cambridge CB2 3RL.

Preface

The aim of the new series of *Medievalia et Humanistica* has been to promote significant scholarship, criticism, and reviews in the fields of medieval and Renaissance studies and to give attention to new directions in humanistic scholarship and to significant topics of general interest. Although previous volumes in the new series have been concerned with particular themes, this volume, which is untitled, is not limited to a particular theme. It presents a range of scholarly and critical articles of significant interest on significant material.

One of the reviewers of Margaret Aston's study of the legacy of Johan Huizinga called it "a beautifully written object lesson in how traditional (political-institutional) historians, literary historians, and historians of a socioanthropological bent can and must mutually influence, benefit, and learn from each other." Her article is both an analysis of Huizinga's ambiguities and stimulating provocations and an exposition of the impact of his book, *The Waning of the Middle Ages,* on the historiography of fifteenth-century English society and culture, wherein cultural history gradually, under Huizinga's stimulus, makes a presence for itself. Along with Maurice Keen's more narrowly focused study of chivalric culture in *Medievalia et Humanistica,* Number 8, Aston's article contributes to a major reevaluation of the subject.

The next two articles share a concern with the relationship of history and literature. Bringing together a number of dispersed texts, Rossell Hope Robbins shows that the open expression of dissent and protest is an honored and honorable stream in Middle English literature. Michael Bath's interesting and well-argued essay on the legend of Caesar's deer lucidly sets forth a new set of observations which are of considerable relevance for the study of *renovatio imperii* at several moments of European history. His investigation is far-reaching and demonstrates convincingly the existence as well as the tenacity of such subliterary traditions and conventions of what might then be called "sub-literary literary iconography."

Betsy Bowden picks up one of the challenges of Francis L. Utley in his article "Must We Abandon the Concept of Courtly Love?" (*Medievalia et Humanistica,* Number 3) and contributes a very thorough study of Latin puns in the *De amore* of Andreas Capellanus. Bowden raises a number of important and valid insights about sexual innuendo in certain

ix

passages of the classic text on Courtly Love and links her discussion to a larger context or level of intent, possible audience reactions, and acceptable ranges of interpretation of these contexts in light of the writer's new insights. Bowden demonstrates both analytical and interpretative flair coupled with an original thesis.

The handling of theological concepts in literature is the concern of the next two essays. Lawrence M. Clopper studies the sources of Langland's Trinitarian analogies, explicates the nature of the relationship among Divine Persons in Trinitarian theology, and then uses this study and explication to illuminate the meaning of the terms of Dowel, Dobet, and Dobest, and the quadripartite relationship among *Visio* and the threefold *Vita*. Theresa Coletti's essay on the Towneley *Play of the Talents* is best described by one member of the editorial board: "Essays on the art of the medieval cycle plays often skate on the surface of a play and ignore intellectual and cultural history; or, conversely, they are all erudition and lack sensitivity to the art of a play. Coletti manages to be both learned and perceptive of textual and artistic matters."

The late fourteenth and early fifteenth centuries have been seen to possess much more originality and importance than late nineteenth-century critics tended to accord the period. Mary Ann Ignatius' article constitutes a positive contribution to the revisionist view of the period and particularly to the importance accorded to the role of Christine de Pizan, who up to now has been considered merely a "feminist" or a writer of questionable literary merit and originality. Ignatius' study is at once broad (focusing on audience and book theory) and specific in its reassessment of one of Christine de Pizan's most important and least understood works.

Chaucer and Malory are the subjects of the next essays. Barry Windeatt amply and pointedly illustrates Chaucer's interest in gesture as broadly defined. This fresh topic enlarges our knowledge of Chaucer's art and should be of general interest to those in related fields. The reader is bound to become enthusiastic about Dhira B. Mahoney's reappraisal of Malory's "Tale of Tristram." The pursuit of worship and the heroic problem it presents is an original and arresting thesis. Mahoney's conclusion that the "Tale of Tristram" is central to the *Morte Darthur* is well argued and convincingly established as against recent major critics.

The use of tradition and convention figures largely in the discussions of the next two essays. Walter M. Gordon throws interesting background and foreground light upon More's *Utopia* and the utopian tradition. One board member sums it up: "I like this essay on More and monasticism very much. It comes to me as a reasonably new idea, and an entirely convincing one. The details of comparison between life in Utopia and in the monastery are right. I was instructed throughout, and find the writing clear and graceful. The author's explanation of the difference between

Plato and More in terms of *laborare est orare* again struck me as profoundly right." R. B. Gill's comprehensive essay on the Renaissance Conventions of Envy surveys the patterns of Envy from the beginnings of time down through the late sixteenth century. The number of examples of the topos here assembled is quite impressive.

A special feature of the new series has been the appearance of review notices. This volume concludes with nine review notices of significant recent publications. In terms of scholarly significance and, I sincerely hope, reader interest, this volume should be especially rewarding.

P. M. C.

MEDIEVALIA ET HUMANISTICA

Paul Maurice Clogan, EDITOR
North Texas State University

Julie Sydney Davis, ASSISTANT EDITOR

EDITORIAL BOARD

Michael Altschul
Case Western Reserve University

David Bevington
University of Chicago

Giuseppe Billanovich
Universita Cattolica del Santo Cuore

Robert Brentano
University of California at Berkeley

Derek Brewer
University of Cambridge

Marvin L. Colker
University of Virginia

John Conley
University of Illinois at Chicago Circle

Giles Constable
Harvard University

Michael Curschmann
Princeton University

Charles T. Davis
Tulane University

Peter Dronke
University of Cambridge

Stanley E. Fish
Johns Hopkins University

Creighton Gilbert
Cornell University

J. R. Hale
University College London

Denys Hay
University of Edinburgh

W. T. H. Jackson
Columbia University

Jean-Claude Margolin
*Centre d'Études Supérieures de la Renaissance
Université de Tours*

Berthe M. Marti
University of North Carolina at Chapel Hill

Ian D. McFarlane
University of Oxford

Stephen G. Nichols, Jr.
Dartmouth College

Rossell Hope Robbins
State University of New York at Albany

Paul G. Schmidt
Universität Göttingen

Richard S. Sylvester
Formerly of Yale University

Jerome Taylor
University of Wisconsin at Madison

Charles Trinkaus
University of Michigan at Ann Arbor

Charles Witke
University of Michigan at Ann Arbor

Articles for Future Volumes Are Invited

Articles may be submitted to any of the editors, but it would be advisable to submit to the nearest or most appropriate editor for consideration. A prospective author is encouraged to contact his editor at the earliest opportunity to receive any necessary advice. The length of the article depends upon the material, but brief articles or notes are not normally considered. The entire manuscript should be typed, double-spaced, on standard 8½- by 11-inch bond paper with ample margins and with documentation held to a minimum. Endnotes, prepared according to *A Manual of Style*, twelfth edition (University of Chicago Press), should be double-spaced, numbered consecutively, and placed at the end of the article. All quotations and references should be carefully verified before submission. The completed article should be in finished form, appropriate for printing. Only the original manuscript (not photocopy or carbon) should be submitted, accompanied by a stamped, self-addressed manuscript envelope.

The addresses of the American editors can be determined by their academic affiliations. The addresses of the editors outside the United States are:

Professor Giuseppe Billanovich, Via Giovanni Rusca 15, Padova 35100, Italia (Medieval and Humanistic Philology)

Dr. Derek Brewer, Emmanuel College, Cambridge, CB2 3AP, England (Medieval Literature)

Mr. Peter Dronke, Clare Hall, Cambridge CB3 9DA, England (Medieval Latin Poetry and Thought)

Professor J. R. Hale, Department of Italian, University College London, Gower Street, London WC1E 6BT, England (Renaissance History)

Professor Denys Hay, Department of History, University of Edinburgh, William Robertson Building, George Square, Edinburgh EH8 9JY, Scotland (Renaissance History)

Professor Ian D. McFarlane, Wadham College, Oxford OX1 3NA, England (Renaissance French and Neo-Latin Literature)

Professor Jean-Claude Margolin, 75 Bld Richard-Lenoir, 75011 Paris, France (Humanism, Renaissance Philosophy and Neo-Latin)

Professor Dr. Paul G. Schmidt, Seminar für Klassische Philologie der Universität, 34 Göttingen, Nikolausberger Weg 9c, West Germany (Medieval Latin Philology)

Huizinga's Harvest:
England and The Waning of the Middle Ages

MARGARET ASTON

Titles, like names, are dangerous. They have a way of coming to exist in their own right to the prejudice, it may seem, of the objects or people who bear them. Study of the relationship of words to things is as old as philosophy itself, but the pursuit of anonymity in literature is relatively recent and no way has yet been found for enabling books, as opposed to authors, to be nameless.[1] Their fortunes may be deeply affected by their titles. Such, I think, has been the fate of Johan Huizinga's most famous book as presented to English readers.

Huizinga's *Herfsttij der Middeleeuwen* was published at Haarlem in 1919 when the author was in his mid-forties. It bore the subtitle of *Studie over levens- en gedachtenvormen der veertiende en vijftiende eeuw in Frankrijk en de Nederlanden*. Literally translated, therefore, the work was entitled "Autumn of the Middle Ages: A study of the forms of life and thought of the fourteenth and fifteenth centuries in France and the Netherlands." When *Herfsttij* was reissued in Dutch in 1921 the author himself, in order to meet the challenge of some of his critics, drew emphatic attention to the subtitle as defining the boundaries of the work's scope and sources. First receptions of the book were not auspicious. On his home ground Huizinga was regarded with some suspicion as unscholarly, if not novelistic.[2] But by 1940, five years before his death, *Herfsttij* had come of age in Europe, and the Italian edition published that year was the sixth translated version.[3] The English edition had been issued long before this in 1924, the same year as the German. But whereas the latter, faithful to the original, was entitled *Herbst des Mittelalters*, the English translation by F. Hopman appeared as we have come to know it under the name of *The Waning of the Middle Ages. A Study of the forms of life, thought and art in France and the Netherlands in the Fourteenth and Fifteenth Centuries*. Huizinga himself had cooperated in this edition. It was, as the preface explained, "not a simple translation of the original Dutch, . . . but the result of a work of adaptation, reduction, and consolidation under the author's directions."[4] The name, therefore, presumably came with Huizinga's own imprimatur, and so perhaps the introduction of the words "and art" was intended to stress once again the book's intentions and its limits. It was *not* (we can read with hindsight) offered as a complete survey covering the whole of political and social affairs, but set out to describe the ways in which people lived, thought, and expressed themselves artistically in France and the Netherlands at the end of the medieval period.

It is obvious (and has often been remarked) that the English title represented a change of meaning. Was "waning" true to the author's intentions? And did this choice of title have any bearing on the influence of the book in English? "Waning," like "Autumn," carries implications about the historical process, but there is an ambiguity in one which the other clearly lacks. Autumn is a season of ripeness and harvest as well as of overripeness and fall; it is a time of fruitfulness as well as of mists presaging winter. And implicitly where there is autumn we have in our minds the consciousness of spring – the past spring and the seeded spring to come. We know that these meanings were in Huizinga's mind when he wrote the book. He thought of his autumnal period between two historical springs. The past spring, the spring of the Middle Ages, was a topic that engaged his attention in the 1930s, when he published several studies on the "pre-Gothic" twelfth century.[5] The future spring of the Renaissance – or perhaps rather summer, since Huizinga's visualizing mind associated Renaissance with summer sunshine[6] – was a continued presence, as much assumed as acknowledged, hanging over the whole of *Herfsttij*.

It is true that in only one place in the book do we find mention of "the celebrated Swiss historian" Jacob Burckhardt, whose pupil Huizinga in effect was, and whose portrayal of the Renaissance was for him both pattern and counterpattern.[7] But the *Waning* cannot be properly understood without setting it alongside Burckhardt's *Civilization of the Renaissance in Italy*. For not only had Burckhardt set Huizinga a model in the writing of cultural history, but it was also a model which he (like others) regarded as greatly needing modification. "In many respects cultural history today has the task of breaking away from Burckhardt, without that breaking away at all injuring his greatness or reducing the debt we owe him."[8] These words appear in the revised version of an address on "Renaissance and realism" which Huizinga delivered the year after the publication of *Herfsttij*, in 1920. This, and his well-known essay on "The Problem of the Renaissance" of the same year, may be read as offshoots from the recently published book and offer invaluable clues as to the place it took in his thinking. They show that we are not wrong to regard *Herfsttij* as one among the various works which gnawed at what Huizinga described as the crumbling edges of Burckhardt's magisterial conception.[9]

We do not have to read far in the *Waning* to see that a main theme of the book is the demonstration that essential features of Burckhardt's southern Renaissance existed earlier in the world of the gothic north. The "craving for individual glory," the origins of which Burckhardt located in fifteenth-century Italy, was "essentially the same as the chivalrous ambition of earlier times, and of French origin."[10] Here, as elsewhere, the Swiss historian had exaggerated and some of the true roots of Renaissance aspiration – emulation of antiquity, quest for glory, hero worship – sprang from the chivalrous ideals of medieval Europe. If Huizinga's book terminated rather than concluded (as one of his sons later indicated), it came to an end with a chapter on "The Advent of the New Form" which made the same point. The assumed antithesis between the Middle Ages and the Renaissance was misconceived, and the contrast between Italy and the north overstated. Classicism "grew up among the luxuriant vegetation of medieval thought," and "the characteristic modes of thought of the Middle Ages did not die out till long after the Renaissance." The last paragraphs of the book harp once more upon the biological metaphor, on renewal, renovation, and the "inward ripening" of the mind.[11]

One passage in "The Problem of the Renaissance" reads almost as a summary of this aspect of the *Waning* and may be cited for the light it throws on one side of the book.

Staring into the violent sunshine of the Italian *quattrocento,* Burckhardt had only been able to see defectively what lay beyond it. The veil he saw spread over the spirit of the Middle Ages was partly caused by a flaw in his own camera. He had seen all too sharp a contrast between late medieval life in Italy and life elsewhere. That beneath the glory of the Renaissance genuinely medieval popular life continued in Italy in the same forms as in France and the Germanic countries had escaped him just as much as that the new life whose advent he hailed in Italy was also emerging in other lands where he could detect nothing but age-old repression and barbarism. He was not well enough aware of the great variety and the luxuriant life of medieval culture outside Italy. As a result he drew all too restricted spatial limits to the emerging Renaissance.[12]

Herfsttij was a demonstration that the "ripeness and fullness"[13] of Italian Renaissance achievements were a matter of quality, not of essence. The seeds of these fruits existed earlier and outside Italy.

Yet autumn is also fall, withering, and decrease. There is certainly no lack of evidence in the book to justify seeing the period as one of decay and decline. The French edition, which after various vicissitudes eventually appeared in 1932, was called simply *Le Déclin du Moyen Age* – though Lucien Febvre thought that "crépuscule," twilight, would have been more appropriate.[14] This seems not unjust when one counts up the number of references to the "declining," "waning," and "expiring" Middle Ages, and the talk of the "decadence of the medieval spirit" with which the book is studded. The very repetition of these phrases is suggestive of the depth to which Huizinga was moved by the spectacle of a culture in decline – whether it was in his own age or in another. Thoughts about America, whose civilization he was considering at the time of composing *Herfsttij*, may well have reflected back onto his views of late medieval culture. "The mentality of the declining Middle Ages often seems to us to display an incredible superficiality and feebleness,"[15] its defects being rooted in the fundamental formalism which Huizinga traced out in its chivalric, religious, and literary manifestations. In all directions he saw discernible features of decline; "the violent sentimentality, the tendency to see each thing as an independent entity, to get lost in the multiplicity of concepts,"[16] were inherent traits of the expiring Middle Ages which had come to the point of inertia and stagnation, endlessly elaborating upon old formulas instead of continuing to grow and develop anew. The prevailing habit of mind showed itself above all in the accentuation of detail. Things were taken to extremes – "developing every thought and every image to the end . . . giving concrete form to every concept of the mind." It was a manifestation of decay. "The art and literature of the fifteenth century in France and in the Netherlands are almost exclusively concerned with giving a finished and ornate form to a system of ideas which had long since ceased to grow. They are the servants of an expiring mode of thought."[17]

From this theory the book was conceived. Huizinga himself relates its inspiration, which had "hit me out of the blue" over ten years before the work was written and published. He was out for one of his regular afternoon walks in the Groningen countryside on a Sunday about 1907, when "the thought suddenly struck me that the late Middle Ages were not so much a prelude to the future as an epoch of fading and decay. This thought, if indeed it may be called a thought, hinged chiefly on the art of the brothers van Eyck and their contemporaries . . ."[18] The interpretation of the van Eycks, as some reviewers perceived, was central. It nearly gave the book its name and it provided the critical link between the work's main strands of thought. For Huizinga's eventual treatment of the art of the brothers van Eyck was as much concerned to disprove the idea that the realism of their painting could be described as "Renaissance," as it was to see reflected in their work the "twilight hour of an age." The naturalism of the van Eycks was the core of his dual response to the ideas of both *La Renaissance septentrionale* and *Die Cultur der Renaissance in Italien.*[19]

One might conclude from all this that while the choice of "waning" was not unjustified, it drew attention to what was in effect only one part of the author's thesis. The final words of the book summarized its ambivalence. "A high and strong culture is declining, but at the same time and in the same sphere new things are being born. The tide is turning, the tone of life is about to change."[20] The ambiguity in the term "Herfsttij' reflected an inherent ambiguity in the book as a whole. But objections could also, of course, be raised to the choice of this original title in Dutch. As Professor Gombrich has pointed out, it implied

Hegelian ideas of cultural evolution which Huizinga himself came explicitly to reject, and he later regretted the title he had hesitantly chosen as being too poetical.[21] This is a point to which I shall return in considering the *Waning*'s importance for English history.

The *Waning* was reviewed at some length by C. L. Kingsford in the *English Historical Review* for 1925. He drew attention to the book's underlying principle: that "we cannot understand the later middle ages unless we appreciate the mental attitude and forms of thought which created the ideals and governed the actions of the men of the time." It was doubtful however, thought Kingsford, whether "any study of fifteenth-century England on similar lines could be equally profitable, since England neither in art nor in literature has anything of equivalent value." Our chroniclers were incomparably thinner; we had no brothers van Eyck. Also, Kingsford implies, the very idea of such a study was somewhat unreal given that "the political and social evolution . . . was the real moving force of the times."[22] But was not this completely beside the point? Had not Huizinga specifically defined his objectives and limits? He did not deny (as he thereafter made clearer) that "the state and its institutions" were "the most important form of all social life," investigated by historians of the law and the constitution.[23] But cultural history was *not* to be regarded as an amalgamation of other disciplines. It may be hard to define – and harder still to write – but it must be seen to exist in its own right. Kingsford's remarks seem to reflect the stubborn conservatism which has dogged so much of the historical writing on England in the later Middle Ages.

A glance back over the writings published on English history of the fourteenth and fifteenth centuries during the last fifty years shows the solid predominance of political and constitutional affairs. The conviction that history is first and foremost the study of political forms and constitutional developments, to which thoughts about intellectual life, literature, and the arts may be tagged on, almost as afterthoughts, has had a long inning and still rides high to this day. One only has to turn to the relevant volumes of the *Oxford History* to see how historians have gone on sharing Kingsford's view.[24] The idea that history without politics is amorphous, tissue without bones, continues to be expressed and as late as 1968 a leading English historian echoed the strictures of Huizinga's contemporary, S. Muller, the archivist of Utrecht, in criticizing the *Waning* for its "failure of structure."[25] The most recently published bibliography on late medieval England reflects these traditional priorities. Constitutional and administrative history, with political history and foreign relations, here have pride of place and between them occupy more than a third of the pages and items. Proceeding via social, economic, agrarian, scientific, and military history we then reach the history of religion (which produces a total exceeding the items of the constitutional and administrative section), and finally, as the last two out of fourteen headings, the history of the fine arts and intellectual history.[26] To arrange is not necessarily to ratify, but even a list can reflect an attitude of mind.

But there have been voices crying in the wilderness, suggesting that politics and the constitution and public life are not all; that the history which looks at "forms of life and thought" may also be a valid form. As long ago as 1937 K. B. McFarlane delivered a series of lectures on "English Society in the Fifteenth Century" which in its first planning was subtitled "Things that get left out of political and constitutional history."[27] The same call came to a later generation in the valuable survey published by Professor Margaret Hastings in 1961. "This generation of historians wants to know about all the levels of past society, not just about rulers and leaders," and "there is room for a new 'high history' of the intellectual and spiritual life of the English people in the later Middle Ages, something to counteract the prejudice which students pick up from the older textbooks which treat this period as a mere interval between the thirteenth century and the Renaissance and Reformation."[28] Historians' failure to meet this challenge meant that old textbooks enjoyed extraordinarily long lives. The third volume of Stubbs's *Constitutional History* (1878) could be regarded in 1963 as "still the indispensable starting point" for study of the period.[29] Things have however changed. "Culture and Society" has become a recognized and respectable topic, not only for renaissance Italy but even for England's Middle Ages. And though the search for wider social history is not the same as the search for cultural history, the replacement of the Hegelian historical pattern by the Marxist pattern has deeply affected approaches to the latter.

How are we to explain England's long failure to build on Huizinga's model? Is it really because, as Kingsford suggested, England (unlike France and the Netherlands) lacks material for *Kulturgeschichte*? As the author of an admirable survey of *English Historical Literature in the Fifteenth Century* published some years before *Herfsttij*, he might certainly be expected to have known, but surely, even so, we must reject this judgment. To be without van Eycks does not mean a lack of painting, sculpture, and architecture; England had no Chastellain, but we have plenty of other literary sources. Indeed, the very differences of historical sources may, as Professor Hay has suggested, reflect and illuminate social and political realities.[30] It was not lack of materials but traditional thinking that dictated Kingsford's response. The first and most obvious explanation for this lack must be the perennial slowness of university studies to adapt themselves to new modes of thought.[31] Inevitably there is always a time lag between the topics that historians are researching and those they are obliged to teach or, come to that, between periodical literature and textbook literature. Probably there is always some gap between what students want to know and what teachers are ready to teach. Fifty years is a long time to wait, but perhaps we are now, thanks to a certain amount of cross-fertilization between disciplines, beginning to shed some of the prejudices that made the *Waning* seem academically questionable. Some of the hesitancies that remain may be laid at Huizinga's door and accounted for by the concept and form of the book itself.

Apart from its isolation from the norms of academic study, Huizinga's *Waning* is unique in the individuality and originality of its vision. "The book remains in one's mind as a *tour de force*," wrote an early reviewer, "a work of learning which can be read easily and which impresses itself on the memory."[32] It does not lend itself to imitation any more than its author was disposed to found a school of historians.[33] Unlike some other sorts of history that have become famous in our age, such as Lewis Namier's *Structure of Politics at the Accession of George III* (which has left its mark on English fifteenth-century history), Huizinga did not hand historians a methodological key which they could appropriate and use to open doors in their own periods.[34] Methodology as such was alien to Huizinga. Cultural history as he described it was not a subject with a technique like, say, statistics or physics, which he saw as diametrically opposed to the discipline of history.[35] There is in fact (as has already been pointed out elsewhere) only one passage in the *Waning* which bears on this question. It occurs near the beginning when the author, illustrating the violent passions of his period from chronicle sources, adds the comment that historians who depended on official documents to the exclusion of contemporary chroniclers would tend to disregard "the vehement pathos of medieval life." "A scientific historian of the Middle Ages, relying first and foremost on official documents, which rarely refer to the passions, except violence and cupidity, occasionally runs the risk of neglecting the difference of tone between the life of the expiring Middle Ages and that of our own days."[36] This sentence must be read, as Professor Hugenholtz has shown, in the context of Huizinga's profession, with its heightened sense of the potentialities of history as science and its overweening respect for documentary studies. Diplomatic spadework establishing the sources sometimes appeared to have become the very essence of history. Huizinga's remark comes in the nature of an aside and perhaps was only intended as such, but it does I think have some bearing on the long-term reception of the English *Herfsttij*. History in this century suffered overlong from the need to justify itself as a discipline in the face of the claim of science. The search for factual "certainty" took precedence over the pursuit of attitudes and opinions. Charters seemed safer than chronicles, and the discovery of new "facts" conferred an academic validation to which fresh readings of literary sources were alien.

Taken as a whole, however, the *Waning* constitutes a model – if not a paradigm – of a form of history which, despite its slowness to gain academic status, has won recognition. Huizinga himself defined the nature of this relatively new branch of history in his essay of 1929 on "The Task of Cultural History." The cultural historian is a seeker after forms of life, thought, knowledge, art. He is not after rules but the "striking significance" of phenomena, whose vividness he grasps by a process of near-revelatory intuitive cognition, and which he conveys to his readers not only as ideas, but as images and individual portraits.[37] Vividness was an essential part of the process of historical understanding, and it resided for Huizinga in the visual and in the particularized individual. His own manner of thinking was instinctively visual, so it was natural for him both to stress the importance of this approach to the past and to settle himself happily into study of a period characterized, as he put it, by the "marked tendency of thought to embody itself in images."[38] Changes in the relationship of art and life were bound therefore, on Huizinga's viewing, to affect people's thoughts about the past. To see and study more works of art opened up new vistas on the periods to which they belonged and to ideas about them. As he judged it, pessimistically, the process led to the swamping of intellectual by aesthetic activities. It may rather seem to us, after another half-century's experience of ways of seeing, that the reverse has been demonstrated, in that seeing more has brought an interest in knowing more. Huizinga, born in the period before the opening of the "Museum without walls," lived long enough to witness its beginnings and to comment on how this altered views of the Middle Ages.

Now, our perception of former times, our historical organ, so to say, is more and more becoming visual. Most educated people of to-day owe their conception of Egypt, Greece, or the Middle Ages, much more to the sight of their monuments, either in the original or by reproductions, than to reading. The change of our ideas about the Middle Ages is due less to a weakening of the romantic sense than to the substitution of artistic for intellectual appreciation.[39]

The visual, however, was only one part of the formulation of Huizinga's cultural history. This history, though it necessarily embraced politics and the whole of society, came down from the outlines of essential forms to individuals, without whom the reality of the historical process could have no existence." He [the cultural historian] not only sketches the contours of the forms he designs, but colors them by means of intuition and illuminates them with visionary suggestion."[40] These forms and colors – the threads and beads of history – could continue to be valid even when the main construction that they served was no longer acceptable. Thus Burckhardt's *Civilization*, even when its central argument had been pruned, lopped down and modified, was (and is) still read for the penetration of its understanding. As Huizinga put it: "Burckhardt's general thesis . . . has . . . had its day. But all the individual forms that he hewed and used as building stones, all his chapters about glory, ridicule and wit, domestic life, and the like, still preserve the value of that transcendent masterpiece intact."[41] And that is surely just as true of our reading of the *Waning*, from which we are separated by exactly the same span of time as Huizinga's contemporaries were separated from Burckhardt's book.

If the "feeling for forms" lies at the heart of cultural history this seems excessively vague. It was not something that could be taught or prescribed. There appears indeed to have been a certain ambiguity in Huizinga's understanding of these essential "forms." On one hand they appear to have been related to the whole "morphology of the human past" which historians are engaged in constructing: the "forms and functions of civilization" in its overall development. Such were the creations of Burckhardt, Spengler, and Huizinga himself, as summarized under the names of "Renaissance," "Decline of the West," and (for English readers) the "Waning of the Middle Ages." Interpretative forms of this kind easily become tendentious – if they do not start that way. Of this Huizinga was himself well aware. He was highly critical of Spengler's "morphology of world history."[42] Yet his own *Herfsttij* bore worrying signs of the Hegelian holism in which art, literature, and life are all to be regarded as manifestations of one "spirit of the age," which was part of an inexorable dialectical process. On the other hand, as his remarks about Burckhardt indicate, Huizinga's cultural history consisted of sectional "building stones." And these other forms, which might more appropriately be regarded as themes, interpretative *topoi*, did not of themselves necessarily carry or imply qualitative historical judgments. One might suggest here that Huizinga, like Burckhardt, bequeathed us building stones ("the hierarchic conception of society," "the idea of chivalry," "the vision of death," "religious thought crystallizing into images"), which have remained valid and fruitful even when his main interpretation of the period has not. The *Waning* is full of "forms" of both kinds, but the reason why we go on reading it is surely because we remain stimulated by the specific themes, while we may be critical of the general interpretation. That said, it has to be admitted that Huizinga shows a tendency to confuse the issue by blurring mental habits and forms of thought (whose study remains the legitimate task of cultural history) with woolly observations about "the spirit of an age" or "the soul of this epoch."[43]

Huizinga, as he himself made clear, was not writing about England (not that that prevented criticism on this score!),[44] but both his methodology – if we can call it that – and his morphology have left their mark on the study of English history. Let us take the methodology first. Historians have here been given a lead by followers of another discipline. If Huizinga's idea of cultural history has commended itself more to students of literature than to historians, one reason is obviously the nature of the sources. The study of attitudes and forms of thought must be concerned with what people composed as well as with what officials recorded. There is a sense in which, as Huizinga said (though he also qualified this statement), "literary history is cultural history."[45] So it is not really surprising to find that departments of literature have made a larger contribution towards the study of late medieval English culture than have departments of history. As one illustration of this one might set the relevant volumes of the *Oxford History of English Literature* alongside those of the *Oxford History of England*.[46] A good survey of fifteenth-century society, based on the *Paston Letters*, was written by a literary historian.[47] Another famous literary study on this period, C. S. Lewis's *Allegory of Love* (1936), though framed as an enquiry into a "dominant form" of literature, may seem to constitute a valid exemplification of one of Huizinga's building forms, by enlarging our understanding of one of the dominant strands of contemporary thought.[48] There are more recent examples. It is surely significant that Gervase Mathew's *The Court of Richard II* (1968), one of the best examples we have yet had of cultural history for this period, emerged from "many years of lecturing for the Oxford English faculty."[49] In the study of the Lollard movement historians have missed a great mass of evidence by neglecting the literary sources, and we have had to wait for a student of literature to remedy the omission which detracted from the value of part of K. B. McFarlane's *John Wycliffe and the Beginnings of English Nonconformity* (1952) and still more from J. A. F. Thomson's *The Later Lollards 1414–1520* (1965).[50] Such has been historians' frequent shortsightedness toward the resources of literature that a recent book investigating the influence of the first phase of the Hundred Years' War on "the thoughts and feelings of Englishmen," voices the very same plea that Huizinga expressed more than half a century ago.

It is unfortunate that historians' just suspicions of the value of chronicles to the study of certain aspects of political and social history should have led to a more general neglect of the genre. Particularly in the history of social and moral ideas and attitudes the evidence of the chronicles is often invaluable . . . The literature of the fourteenth century is evidently a *terra incognita* for many historians.[51]

The narrowing effects of academic boundaries have made students of literature more in touch with Huizinga's aims than historians themselves have been. If an "image" in literature is comparable to a "fact" in history, the realms of elucidating the two may be wholly different. Literary formulas cannot be accounted for without some reference to forms of thought, whereas historians may find it possible to "explain" past events by the arrangement and manipulation of further "facts" and events. One has the impression that the discussion of ideas and forms of thought are commoner currency in the study of literature than they are in the study of history, so it does not seem to be coincidence that Huizinga's task has been taken up more readily by specialists in literature and the arts than by historians. It is not simply that Huizinga made predominant use of art and literature to excavate his building stones. It is also because historians have tended to be too economical, not to say one-sided, in their quarrying of materials.

Considerations of Huizinga's morphology brings us back to his title. The implications of "waning" and "decline" have both overawed and provoked historians. England was historiographically prejudiced – almost, one might say, from the start – to regard the fourteenth and fifteenth centuries as a period of decline and decay. Tudor justificatory propaganda, which rose to the level of a national myth, exaggerated the scale of fifteenth-century disorder for the benefit of the new dynasty, and Shakespearean assumptions long governed views of the late medieval scene. Under the shadow of the Wars of the Roses and the social and economic dislocation associated with them, the later Middle Ages were all too readily written off as a time of anarchy and degeneration, in church and state alike. Even when the partisan nature of the "Tudor myth" came to be recognized, there still remained one seemingly incontrovertible aspect of decline: population decline. Could the considerable reduction in population effected by the Black Death and subsequent plague and disease have resulted in other than an overall recession: retreat from marginal lands, urban shrinkage, diminished total production? Economic recession was linked with general cultural decline. There seemed every reason to endorse Huizinga's thesis, even though he had himself (remarkably) said nothing of plague or economic depression.[52] "The verdict pronounced by Huizinga in his famous study, *The Waning of the Middle Ages*, that the Middle Ages had dragged out their last years in gloom and decay, was thus endorsed, apparently, by every fresh piece of research that was done."[53] Rather ironically, then, although his book was in a sense quite marginal to English history, it struck peculiarly sympathetic resonances in England where, thanks to the emphasis conveyed by its title, it contributed to the preexisting negative view of the period. The *Waning* helped to imprint the "myth of decline." The terms which seemed most appropriate for fifteenth-century England were "waning, sterility, abuse, corruption and decline . . . it was seen as an age of exceptional violence and lawlessness . . . an age of cultural barrenness between the time of Chaucer and Langland at one end and the Tudor poets and humanists at the other. Huizinga had done his best for France and Burgundy, but this was not England; his very title, *The Waning of the Middle Ages*, had set an oppressive and negative tone . . ."[54]

Exaggerations, like great errors, may themselves be productive. Dialectic is no more necessary in historiography than it is in history, but its processes may promote study. The very overstatement of decline has led to reactions in the other direction. At every point we have had to revise or modify older views. The old clichés about the Wars of the Roses which helped, as McFarlane put it, to make the later fifteenth century repulsive "to all but the strongest-stomached" have been rebutted.[55] The domestic fighting of the fifteenth century did not decimate the old nobility, nor did it cause great disruption of life. It may now seem like a misnomer to use the term civil war at all for disturbances in which, as Commines pointed out, no buildings were destroyed, and our view of the disorderliness of late medieval society at large must be seen to be owed in part to the very richness of its documentation. As regards fighting overseas, the idea that the Hundred Years' War contributed to the wastage of native resources has been questioned in the light of more knowledge of the rewards, profits, and investments which came from England's commitments in France. And in the English economy as a whole it has been realized that an overall reduction of population and cultivated land is consistent with the increasing prosperity of certain classes. The improved situation of wage earners and leaseholding farmers may have been accompanied by greater output per head, as well as by enlarged per capita wealth or income. A. R. Bridbury's *Economic Growth: England in the Later Middle Ages* (1962) presented a picture the very opposite of decay, of an England "vivid with promise," including urban and industrial prosperity, in which the later Middle Ages have become "a period of tremendous advance not only constitutionally, but also in social and economic affairs."[56] Where literature is concerned, Huizinga has been taken to task for the bleak impression he conveyed, which hardly left room for belief "that England could have produced in this period in Chaucer not only one of her greatest poets but one of the sanest and most humane."[57] As for spiritual affairs, the phenomenon of dissent seems a symptom of vitality, not of decay. "The chief characteristic of English religious life in the fourteenth century is the growth of moral fervour among the laity," and the emergence of Lollardy needs to be set in this context, as does the significant figure of Reginald Pecock, whose abortive endeavors point not "to the spiritual deadness of the age but to the preponderance of the English devotional tradition."[58] The last sentence of Professor Jacob's *Fifteenth Century* summarizes this change of interpretation. "So far from running down in this period, religion, not merely in literary and artistic forms, but in the fervour of corporate devotion and in popular appeal achieves a place in the ordinary life of the country which it has seldom been accorded by historians of pre-Reformation England."[59] Vigor, vitality, growth, fervor; these are the chosen words in use today. The difference in judgment is reactive, signalized by bows towards Huizinga. Far from being on the wane or in decline, English society in the fifteenth century is represented as vigorous and expanding, thanks to its inner resilience.[60]

Yet at the same time that Huizinga's descriptive title has been discarded, historians (and others) have freely made use – as Huizinga would have wished – of his "building stones." Certain ideas and themes of *Herfsttij* have proved fertile in germinating further study, to the extent that the book must be recognized as seminal for the cultural history of the period, in England as well as further afield. Attention has been given to courtly culture and royal pageantry and propaganda. Besides Mathew's book on Richard II's court mentioned above, we have for the very end of the period Sydney Anglo's *Spectacle, Pageantry, and early Tudor Policy* (1969) and John Stevens's *Music and Poetry in the Early Tudor Court* (1961), works that show what remains to be done for the intervening years, which have only been examined piecemeal.[61] On the theme of chivalry, while the idea and the ideal have continued to be studied as Huizinga viewed them, as elements of social life which held both ethical and aesthetic significance, advances have been made in what might be called the cultural history of the Hundred Years' War. Understanding of the essential framework of the laws of war – laws which themselves embodied chivalric convention and towards which Huizinga had taken some tentative steps – was greatly enlarged by the publication of Maurice Keen's *The Laws of War in the Late Middle Ages* (1965). There have been increasing efforts to place the war in its social context, to examine not only its connection with social change, but also the implications of changing attitudes towards it. "Mind and Outlook" formed a part of the consideration of war in H. J. Hewitt's *The Organization of War Under Edward III, 1338–62* (1966), and two other recent books reflect this interest. In *Society at War: The Experience of England and France During the Hundred Years War* (1973), C. T. Allmand explored (through assembled texts), alongside the practices and enticements of the war, late medieval thinking about it and the impact of the conflict on the civilian population. John Barnie's *War in Medieval Society: Social Values and the Hundred Years War* pursued the attitudes and ideas of the English as they responded to the first sixty years of war through aristocratic, knightly, and chivalric conventions, in a fresh spirit of patriotism, or debating the pros and cons of war.[62] Another sphere in which Huizinga's perceptions have been taken further – not specifically in the English context – is "The Vision of Death." "No other epoch has laid so much stress as the expiring Middle Ages on the thought of death," wrote Huizinga.[63] His omission in this context of the impact of contemporary plague and mortality has been remedied by various studies, while the relevance of Huizinga's views for English medieval poetry on "Death and the Last Things" has lately been critically assessed by Douglas Gray in his *Themes and Images in the Medieval English Religious Lyric* (1972).[64]

This is not a bibliographical survey, but these fairly random examples show that the influence of Huizinga's *Waning* remains pervasive, even if no longer persuasive. We have continued to work, topically at least,

along his outlines, and there are signs that historians are learning greater
respect for his ideas of history. Cultural history, despite the remaining
hesitancies towards it, is becoming more acceptable in that the study of
the past now seems to demand some concern for forms of thought and
attitudes and, along with that, an ear for literary sources. Professor
F. R. H. Du Boulay's *An Age of Ambition: English Society in the Late
Middle Ages* (1970) is an excellent exemplification of this, with its exploration of "attitudes towards authority" and its full use of such sources
as *Piers Plowman*, the *Paston Letters* and the *Plumpton Correspondence.*[65]
It is easier now than it was in the early 1960s, at the time of Professor
Hastings's article, for students of history to find out about all levels of
society and to learn something of contemporary "forms of life and
thought." We have done a little to rectify the overexclusive concentration which previous generations gave to political history. C. T. Allmand's
remarks about the study of the Hundred Years' War are symptomatic of
a wider trend. "There is a need to study wars in terms of the societies in
which they were fought, to underline the fact that wars not only affected
the historic development of societies and social groups, but were often
less affected by the principles over which they were fought than by the
needs of people who became involved in them . . . Attitudes to war
were undergoing a change."[66]

We may have moved towards Huizinga by employing some of his
building tools. But have we moved away from him in the architectural
plan? If no real equivalent of the *Waning* has been written for late
medieval England, perhaps this has to do with the difficulties that have
been found in endorsing Huizinga's historical aims. Does rejection of the
idea of the "declining Middle Ages" imply rejection of any attempt at a
cultural survey as gross oversimplification? Is it indicative of historians' approaches to the period that in shying away from "waning" and "decline"
as descriptive of England in these centuries, they have failed to substitute
any convincing alternative? It has seemed easier to plump for the double
bill with paradoxical implications. Kingsford's *Prejudice and Promise in
XVth Century England* (1925) does not stand alone; there is J. R. Lander's *Conflict and Stability in Fifteenth-Century England* (1969), and
A. R. Bridbury's title, *Economic Growth: England in the Later Middle
Ages*, straightforward though it may sound to the uninitiated, reads as
a challenging paradox to anyone familiar with once prevalent concep-
tions of the period. Professor Du Boulay's *Age of Ambition* could
seemingly just as well have been named "An Age of Anxiety."[67] Prejudice, promise; conflict, stability; anxiety, ambition; title, profit; ostentation, retirement; ruthlessness, piety; decay, growth: it is not hard to
multiply the conflicting qualities which confront us in the fourteenth and
fifteenth centuries. Huizinga's portrayal of the age presented vividly this
coexistence of opposites, and historians, albeit perhaps unconsciously,

private chapels in the houses of the laity, the privilege of appointing one's own confessor with a portable altar and no parochial responsibility – and hence independence of episcopal surveillance . . . The contemporary spirit in religion was puritan, biblical, evangelical, anarchic, anti-sacerdotal, hostile to the established order in the Church." Such support as the Lollards gained from the knightly class represented "a moral revolt by the laity against the visible Church, a rejection of sacerdotalism in favour of the personal, immediate contact between the believer and his Creator."[76] The same motivations are evident in the lives of late medieval mystics or near-mystics – Richard Rolle or Margery Kempe – and in the most popular form of contemporary religious foundation, the chantry, which represents an institutionalized form of the services of the personal household chaplain. We might even regard the increasing pursuit of literacy, in certain of its manifestations, as part of this same phenomenon of dissatisfaction with the rituals of existing forms and withdrawal into private spirituality.

Within or alongside traditional hierarchical links there grew up other forms of association that strike us as more personal, collateral, or horizontal. "Bastard feudalism" was a more personal form of contractual relationship than the tenurial bond which it superseded. The pursuit of profits and security, spiritual or material, often seemed to be achieved most effectively by relationships in which the idea of lordship was set aside in favor of a bond more domestic and familial. Confraternities flourished in this age; brotherhood-in-arms though not new to the period was a valued form of affiliation for legal or illegal ends, sometimes formed of bands of blood brothers, at others through contracts drawn up for services in war or business partnership. One wonders if it is significant of more than the gaudy spirit that the company of escapists who left plague-ridden Florence for the pleasures related in the *Decameron* formed a single youthful age-group. Already too, we can detect the beginnings of another comparable development which was to become more marked in the future, namely the transference of religious aspiration to the domestic household group. The spectacle of Thomas More, turning his Chelsea household into a community which as nearly as possible followed monastic observance, has earlier precedents. There was John Gerson, endorsing the aim of his sisters to pursue a religious life in their family home, or the communities of English Lollards and German Waldensians, whose spiritual calling seems largely to have been followed and transmitted in domestic circles.[77] Spiritual lordship may have become suspect; spiritual fatherhood was another matter.

Social history is no more cultural history than is literary history. But we have to start somewhere and Huizinga himself told us that "the true problems of cultural history are always problems of the form, structure, and function of social phenomena."[78] It seems clearer than ever now that forms of thought have to be studied in connection with social experience. As a guide Huizinga has done much for us, and we can still learn from him.[79] To assess the influence of his *Waning* is not easy for, as Edmund Wilson said, "it is hard to judge very brilliant books," and it may be a long while after publication before the resonances of a splendid synthesis begin to be registered.[80] Huizinga's *Waning of the Middle Ages* has undoubtedly made one thing clear to us: naming a period resolves nothing, but may make historians more aware of their own uncertainties. Yet books, like people, have to live with their labels and, since we all suffer from the feeling that to be nameless is to be nonexistent, it also seems that to find a name is – at least to some degree – to find a character. "Waning" appeared to have done for the late medieval north something of what "Renaissance" had done for the south: to have made its essence recognizable. Both titles give cause for argument. And whether or not there are more genuine elements of contradiction in northern culture than there are in that of the south, they have certainly come to seem more evident than they did in Huizinga's day. We have rejected "waning" as a satisfactory descriptive title, but we still value *The Waning* as a book. And neither the name nor the book has yet found its replacement. We may leave the last word with Huizinga. "We can give it [the quality of an age] a name by means of which we can more or less understand one another, but we cannot determine it. And in this indeterminateness of its supreme object the close connection between historical knowledge and life itself is revealed anew."[81]

NOTES

I wish to thank Dr. John Bossy for his comments on this article.

1. Anonymity (like the title page) is presumably a result of the advent of printing. For play on the possibility of a book with "no title at all" see Max Beerbohm, *Seven Men* (London, 1919), p. 9. See also Maurice Keen, "Huizinga, Kilgour and the Decline of Chivalry," *Medievalia et Humanistica*, No. 8, 1977, 1–20.

2. Kurt Köster, *Johan Huizinga, 1872–1945* (Oberursel, 1947), pp. 99–103, lists the editions and reviews of the book; for contemporary receptions of the various editions see F. W. N. Hugenholtz, "The Fame of a Masterwork," in *Johan Huizinga, 1872–1972*, eds. W. R. H. Koops, E. H. Kossmann, and Gees van der Plaat (The Hague, 1973), pp. 91–103.

3. The Italian version, preceded by the German, English, Swedish (1927), Spanish (1930), and French (1932), was called *Autumno del Medioevo*. Köster, *ibid.*, p. 100.

4. *The Waning* (London, 1924), pp. v–vi. I have not attempted to explore this editorial revision, and the remarks which follow are based on this English edition, which had been reprinted eight times (in hardback) by 1967. Karl J. Weintraub, *Visions of Culture* (Chicago and London, 1966), p. 212, n. 13, regards the translation as a "very inferior, crippled version" of the Dutch original, and it is a pity that the fairly full annotation was

omitted in the English version, leaving the reader disconcertingly up in the air.

5. Huizinga's essays on Alanus de Insulis, John of Salisbury, and Abelard appeared in 1932, 1933, and 1935 (Köster, *op. cit.*, pp. 129, 132, 141); the latter two are translated in *Men and Ideas: Essays by Johan Huizinga*, trans. J. S. Holmes and H. van Marle (New York, 1959). Were these essays conceived as part of a larger work to be called "The Spring of the Middle Ages"? E. H. Gombrich, "Huizinga's *Homo ludens*," in *Johan Huizinga, 1872–1972*, p. 142, reads this, though it seems unwarrantably, into a remark of Pieter Geyl, "Huizinga as Accuser of his Age," *History and Theory*, II (1962–3), p. 255.

6. For such images of sunshine and summer see *Men and Ideas*, pp. 89–90, 179, 252, 260, 305; *Waning*, p. 308.

7. *Waning*, pp. 58–9. R. L. Colie, "Johan Huizinga and the Task of Cultural History," *American Historical Review*, LXIX (1964), pp. 608, 611. Huizinga has been described as "the Dutch Burckhardt," and the latter's influence on the former was lifelong. See H. R. Guggisberg, "Burckhardt und Huizinga: Zwei Historiker in der Krise ihrer Zeit," in *Johan Huizinga, 1872–1972*, pp. 155, 163, 173.

8. *Men and Ideas*, p. 289; H. Gerson, "Huizinga und die Kunstgeschichte," in *Johan Huizinga, 1872–1972*, p. 206.

9. *Men and Ideas*, p. 289; Werner Kaegi, *Das historische Werk Johan Huizingas* (Leiden, 1947), pp. 16–17.

10. *Waning*, p. 59.

11. *Ibid.*, pp. 297, 307. Leonard Huizinga's evaluation is quoted by Hugenholtz, *op. cit.*, pp. 100–101.

12. *Men and Ideas*, p. 260; cf. pp. 253–4, 267, 278–80, 285–6, where the same point is harped on.

13. *Ibid.*, p. 286; cf. p. 183 for the description of the twelfth-century Renaissance as "a ripening, a coming of age."

14. Hugenholtz, *op. cit.*, p. 101; Lucien Febvre, "Un Moment avec Huizinga," *Annales*, 6 (1951), p. 493, cited by Colie, *art. cit.*, p. 626, n. 61. Cf. *Waning*, p. 237 on "that serene twilight hour of an age," as seen in Jan van Eyck's Arnolfini portrait.

15. *Waning*, p. 214, cf. pp. 82, 121, 124, 181, 227, 241. See Geyl, *art. cit.*, and George Steiner's introduction to the Paladin edition of *Homo Ludens* (London, 1970), p. 13. Cf. Huizinga's remarks in his critique of Spengler, about "the autumn of our Western culture" (viewing autumn as both maturing and a time of approaching decline), in *Dutch Civilisation in the Seventeenth Century and other essays*, sel. Pieter Geyl and F. W. N. Hugenholtz, trans. A. J. Pomerans (London, 1968), pp. 167, 174, 186. For Huizinga's views of cultural imbalance in both his essays on America and in the *Waning* see Weintraub, *op. cit.*, pp. 235–6.

16. *Waning*, p. 244.

17. *Ibid.*, pp. 255–6, 253.

18. From "My Path to History," in *Dutch Civilisation*, pp. 272–3, and cf. *Waning*, Preface, p. v. (Huizinga's words recall Petrarch's remark about the power of the countryside to promote in him "great thoughts . . . if indeed a great thought ever does occur to me.")

19. *Waning*, pp. 237, 241–4, cf. pp. 262–3, 290–1. See *Men and Ideas*, pp. 244, 265, 289, 297, 303 for further remarks about the van Eycks in the two 1920 essays on the Renaissance. The Preface to the Dutch edition which explains this role of the van Eycks and Burgundy as Huizinga's starting point was

unfortunately curtailed in the English edition. A. G. Jongkees, "Une génération d'historiens devant le phénomène bourguignon," in *Johan Huizinga, 1872–1972*, p. 75, points to the probability that at the time when the idea struck him Huizinga had been reading H. Fierens-Gevaert, *Études sur l'art flamand. La Renaissance septentrionale et les premiers maîtres des Flandres* (Brussels, 1905). See also Gerson, *op. cit.*, pp. 210–12, and E. H. Gombrich, *In Search of Cultural History* (Oxford, 1969), pp. 28–9 (my debts to this invaluable paper are greater than the following notes might indicate).

20. *Waning*, p. 308. On this dualism in the *Waning* see Paul L. Ward, "Huizinga's Approach to the Middle Ages," in *Teachers of History: Essays in Honor of Laurence Bradford Packard*, ed. H. Stuart Hughes, et al. (Ithaca, 1954), pp. 168–95, esp. pp. 177–8, 186–9.

21. Gombrich, *Search*, p. 29; *idem*, "Huizinga's *Homo ludens*," p. 140; Jongkees, *op. cit.*, pp. 78–9. Huizinga had toyed with the titles "In the Mirror of van Eyck" and "The Age of Burgundy"; Gerson, *op. cit.*, p. 210; see also Huizinga, *Verzamelde Werken* (Haarlem 1948–53), III, p. 4 for the Preface to the 1919 Dutch edition, and IV, p. 450, n. 1, for the regret about the choice of title expressed in the context of criticism of Spengler's metaphysical view of cultural autumn and winter.

22. *Eng. Hist. Rev.*, XL (1925), pp. 273–5. Professor Hugenholtz, *op. cit.*, p. 98, rather mysteriously finds Kingsford's review "so confused and incoherent" as to be incomprehensible, though he points to the significance of this remark.

23. "The Task of Cultural History" (published 1929, after a 1926 speech), in *Men and Ideas*, p. 64.

24. May McKisack, *The Fourteenth Century, 1307–1399* (Oxford, 1959); E. F. Jacob, *The Fifteenth Century, 1399–1485* (Oxford, 1961). Cf. the reviews by Y. Renouard, *Eng. Hist. Rev.*, LXXVII (1962), pp. 525–30, H. G. Richardson, *Eng. Hist. Rev.*, LXXVIII (1963), pp. 552–7, and S. B. Chrimes, "The Fifteenth Century," *History*, XLVIII (1963), pp. 18–27.

25. E. F. Jacob, "Huizinga and the Autumn of the Middle Ages," in *Essays in Later Medieval History* (Manchester, 1968), p. 150; Hugenholtz, *op. cit.*, p. 97; Geyl, *art. cit.*, pp. 244–5. For remarks on the primacy of political history see Herbert Butterfield, *Man on his Past. The Study of the History of Historical Scholarship* (Cambridge, 1955), pp. 41, 84, 116ff.

26. DeLloyd J. Guth, *Late-medieval England 1377–1485* (Cambridge, 1976). My calculation of these proportions is based on sections iv to xiv (omitting the first three general headings). Religious History occupies 581 items on 27 pages, compared with 449 items and 21 pages on Constitutional and Administrative History.

27. K. B. McFarlane, *The Nobility of Later Medieval England* (Oxford, 1973), p. xvi.

28. Margaret Hastings, "High History or Hack History: England in the Later Middle Ages," *Speculum*, XXXVI (1961), pp. 228, 251 (reprinted in *Changing Views on British History. Essays on Historical Writing since 1939*, ed. E. C. Furber [Cambridge, Mass., and London, 1966], pp. 58–100).

29. Chrimes, *art. cit.*, p. 18. Cf. F. R. H. Du Boulay, *An Age of Ambition: English Society in the Late Middle Ages* (London, 1970), p. 179 where Stubbs heads the bibliography.

30. Denys Hay, "History and Historians in France and England during the Fifteenth Century," *Bulletin of the Institute of Historical Research*, XXXV (1962), pp. 111–27. Kingsford's *English Historical Literature in the Fifteenth Century* (Oxford, 1913, rep. New York, 1963) is still the best survey

of the sources. In his review of the *Waning* Kingsford had indicated the value that English collections of private letters could have for revealing "the practical life of the people."

31. For comments on this point see Gombrich, *Search*, p. 45ff.; Keith Thomas, "History and Anthropology," *Past and Present*, 24 (1963), p. 15ff.; R. W. Southern, *The Shape and Substance of Academic History* (Oxford, 1961).

32. C. G. Crump, *History*, X (1925–6), p. 164.

33. On Huizinga's independent spirit and untransferable originality see Colie, *art. cit.*, pp. 621–2.

34. John Brooke, "Namier and Namierism," *History and Theory*, III (1964), pp. 331–47. McFarlane (*Nobility*, pp. xii, xviii, xxxvii, 296–7) was among those who believed in the value of applying prosopography to late medieval studies. The historian to achieve most in this field has been J. S. Roskell with *The Commons in the Parliament of 1422* (Manchester, 1954), *The Commons and their Speakers in the English Parliaments 1376–1523* (Manchester, 1965), and other studies.

35. See "The Task of Cultural History," *Men and Ideas*, p. 21.

36. *Waning*, p. 7; Hugenholtz, *op. cit.*, p. 93ff.

37. *Men and Ideas*, p. 59, cf. pp. 52–55 and for remarks on individuals in history, "The Aesthetic Element in Historical Thought," in *Dutch Civilisation*, p. 231. Jacob, "Huizinga and the Autumn," pp. 142–3, comments on Huizinga's moments of illumination.

38. *Waning*, p. 136; cf. Huizinga's remarks on the visual element in historical understanding in *Dutch Civilisation*, pp. 226, 237, 241, 249, 263, 269. See also Gerson, *op. cit.*, pp. 208–9; Weintraub, *op. cit.*, pp. 229–30; Gombrich, "Huizinga's *Homo ludens*," pp. 137–9.

39. *Waning*, pp. 222–3 on the decline of romantic interpretations. In "My Path to History" Huizinga described his youthful activity in mounting art exhibitions, including an illustrated lecture of 1897 based on travel photographs of Italian art. "It is hard to imagine today," he wrote in the 1940s, "how hard it was to get good reproductions of old masterpieces"; *Dutch Civilisation*, p. 259: cf. pp. 9–10, 46, 64–5 and Gerson, *op. cit.*, p. 221 for Huizinga's association of intellectual laziness with increased visual material, and on the damage done to art by photographic reproduction *Homo Ludens* (Paladin ed., 1970), pp. 228–9.

40. *Men and Ideas*, p. 59.

41. *Ibid.* (Burckhardt's *Civilization* was first published in 1860).

42. *Ibid.*, pp. 60, 65; "Two Wrestlers with the Angel," in *Dutch Civilisation*, pp. 165–6; Gombrich, *Search*, pp. 29–30, 32, 46; Geyl, *art. cit.*, p. 247.

43. E.g., *Waning*, pp. 47, 206, 217, 237, 307. For criticism of Huizinga's "specific morphology" (in its narrowest sense) see Geyl, *art. cit.*, p. 255.

44. It seems a little unfair that Professor Jacob, whose own book on the fifteenth century contained so little on the growth of English dissent (for which he was criticized by H. G. Richardson in the review mentioned above, n. 24), should have charged Huizinga for this omission. "Huizinga and the Autumn," pp. 148–9.

45. *Men and Ideas*, p. 85, cf. p. 65.

46. I.e., comparing the works mentioned in n. 24 above with H. S. Bennett, *Chaucer and the Fifteenth Century* (Oxford, 1947), and (though with less advantage) E. K. Chambers, *English Literature at the Close of the Middle Ages* (Oxford, 1945).

47. H. S. Bennett, *The Pastons and their England: Studies in an Age of Transition* (Cambridge, 1922, rev. ed. 1932).

48. C. S. Lewis, *The Allegory of Love. A Study in Medieval Tradition* (Oxford, 1936).

49. G. Mathew, *The Court of Richard II* (London, 1968), Foreword. The original suggestion for a book combining "political history with an analysis of social ideals" was made to the author by F. M. Powicke.

50. For the various valuable articles of Anne Hudson, see her *Selections from English Wycliffite Writings* (Cambridge, 1978) and Guth, *op. cit.*, Nos. 1857, 1881, 2076 and recent numbers of the *Annual Bulletin of Historical Literature* (Historical Association, London).

51. John Barnie, *War in Medieval Society: Social Values and the Hundred Years War 1337–99* (London, 1974), p. xi.

52. As pointed out by Peter Burke in his account of Huizinga published in *The Listener*, 22 February 1973, p. 242.

53. A. R. Bridbury, *Economic Growth: England in the Later Middle Ages* (London, 1962, new ed. 1975), p. 20.

54. From Chapter 1, "The Myth of Decline," in F. R. H. Du Boulay, *op. cit.*, (above n. 29), p. 11.

55. K. B. McFarlane, "The Wars of the Roses," *Proceedings of the British Academy*, Vol. L (1964), p. 87. Also on this revision see McFarlane's *Nobility*, pp. 15, 146–9; S. B. Chrimes, *Lancastrians, Yorkists and Henry VII* (London, 1964), pp. xi–xiv; J. R. Lander, *The Wars of the Roses* (London, 1965); Charles Ross, *The Wars of the Roses. A Concise History* (London, 1976).

56. Bridbury, *op. cit.*, pp. 22, 108.

57. Douglas Gray, *Themes and Images in the Medieval English Religious Lyric* (London and Boston, 1972), p. 30, cf. pp. 27–8.

58. K. B. McFarlane, *Lancastrian Kings and Lollard Knights* (Oxford, 1972), p. 224; E. F. Jacob, "Reynold Pecock, Bishop of Chichester," in *Essays in Later Medieval History*, p. 34. Cf. the remarks of V. H. H. Green, *Bishop Reginald Pecock* (Cambridge, 1945), pp. 73, 75, trying to fit Pecock's character into Huizinga's "waning" model.

59. Jacob, *Fifteenth Century*, p. 687. (Cf. n. 44 above.)

60. *Idem*, "Huizinga and the Autumn," p. 153. For a summary of this overall reinterpretation (also looking back to Huizinga) and the replacement of ideas of decline and decadence by vigor, vitality, and progress, see Bertie Wilkinson, "The Historian and the Late Middle Ages in England," in *Essays on the Reconstruction of Medieval History*, ed. V. Mudroch and G. S. Couse (Montreal and London, 1974), pp. 133–45.

61. The two books mentioned here were published at Oxford and London respectively. See Stevens, pp. 153, 188, 235 for acknowledgments to Huizinga, especially his chapters on courtly love. On the fifteenth century there are several articles by J. W. McKenna (Guth, *op. cit.*, Nos. 635, 799) including "Popular Canonization as Political Propaganda: The Cult of Archbishop Scrope," *Speculum*, XLV (1970), pp. 608–623; and P. E. Gill, "Politics and Propaganda in Fifteenth-Century England: The Polemical Writings of Sir John Fortescue," *Speculum*, XLVI (1971), pp. 333–47.

62. Of these works, Hewitt's was published in Manchester, Allmand's in Edinburgh, the others in London. See Keen, p. 239, for a signal of debt to Huizinga. Despite the contribution of works such as John Harvey's, including his *Gothic England. A Survey of National Culture 1300–1500* (London, 1947), and V. J. Scattergood's recent *Politics and Poetry in the Fifteenth Century* (London, 1971), we still have no adequate general assessment of the architectural and literary impact of the war.

63. *Waning*, p. 124. Among the works that have pursued this theme mention

may be made of James M. Clark, *The Dance of Death in the Middle Ages and the Renaissance* (Glasgow, 1950); A. Tenenti, *La vie et la mort à travers l'art du XVe siècle* (Paris, 1952); T. S. R. Boase, *Death in the Middle Ages: Mortality, Judgment and Remembrance* (London, 1972). Cf. also Philippe Ariès, "Huizinga et les thèmes macabres," in *Johan Huizinga, 1872–1972*, pp. 104–15.

64. Chapter 10, pp. 176–220, esp. 179ff.

65. See n. 29 above.

66. Allmand, *op. cit.*, p. 192, cf. p. 13.

67. Kingsford's book (the Ford Lectures for 1924, published at Oxford) was a collection of essays which describe some of the "promising" expansive aspects of the period to demonstrate Tudor prejudice. Lander's (published London) is a more general survey, to which may be added the introduction to his reprinted essays, *Crown and Nobility 1450–1509* (London, 1976), pp. 1–56. Du Boulay, *op. cit.*, p. 40 (on Bridbury) and pp. 66–67, 145, 156, 160–62 (on the anxieties of the age).

68. Gombrich, *Search*, p. 30 et seq.

69. For Huizinga's reading in his late teens of E. B. Tylor's *Primitive Culture* (1871) which, he later said, "opened up perspectives that, in a sense, have inspired me ever since," see *Dutch Civilisation*, p. 250; Gombrich, "Huizinga's *Homo ludens*," p. 138. Anthropological findings featured conspicuously among the widely ranging material Huizinga drew on for *Homo Ludens*. On the pioneering work of Tylor (1832–1917) see Mary Douglas, *Purity and Danger* (London, 1966), p. 13ff.

70. Colie, *art. cit.*, p. 623; Ward, *op. cit.*, p. 171. Obviously this is not true of all anthropology; cf. the general remarks on history and anthropology in Thomas, *art. cit.*, pp. 4–5, and the Conference Report on "History, Sociology and Social Anthropology," *Past and Present*, 27 (1964), pp. 102–8.

71. See for example Professor Duby's remarks about the models of the perfect knight and the perfect clerk in France from the twelfth to the fourteenth centuries. Georges Duby, "The Diffusion of Cultural Patterns in Feudal Society," *Past and Present*, 39 (1968), pp. 8–10. Cf. also the questions raised about the role of the "formalized social past" by E. J. Hobsbawn, "The Social Function of the Past," *Past and Present*, 55 (1972), p. 3ff.

72. *Waning*, p. 48 (cf. Pelican Edition, p. 58).

73. Mary Douglas, *Natural Symbols: Explorations in Cosmology* (London, 1970), pp. viii, xvi.

74. McFarlane, *Nobility*, p. 217; Christopher Dyer, "A Redistribution of Incomes in Fifteenth-Century England," *Past and Present*, 39 (1968), pp. 11–33.

75. Douglas, *Natural Symbols*, p. 14, cf. pp. 8, 19.

76. McFarlane, *Lancastrian Kings and Lollard Knights*, p. 225.

77. My indebtedness here, and perhaps elsewhere, is to John Bossy's stimulating review article "Holiness and Society," *Past and Present*, 75 (1977), pp. 119–37.

78. *Men and Ideas*, p. 59.

79. Cf. the recent plea to medieval historians to take a wider view and study society and culture as a whole, advanced by Norman F. Cantor, "The Interpretation of Medieval History," in *Essays on the Reconstruction of Medieval History*, pp. 16–17. But I would not go so far as Professor Cantor who calls the *Waning* "the one book which makes any sense of the bizarre political history of France and England in the late fourteenth and fifteenth centuries."

80. Edmund Wilson, *The Bit Between My Teeth* (New York, 1966), p. 137.

After forty years, remarked E. F. Jacob ("Huizinga and the Autumn," p. 144), the *Waning* "seems more significant than it did when it appeared."

81. *Men and Ideas*, p. 76 (the end of the essay on "The Task of Cultural History"). Huizinga had a good deal to say about the effects of naming periods with terms such as "Renaissance" or "Baroque"; cf. *ibid.*, pp. 183, 243ff.; *Dutch Civilisation*, pp. 11–13, 97–8, 103; *Homo Ludens*, pp. 207–8; and see Gerson, *op. cit.*, pp. 215–6.

Dissent in Middle English Literature:

The Spirit of (Thirteen) Seventy-six

ROSSELL HOPE ROBBINS

If 1976 was a great year for an anniversary, all medievalists might well have celebrated the sesquimillennial of the beginning of the Middle Ages. On the ending of the Middle Ages they would have shown less unanimity. Middle English scholars, who generally extend it, might agree, however, that a satisfactory *terminus ad quem* would be the discovery (or rediscovery) of the Americas in 1492. While a scholar whose academic world ends then cannot be held responsible for any implications in the title of this article, "The Spirit of (Thirteen) Seventy-six," he nevertheless may find some links between dissent in the medieval period in England and dissent in the Colonial period in America, between 1376 and 1776.

One grievance makes the whole world kin. The major grievance common to feudal England in 1376 and to Colonial America in 1776 concerned high taxes. In April, 1376, Sir Peter de la Mare, chosen speaker for the Commons in the so-called "Good" Parliament, complained that the Commons had been oppressed by taxation of fifteenths and tenths, and refused to grant the king fuller subsidies without redress.[1] But apart from a riot in London, over a quite different issue, the taxes did not lead to revolution in that year. Nevertheless, the continuing imposition of taxes not acceptable to the Commons, and a poll tax in 1377, renewed periodically, culminated in the Peasants' Revolt of 1381. Added to many other grievances, the tax was the last straw, as a macaronic poem, not sympathetic to the rebels, points out:

> The taxe hath tened vs alle,
> > probat hoc mors tot validorum;
> The kyng therof had small,
> > ffuit in manibus cupidorum.[2]

Poems protesting taxes were nothing new, and a farmer's complaint about 1300 indeed uses very similar words.[3]

Despite the intensity and extent of the Peasants' Revolt, it had relatively little impact on following decades, nor was it often recalled as a shining example by later radicals. Even the Levellers and Diggers of the English Revolution of 1642 did not regard John Ball or Wat Tyler as their spiritual forbear or political ancestor. The main spokesmen of the American

Revolution were essentially in the Whig tradition and more apt to go back to Anglo-Saxon England and to Magna Carta or to earlier seventeenth-century examples than to the feudal period, which they regarded with some distaste as a time when English liberty was perverted.

Only at the very end of the eighteenth century did 1381 attract attention. Looking back on the conditions in fourteenth-century England, both European and American philosophers and politicians observed certain parallels. When Edmund Burke's "Appeal from the New to the Old Whigs" appeared in 1791, Thomas Paine almost predictably responded. Burke had compared the Peasants' Revolt of 1381, not with the American Revolution of 1776, but with the French Revolution of 1789, equating John Ball's "sapient maxim" (as he disparagingly termed it):

> When Adam delved and Eve span,
> Who was then the gentleman?

with the French National Assembly's insistence on man's equal rights.[4] Paine took up the cudgels on behalf of the English rebels:

Several of the Court newspapers have of late made frequent mention of Wat Tyler. That his memory should be traduced by Court sycophants and all those who live on the spoil of a public is not to be wondered at. He was, however, the means of checking the rage and injustice of taxation in his time, and the Nation owed much to his valour.[5]

At this point, Paine tells the legend of how Wat Tyler, incensed by a tax collector's clinical inspection of his fifteen-year-old daughter to see if she were taxable (as an adult), "struck him with a hammer that brought him to the ground, and was the cause of his death." Paine concludes with evaluating Wat Tyler as patriot:

Tyler appears to have been an intrepid disinterested man with respect to himself. All his proposals made to Richard were on a more just and public ground than those which had been made to John by the Barons, and notwithstanding the sycophancy of historians and men like Mr. Burke who seek to gloss over a base action of the court by traducing Tyler, his fame will outlive their falsehood. If the Barons merited a monument to be erected at Runnymede, Tyler merits one in Smithfield.[6]

So much by way of prologue.

Middle English protests against specific evils like the poll tax are rare; more common are complaints about general grievances. These, however, present certain problems in interpretation: Do they refer to an actual topical abuse or are they aphoristic and proverbial?[7]

In 1311, a poet criticized Edward II for breaking the Ordinances he had signed in October, but the barons did not need a *carmen rebelli* to break into armed revolt less than two months later. The "chaotic mismanagement" of that year, however, adds immediacy to the convention that "Engelond is shent":

> ffor miht is right, þe lond is laweles;
> ffor niht is liht, þe lond is lore-les;
> ffor fiht is fliht, þe lond is name-les.[8]

A scrap in the *Fasciculus Morum,* a little later, similarly explains why "England may say and syng, Allas, allas":

> Syn lawe for will begynnes to slaken,
> and falsed for sleyth now is taken,
> Robbyng and rewyng is holden purchas,
> and of vnclennes is made solas.[9]

About 1400, another jeremiad listed what was then wrong with England. Things didn't seem to have changed much:

> richesse is clepud worþynes . . .
> robberie good wynnynge . . .
> enuye and wraþþe men clepen riȝtfulnes . . .
> lesinges and fables ben clepude good lore.[10]

One poem in the mid-fifteenth century describes conditions that "now regnethe in Ingeland" under Henry VI:

> This lond ys now full of inyquyte . . .
> Untrowthe regnyth in many a syde . . .
> Meed and falseheed assocyed are.[11]

Another says: "Truthe is set at lytyl prys . . . Robberys now rewle ryȝtwysenesse."[12] In a late fifteenth-century poem the homilist is on the same tack, still complaining of the disregard for law and order; his words were considered sufficiently pertinent to be copied in the early sixteenth century:

> Now ys Yngland alle in fyght;
> Moche peple of consyens lyght;
> Many knyghtes, and lytyl of myght;
> Many lawys, and lytylle ryght;
> Many actes of parlament;
> And few kept wyth tru entent.[13]

Such verses are ubiquitous: two hundred years later, the descendant of the moralist of 1311 is expressing the same point of view and using even the same rhymes as his literary great-great-grandfather. What was amiss in 1300 was still amiss in 1500. No doubt the catalogue of Evils had become "an abstract or conceptual tradition,"[14] or a kind of ritual *nostra culpa,* or a literary topos on the *De Contemptu Mundi* theme.[15] Only occasionally does a poem allude to a verifiable incident; thus the lines "He ys louyd þat wel can lye; / And theuys tru men honge," in a poem whose chronology can be fixed,[16] refer to a notorious case of an "appealer," recorded in a contemporary chronicle in 1456.[17] Generally, however, the Abuses of the Age comprise a traditional formula, a variant of a Latin text variously ascribed to Cyprian, Augustine, or Origen, first translated in Aelfric's *Homilies*, and spread through the *Speculum Christiani* or the *Gesta Romanorum*, "Munus fit iudex, fraus est mercator in urbe, non est lex dominus."[18] Their immediate ancestors are the "pleintes Jeremie" that circulated in England in the thirteenth century and earlier:[19]

> Mundi status hodie multum variatur,
> Semper in deterius misere mutatur . . .
> Regnat nunc impietas, pietas fugatur.[20]

If these complaints are more topoi than topical, they must be devaluated as expressions of protest. Similar caution has to be exercised with the topos of gentility on moral worth rather than on ancestry.[21]

Where then, if the traditional Evils of the Times ignore the facts of real life, are elements of dissent and protest to be found in Middle English literature? Ironically, the most dangerous and far-reaching manifestations of dissent are to be found, not so much in the tags current in the Peasants' Revolt, but in the works of pro-Establishment writers. The best examples come in the *unconscious* formulations by men like Langland and Wyclif, both fundamentally conservative, of basically dissident positions that only later moved from philosophical criticism and genteel reform to open rebellion.[22] It took the medieval "establishment," which had let Wyclif die in peace, some thirty years to realize that his doctrines were being misused for subversion and ultimately to exhume and burn his remains.

In this paper, I will discuss first the pervasiveness of the Three Estates theory in Middle English literature, especially in Gower, Hoccleve, and Langland, and in the near propaganda of Peter Idley and Lydgate.

Second, the long-range implications of the latent dissent in reformist supporters of the Establishment, like Wyclif.

Third, the head-on but short-lived protest of John Ball and the Peasants' Revolt against the Estates Theory.

Fourth and finally, I will mention some Middle English poems that by various forms of satire nibble away at the *status quo* advocated by the Estates Theory.

The medieval Establishment sought unquestioning acceptance by all classes of society of the basic theory of the Three Estates, current throughout Western Europe and persisting far into the Renaissance. Citations here will be limited to writings in Middle English.

In medieval England, of course, there could be no equivalent to what an American president once classified as the Establishment: the political-industrial-military complex. In medieval England the military classes (the nobles) were in no way united, as their lukewarm support for John of Gaunt's Spanish venture indicated; and an embryonic industry (the gilds) was split by conflicting interests of victuallers and clothiers. Nevertheless, some sort of medieval consortium of vested interests did in fact exist.

Despite the fluidity and interchange possible between the various social classes,[23] and despite their internal rivalry, the ruling class, or the Establishment, was exceptionally conspicuous: the higher echelons of the Clergy (who owned about one third of England) and the Nobles (who owned the remaining two thirds), supported to a large extent by the lesser clergy and gentry[24] (the so-called Commons). As non-persons, the rural populace (peasants, villeins, yeomen) as well as the urban (apprentices, townsmen, and traders) had little voice. A fifteenth-century tract contrasted the two ruling classes, "men of holi cherche" and "lordis and ladies [whom God] hathe sette in this worlde in weelthe and likyngis," with "tillynge men and laboreris" who "bothe dike and delve."[25] These categories formed the traditional Three Estates.

All society was imbued with the philosophy of the Three Estates. In his earlier writings, Wyclif could conceive of no other type of social organization, and divided the Church militant into "þese þre partis; – in prechoures, and deffendoures, and þo þridde part ben laboreris."[26] Their divine sanction was clearly confirmed by their correspondence with the three persons of the Trinity: "Almyȝty god þe trinyte, fadir, sonne and holy gooste, boþe in þe olde lawe and þe newe haþ fowndid his chirche up-on þre statis, awnswerynge or acordynge to þes þre persones and her propirtes."[27] By this analogy, the secular nobility was equated with God the Father, the clergy with the Son, and the Commons, "þe whiche owiþ true loue and obedyente wille to þe statis of lordis and prestis,"[28] with the Holy Ghost. Of course, when yeomen rose to the wealth of country gentlemen and gildsmen to the wealth of nobility, they might become assimilated by enforced nobility or "distraint of knighthood,"[29] an ongoing custom satirized by Langland:

> For made neuere kyng no knyȝt but he hadde catel to spende
> As bifel for a knyȝt, or foond hym for his strengþe.[30]

When Richard II in 1392 attempted to force every citizen with real property worth ten pounds or more to buy his title of knight, he was but anticipating the pawns' purchase of promotion to knights in Caxton's *Game of Chess!*

Two features are central to the theory of the Three Estates:
The division of worldly duties among separate social classes was divinely ordained: it was the duty of the clergy to praise God and pray for the world; it was the duty of the hereditary nobility "ȝif þat Batayle come in to londe / [to] Defende hit faste wiþ fiht";[31] and it was the duty of the peasants to labor and produce the necessities (and luxuries) of life for the clergy and nobles. Chaucer's parson was very explicit: "God

ordeyned that som folk sholde be moore heigh in estaat and in degree, and some folk moore lough, and that everich sholde be served in his estaat and in his degree."[32] And so Lydgate warned:

> A knaue also, by hys werkyng,
> Sholde ben Egal wyth the kyng;
> The wych (who wysly kan espye,)
> Ne wer no maner polycye,
> But rather a confusioun
> In every maner Regioun.[33]

Similarly Wyclif: "And so þes þre statis ben, or schulde be, sufficient in goddis chirche; or ellis men mosten say þat god is and was fawty in ordenance of boþe his lawis."[34] Whereas in classical writings, one's estate was the result of fortune, in medieval Christendom, slavery was the consequence of sin; the freeman, therefore, had more virtues than a slave, and a prince most of all.[35] "No beggere ne boye amonges vs," said Langland, "but if it synne made."[36]

The successful and efficient ordering of feudal society, so the theory ran, depended on all members of each estate being content with the earthly condition into which they were born and pursuing the specific aim and duties of their own estate. A breakdown of society would come about when the "contract theory" failed, and men did not know their place.[37] Gower, in the Prologue to his *Confessio Amantis*, lamenting in 1392 the axiom that "the world stant evere vpon debate / So may be seker no estat," longed for the mythical Golden Age: when, in the phrase of Marsilius of Padua,[38] each citizen "participate . . . secundum gradum suum":

> Tho was knyhthode in pris be name . . .
> Justice of lawe tho was holde,
> The privilege of regalie
> Was sauf, and all the baronie
> Worschiped was in his astat.[39]

The punch came in the following lines: "The citees knewen no debat, / The poeple stode in obeissance / Under the reule of governance."[40]

Poems in the fourteenth and fifteenth centuries continually emphasize the need for members of all three classes to do their duty if stability is to be maintained. Not even Langland, who overstressed the primacy of the king,[41] wished the specialized duties of the Three Estates to become blurred, and when the search for Truth was joined, Piers exempted the Knight, the representative of the nobility, from manual labor;[42] and in the C-Text, Piers upheld the clergy's freedom from manual work[43] – it was for "knaues vncrouned [untonsured] to cart and to worche."[44] Wyclif's works provide similar illustrations. In "Of Servants and Lords," written soon after the 1381 Revolt, for example, he indignantly disclaimed "socialist doctrine": "First, seruauntis schullen trewely and gladly serue to here lordis or maistris . . . but holde hem paied of þe staat of seruauntis, in whiche god haþ ordeyned hem for here beste."[45]

As the Middle Ages advanced, two developments of the Three Estates theory evolved that foreshadowed Tudor and Stuart absolutism:

First, the king had for long been considered the arbiter to keep a peaceful balance between the Three Estates. The celebrated lawmaker, Bracton, possibly influenced by new trends in France, had been advocating in the mid-thirteenth century that "the king was created and chosen for this: that he should make justice for all, and that in him the Lord should sit, and that he himself should decide his judgments, and that he should sustain and defend what he has justly judged."[46] The function of a monarch to cherish all three Estates is a theme often found in Middle English literature, as in Chaucer:

> A kyng to kepe his leeges in justice,
> Withouten doute, that is his office.[47]

or as in Gower: "And it is proper for the king to guide the people entrusted to him and govern them with just law,"[48] or as in "The Crowned King," a poem addressed to King Henry V.[49] Beyond this, however, the office of king, possibly enhanced by a consecration that assumed the proportions of an eighth sacrament, began to assume a divine right.[50] Gower provides the most advanced expression of this emerging divine right of kings in his *Confessio Amantis*, which John Fisher sees as the real conclusion of the whole poem:

> To him belongith the leiance
> Of Clerk, of knyght, of man of lawe;
> Undir his hond al is forth drawe
> The marchant and the laborer;
> So stant it al in his power
> Or forto spille or forto save.[51]

The second development, inevitable with the shift from a land-oriented to a money economy, was the rise in power of a section of the Commons, the rich merchants of the major cities of England. Some of the London merchants were actually more wealthy than many noblemen. "Merchants and moneyed men reckon themselves 'ennobled' and on the road to enrichment," says a fifteenth-century preacher, "when they are seen to have friendship with the nobility, when they can wear their robes and are summoned to their banquets, and when they can go a-hunting with them."[52] Mutual alliances between king and merchants appeared with increasing frequency, with the townsmen funding the king when the lords were tardy raising their levies.[53] The merchants were not entirely different in origin and manners from the old nobility, for many of them were younger sons of landed gentry and expected to acquire estates of their own.[54] Gower, "almost unique in [his] time,"[55] saw a divine origin for a new estate of merchants:

> Dieus establist, et au bon droit,
> Qe l'une terre en son endroit
> Del autry bien busoignera:
> Sur quoy merchant dieus ordina,
> Qui de q'en l'une ne serra
> En l'autre terre querre doit;
> Pour ce qui bien se gardera,
> Et loyalment marchandera,
> De dieu et homme il est benoit.[56]

In medieval England, along with the major realignments taking place in the social order, major changes were also coming in the technological and economic order. By the middle of the fourteenth century, the Estates theory was vulnerable for a very pressing reason: it no longer accorded to practice. Crécy in 1346 and Poitiers in 1356 showed that a peasant with a longbow was more than a match for a nobleman with a lance. Yet political and moral philosophy were still couched in terms of twelfth-century agricultural society.[57] At some point the realization of the obsolence of the dominant philosophy will be expressed in reform or revolt. Sooner or later the gap becomes intolerable, and society has either to change peaceably or undergo surgery. The 1381 Rebellion was premature; 1776 came at the right time.

Such was the concept of society which formed the conscious and unconscious underpinning of writings in Middle English. The viewpoint of the Establishment, even when no longer representative of the way society functioned, was omnipresent and prevailed because writers either belonged to it by birth, had been trained in it, or were employed by it. The aspirations of the working class, if reported at all, issued almost invariably from hostile and biased lips. Their legitimate complaints, even if presented, were rarely examined.[58] Medieval England had no counter-culture.

Just what the medieval Establishment stood for in practice, and how the philosophy of the Three Estates filtered down, may be gathered from the numerous sets of instructions that prepared young people to take their place in the world, like "How the Wise Man Taught his Son," that warned against the tavern, dicing, common women, and recommended prompt payment of tithes.[59] On the other hand, Peter Idley's *Instructions to his Son* is far more than the usual courtesy book. It is an illustration of Establishment polity; its author, Peter Idley, a minor royal official, is representative of and spokesman for the fifteenth-century country gentry, like the Stoners and Pastons and Celys, the permanent cadre, one might call them, of the Establishment.

Much of Idley's advice follows the common European tradition, paraphrasing Albertanus but angled to promote unquestioning obedience to the ruling powers: "First God and thy kyng þou loue and drede; / Aboue all thyng þou this preserue."[60] Anything that upsets the *status quo* is frowned on; the twin props, the monarchy and the church,[61] must never be questioned:

> Trust not to moche to thyn owne reason,
> Dispute not thy feith ne the power of thy kyng.
> Thow myght happe to stumble and falle into treason.[62]

Particularly notable is Idley's acceptance and support of institutions and customs that other equally conservative but more idealistic writers condemned. The law, says Idley, "must nedis be kept / Or elles the londe were soone ouerthrowe." But how is law and order to be kept? By Catholic faith and Reason? Oh no, the law is to be kept by Bribery or – in Middle English terminology – by "Meed," because this is the only practical way "A carte goith more easily when he is greesed," Idley observes,[63] and in three successive stanzas he details the steps to worldly success: In appearing before a commission, "Thenke redelie that without mede / Thow art like in fewe maters forto spede." Even in obtaining the services of a physician, "But þou paie freely or þou goo / Thus must þou lerne to synge 'Si dedero.' " In fact, for any services or assistance, "with empty hande men may no hawkes lure" – a proverb quoted by the Pastons[64] – "But if þou redelie paie hem their fee, / At thy most nede þou shalt hem lacke."

An example of more blatant propaganda based on the Three Estates theory is Lydgate's paraphrase of *De Casibus Virorum*, Boccaccio's guide for rulers. "To Boccaccio, princes, spiritual or temporal," wrote Ruth Mohl,[65] "were fit only for his scorn. In his dedicatory epistle he said that no pope, emperor, or king was worthy of his dedication – they all 'made him sick' ['quadpropter nausea quadam vexatus . . . ab indagine destiti']. The corruptions of the world were due to its rulers. The people were contaminated by their example." For his *Fall of Princes* Lydgate also used the French translation of Boccaccio by Laurence de Premierfait, who softened the passages against the nobility. Lydgate (as a monk) muffled the criticism against the Church, and omitted the passages (both in Boccaccio and Premierfait) that subjects owe no obedience to a ruler who fails in his reciprocal obligations and duties.[66] The version of Lydgate, the laureate of the English Establishment, as Ruth Mohl wrote, "changes from a treatise written in scorn of rulers to one equally disdainful of the people they rule; it begins with the belief that no ruler is fit to rule and therefore fails, and ends with the belief that subjects of rulers exist to be ruled and for their benefit."[67]

With the Establishment so firmly entrenched, and with the *inferiores* voiceless, it is not surprising that Middle English has very little overtly subversive literature, certainly nothing with the depth and range of a Rabelais or a Cervantes. For who would dare utter a subversive word, which might be considered oral treason, when the Establishment would crack down with violence. In 1401, for example, William Clerk, a writer of Canterbury, who had "uttered against the king wicked words, laying them to the charge of others . . . was condemned by judgment of the court military, and was first reft of his tongue . . . and then of his right hand . . . and lastly by penalty of talion, because he had not made good his charges, was beheaded at the Tower."[68] In 1465, John Holton attacked the king's person "per scripturam billarum"; he was apprehended, drawn, hanged, and quartered.[69] Earlier, in 1384, a "bill" deriding Catesby,[70] Ratcliff, and Lord Lovell, the dominant advisers of King Richard II, whose cognizance was the white boar or "hog," was posted on the doors of St. Paul's Cathedral:

> The Cat, the Rat, and Lovel our dog
> Rule all England under a Hog.[71]

For this "immortal couplet," its author, Wyllyam Colyngbourne, was

put to the most cruel deth at the Tower Hylle, where for hym were made a newe payer of galowes. Vpon the whiche, after he hadde hangyd a shorte season, he was cutte down, beynge alyue, and his bowellys rypped out of his bely, and cast into the fyre there by hym, and lyued tyll the bowcher put his hande into the bulke of his body; insomuch that he sayd in the same instant, "O Lorde Ihesu, yet more trowble," and so dyed to the great compassion of moche people.[72]

The gravest attack on medieval society came not from works of direct protest and dissent, but from Wyclif, who in fact supported the secular feudal aristocracy. Wyclif, because of his public position, had a more decisive impact on English history than Langland or Gower. On one level, like Langland, he stressed personal holiness and advocated religious reform; on another, quite unconsciously, he advocated political and social change. For the first time in England, Wyclif brought together a body of reformist views previously expressed only separately, and by coalescing them revealed their latent radicalism. Most of his opinions were already current coin of the fourteenth century, but together they created England's first heresy.[73] Grosseteste had challenged the claims of the papacy, castigated the worldliness of the clergy, and had emphasized preaching and the appeal to the Bible.[74] William of Ockham, whom Wyclif claimed as his precursor, not only opposed the abuses of the papacy, but questioned its underlying principles.[75] Bishop Richard Fitzralph of Armagh, Wyclif's former teacher at Oxford, had promoted the doctrine of dominion in opposing the friars, for which he had to defend himself before the Pope in Avignon in 1357.[76] Wyclif's use of these theologians may have encouraged translations of the Latin originals. John de Trevisa, for example, who followed Wyclif as canon of Westbury, translated Fitzralph's *Defensio Curatorum*[77] as well as William of Ockham's *De Potestate Ecclesiastica et Saeculari*.[78]

From his theological bases, Wyclif drew major conclusions, basically theological but all fraught with sociological overtones. He questioned the value of the sacraments (including baptism) as essential to salvation;[79] he argued that the sacrifice of the mass was commemorative;[80] he rejected transubstantiation;[81] he said priests had no special mediating function, that the sacraments could be administered by laymen,[82] that the papacy had no authority from Christ, that the Bible should be available in the vernacular,[83] and that preaching was the most important function of a priest.[84] By denying the sacramental principles, Wyclif placed the individual into direct relationship with God, "a lyne streght unto heven."[85]

Many nobles supported Wyclif in his attacks on the papacy and the friars, on indulgences, on simony.[86] They supported him as well in advocating withholding tithes and offerings, and the removal of the temporalities from the clergy,[87] and approved of these "reforms." Few realized the political implications of his condemnation of purely religious practices.[88] Philosophically, as it turned out, Wyclif was more dangerous to the Establishment than John Ball. By abolishing the doctrinal distinction between clergy and laity,[89] Wyclif obliterated one of the Three Estates, on which, according to traditional theory, not only the well-being but the very existence of a nation rested:[90]

Crist wole ordeyne to his chirche prestis and ordre þat is nedeful . . . whanne þe pope was deed and cardenals weren not ȝit sprongun, in whois hond was þe chirche þat wandriþ heere vpon erþe? certis in cristis hond, þat dwelliþ euere heed of hooly chirche; and he mut nedis ordeyne prestis . . . and ȝif þou axe who shulde make þes prestis, and bi what wordis and whois autorite, certis bileue nediþ vs to seye þat crist mut make þes prestis, oþer bi wordis hid to vs or bi grace wiþ-oute wordis.[91]

The introduction into religion of the concept of the worthiness or unworthiness of the recipient of God's dominion, whereby a Christian man was not bound to obey an unworthy bishop or pope, was capable of transfer to an unworthy nobleman or king. And a man who refused to pay tithes to a sinful priest might easily refuse rent to a sinful lord.[92] Wyclif was blind to the parallel and denounced such advocacy as "a feyned word of anticristis clerkis." Nevertheless, the Archbishop of Canterbury and the Bishop of London, in presenting the papal condemnation of 1377, warned of these wider implications.[93] In fact, the theological charges (such as Wyclif's heresies on the Incarnation or on the imperishability of matter) were never mentioned. A reply to Wyclif, commissioned by Archbishop Arundel, noted that by his teachings, "the people could lawfully remove the possessions of kings, dukes, and their lay superiors, whenever they habitually offended."[94] And the Dominican Roger Dymoke in 1395 feared that "no one thenceforward in this kingdom would possess his lordships in safety, since anybody would be able to rise against another when he wished."[95]

On the ultimate influence of Wyclif's teaching, Workman concluded: "The Peasants' Revolt was but the rude translation into a world of practice of a theory of 'dominion' that destroyed the 'lordship' of the wicked, and exalted communism into the inalienable right of the saint." [96]

While Wyclif himself was unwilling to apply the same standards to clergy and nobles alike, accommodating himself to an uneasy dualism, once the criterion of *dominium* had been introduced, others took over. William Thorpe, a Lollard priest, was interrogated by Archbishop Arundel in 1407, and the questioning turned to secular affairs:

"Why losell! wilt not thou and others that are confedered with thee, seek out of Holy Scripture and of the sentence of Doctors, all sharp authorities against Lords and knights and Squires, and against other secular men, as thou dost against priests?"[97]

Wyclif's conservative supporters too became frightened after 1381,[98] seeing his influence, however unpremeditated, on John Ball: "Docuit et perversa dogmata perfidi Johannis Wiclyf, et opiniones quas tenuit, et insanias falsas, et plura quae longum foret recitare."[99] The more radical, however, intensified their opposition to the Establishment.[100] The Lollards, not so called until after 1383, actually did attempt to overthrow society. Lord Cobham, Sir John Oldcastle, who led the revolt in 1414, wished "quam status et officium p̄lacie Dignitatis infra Regnum Anglie, in prosperitate perseverarent, falso et proditorie machinando tam statum Regium, quam statum et officium Prelatorum, necnon ordines Religiosorum infra dictum Regnum Anglie penitus adnullare."[101] Later, Ralph Mungyn was accused of advocating that "all goods should be held in common, and no one ought to be allowed to have property."[102] By 1417, rioters were considered prima facie "verrai semblables d'estre de l'opinion des Lollardes, Traitours, et Rebelx, tout ditz maliciousement gisantz en agaite, et traitouresment purposantz de faire insurrection, ou subversion de la foy Catholique, destruction du Roy notre soveraigne Seigneur, et de son Roiaume."[103] In 1431 Lollards were again described as traitors.[104] The russet-clad "poor preachers" whom the evangelical Wyclif had been sending out to preach the Gospel since 1377, says the *Rotuli Parliamentorum*, "prechent . . . diverses Predications conteignantz Heresyes et Errours notoirs, a grant emblemissement de la Foy, et destruction des Loys et de l'estat de Seinte Esglise, a grant peril des Almes du poeplee et de tout le Roialme d'Engleterre."[105] A polemic about 1415, the sole Middle English poem dealing exclusively with the Lollards, added to a manuscript of *Piers Plowman*, makes the same changes in verse:

> and vnder colour of suiche lollynge
> To shape sodeyn surreccion
> Agaynst oure liege lord kynge
> with fals ymaginacion.[106]

The Abuses or Evils of the Age, as previously noted, were seldom specific: a king or bishop or judge was unworthy; the abuse was chronic, and the complaints generally end with pious resignation, like "Be thou pacient in thyn aduersite / ffor when god wyll better may be."[107] Seeing the differences in attitude between the homilists and the activists, we are reminded of Carlyle's anecdote: "Well, well, God mend all!" "Nay, by God, Donald, but we must help Him to mend it."

It was left to John Ball, the priestly theoretician – if one may call him that – of the Peasants' Revolt[108] to "mend it" and turn the topos of the Evils of the Age into justification for the overthrow of the government:

> now raygneth pride in price,
> couetise is holden wise,
> lechery without shame,
> gluttonie without blame,
> enuye raygneth with reason,
> and sloath is taken in great season.[109]

For a campaign piece, Ball added to this ineffectual catalogue one line, "God doe bote for nowe is time," and thereby transformed it into a summons to man the barricades. For a moment it was victory for "Freedom Now."[110] A similar catalogue ends limply with a hoped-for change, but "whanne hit shal be, we knowen not!"[111] How accurate was the Earl of Salisbury's realization, according to Froissart, that for the nobility, "if [we] can appease them by fair words, it will be so much the better, and good humouredly grant them what they ask; for, should we begin what we cannot go through, we shall never be able to recover it: it will be all over with us and our heirs, and England will be a desert."[112]

While some of the eleven planks of the Great Society grew out of a coherent philosophy of radicalism, like the primitive republicanism of Marsilius of Padua,[113] in the main the Rebellion was an *ad hoc* affair, touched off by unbearable injustices. "Ubi cum venissent conquesti sunt regi se multiplici et intolerabili servitute et vexatione graviter oppressos, nec posse nec velle ulterius sustinere."[114]

It was to this sense of "intolerable servitude" that Ball appealed when he preached his famous sermon on June 13, 1381, at Blackheath to the rebel forces before they took London. For his theme he used a Latin proverb: "Cum vanga quadam tellurem foderit Adam / Et Eva nens fuerat, quis generosus erat?"[115] It was common in other tongues as well as English: "When Adam delved and Eve span / Who was then a gentleman?"[116] This catchy couplet is probably the most compressed bit of anti-Establishment writing in Middle English, for by attacking head-on the whole theory of the Three Estates, it advocated a new form of classless society.[117] And, again according to Froissart, Ball did indeed preach a new order:

My good friends, things cannot go on well in England, nor ever will until every thing shall be in common; when there shall neither be vassal nor lord, and all distinctions levelled; when the lords shall be no more masters than ourselves. How ill have they used us? and for what reason do they thus hold us in bondage? Are we not all descended from the same parents, Adam and Eve?[118]

Contrasting the riches and luxury and ease of the lords with the poverty and misery and subjugation of working people, Ball drew the astute political conclusion: "it is from our labour they have wherewith to support their pomp."[119] Then he asked the key question: "And what can [the lords] shew, or what reasons give, why they should be more the masters than ourselves?"[120]

Apologists for the aristocracy might answer that while originally every man had been equal, some proved wiser or better leaders for ensuring peace, and to them the others voluntarily gave precedence and rewards. A Tudor interlude, *Of Gentleness and Nobility, a Dialogue between the Merchant, the Knight, and the Ploughman, Disputing who is a very Gentleman* (about 1529), discusses Ball's question at some length. The Ploughman paraphrases Ball's sermon against the "robber barons":

> All possessions began furst of tyranny
> For when people began furst to encrece
> Some gafe them self all to Idylnes
> And wold not labour but take by vyolence
> That other men gat by labour and dylygence . . .
> So possessyons began by extorcyon
> And when such extorsyoners had oppressyd
> The labouryng people than they ordeynyd
> And made laws meruelous strayte and hard
> That theyr heyres myght inioy it afterward.[121]

Though the Great Revolt failed, it was not without some permanent effect.[122] It crystallized the identity of unorthodoxy in both politics and religion. It was testimony to the coming of age of the peasant as no longer serf, but as freeman in spirit and outlook. A contemporary poem, "The Course of Revolt," worries that the peasants "dred no man."[123] Some rhymes from Yorkshire in 1392 stress the independence of a man who claims respect and dignity by virtue of his common humanity, a far cry from the generalized laments of 1311:

> but hething will we suffer non –
> neither of hobb nor of Ion,
>   with what man he be . . .
> who-so doth vs any wrong . . .
> yet he might als weele . . .
>   Doe againe us all.[124]

This paper has emphasized those writings which attack the very heart of the Establishment, the theory of the Three Estates, which was used to justify almost any abuse, evil, wickedness, corruption. Other attacks – on dress, cosmetics, luxuries, all concerned with personal morality – are tangential or peripheral, even though they may make agreeable *vers de société*. Squibs and lampoons will bring about no change in the distribution of power, and exposés of such blemishes constitute no clear and present danger – and that is why these were tolerated. Their range extends from popular carols on the misuse of wealth, from mystery plays like the First and Second Shepherds' Plays in the *Towneley Cycle* which oppose the high taxation, the Robin Hood ballads (in their present form Tudor, though they are known by the late fourteenth century),[125] and topsy-turveydom nonsense verses to political prophecies, polemical tracts, and the more elaborate poems outfitted with "I and O" refrains or allegoric figures descended from the *Roman de la Rose*.

Satires against clerics serve their turn when they whittle away the privilege and power of the most organized Estate in medieval society.[126] One weapon may be polemic: "Why I can't be a Nun," early fifteenth century, is an elaborate development of a *chanson de nonne*, progressing from the confessions of a girl, Katherine, who is learning from her father and the commissioners about the actual state of the nunneries.[127] Another weapon may be ridicule: the contempt of impotent old men in "Lyarde" is bracketed with scorn of lecherous friars, who admit no one to their order "bot if he may wele swyfe . . . twyse or thrise at the leste on a schorte somer nyghte."[128] Humor and ridicule also come within the purview of the anti-Establishment in *Le Ordre de Bel-Eyse*[129] and *The Land of Cokaygne*.[130] In the laughter over the wiles of the young friars flying about like birds and trying to catch a naked young nun bathing in the river to teach her – the poem says – an orison "wiþ iambleue vp and dun," and the abbot recalling his flock by taking "a maidin of þe route / and turniþ vp har white toute, / and betiþ þe taburs wiþ is hand," one can also detect a strong motif for a new society, when clergy – no longer granted the exemption from manual labor even Langland would allow them – must do all the dirty work of the lowest type of manual worker as penance before gaining admission to Cokaygne:

> Whose wl com þat lond to,
> ful grete penance he mot do:
> Seue ȝere in swine-is dritte
> he mote wade, wol ȝe iwitte,
> al anon vp to þe chynne,
> so he schal þe lond winne.[131]

Whether this gay mockery had the social impact of *Pierce the Ploughman's Crede* in downgrading the clerical establishment is a question. This first and best imitation of *Piers Plowman* presents some of the most intense exposés of the luxuries of the mendicants in all Middle English literature, as well as a terrifying picture of poverty, the ploughman's wife in tatters, her bare feet leaving blood tracks on the ice.[132]

The Estate of the nobles was also satirized. "The Tournament of Tottenham," about 1450, describes a mock tournament by a group of appren-

tices for the hand of Tyb, daughter of Randolf the Reeve.[133] Bishop
Thomas Percy, who first popularized the poem in 1765, had high praise
for it. "Two of our writers in the rudest times could see through the
false glare that surrounded them, and discover whatever was absurd in
them both [Chivalry and Romance]. Chaucer's *Sir Thopas* ridicules Romance; *Tournament of Tottenham* burlesques the former." Bishop Percy
continued: "Our poet . . . easily perceived that inveterate opinions must
be attacked by other weapons beside proclamations and censures; he accordingly made use of the keen one of ridicule."[134] Of course, while
mocking the tournament, the typical knightly sport of the nobility,[135]
the poet also mocked the low-bred "parcel of clowns" who aspire to the
manners of knights. In many ways, the skit anticipates *Ralph Royster
Doyster* or *The Knight of the Burning Pestle.*

Over the three hundred years of Middle English literature, a small
stream of writings like these was creating a tradition of protest and
dissent;[136] alongside major works by Langland and Wyclif, these are
minor items, but all are asking questions to which the Establishment
could provide no ready answers and are slowly subverting old accepted
standards.

Two conclusions may be drawn from the foregoing discussion:

First: In certain respects Middle English literature itself, by its very
existence, advocated dissent. It is in the vernacular. To break away from
Latin or French and use English was a major act of rebellion. "Holy writ
in Englische wole make cristen men at debate, and sugettis to rebelle
ageyns her sovereyns."[137] The vernacular destroyed the intellectual and
political control of the aristocrats of church and state. With the vernacular, ordinary people could approximate the knowledge and skills of the
ruling class. Not merely religion, which formed the battleground where
the right to read in the vernacular was won, but law, politics, history,
science, and medicine were opened up to the English people at large. The
extent of this revolutionary change may be gauged by the estimate that
for every page of English written in the thirteenth century, ten were
written in the fifteenth.[138]

Any government bent on preserving the *status quo* has to be repressive.
The written word had to be restricted, for the subversion inherent in it
was clear. "Preachers are warned, if they are preaching to the people
to alter stories reflecting on the monks so as to make them of general
application; otherwise the religious will be brought into contempt."[139]
The Lambeth Council of 1407–8 decreed: "The licensed preacher may
preach to the laity only against layfolk's sins; he may preach against clerical sins only in select clerical assemblies."[140] Since it is preserved in a
Franciscan manuscript, *The Land of Cokaygne* was probably originally
an in-joke among the friars themselves. Even to learn the written word
was subversive. Lords fined fathers for daring to send their sons to

school.[141] Any author who selected the native tongue as his medium, up to the end of the fourteenth century, when Gower was writing with equal facility in Latin, French, and English, was in effect supporting dissent.[142]

Second: The nature of a writer is to portray accurately what he sees, no matter what political persuasion he supports. The chasm between precept and practice, between the idea and the institution, between justice and law, love and marriage, religion and the Church, makes the works of any author who tries to show life the way it is – any time, anywhere – inevitably radical. Sir John Fortescue, a man of quality and education, could describe the misery of the French peasants with the empathy of a Kingsley and pinpoint the cause with the acumen of a Marx:

> Thai drinken water, thai eyten apples, with brede right browne made of rye; thai eyten no flesshe but yf it be right seldon a little larde, or of the entrales and heydes of bestis slayn for the nobles and marchauntes of the lande . . . Thair wyfes and children gone bare fote; thai mowe in no oþer wyse leve . . . But verely thai liven in the most extreme pouertie and miserie, and yet dwellyn thei in on the most fertile reaume of the worlde.[143]

No matter that Fortescue needed such a description to emphasize the superiority of the English *ius politicum et regale* over the French *ius regale*. No matter what his purpose, his little vignette inadvertently sowed the seeds of doubt and questioning: Why Poverty in the midst of Plenty? And did the moralist Langland, drawing his heartrending sentimental picture of the poverty of an English family, realize his verses might lead some to doubt the morality of an Establishment that had so long condoned it:

>   . . . and poure folke in Cotes
> Charged with children and chef lordes rente . . .
> Al-so hem selue suffren muche hunger,
> And wo in winter-tyme with wakynge a nyghtes
> To ryse in þe ruel to rocke þe cradel . . .
> The wo [of] þese women þat wonyeþ in Cotes . . .
> And beth abasshed for to begge and wolle nat be aknowe
> What hem needeþ at here neihebores at non and at euen.[144]

Passages like these can be linked with the general disaffection and run parallel to the underground manifestos of the rebels of 1381, with their code words of "Do Wel" and "Do Bet" and "Piers the Plowman."[145] But all Langland could see in working-class poverty was not exploitation, but (like Gower) uppity laborers demanding exorbitant wages for little work.[146]

The value of protest and dissent in Middle English literature is this: the writers take an extant European tradition,[147] turn it into English, make it national, and manage to ask significant questions under the very nose –

might one say noose? – of the Establishment, and form a body of writing that continued to grow through the centuries. The ghost of Langland stands behind Lilburne, and the ghost of Wyclif behind Winstanley. One might fantasize that the Lollard Payne was reincarnated four hundred years later with the same surname.[148] Slowly an ideology was built up that gave intellectual justification for the successful English Revolution of 1642, and in the dismal years of the nineteenth century inspired the Chartists (who formed a "Wat Tyler Brigade") and produced a spark that set Southey and Morris aflame with the spirit of 1381:

> Men of England, wherefore plow
> For the lords who lay you low?

Every man tries to do what he can to build a world nearer the heart's desire. There is no point in berating Bishop Reginald Pecock who wrote the memorable English quatrain[149] which so well summarized his theological quandary:

> Witte hath wondir that resoun ne telle kan,
> How maidene is modir, and God is man.
> Leve thy resoun and bileve in the wondir,
> For feith is aboven and reson is undir.[150]

It served him little that he was a strong anti-Lollard; he dared use the Lollard rationale. Pecock was compelled to recant, accept solitary confinement, and on December 4, 1457, watch his books instead of his body being burned:

I am in a strait betwixt two, and hesitate in despair as to what I shall choose. If I defend my opinions and position, I must be burned to death; if I do not, I shall be a byeword and a reproach.[151]

Pecock's decision, however, might be contrasted with that of the four Lollards in 1496 who chose burning at St. Paul's Cross, "with the Bookes of their lore langyng abowte theym."[152]

One cannot but admire the anonymous dissenters who have left no memorial and of whom only an occasional name or occasional memento has survived. The words of a typical dissenter should make medievalists proud, one might submit, that the open expression of protest and dissent in an honorable and honored stream in Middle English literature. William Grindcobbe had been captured in the 1381 revolt of St. Albans, and he suffered the fate Bishop Pecock managed to avoid. Walsingham's report of his final words form a fitting conclusion to the medievalists' contribution to the American Bicentennial:

Fellow citizens, you whom a newborn freedom has released from longstanding oppression, stand firm while you can. Have no fear of my execution. And if I must die, I shall count myself happy to end my life by such a martyrdom.[153]

This is the true spirit of seventy-six – in any century.

NOTES

This article is based on a paper presented to the Mediaeval Academy of America on March 27, 1976, at Tulane University. Because it was specifically requested by the Academy as a contribution to the Bicentennial celebrations, I have retained some of the introductory prologue and the title. Several sections, in much abridged form, were read at the XI Conference of the Fédération international des langues et littératures modernes in Islamabad, Pakistan, in September 1969, but not published. A detailed account of some Middle English verse appeared in my "Middle English Poems of Protest," *Anglia*, 78 (1960), 193–203; and in my description and bibliography of over 300 items, "Poems on Contemporary Conditions," in *A Manula of the Writings in Middle English 1050–1500*, ed. Albert E. Hartung (New Haven, 1976), V, 1385–1536, 1631–1725.

1. *Rotuli Parliamentorum* (London, 1710), III, 322, 356. *The Brut*, ed. F. W. D. Brie, EETS, O.S. 136 (London, 1908), II, 329: "þey myȝte no longer suffre non such berþes ne charges." Detailed account in *The Anonimalle Chronicle 1333 to 1381*, ed. V. H. Galbraith (Manchester, 1970), pp. 79–100.
2. *Historical Poems of the XIVth and XVth Centuries*, ed. Rossell Hope Robbins (New York, 1959), p. 55.
3. *Ibid.*, p. 2.
4. *Works of Edmund Burke*, (Oxford, 1907), V, 103–4: "[John Ball,] that reverend Patriarch of sedition, and prototype of our modern preachers, was of the opinion with the French [National] Assembly, that all the evils which have fallen upon men had been caused by an ignorance of their 'having been born and continued equal as to their rights.' "
5. Thomas Paine, *Rights of Man* (London, 1915), pp. 236–7.
6. *Ibid.*
7. See Thomas J. Elliott, "Middle English Complaints against the Times: To Contemn the World or to Reform it?" *Annuale Medievalia*, 14 (1973), 22–34.
8. Robbins, *Historical Poems*, pp. 141, 324. See also V. J. Scattergood, "Political Context, Date and Composition of *The Sayings of the Four Philosophers*," *Medium Aevum*, 37 (1967), 157–65; Thomas L. Kinney, "The Temper of Fourteenth-Century Verse of Complaint," *Annuale Medievalia*, 7 (1966), 75–89.
9. Robbins, *Historical Poems*, pp. 145–6.
10. *Ibid.*, p. 145.
11. *Political Poems and Songs Relating to English History*, ed. Thomas Wright, Rolls Series, 14 (London, 1859, 1861), I, 238–42.
12. Robbins, *Historical Poems*, p. 128.
13. Wright, *Political Poems*, II, 252; later version in Robbins, *Historical Poems*, pp. 149–50.
14. John Peter, *Complaint and Satire in Early English Literature* (Oxford, 1956), p. 59. Similarly Morton W. Bloomfield, *Piers Plowman as a Fourteenth-Century Apocalypse* (New Brunswick, 1961), p. 29. For an opposing view see Elliott, *Annuale Medievalia* 14, 34.
15. One can never be certain. A Yorkist poet in 1462 laments "Woo be to þat Regyon / Where ys a kyng vnwyse or Innocent" (Robbins, *Historical Poems*, p. 224, vv. 49–50). Is he echoing the traditional signs of trouble of Ecclesiastes 10:16: "Woe to the land when the king is a child?" But in

1461 Henry VI was not a child, but surely unwise. Is this poem then a direct partisan attack, a popular protest, or an aphorism? See John W. McKenna, "Henry VI of England and the Dual Monarchy: Aspects of Royal Political Propaganda, 1422–1432," *Warburg and Courtauld Institute Journal*, 28 (1965), 145.

16. Robbins, *Historical Poems*, p. 129. For a full discussion see Rossell Hope Robbins, "On Dating a Middle English Moral Poem," *Modern Language Notes*, 70 (1955), 473–6.

17. *The Historical Collections of a Citizen of London in the Fifteenth Century*, ed. James Gairdner, Camden Society, N.S. 17 (London, 1876), 199–202.

18. See Robbins, *Historical Poems*, pp. 143, 326.

19. *The Political Songs of England*, ed. Thomas Wright, Camden Society 6 (London, 1839), 14–8, 27–36, 42–4, 46–51, 133–6.

20. *Ibid.*, pp. 47, 48.

21. See Kenneth W. Cameron, *Authorship and Sources of "Gentleness and Nobility"* (Raleigh, N.C., 1941); Ruth Kelso, "Sixteenth Century Definitions of the Gentleman in England," *Journal English and Germanic Philology*, 24 (1925), 370–82; John E. Mason, *Gentlefolk in the Making: Studies in the History of English Courtesy Literature and Related Topics from 1531 to 1744* (Philadelphia, 1935); George McGill Vogt, "Gleanings for the History of a Sentiment: Generositas virtus, non sanguis," *Journal English and Germanic Philology*, 24 (1925), 102–24.

22. Even Chaucer, a paid servant of the Court, the martyrologist John Foxe considered "a right Wicleuian" – quoted in Caroline F. E. Spurgeon, *Five Hundred Years of Chaucer Criticism and Allusion 1357–1900* (Cambridge, 1925), I, 106. Nearly 600 years later, a United States investigating committee trembled lest Chaucer again inspire subversion: committee agents, banned from Westminster Abbey, had to settle for burning *The Canterbury Tales*, with ten other books (John Foster Dulles "did not know" which) in March/April, 1953, in New Delhi, Bombay, or Calcutta. See "Books Are Burning," *Nation*, June 20, 1953, p. 515, referring to the edition illustrated by Rockwell Kent.

23. See Sylvia L. Thrupp, "The Problem of Conservatism in Fifteenth-Century England," *Speculum*, 18 (1943), 366, 367.

24. According to Thrupp, *loc. cit.*, p. 364, the gentry numbered "several thousand" families.

25. A. I. Doyle, "A Treatise of the Three Estates," *Dominican Studies*, 3 (1950), 356–7.

26. *Select English Works*, ed. Thomas Arnold (Oxford, 1869–71), III, 130.

27. *The English Works of Wyclif Hitherto Unprinted*, ed. F. D. Matthew, EETS, O.S. 74 (London, 1880), 362 (The Clergy May Not Hold Property). Perhaps not by Wyclif, p. 359. See also Sheila Delany, "Substructure and Superstructure: the Politics of Allegory in the Fourteenth Century," *Science & Society*, 38 (1974), 257–80.

28. Matthew, *EETS* 74, 363.

29. May McKisack, *The Fourteenth Century 1307–1399*, Oxford History of England, 5 (Oxford, 1959), p. 468. On the other hand, the nobility was so worried about upward mobility that sumptuary laws were passed to prevent rich townspeople from dressing like lords and ladies; see Elspeth M. Veale, *The English Fur Trade in the Later Middle Ages* (Oxford, 1966), pp. 3–5.

30. *Piers Plowman: The B Version*, ed. George Kane and E. Talbot Donaldson (London, 1974): B. XI. 294–5. See also *The Vision of William Concerning*

Piers the Plowman, ed. Walter W. Skeat, EETS, O.S. 54 (London, 1973), C. VI. 77.

31. *The Minor Poems of Vernon MS.*, ed. F. J. Furnivall, EETS, O.S. 117 (London, 1901), I, 561 (Little Cato), vv. 103–04.

32. *The Complete Poetry and Prose of Geoffrey Chaucer*, ed. John H. Fisher (New York, 1977), *CT*, X. 770. Similarly Lydgate: "Remembre you how god hathe sette you, lo / And doo your parte, as ye ar ordeynd to" – Robbins, *Historical Poems*, p. 233.

33. Lydgate's trans. of Guillaume de Guileville's *Pelerinage de la vie humaine*, *The Pilgrimage of the Life of Man*, ed. F. J. Furnivall, EETS, E.S. 77, 83 (London, 1899, 1901), 311 (vv. 11375–80).

34. Matthew, *EETS* 74, 364. Another common analogy was the body-state, found widely; full documentation in Maud Elizabeth Temple, "Fifteenth Century Idea of Responsible State," *Romanic Review*, 6 (1915), 402–433.

35. St. Augustine, *De Civitate Dei*, XIX. 17; adopted by Gower, *Vox Clamantis*, in *The Major Latin Works of John Gower*, trans. and ed. Eric W. Stockton (Seattle, 1962), p. 105 and passim.

36. *Piers Plowman*, B. XI. 204.

37. So Langland, who approved restrictions forbidding ordination to "Bondmen and bastardes and beggers children / Thuse by-longeþ to labour and lordes kyn to seruen" – C. VI. 65-6, Skeat, *EETS* 54, 85.

38. Marsilius of Padua, *Defensor Pacis*, ed. C. W. Previté-Orton (Cambridge, 1928), I, xii, 4, quoted by R. H. Bowers, "The Middle English Obey Your King and Lord," *Southern Folklore Quarterly*, 16 (1952), 224. Description and bibliography in Rossell Hope Robbins, "Poems on Contemporary Conditions," in *A Manual of the Writings in Middle English 1050–1500*, ed. Albert E. Hartung (New Haven, 1976), V, 1500, 1701-2 (No. 242). See Alan Gewirth, *Marsilius of Padua The Defender of Peace* (New York, 1951), I. 191.

39. *The English Works of John Gower*, ed. G. C. Macaulay, EEST, E.S. 81 (London, 1900), I, 7 (Pro., vv. 99, 102–5).

40. *Ibid.*, Pro., vv. 106-8. And see Pro., vv. 127-32.

41. *Piers Plowman*, B. XIX. 467: "Ye ben but membres and I aboue alle . . . for I iugge yow alle."

42. *Piers Plowman*, B. VI. 24-36.

43. *Piers Plowman*, C. VI, 54-7; Skeat, *EETS* 54, 85: "For by lawe of leuitici þat oure lord ordeynede / Clerkes þat aren crouned of kynde vnderstondyng / Sholde noþer swynke ne swete."

44. *Piers Plowman*, C. VI. 59; Skeat, *EETS* 54, 85.

45. Matthew, *EETS* 74, 227; and see note, p. 226. See also Sermon XXV in Arnold, *Select English Works*, II, 296 (obedience is due even to unworthy lords); *Wimbledon's Sermon*, ed. Ione Kemp Knight (Pittsburgh, 1967), esp. pp. 62–68.

46. Henry de Bracton, *De Legibus et Consuetudinibus Angliae*, ed. George E. Woodbine, (New Haven, 1922), II, 305. Translation by Fisher, *Gower*, pp. 181-2.

47. *LGW*, Pro. F, vv. 382-3.

48. *Vox Clamantis*, VI. 581, in Stockton, *Major Latin Works*, p. 233.

49. Robbins, *Historical Poems*, pp. 227-32.

50. So Lydgate, *Fall of Princes*, ed. Henry Bergen, EETS, E.S. 123, III, 889: "Thestat of kynges gan be permyssioun / Of Goddis grace and of his purueyaunce." For general summary see Fritz Kern, trans. and ed. S. B. Chrimes, *Kingship and Law in the Middle Ages* (Oxford, 1939), pp. 140-1;

for development of theory and relations of Richard II and Wyclif see John Neville Figgis, *The Divine Right of Kings* (Cambridge, 1914), pp. 68–80.

51. *Confessio Amantis,* Macaulay, EETS E.S. 82, II, 472 (VIII, vv. 3058–63); Fisher, *Gower,* p. 192.

52. Bromyard, trans. G. R. Owst, *Literature and Pulpit in Medieval England* (Cambridge, 1933), p. 352.

53. Except for Richard II's call in 1385, the feudal levy had not been summoned for over half a century; see J. J. N. Palmer, "The Last Summons for a Feudal Army in England (1385)," *English Historical Review,* 83 (1968), 771.

54. Together with lawyers, "they usurp in time the place of the old feudal nobility." See Ritchie Girvan, "The Medieval Poet and his Public," *English Studies Today,* ed. C. L. Wrenn and G. Bullough (Oxford, 1951), p. 87.

55. Mohl, *Three Estates,* p. 278.

56. *Mirour de l'Omme* (vv. 25192–9), *The Complete Works of John Gower: Vol. I, The French Works,* ed. G. C. Macaulay (Oxford, 1899), p. 278. Translation by Fisher, *Gower,* p. 348: "God established rightly that one country should have need of another. Therefore God ordained merchants who should search in other lands for what one doesn't have. Therefore one who looks to himself and trades honestly is blessed by God and man."

57. See Margaret Schlauch, "Chaucer's Doctrine of Kings and Tyrants," *Speculum,* 20 (1945), 141: "The spokesmen of a mediaeval hierarchic society were using the formulations of an earlier age to confirm practices of their own, and in doing so they retained the irrelevant with the relevant."

58. See Robbins, *Anglia* 78, 194–5.

59. *How the Wise Man Taught hys Sone,* ed. Rudolf Fischer, Erlanger Beiträge zur Englischen Philologie, 2 (Erlangen, 1889), pp. 29, 33.

60. *Peter Idley's Instructions to his Son,* ed. Charlotte d'Evelyn (Boston, 1935), p. 81.

61. Archbishop Arundel in 1407–8 had ordered that "schoolmasters must not permit their pupils to discuss the Faith, even in private." G. G. Coulton, *Inquisition and Liberty* (London, 1938), p. 280.

62. d'Evelyn, *Idley's Instructions,* p. 94.

63. d'Evelyn, *Idley's Instructions,* p. 90. For overall survey of Middle English venality satire see John A. Yunck, *The Lineage of Lady Meed* (Notre Dame, 1963), pp. 227–73.

64. d'Evelyn, *Idley's Instructions,* p. 90. Proverb in *The Paston Letters 1422–1509 A.D.,* ed. James Gairdner (London, 1907), III, 65. For detailed discussion of French (and Latin) satires on Dan Denier, see John A. Yunck, "Medieval French Money Satire," *Modern Language Quarterly,* 16 (1960), 73–82, and suggestion (p. 82) that venality satire forms "a significant part of the conservative protest" at the rise of a money economy.

65. Ruth Mohl, *Three Estates* (New York, 1933), pp. 116–7.

66. "Lydgate goes out of his way to avoid anything that might undermine the position of a monarch." Herbert Gladstone Wright, *Boccaccio in England from Chaucer to Tennyson* (London, 1957), p. 13. Later, Lydgate asserted "to moordre a prince, it is a pitous thyng" (*Fall of Princes,* IV, 1941).

67. Mohl, *Three Estates,* p. 117.

68. *Chronicon Adae de Usk A. D. 1377–1421,* ed. and trans. Sir Edward Maunde Thompson (London, 1904), pp. 58–9 (Latin), p. 222 (English trans.).

69. *Registrum Abbatiae Johannis Whethamstede,* ed. Henry Thomas Riley, Rolls Series 28, Part VI, Vol. I (London, 1872), pp. 247–8.

70. For detailed account of William Catesby, see J. S. Roskell, "William Catesby, Counsellor to Richard III," *Bulletin John Rylands Library*, 42 (1959), 145–74; couplet quoted, p. 168. See also James H. Ramsay, *Lancaster and York* (Oxford, 1892), II, 528–9.
71. Rossell Hope Robbins and John L. Cutler, *Supplement to the Index of Middle English Verse* (Lexington, Ky., 1965), No. 3318.7.
72. *Robert Fabyan: The New Chronicles of England and France*, ed. Henry Ellis (London, 1811), p. 672.
73. Yet Wyclif's opponents never refer to earlier heresies. See Gotthard Lechler, trans. and ed. Peter Lorimer, revised S. G. Green, *John Wycliffe and his English Precursors* (London, 1884), p. 54. See also H. G. Richardson, "Heresy and the Lay Power under Richard II," *English Historical Review*, 51 (1936), 1–4; George R. Coffman, "John Gower, Mentor for Royalty: Richard II," *PMLA*, 69 (1954), 956.
74. Edward A. Block, *John Wyclif Radical Dissenter* (San Diego, 1962), pp. 51–2. For "Wyclif and the Middle English Sermon," see Clifford Davidson, *Universitas*, 3 (1965), 92–9.
75. *The De Imperatorum et Pontificum Potestate of William of Ockham*, ed. C. Kenneth Brampton (Oxford, 1927), pp. xi, xxviii. See Reginald Lane Poole, *Illustrations of the History of Medieval Thought and Learning*, 2nd. ed. (London, 1920), p. 244; *John Wyclif's Polemical Works in Latin*, ed. Rudolf Buddensieg, Wyclif Society (London, 1883), I, 91–2.
76. For influence of Oxford scholars on Wyclif, see Herbert B. Workman, *John Wyclif: A Study of the English Medieval Church* (Oxford, 1926), I. 114–34.
77. For dependence of Wyclif on Fitzralph see *De Pauperie Salvatoris*, ed. R. L. Poole (with *De Dominio Divino*), Wyclif Society (London, 1890); Workman, *Wyclif*, I, 131; Gordon Leff, *Richard Fitzralph Commentator of the Sentences* (Manchester, 1963), p. 3; Aubrey Gwynn, *The English Austin Friars in the Time of Wyclif* (Oxford, 1940), pp. 59, 72–3.
78. *Dialogus inter Militem et Clericum, Richard Fitzralph's Sermon: "Defensio Curatorum,"* ed. Aaron Jenkins Perry, EETS, O.S. 167 (London, 1925).
79. Wyclif's *The Wycket* was first printed in 1546, and ed. R. Potts (Cambridge, 1851), quoted Block, *Wyclif*, p. 18.
80. *Joannis Wiclif Trialogus*, ed. G. Lechler, (Oxford, 1869), IV. 261. Matthew, *EETS* 74, 466.
81. Block, *Wyclif*, p. 15 (quoting Wycket); Lechler, *Trialogus*, IV. 272. In 1355 Ralph de Tremur had been denounced for these views by Bishop Grandison of Exeter (Coulton, *Inquisition and Liberty*, p. 265).
82. Lechler, *Trialogus*, IV, 280; see also R. L. Poole, *De Civili Dominio*, Wyclif Society (London, 1885), I, 377–8.
83. See Margaret Deanesly, *The Lollard Bible* (Cambridge, 1920), chaps. 9, 10; Workman, *Wyclif*, II, 150–88 (with detailed references); *Chronicle of Henry Knighton*, ed. Joseph Rawson Lumby, Rolls Series 92 (London, 1895), II. 152; John Purvey, "On Translating the Bible," in *Fifteenth Century Prose and Verse*, ed. Alfred W. Pollard (Westminster, 1903), pp. 191–9.
84. For references see Block, *Wyclif*, p. 37. See also fifteenth-century tract: "it is more profytable to here goddes worde in prechynge than to here ony masse." Anne Slater, "Dives and Pauper: Orthodoxy and Liberalism," *Journal of Rutgers University Library*, 31 (1967), 4.
85. Arnold, *Select English Works*, III, 407.
86. Arnold, *Select English Works*, III. 363; Matthew, *EETS* 74, 229.

87. Thompson, *Chronicon Adae de Usk,* p. 4 (Latin), p. 141 (English).
88. See Workman, *Wyclif,* II. 221; W. A. Pantin, *The English Church in the Fourteenth Century* (Notre Dame, 1962), p. 184; K. B. McFarlane, *John Wycliffe and the Beginnings of English Nonconformity* (London, 1952), pp. 58–9; K. B. McFarlane, *Lancastrian Kings and Lollard Knights* (Oxford, 1972), pp. 139–41; Joseph H. Dahmus, *The Prosecution of John Wyclif* (New Haven, 1952), p. 82.
89. Poole, *De Civili Dominio,* I. 392, and elsewhere.
90. So Margaret E. Aston, "Lollardy and Sedition 1381–1431," *Past and Present,* 17 (1960), 1–2: "The structure of medieval politics and political theories were such that extreme and penetrating statements on the nature of the church and the priesthood could hardly fail to have some bearing upon society and the state."
91. Matthew, *EETS* 74, 479.
92. *Ibid.,* p. 229.
93. *Chronicon Angliae,* ed. Edward Maunde Thompson, Rolls Series, 64 (London, 1874), p. 176.
94. Quoted by Aston, *Past and Present* 17, 9, note 36.
95. *Ibid.,* note 38. Although Wyclif argued against serfdom as a matter of justice and "hinted that women might have votes at a General Church Council" (Coulton, *Inquisition and Liberty,* pp. 268, 227), he retreated to orthodoxy at the point where he might be preaching rebellion. He had never argued, as did John of Salisbury, that resistance to tyranny was justified (Schlauch, *Speculum,* 30, 134). Wyclif emphasized the good medieval doctrine that an oppressed servant owed "mekenes" to lords unworthy and masters tyrannical (Arnold, *Select English Works,* II, 196; III, 207).
96. Workman, *Wyclif,* II, 240.
97. Pollard, *Fifteenth Century Prose and Verse,* p. 148.
98. The "safe distance between ideology and practice" no longer held; see Herbert Marcuse, *A Critique of Pure Tolerance* (Boston, 1965), p. 111. See Leslie Mahin Oliver, "Sir John Oldcastle: Legend or Literature," *Library,* Series 5, 1 (1946–7), 183: "The objections to Lollardy, it must be remembered, came from above; the people themselves were kindly disposed towards it."
99. Thomas Walsingham, *Historia Anglicana,* ed. Henry Thomas Riley, Rolls Series, 28 (London, 1864), II, 32; see also *Fasciculi Zizaniorum Johannis Wyclif cum Tritico,* ed. W. W. Shirley, Rolls Series, 5 (London, 1858), p. 275.
100. Workman, *Wyclif,* II, 225, note 3.
101. *Rotuli Parliamentorum,* IV, 108. Similarly, in P.R.O. document quoted by Aston, *Past and Present* 17, 19. See also W. T. Waugh, "Sir John Oldcastle," *English Historical Review,* 20 (1905), 434–56, 637–58.
102. Aston, *Past and Present* 17, 23, quoting *The Register of Henry Chichele,* ed. E. F. Jacob (Oxford, 1943), III, 197, 200, 202–4.
103. *Rotuli Parliamentorum,* IV, 114.
104. See John A. F. Thomson, *The Later Lollards 1414–1520* (Oxford, 1965), p. 249.
105. *Rotuli Parliamentorum,* III, 124–5, No. 17. For "A Fifteenth-Century Lollard Sermon Cycle," after Lollard doctrine had been declared heretical, see Ernest William Talbert, *Texas University Studies in English,* 19 (1939), 5–20. "Hence such attacks on clerical vices, in vernacular sermons containing definitely Lollard doctrine in the pro-themes, certainly seem to be the result of more than 'the indiscreet zeal of the orthodox'" (p. 16).
106. Robbins, *Historical Poems,* p. 156.

107. Curt F. Bühler, "Patience in Adversity," *Anglia*, 78 (1960), 418, a variant couplet heading each of four stanzas and repeated at end.

108. Similar revolts took place in the same year at Ghent, Paris, Rouen, and Florence. At Florence, Venice, and Milan, the revolts led to the governments of "tyrants." See Workman, *Wyclif*, II, 239.

109. Robbins, *Historical Poems*, pp. xlii, 54.

110. Richard II said he would "confermer et graunter a euz destre free." Galbraith, *Anonimalle Chronicle*, p. 144.

111. Robbins, *Historical Poems*, pp. 144–5.

112. *Sir John Froissart's Chronicles*, trans. and ed. Thomas Johnes (London, 1808), V, 349. See Robbins, *Anglia* 78, 197.

113. Previté-Orton, *Defensor Pacis*, p. xi: "An anti-clerical ideal of a republic only native then [1324] to North Italy."

114. *Chronicon Henrici Knighton*, ed. Joseph Rawson Lumby, Rolls Series, 92 (London, 1895), II, 133.

115. Harley MS. 3362, f. 7ʳ.

116. Carleton Brown and Rossell Hope Robbins, *The Index of Middle English Verse* (New York, 1943), and Robbins-Cutler, *Supplement*, No. 3922; *Manual*, V, pp. 1511, 1710 (No. 255) for full documentation.

117. Sir George Sitwell, "The English Gentleman," *The Ancestor*, No. 1 (April, 1902), suggests that the definition of "gentleman" became important in 1413, when an act was passed that in cases involving outlawry, the "estate, degree, or mystery" of defendants had to be specified. See also Mason, *Gentlefolk in the Making*, p. 305, note 17.

118. Johnes, *Froissart's Chronicle*, V, 333–4.

119. Marsilius of Padua had suggested that "the laity should reduce their revenues to a reasonable salary in each case, and employ the surplus on more useful purposes" (Coulton, *Inquisition and Liberty*, p. 227).

120. Johnes, *Froissart's Chronicle*, V, 334. See Owst, *Literature and Pulpit*, p. 290. For Ball see also G. G. Coulton, *Medieval Panorama* (Cambridge, 1933), p. 80; Hope Emily Allen, *Writings Ascribed to Richard Rolle* (New York, 1927), p. 176, note 1.

121. *Early English Dramatists: John Heywood*, ed. John S. Farmer (London, 1908), p. 453; also in *Malone Society Reprints*, vv. 608–12, 616–20.

122. Even John Stowe, *Annales* (London, 1631), p. 293, included Ball's arguments: "All were made alike by nature, and bondage or seruitude was brought in by vniust oppression of naughty men, against the will of God: for if it had pleased God to haue made bond-men, hee would haue appointed them from the beginning of the world, who should haue beene slaue, and who Lord."

123. Robbins, *Historical Poems*, p. 56.

124. *Ibid.*, p. 61.

125. Recent discussion and documentation in R. B. Dobson and J. Taylor, *Rymes of Robyn Hood* (London, 1976).

126. Previté-Orton, *Political Satire*, p. 8.

127. Robbins-Cutler, *Supplement*, No. 316.3; F. J. Furnivall, *Early Poems* (Berlin, 1862), pp. 138–50.

128. Brown-Robbins, *Index*, No. 2026; *Manual*, V, 1146, 1674 (No. 107). My transcription from manuscript.

129. Wright, *Political Songs*, pp. 137–148.

130. Robbins, *Historical Poems*, pp. 121–7.

131. See A. L. Morton, *The English Utopia* (London, 1952), pp. 11–24.

132. *Pierce the Ploughmans Crede*, ed. Walter W. Skeat, EETS, O.S. 30 (London, 1867). Documentation in *Manual*, V, 1447, 1676–7 (No. 109).

133. Brown-Robbins, *Index*, and Robbins-Cutler, *Supplement*, No. 2615.
134. Thomas Percy, *Reliques of Ancient English Poetry* (London, 1876), I, 254.
135. After 1530, of course, a tournament had no value as training for combat. See Noel Denholm-Young, "The Tournament in the Thirteenth Century," *Studies in Medieval History Presented to F. M. Powicke* (Oxford, 1948), pp. 240–1.
136. Robbins, *Anglia* 78, 193–203.
137. Aston, *Past and Present* 17, 39, quoting J. Forshall and F. Madden, eds., *The Holy Bible* (Oxford, 1850), I, 49.
138. In similar fashion, perhaps the current acceptance of Liverpool scousers' slang (to say nothing of more recent illiterate infelicities) on a par with the King's English or our own mid-Atlantic may turn out to be the most subversive act of the twentieth century.
139. A. G. Little, *Studies in English Franciscan History* (Manchester, 1917), p. 154 (re *Liber Exemplorum ad usum Praedicantium*).
140. Coulton, *Inquisition and Liberty*, p. 280.
141. Workman, *Wyclif*, II, 230; A. F. Leach, *The Schools of Medieval England* (London, 1915), pp. 206–7; A. W. Parry, *Education in England in the Middle Ages* (London, 1920), p. 51.
142. John Taylor, "Notes on the Rise of Written English in the Late Middle Ages," *Leeds Philological and Literary Society Proceedings*, 8, Part II (1936), 133, notes retention of Latin and French in many fifteenth-century local documents, and retention of Latin in Pipe and Plea Rolls to mid-seventeenth century.
143. *The Governance of England*, ed. Charles Plummer (Oxford, 1885), p. 114.
144. *Piers Plowman*, C. X. 72–87; EETS 54, 161–2.
145. See *Manual*, V, 1511–2, 1710–2 (No. 256).
146. See Fisher, *Gower*, p. 349, note 57. Also *Piers Plowman*, B. VI. 307–9: "Laborers þat haue no lande to lyue on but hire handes, / Deyneþ nouȝt to dyne a-day nyȝt olde wortes. / May no peny ale hem paie ne no pece of bacoun."
147. Clearly seen in the Harley MS. 2253 lyrics: Robbins, *Historical Poems*, pp. 7–9, 24–27, the former "alive with its passionate despair and sincerity of utterance" (J. P. Oakden, *Alliterative Poetry in Middle English* [Manchester, 1935], II, 10), similar to the Latin and Anglo-Norman poems of the earlier thirteenth century, as in Wright, *Political Songs*, pp. 14–18, 42–44, etc. The first "proletarian" literature might be said to be that of Sketon; see Maurice Pollet, *John Skelton* (Paris, 1962), pp. 225–35; and trans. by John Warrington (London, 1971), pp. 186–202; *The Complete Poems of John Skelton*, ed. Philip Henderson (1931; London, 1964), p. xvii.
148. See James Baker, *A Forgotten Great Englishman or the Life and Work of Peter Payne the Wycliffite* (London, 1894).
149. Pecock's troubles were in part due to his circulating criticism of the authority of Church Fathers in English, "the common peplis langage," thereby alienating his fellow bishops. See *The Folewer to the Donet*, ed. Elsie Vaughan Hitchcock, EETS, O.S. 164 (London, 1920), p. xxii, note 4.
150. Carleton Brown, *Religious Lyrics of the Fifteenth Century* (Oxford, 1952), p. 186.
151. *The Repressor of over much Blaming of the Clergy*, ed. Churchill Babington, Rolls Series, 19 (London, 1860), I, xlvi; also Emmet A. Hannick, *Reginald Pecock* (n.p., 1922), pp. 72–4; V. H. H. Green, *Bishop Reginald Pecock* (Cambridge, 1945), p. 6.

152. Charles Kingsford, *Chronicles of London* (Oxford, 1905), p. 211: "And among their Erronyous oppynyons one was, that the Sacrament of the Awter was but Materiale breed."

153. *Gesta Abbatum Monasterii Sancti Albani a Thome Walsingham*, ed. Henry Thomas Riley, Rolls Series, 28, Part IV (London, 1869), III, 341: "Concives, quos jamdudum parta libertas de oppressione diutina relevavit; state modo, dum stare licebit, et de mea mulctatione minime timeatis; qui in causa libertatis adquisitae moriar, si tunc contingat occumbere, felicem me reputans per tale posse martyrium vitam finire."

Piedmont College Library
Demorest, Georgia

The Legend of Caesar's Deer

MICHAEL BATH

The legend that Caesar put a collar round the neck of a deer which survived to a miraculous age may be familiar to scholars from an allusion in a well-known sonnet of Petrarch's, which was imitated by Sir Thomas Wyatt. The sources of this legend have never been thoroughly studied however and its provenance and meaning remain shrouded in mystery. It is possible to distinguish a number of more or less distinct iconographic traditions concerning the deer in the Middle Ages, and it may be useful to summarize these before focusing attention on the specific motif of the collared deer. The most familiar and, in terms of its influence on medieval literature, the most important is what Marcelle Thiébaux has called "the stag of love."[1] The white hart which figures in Arthurian romances is a close relative and plays a role as guide or messenger which is shared by the cruciferous stag which leads the future St. Eustace, and a number of other saints whose legends were modeled on his, to conversion or baptism.[2] The text of Psalm 41 (Quemadmodum desiderat cervus . . .) was traditionally explained as a reference to the belief found in classical zoology and perpetuated by the Bestiaries that the aging or the ailing stag ate snakes and ran to the waterbrooks to counteract the effect of the venom.[3] Commentaries on the Psalms gave an allegorical explanation to this text in which the snake was identified with the devil or sin, the waterbrooks were the fount of Christian doctrine or the saving waters of baptism, and the stag was the Christian soul or more particularly the catechumen. Versions of this symbolism are given in the Bestiaries themselves, and it is reflected in ecclesiastical monuments from the fifth century onward. Pseudo-Bede's commentary on Psalm 41 identifies the stag with Christ himself.[4] A much later tradition enjoyed a vogue throughout the Renaissance period, in which the stag represents the human soul beset by the hounds of earthly temptation or adversity.[5]

The legend of Caesar's deer, as it appears in medieval sources, has occasionally been influenced by these other traditions, but I believe it was distinct from them and that it preserved from the earliest times a significance which is neither amatory nor religious, but rather political and ethnogenic. Its classical versions have to do with dynastic fables relating to the Homeric founders of ancient cities. It is not my purpose here to embark on an exhaustive examination of these few classical sources, but simply to provide a gloss which will allow their historical significance to emerge. The account from Pausanias will stand as an epitome of the legend.

[Arcesilaus] dwelling at Lycosura, beheld the sacred deer of the mistress (as they call her); the deer was old and frail, and on its neck there was a collar, and on the collar were these words: – I was caught as a fawn when Agapenor was at Ilium. The story shows that a deer is a longer lived animal by far than even an elephant.[6]

Agapenor was, of course, the legendary ancestor and leader of the Arcadians in Homer. The Goddess known as "the Mistress" was a local chthonic goddess associated with Demeter and connected with Arcadian patriotism in local cults centering on Lycosura, where her temple was. A similar tradition is recorded in the pseudo-Aristotelian *De Mirabilibus Auscultationibus,*

Among the Peucetini they say that there is a temple of Artemis, in which is dedicated what is called a bronze necklet, bearing the legend "Diomedes to Artemis." The story goes that he hung it about the neck of a deer, and that it grew there, and in this way being found later by Agathocles, king of the Siciliots, they say that it was dedicated in the temple of Zeus.[7]

Diomedes was celebrated in this part of Italy as the Homeric founder of the colonies of Magna Graecia, of such cities as Canusium, Sipontum, Beneventum, Brundisium and Argyrippa. He was regarded as the rival of Aeneas on the Italian mainland; thus in Book viii of the *Aeneid*, Turnus sends to "the city of Diomedes" for aid against Aeneas.[8] Livy tells how before the Roman defeat at Cannae a seer warned the Romans, "descendants of Troy," not to do battle on the Plain of Diomedes.[9] Clearly it was felt as inauspicious to fight on the territory colonized by their legendary enemy. Agathocles, who in this case recaptured the deer, was tyrant of Syracuse, and at the end of his life champion of Hellenic imperialism in its doomed struggle with the expanding power of Rome on the Italian mainland. His successor was the better known Pyrrhus. Pyrrhus, indeed, regarded himself as a descendant of Achilles, and the Romans accordingly developed a counter-claim of their own Trojan origins. By the third century B.C., the story of the foundation of Rome by Aeneas had already taken its place in, for example, the Roman history of Fabius Pictor.[10] We may surely see in the story of Diomedes's deer an echo, however faint, of Agathocles's claim to be heir to Greek imperial tradition, and a parallel myth to the ethnogenic fable about Aeneas.

A story told by Silius Italicus bears a superficial resemblance to the well-known story of Sertorius's tame deer in Plutarch, but it clearly shows the same ethnogenic pattern as the collared deer in the previous examples. Silius Italicus tells how at Capua there was a rare white hind which had been tamed by Capys when he was tracing out the walls of the city with his plough. The hind survived its patron and became a deity of the city; it lived a thousand years, "and numbered as many centuries as the city founded by the Trojan exiles."[11] It was inauspiciously killed by enemy soldiers who were besieging the city. This charming anecdote is possibly a composite of various influences, showing traces of the zoological belief in cervine longevity and albinism, and the Cadmean type of animal foundation legend.[12]

Why, we may ask, should the deer have been associated with ethnogenic fables in classical times? One answer may be the ancient opinion of the stag's longevity. Hesiod was the source of a well-known proverb on the longevity of animals, and Aristotle records that stories were told of the age of stags, though he questions their truth.[13] The *Physiologus* account of the serpent-eating stag, though based primarily on a folkloric motif which is found as far afield as the near East and China, may also preserve a trace of the same belief, for the Bestiaries explain that the stag lives for fifty years before eating snakes and rushing to the water, after which he lives for another fifty years, otherwise he dies.[14] It is however Pliny the Elder who provided the major literary channel for the transmission of a belief in the longevity of stags to the Middle Ages, along with another example of the collared stag, which was destined to become familiar to later writers,

Stags are commonly acknowledged to live for a long time, some having been recaptured a hundred years later with gold necklaces which Alexander the Great had put on them, which were by then covered in folds of skin.[15]

As late as the seventeenth century writers on zoology will be found affirming that stags live to a great age, and citing Alexander's deer as evidence.[16]

Among the best-known medieval versions of the legend of Caesar's deer is that associated with Charles VI of France. The early annalists of the reign record that when Charles was at Senlis in his youth, a deer was captured bearing the inscription "Caesar hoc mihi donavit." Thereafter he adopted the winged deer wearing a collar as his personal badge, *le cerf volant couronné d'or*.[17] Froissart fancifully elaborates this story, recounting how, after losing his hawk the King dreamed he saw a marvelous winged deer on whose back he climbed and flew up into the heavens to retrieve his hawk.[18] Froissart's invention may be explained as an attempt to account for the unexpected detail of the wings, which are more likely to be a simple iconographic motif denoting swiftness, thus at least a seventeenth-century writer on emblems interprets the wings added to stags, "the adjunct emphasizes their natural swiftness."[19] The *cerf volant* becomes an important motif in the literature of late-fourteenth-century

France. Philippe de Mézières's *Songe du Vieil Pelerin,* which was written and presented to Charles VI to persuade him to undertake the great moral and spiritual reforms which were necessary if France was to fulfil Philippe's lifelong ambition of uniting Christendom against the infidel, figures the king throughout in the guise of *le Cerf Volant, couronné d'or.*[20] On Charles he pins his hopes, not just for a new crusade, but for uniting the West, reaching Jerusalem, and realizing the City of God. Eustace Deschamps figures Charles as the *cerf volant* in several *balades,* particularly in an elaborate beast allegory, in which Merlin's prophecy of the destruction of Albion is used as a pledge of the eventual triumph of the *cerf volant* over other regal animals opposed to French interests in the Hundred Years' War. In another *balade* Deschamps associated the motif with the world of the Reynardian beast fables, as he bestows on Charles, as *cerf volant,* the name Briquemer, which is the name of the stag in the *Contes de Renard.*[21]

After Charles's death, the badge was adopted by Charles VII. Christine de Pisan refers to it in her *Ditié de Jehanne d'Arc* in a stanza which picks up the idea of political prophecies which Deschamps had emphasized, and proceeds naturally to an imperial allusion,

> Car ung roy de France doit estre
> Charles, filz de Charles, nommé
> Qui sur tous rois sera grant maistre
> Propheciez l'ont surnommé
> "Le Cerf Volant," et consomé
> Sera par cellui conquereur
> Maint fait (Dieu l'a à ce somé)
> Et en fin doit estre empereur.[22]

The *cerf volant* puts in an appearance during the elaborate ceremonies marking Charles's triumphant entry into Rouen in 1449. Mathieu de Coussy's chronicle makes it clear that this, the liberation of the capital of Normandy in which not long before Joan of Arc had been burnt at the stake, was a reassertion of France's traditional sovereignty.[23] As Charles entered the celebrating city, he was greeted with a number of ceremonial and symbolic tableaux, in the manner of a Renaissance Triumph, the style of which was already established in France, as recent research has shown.[24] Near the church of Notre Dame, there was a *cerf volant,* probably some kind of automaton, with a crown round its neck and two maidens holding it on silken leads. As the King passed, the stag knelt down. The same episode is described by Martial d'Auvergne,

> Puis au carrefour de l'Eglise
> Y avoit un beau cerf volant,
> Portant en son col par devise,
> Une couronne d'or boullant.
> Et quant le Roy illec alla
> Dire ses graces en l'Eglise,

Ledit cerf si s'agenoulla,
Par honneur, et plaisance exquise.[25]

The most unexpected reappearance of the *cerf volant* is in an initial illumination to a title page of the household accounts of Queen Elizabeth I of England in the Bodleian Library.[26] The annual household accounts had decorative and emblematic titles, one of which shows a stag springing up on its hind legs, a crown round its neck and another above its head. It has fully feathered wings, and a scroll from its mouth is inscribed "Hoc Caesar me donavit." This, of course, is the motto inscribed on the collar of Charles VI's deer at Senlis. What, we may ask, is the royal badge of the kings of France doing in Queen Elizabeth's household books? The answer may lie on the title page itself, for there the Queen is described as "Dei gracia Angliae, Franciae et Hiberniae Regina." It is presumably the traditional pretensions of the English sovereigns to the throne of France which account for the choice of the winged stag.

Elizabeth was, after all, not the first English sovereign to adopt a French royal badge, for, as M. V. Clarke has shown, the livery collar of broom cods which the Plantagenet English kings favored, and which features so prominently in the Wilton Diptych, was a gift from Charles VI to Richard II on the occasion of the latter's marriage to his daughter Isabella in 1396.[27] Although there is nothing which explicitly connects Richard's own badge of the white hart with the legend of Caesar's deer, it seems plausible that he was aware of its legendary significance. Those who have discussed the iconography of the Wilton Diptych have frequently speculated on the origins of the white hart.[28] There is some evidence that it was the badge of his mother, the Maid of Kent, which appears on seals of her son, the earl of Holland in documents dated 1387 and 1396. It is, however, pertinent to note that the collared stag was adopted at about the same time by the French king. It is true that the postures and attributes are different, for the winged stag of Charles VI is upreared on its hind legs, whereas the white hart is *lodged* – the Wilton Diptych shows it seated in green pasture. Such evidence, however, is less than decisive, and before accepting any dogmatic conclusions on the origin of the badges, it would be well to be sure that one had all the heraldic sources. A French seal, for instance, attributed to Jean II of France, c. 1362, shows a hart *lodged*, with collar and chain, the end of the chain held in the claws of an eagle.[29] In the course of time the heraldic addition of collar and chain, the tendency to show various animals regally gorged, became merely conventional, and it may be that already by the time of Richard II this detail has no significance for our legend. At any rate the badge of the white hart became widely dispersed among Richard's followers, as the poet, possibly Langland, laments in *Richard the Redeless*, until eventually it found its way onto inn signs up and down the country, where it is still a familiar sight with collar and chain attached, but, alas, no inscription to Caesar.

A version of the legend from Lübeck attributes the deer to Charlemagne. According to an inscription on the walls of the cathedral, Charlemagne put a collar on the neck of a stag, which he had captured in the woods of Holstein. Four hundred years later this stag was killed by Henry the Lion, Duke of Saxony, who built a cathedral on the spot.[30] An additional feature of this version is the mention of a golden crucifix which Henry noticed between the antlers of the stag. The inscription dates from 1646 and is illustrated by murals, one depicting a stag with a golden collar and a cross above its forehead, and another showing Henry aiming his bow at the deer. This example is primarily a foundation legend, whose purpose is to account for the origins of the cathedral. It has clearly suffered various pious accretions which have nothing to do with the legend of the collared deer. The golden cross between the stag's horns will be familiar to us from the legends of St. Eustace and St. Hubert, in each of which the saint is confronted, while hunting, by a cruciferous stag, which acts as an agent of conversion.[31] The function of the deer as divine messenger is a feature of such legends and of a large number of less familiar examples which were probably modeled on them. It was likewise a deer which showed the Duke of Anségise where he should found the Abbey of Fécamp; St. Berachus was told in a vision that he should load his baggage on a deer and follow it. The saint built his church at the predetermined spot where the deer stopped.[32] The legend of St. Giles is of the same type, as is a story of David I of Scotland, albeit somewhat garbled, which tells how on a hunt the King was attacked by a white stag and saved by a cross mysteriously presented to him by a magic hand, a circumstance which led to the foundation of Holyrood Abbey in Edinburgh.[33] Raimbert de Paris tells us that a deer *blans comme nois* showed Charlemagne the St. Bernard Pass;[34] in *Les Saisnes* a deer leads Charlemagne to the only crossing of the dangerous Rune, and is taken as a sign from God;[35] a version of the *Chronicle* of Turpin tells how a stag miraculously assists Roland in crossing the river Gironde.[36]

The number of examples of the deer as guiding animal in Arthurian literature is too extensive and familiar to bear much repetition. Malory's comment on such legends deserves to be quoted, however, since he tells us what the deer means in them,

> And well ought oure Lorde be signifyed to an harte.
> For the harte, whan he is olde, he waxithe yonge agayne
> in his wyght skynne. Ryght so commyth agayne oure
> Lorde from deth to lyff, for He lost erthely flesshe,
> that was the dedly fleyssch whych He had taken in the
> wombe of the Blyssed Virgyne Mary. And for that cause
> appered oure Lorde as a whyghte harte withoute spot . . .

for oftentymes or thys hath oure Lord shewed Hym to
good men and to good knytes in lykeness of an herte . . .[37]

It is interesting to note that a number of Westphalian folktales preserve the motif of the cruciferous stag, suggesting that the detail of the
cross in the Lübeck inscription may have been influenced not so much
by the legend of St. Eustace, as by local tradition.[38] One such concerns
a huntsman who is rash enough to go hunting on Good Friday. When he
fails to catch anything, he wishes angrily that he could catch a stag with
a cross between its horns. His wish is miraculously granted, but when he
shoots it and sees the blood pouring from its side, he is overcome with
remorse and tries to stem the flow with his hand. It is too late, however,
and he is condemned to a perpetual hunt. Other Westphalian folktales of
sacrilegious hunters preserve this detail.

A double of the Lübeck deer was found at Magdeburg. Opposite the
statue of Roland in the square, there stood on a plinth a stag with a golden
collar, which local tradition claimed Charlemagne had hung there. The
collar showed a cross and the words,

> Lieber Jäger, lass mich leben,
> Ich will dir mein Halsband geben.[39]

The stag was recaptured in the time of Frederick Barbarossa. There is
no mention of Henry the Lion, and it may be that "captured in the time
of" means originally "captured by." Clearly the story of a stag captured
"in the time of" Frederick the Great was not confined to Lübeck, though
in Lübeck it would be natural to attribute the recapture to the city's
patron and founder of its cathedral. The Hohenstaufen period showed
a strong revival of the idea of Empire, as Robert Folz and others have
shown, for Frederick claimed to be the successor of Charlemagne and,
through him, of the authority of the first Caesars. This revival culminated
in the canonization of Charlemagne in 1165. One of the reasons why
Henry the Lion was left to rule his extensive territories, stretching at
one time from the North Sea to the Adriatic, was because Frederick left
his country to receive the imperial crown at Rome. It may be that the
recapture of Charlemagne's deer reflects some hint of this imperial
renovatio. At the same time there are a number of additional features
which should be remarked – the insidious intrusion of the pious detail of
the cross, for instance, or the connection, if it is a connection, with the
statue of Roland. Roland statues are found in a number of north German
cities. That in Bremen is identified with the fortunes of the city: "As long
as Roland stands, the city will be free," runs a local saying.[40] The statue
of Roland appears to have acquired a civic meaning not far removed
from that of the legendary Capuan deer.

Local tradition in England also preserves a record of Caesar's deer. I
have discovered three versions recorded at widely separate intervals. The

earliest is in Nicholas Upton's *De Studio Militari* (c. 1445). In discussing the deer as a heraldic device, Upton sets out the known zoology of the animal, paraphrasing Isidore and Pliny the Elder, and he quotes Pliny's anecdote about Alexander's deer as the standard piece of evidence on longevity. He then goes on to supply an example of his own, concerning a stag killed near Besastine in Windsor forest, with a golden collar bearing the following inscription,

> Julius Cesar quant jeo fu petis
> Ceste coler sur mon col ad mys.[41]

Upton does not pause to consider how Caesar came to write in Old French, indeed with an engaging ingenuousness he translates the motto into Latin for his modern readers. Some two hundred years after Upton, the celebrated English naturalist John Ray was visiting Yorkshire on one of his Itineraries. On the third of August, 1661, he was near Leeds at a place called Rothwell Haigh,

where (according to the vulgar tradition) was once found a stag, with a ring of brass about its neck, bearing this inscription:

> When Julius Caesar here was king
> About my neck he put this ring:
> Whosoever doth me take
> Let me go for Caesar's sake.[42]

Two hundred years after Ray, the same verses were recorded in Dorset, three hundred miles to the south. Not far from the town of Sherborne, there is a small village with the unusual name of King's Stag. It lies in the Vale of Blackmore, otherwise known as Vale of the White Hart, which in medieval times was a royal deer forest. A local anecdote, first recorded in Camden's *Britannia* (1637), tells of a white hart which king Henry III had run down and spared. The hart was later killed by a local gentleman, one Thomas de la Lynde. In his anger the king imprisoned de la Lynde and placed a fine on his lands, and, indeed, a fine known as White Hart Silver was paid into the exchequer by certain Dorset estates until the mid-nineteenth century, when the Victorian revenue authorities finally decided that enough was enough. Outside the village inn there used to hang a sign displaying a stag with a gold collar, and on the reverse the following rhyme,

> When Julius Caesar landed here
> I was then a little deer:
> When Julius Caesar reigned king
> Round my neck he put this ring.
> Whoever shall me overtake
> Spare my life for Caesar's sake.[43]

I have no ready explanation as to how these verses were disseminated, but it seems necessary to posit the existence of a popular and otherwise unrecorded tradition. That the Windsor anecdote directly inspired the Yorkshire verses and the Dorset inn sign seems quite improbable.

Whereas in England the legend seems to have been part of folklore, in Italy its popularity derived from a famous sonnet in which Petrarch compared Laura to a white hind, inviolable because dedicated to Caesar.[44] The sonnet inspired imitations by Romanello and Sir Thomas Wyatt, while the commentaries of Petrarch's editors occasionally show some familiarity with the legend and its sources. It is clear that in Petrarch's poem the deer has lost any ethnogenic or political significance it may have had and its meaning is to be understood in the light of the amatory and the religious traditions of cervine iconography, for the white hart has not only changed its sex, but Caesar, as most of the commentators recognize, is God. The motto in Petrarch's poem is given in Italian,

> "Nessum mi tocchi," al bel collo d'intorno
> Scritto avea di diamanti e di topazi;
> "Libera farmi al mio cesare parve."

but his editors quote a Latin formula which was to become extremely well known, and whose origins I cannot discover, "Noli me tangere, Caesaris enim sum." By the sixteenth century this motto seems to have become proverbial, for John Anstis, citing Menestrier, says that "the family of Pompei in Italy use two Harts for their Supporters collared with the Letters N.M.T. in memory of one taken, on whose Collar as is said, were these words Nemo me tangere, Caesaris sum."[45] Pier Mattioli quotes the motto and alludes to Pliny's story of Alexander's deer in his commentary on Dioscorides.[46] In this Renaissance literary tradition, it is the elusiveness and inviolability of the deer which is of primary significance; its whiteness is emblematic of purity, its collar of chastity. We have entered into a more conscious and sophisticated iconographic world.

It is no part of my purpose here to solve the hermeneutic problems raised by Petrarch's sonnet or its imitations, but it is of some interest to note the ways in which Petrarch's commentators understand the symbolism of his white hind. As Patricia Thomson has pointed out, there is a certain lack of unanimity among them.[47] They seldom miss the opportunity to spell out the allusion to Caesar's deer, though they seldom give sources. Gesualdo, it is true, speaks of the ancient custom of putting collars on deer, such as those which Alexander the Great had ringed, and Daniello da Lucca quotes the whole of Robert Gaguin's account of Charles VI's deer from the *Gesta Francorum*.[48] There is a general consensus among commentators that the deer stands for chastity and that her flight is from carnal passion. Caesar, however, gives some difficulty. Venaphro affirms that Caesar is God, but Squarciafico believes he is the lady's husband, and Gesualdo elaborates what Patricia Thomson calls the "fantastic notion" that the reference is to the law *de adulteris* promulgated by Julius Caesar.[49] With a fine disregard of the text he goes on to dedicate the deer to Diana, goddess of chastity, and supports this by citing two classical anecdotes about deer, neither of which has anything to do with Petrarch's poem. The first is the story of Iphigenia at Aulis, where Artemis substitutes a deer for sacrifice in place of Iphigenia; the second is the tale of Sertorius's deer from Plutarch. Petrarch's deer is probably to be understood more in the spirit of St François de Sales, who, speaking of the natural inclination of the human heart to love God, says that this inclination binds us just as the inscribed collars bind deer to those *grans princes* who have captured them and set them free in the forests, bearing their arms, and the motto "Caesar m'a lasché."[50]

It has been noted that the opening words of the inscription which the Italians hung round the neck of Caesar's deer are those of the resurrected Christ to Mary Magdalene (John 20:17). However, Petrarch does not quote the Vulgate wording, since his motto is in Italian. His commentators do not spell out any such allusion, and although Wyatt used the "Noli me tangere" motto, such an allusion would be quite alien to the spirit and meaning of his poem,

> *Noli me tangere,* for Caesars I ame
> And wylde for to hold, though I seme tame.

It has been suggested that Wyatt's Caesar is not Julius, nor Augustus, nor God, but Henry VIII, and that the poem refers to an affair between Wyatt and Anne Boleyn. The evidence is inconclusive, however. What in Petrarch is a particular case and a unique vision, becomes in Wyatt, characteristically, a general condition, from which, despite the concluding resolution, there is no escape. Wyatt seems tied to the deer by his own alliteration, "Faynting I folowe." Giovanni Antonio Romanello's fifteenth-century imitation ("Una cerva gentil, che intorno avvolto") appeared in his *Rythmorum Vulgarum* (Verona, n.d., Soneto iii) and in early editions of Guisto de' Conti's *La Bella Mano.*[51] Romanello forgets the purpose of the deer's collar, which is to record Caesar's message, and he makes the deer speak in a *voce altera* – a "haughty voice." Love leads Petrarch through every toil (*ogni lavoro*), whereas it entices Romanello away from his duty (*degno lavoro*). Wyatt puts a less brave face on it, love for him is itself a "vayne travail."

The most bizarre analogue of this legend is the story of the Emperor's pike. According to the naturalist Conrad Gesner, citing Conradus Celtis, a pike was caught in a pool near Heilbrunn, in the gills of which was found a ring of copper with a Greek inscription, to the effect that it had been caught and released by the Emperor Frederick the Great in 1230. Gesner says that clearly the Emperor was imitating Alexander who put collars on deer, according to Pliny, whom he quotes verbatim. The celebrity of this pike is suggested by the fact that paintings were made of it, one of which still hangs in the Department of Natural History at the British Museum. The skeleton of the fish was long preserved in the Cathedral at Mannheim and measured nineteen feet. It was examined by a German anatomist who counted its vertebrae, and, finding too many, pronounced it a fake.[52]

I believe my last example clinches the case which I am arguing. It occurs in a folktale from Denmark, the tale of King Frode's hart. In the reign of King Christian IV of Denmark (1577–1648) a hart was captured at Skoven which King Frode had caught, on the neck of which hung a costly ring, on which Frode had written these words, *Freg mig! Frode freded' mig!*, "Protect me! Frode protected me!"[53] It is remarkable that this late version from seventeenth-century Denmark should preserve complete and unfragmented the essential features of the very earliest classical versions concerning the Homeric ancestors of ancient cities. For Frode is none other than Frothe, the Peace King, one of the legendary kings of Denmark. The early dynastic rolls of the Danish kings date his reign as contemporary with the birth of Christ, *Post hunc regnavit Frothi puer bonus. In cujus temporibus Redemptor mundi carnem suscepit humanam.*[54] He is claimed to have subjugated all the surrounding kingdoms as far as Greece and to have created such a respect for peace and law in his kingdom that he hung golden rings above the public highway, which were never stolen; hence his title, Pacificus. King Christian IV was a scholarly king. In the intervals of his reign when he was not drawn into wars with Sweden or the Empire, he spent his energies cultivating the arts of peace. He founded cities at Christianopel in Blecklingen, Christianstadt in Schonen and Christiana in Norway, modern Oslo. He re-established the Academy at Soroë, established the cloth industry, developed silver mines, and saltpeter mines, founded a postal service and supported an expedition to India. It is not surprising that such a king should be associated with his predecessor Frothe, the Peace King. The stuffed hide of a stag claiming to be that recaptured by Christian IV was preserved in the Royal collection and can still be seen in the museum at Hørsholm, Denmark, with clear marks as of a collar on the skin of the neck. In 1740 Queen Sophie Magdalene carried on the tradition when she released a stag which had strayed into the palace garden, on which she put a collar with a verse inscription.[55]

We clearly have a pattern here which confirms the essential and most ancient bearing of the legend of the collared deer, a bearing which had become obscured or fragmented in so many of the intervening examples. Evidently Christian IV, or those who propagated the legend of Frode's deer, knew what the collared deer signified, even though none of the written sources, as far as I can tell, during the Middle Ages and Renaissance had spelled it out. It seems unlikely that the seventeenth-century Danes were imitating such obscure ancient texts as the *De Mirabilibus*

Auscultationibus or the anecdote in Silius Italicus. Pliny they might well have known, but what Pliny says about Alexander's deer does not provide any basis for interpreting the deer as a symbol of dynastic *renovatio*. I think we must posit some kind of popular tradition – a tradition lasting from at least the second century B.C. to the seventeenth century of our era – in which the popular imagination of several European countries understood the collared deer as a symbol of dynastic continuity, as a pledge of the survival of the heroic figures of the past in their modern successors, which associated the deer with the founders of cities, abbeys or empires, and which saw its inviolability as a sign of the sanctity and endurance of the national identity.

NOTES

1. Marcelle Thiébaux, *The Stag of Love: The Chase in Medieval Literature* (Ithaca and London, 1974), reviewed by P. E. Beichner, *Medievalia et Humanistica* No. 6, 1975, pp. 218–19.
2. R. S. Loomis, *Arthurian Tradition and Chrétien de Troyes* (New York, 1949), pp. 60–70. K. G. T. Webster, *Guinevere* (Milton, Mass., 1951), ch. 6, "The White Stag," pp. 89–104.
3. The most recent study of the serpent-eating stag is Herbert Kolb, *Medievalia Litteraria: Helmut de Boor Festschrift* (Munich, 1971), pp. 583–610. Kolb confines his attention to Psalm commentaries. The iconographic variations are well set out in a wider ranging study by Jean Bayet, "Le symbolisme du cerf et du centaure à la porte rouge de Notre Dame de Paris," *Revue Archéologique*, 44, pp. 21–68. The classic study of the ecclesiastical monuments is still Henri-Charles Puech, "Le cerf et le serpent: note sur le symbolisme de la mosaïque découverte au baptistère de l'Henchir Messaouda," *Cahiers Archéologiques*, 4 (1949), pp. 17–60. Richard Ettinghausen, "The 'snake-eating Stag' in the East," *Late Classical and Medieval Studies: Albert M. Friend Festschrift* (Princeton, 1955), pp. 272–86, shows the development of the motif in Islamic texts.
4. For the fullest references to commentaries on Ps. 41 see Bayet, *ibid.* The most influential are St. Augustine, *PL*, xxxvi, 464; St. Jerome, *PL*, xxvi, 949, xl, 1205; Bede, *PL*, xciii, 702. See also Hugh St. Victor, *PL*, clxxvii, 64.
5. See E. Picot, "Le cerf allégorique dans les tapisseries et les miniatures," *Bulletin de la Société Française de réproductions de manuscrits à peintures* (1913), pp 57–67; Thiébaux, *op. cit.*, p. 146 et seq.
6. *Arcadia*, x. 10. trans. J. G. Fraser in *Works* (London, 1898), vol. 1, p. 387.
7. Aristotle, *De Mirabilibus Auscultationibus*, 110, trans. W. S. Hett, *Minor Works* (Loeb edition).
8. *Aeneid*, viii, 9. Servius in his commentary identifies this city as Argyrippa. See also x, 29.
9. Livy, xxv, 12, 5.
10. See W. Warde Fowler, *Aeneas at the Site of Rome* (Oxford, 1918), p. 52.
11. xiii, 115–37.
12. The sources of such foundation legends are examined by Francis Vian, *Les Origines de Thèbes* (Paris, 1963), ch. 3.
13. Hesiod, *The Precepts of Chiron*, 3; Aristotle, *Historia Animalium*, 6, 29.

14. See "Physiologus," ed. James Carlill in *The Epic of the Beast*, ed. William Rose (London, n.d.), p. 179; Richard Ettinghausen, *op. cit.*

15. *Naturalis Historia*, viii, 50, 119.

16. E.g., Topsell, *The History of Foure-Footed Beastes* (London, 1607), p. 130. Alexander's deer became the standard classical *exemplum* of cervine longevity, and is singled out as such by Sir Thomas Browne in the course of his refutation of this particular "vulgar error." (*Pseudodoxia Epidemica* [1640], III, 9.) As late as 1774 Oliver Goldsmith apparently felt the necessity of singling out Charles VI's deer at Senlis as an example of "the credulity of ignorance" which had attributed great age to stags (*An History of the Earth and Animated Nature* [1774, London, 1818, vol. 2, p. 95]).

17. Juvenal des Ursins, ed. Michaud, *Nouvelle Collection de Mémoires Relatifs à l'Histoire de France* (Paris, 1857), tom. 2, 343–4. Robert Gaguin, *Rerum Gallicarum Annales* (1577), ix, 3, p. 165.

18. Froissart ed. Lettenhove (repr. Osnabruck, 1967), tom. 10, pp. 68–71.

19. Ercole Tasso, *Della Realtà e Perfezione delle Imprese* (Bergamo, 1612), p. 403. Cited by Mario Praz, *Studies in Seventeenth Century Imagery* (Rome, 1964), p. 69.

20. Philippe de Mézières, *Le Songe du Vieil Pelerin*, ed. G. W. Coopland (Cambridge, 1969). For a graphic illustration of the *cerf volant* see frontispiece to vol. 2 of Professor Coopland's edition showing an illumination from Arsenal MS 2682–3, f. 341.

21. See *Oeuvres Completes* published by the *Soc. des Anc. Textes Françaises*, tom. 2, pp. 164–5, and 350n. The prophecy theme is developed in Balades de Moralitez, nos. lxvii, clxxx, clxxxii, cxcii, ccxi, cclxxxiv. For Briquemer see Chanson Royale no. ccccv.

22. *Ditié de Jehanne d'Arc*, stanza 15, ed. Angus Kennedy and Kenneth Varty, *Nottingham Medieval Studies*, vol. 18 (1974), pp. 29–55.

23. J. A. Buchon, *Collection des Chroniques* (Paris, 1826), tom. 10, pp. 205–06.

24. See M. G. A. Vale, *Charles VII* (London, 1974), ch. 7; and the series of Renaissance Triumphs issued under the general editorship of Margaret McGowan (New York, 1976).

25. "Les Vigilles de Charles VII," *Poésies*, Gottfried von Leibniz, ed. (Paris, 1724), tom. 2, p. 78.

26. MS Douce b.1, fol. 2.

27. M. V. Clarke, *Fourteenth Century Studies* (Oxford, 1937), ch. 8, "The Wilton Diptych."

28. John Gough Nichols, "Observations on the Heraldic Devices . . . in Westminster Abbey," *Archaeologia*, vol. 29, 1840, pp. 32–41. Francis Wormald, "The Wilton Diptych," *Journal of the Warburg and Courtauld Institutes*, vol. 17, 1954, pp. 191–203.

29. The seal is illustrated in *Le Bestiaire des Monnaies, des Sceaux et des Médailles*, published by the Hotel de la Monnaie (Paris, 1974), fig. 228, p. 236.

30. A transcript of the Latin inscription, with a German verse translation, can be found in (Lebermann) *Die Beglückte und Geschmückte Stadt Lübeck* (Lübeck, 1697), pp. 164–7.

31. See Thomas J. Hefferman, "An Analysis of the Narrative Motifs in the Legend of St Eustace," *Medievalia et Humanistica*, n.s. 6, 1975, pp. 63–89.

32. The standard survey in this field is Alexander Krappe, "Guiding Animals," *Journal of American Folklore*, vol. 5, 1942, pp. 228–46.

33. K. G. T. Webster, *op. cit.*, p. 103.

34. *Le Chevalerie Ogier de Danemarche*, ed. Barrois (Paris, 1842), pp. 11–12.

35. Ed. Menzel and Stengel (Marburg, 1906), pp. 190–1.
36. C. Meredith-Jones, "The Chronicle of Turpin of Saintonge," *Speculum*, xiii, 1938, pp. 160–79.
37. *Works*, ed. Vinaver (Oxford, 1967), vol. 2, p. 999.
38. A. Kuhn, "Der Schuss des wilden Jägers auf den Sonnenhirsch," *Zeitschrift für Deutsches Philologie*, vol. 1, 1869, pp. 89–119.
39. Grimm, *Deutsche Sagen* (Berlin, 1818), II, 110, sect. 440.
40. I am indebted to Frau U. Edge for this information.
41. Ed. Edward Bysse (London, 1654), p. 159.
42. *Memorials of John Ray*, ed. Edwin Lankester, Ray Society Publications (London, 1846), pp. 139–40.
43. William Camden, *Britannia*, trans. Philemon Holland (London, 1637), p. 213. The verses on the inn sign were first recorded in a newspaper in 1829, and they can be found in the third edition of Hutchins, *History of Dorset* (London, 1861), vol. 3, pp. 737–8. See my paper, "King's Stag and Caesar's Deer," *Proceedings of the Dorset Natural History and Archaeological Society*, vol. 95, 1974, pp. 80–3.
44. *In Vita*, cxc.
45. John Anstis, *Register of the Garter* (London, 1824), vol. 1, p. 113n.
46. Pier Andrei Mattioli, *Commentaire sur Dioscorides*, trans. Antoine Pinet (Lyons, 1580), II, 52, pp. 162–3.
47. Patricia Thomson, *Sir Thomas Wyatt and his Background* (London, 1964), pp. 196–200.
48. Petrarcha, *Opere*, ed. Giovanni Andrea Gesualdo (1533, repr. 1553); Daniello da Lucca, *Sonetti, Canzoni, e Triomphi di . . . Petrarcha* (Venice, 1541), f. 120v.
49. *Il Petrarcha*, ed. Sylvano Venaphro (1533), f. 142r; Thomson, *op. cit.*, p. 200.
50. *Oeuvres* (Annecy, 1894), tom. 4, "Traitté de l'Amour de Dieu," p. 84.
51. Bologna, 1472.
52. *Historia Animalium* (Lausanne, 1558), "Epistula Nuncupatoria," p. 5. See J. R. Norman, "The Emperor's Pike: a Fish Story," *Natural History Magazine*, vol. 2, 1930, pp. 179–83.
53. J. M. Thiele, *Danmarks Folkesagn* (Copenhagen, 1843), vol. 1, p. 16.
54. Langebeck, *Scriptores Rerum Danicarum* (Hafniae, 1772), p. 21; cf. pp. 2, 68, 153.
55. I am indebted to Mr. Knud Paludan, Curator, Jagd- og Skovbrugsmuseet, Hørsholm for this information, and for a photograph of the stag; and to the editorial board of *Medievalia et Humanistica* for helpful advice.

The Art of Courtly Copulation

BETSY BOWDEN

No one feels comfortable around Andreas Capellanus. His treatise on "courtly love" seems too serious to be funny, too funny to be moral, and at the end too moral to be serious. One ingredient in its tone has gone unnoticed, however, one that helps place *De amore* in its seldom-studied context of scholastic humor: Andreas is playing word games with explicit sexual allusions, including obscene Latin puns. John Jay Parry's standard English translation demonstrates the subconscious but systematic bowdlerization with which Andreas has been interpreted.[1]

Few of Andreas's double entendres form perfect puns, wherein the word makes sense both in its nonsexual and its suggested sexual usage, or even bad puns, wherein the suggested sexual word differs slightly in spelling or pronunciation from the given word. Much commoner in *De amore* are passages that make little sense if understood nonsexually, passages that Andreas has contrived solely as vehicles for his suggestive wordplay. Why, for example, does a male wooer declare that showers of dew fall on him whenever he dreams about his lady? Does he sleep out of doors? Why does the lady, theretofore a patient listener, suddenly refuse to hear any more about the man's good deeds or his uprightness? And why do the characters go on and on so about punishments, about *poenis* – punishments of lovers and of nonlovers, for women and for men, the hard punishments of the man whose love is refused, the diminishing punishments of the man who has entered the doorway to the court of love?

Medievalists studying *De amore* have never remarked on the wordplay and have seldom focused on any textual details that make the treatise's tone so oddly frivolous. Most recent commentators would agree that Andreas's intention seems as oddly frivolous as the tone, however, and that the treatise represents one man's work, not the typical medieval mind. Only a few critics would still try to force *De amore* into some schema preconceived to explain all medieval literature.

For example, somewhere in the back of every medievalist's mind lurks C. S. Lewis. And rightly so – for along with his bewitching prose come striking insights into literature and human nature, insights that unfortunately get deflected by the rose-colored glasses he dons to view the Middle Ages as a time when all men, no matter what they said, really meant that they loved God best. Lewis could even explain such schizophrenia: *De amore* represents the religion of love, which aims its devotees toward the highest ideals of society. "But, rising like a sheer cliff above and behind this humane or secular scale of values" is the divine scale. "Love is, *in saeculo*, as God is, in eternity."[2]

Sharing this eagerness to excuse Andreas's apparent unorthodoxy, a more recent commentator shares also Lewis's presupposition that the medieval mind was always devout and God-directed. Douglas Kelly essentially takes Lewis's striking image of a cliff and converts it to the scholarly abstraction "gradualism": "It was customary for medieval writers who reveal gradualistic views, when striving to convince their readers to lead a better life, to attack violently those levels of existence that are further removed from God, at the same time they affirm that, as God's creations, they possess a certain measure of good."[3]

Otherwise, the last gasp for Andreas's orthodoxy came a quarter century ago, during one of D. W. Robertson's dredgings for irony.[4] Excusing the contradictions, Robertson finds "no doctrinal inconsistency in the *De amore* as a whole."[5] In the first two books, whenever Andreas appears to praise carnal love he in fact condemns it; in the third book, when he appears to condemn carnal love he in fact condemns it. Like Lewis and Kelly, Robertson thus argues from an extreme overemphasis on Andreas's brief and perfunctory third book, which in proper scholastic form lists some arguments against the proposition that Andreas had proved, for 312 pages of Trojel's edition,[6] the proposition that a young man ought to practice love.

Another, more constant course of *De amore* commentary has assumed that Andreas's young man practicing love did so in the sociohistorical reality of late-twelfth-century France.[7] And in an outgrowth, two social psychologists have gone to *De amore* to describe "courtly love" behavior as a common medieval neurosis analyzable in Freudian terms.[8] John Halverson vehemently opposes such historical readings. "The closest Andreas may have come to reality is the possibility that the 'courts of love' of Queen Eleanor and her daughter Marie may in fact have been a court game . . . But even for this there exists no evidence outside the *De amore* itself."[9] His own analysis then concludes that Andreas (as an individual) was sublimating his eros by converting the sexual impulse into sterile intellectual games.

A more literary analysis of Andreas's psyche comes from Nevill Coghill, who seems almost to reel in disgust before Andreas's "unhealthy [and unholy] hatred of sexuality."[10] But Coghill simply rejects Robertson's farfetched irony without going on to consider the possibility of another sort of humor, the dirty joke, which then and now can be said to show the simultaneous hatred of and fascination with female sexuality that Coghill sees in Andreas.

I will later discuss other critics' suggestions about Andreas's intentions and his place in literature. But because no modern medievalist has argued for or against the presence of obscene puns in *De amore*, let us look first to a medieval commentator.

Written about 1170, *De amore* was first blacklisted in 1277. Etienne Tempier, Bishop of Paris, condemned it and a treatise on black magic as preface to a list of 219 Averroist and Aristotelian propositions declared heretical.[11] Only thirteen years later, in 1290, some friends of one Drouart la Vache showed him a copy of Andreas's outlawed treatise,

> In Latin. When I had seen it
> And he had read a little of it,
> The matter very much
> Pleased me, know this, certainly,
> So much so, that I began to laugh at it.[12]

Why is this man laughing? His friends, he continues, then urged him to translate it into French. And he complied – though condensing, changing, or omitting certain parts. What does Drouart leave out, and why? Then in his closing remarks, he makes a readership analysis that seems strange:

> For I have for clerics made this book,
> Which is, as it should be, handsome and good-looking,
> Rather than for lay people
> Who are a little naive and foolish,
> For in the book are many words
> Which lay people could not understand,
> Even if one were to (threaten to) drown or hang them.
> But the clerics who think about it,
> Will well understand the book,
> For in it there is much delight.[13]

No one has speculated as to why Drouart la Vache, translating from Latin to vernacular, would insist that his doing so delights churchmen. Several critics though, interpreting Andreas, have mentioned Drouart's "j'en commençai a rire." Robertson, for instance, has Drouart laughing at subtle ironic overtones that arise from his thorough knowledge of Aildred of Rievaulx, Peter Lombard, Boethius, and what Ernst Robert Curtius calls "the hermetic-Neo-Platonic speculation of Bernard Silvestris."[14] And Douglas Kelly opines, instead, that Drouart would not have laughed; he would have smiled in approval at Andreas's moral orthodoxy.[15] Other critics cite Drouart as evidence for the frivolity of Andreas's intentions – E. Talbot Donaldson, for example.[16]

But only two critics have ever speculated about the changes and omissions Drouart made. In 1892 E. Trojel, prefacing what is still the standard edition of *De amore*, says that Drouart condenses Andreas's dream sequence with palace of love, afterlife of lovers, and twelve precepts of love (pp. 89–108 in Trojel, pp. 72–83 in Parry) into a bland generalization (pp. 81–3 of Bossuat's edition). Drouart also omits the tale of the Breton knight; part of the initial definition of love; the chapters on love of clergymen and nuns; and every mention of Walter, Andreas, or Capellanus. Trojel weakly suggests that Drouart left out whatever did not translate easily into French poetic meter (p. xvii).

Robert Bossuat's 1926 explanation is almost as weak.[17] Detailing those same omitted passages, he adds other contrasts as well: Drouart, for example, eliminates many terms of formal scholastic argument. Bossuat believes that Drouart was modernizing the book for his thirteenth-century audience, for readers who no longer participated in courts of love presided over by the court chaplain. Thus Bossuat, like others after him, reads Andreas's Ovidian imitation as twelfth-century social history.

The clarifications Bossuat outlines do modernize the work. But Drouart's motivation for modernization, I suggest, is not his recognition of social change but rather his immediate wish to put out a book that censors could not easily identify with the blacklisted one. Drouart uses less formal scholastic terminology, eliminates names, and changes opening and closing, simply because these elements characterize *De amore* on the bishop's list. The omitted portion of the definition of love mentions *praecepta amoris;* the two omitted allegorical passages list precepts of love, many identical to the 219 condemned propositions. And Drouart seems also to have eliminated parts most overtly opposed to official church morality.

One of those omitted parts, retranslated, has proven quite amoral. In the fifth dialogue, which includes the dream sequence mentioned, a man who is arguing a woman into having sex with him tells her his wet dream. The carnal imagery is explicit; the double entendres, usually uninspired ones like rod for penis and door for vagina, are occasionally even clever.

Andreas's treatise exemplifies the oft-documented fondness of twelfth-century clerics for Ovidian didacticism. Ovid's three books on the *Art of Love* tell how a man acquires a lover, how he retains her affections, and how a woman attracts a lover. His *Remedia amoris*, then, tells how a man can get rid of a lover.

To this precedent, Andreas brings the techniques of dialectical debate, a conglomeration of commonplaces and ambitions greater than his imagination. Having apparently set out to follow Ovid's structure, Andreas first devotes 234 pages (in Trojel's edition) to the acquisition of love. His advice is very unlike Ovid's practical hints that a man, for example, get to know his lady's handmaiden. As a glance at Parry's table of contents shows, Andreas discusses the theoretical acquisition of love. Like any abstraction, love must first be defined, classified, analyzed, dissected. But the bulk of Book I consists of debates, loosely hung on a structure of social ranks.[18] Andreas teaches Walter how to argue, not seduce, ladies into bed. The passion for dialectical debate that swept twelfth-century schools, regarded by many elders as a fad that kept students from learning their *auctoritates*, here overwhelms in spirit its Ovidian model's pragmatism.

Andreas's Book II, a third the length of Book I, pieces together various traditions (including Ovid's Book II and *Remedia*) with little attempt at organization or elaboration. His Book III, shorter still, gives a perfunctory list of twenty possible arguments against love – some with biblical reference, others social or physiological. Andreas, like other students, had learned how to debate both sides of a question.

And like other twelfth-century students, Andreas had learned how to play with Latin words.[19] The wordplay I will examine in detail occurs in the fifth dialogue of Book I. Because there are three bulky components – Trojel's Latin text (pp. 80–110), Parry's translation (pp. 68–83), and my evidence and comments – a summary of the dialogue is essential.

A nobleman asks a noblewoman if he may speak his heart. He says that although he sees her rarely in the flesh, he sees her constantly in dreams. Because his life is painful, he appreciates sleep and its showers of release. The woman replies that he may visit her oftener.

He calls her offer one of false hope; it might prolong his tormented life but will not prevent his death. He asks her to open the way of all goodness. She has resolved to avoid the service of Venus, she retorts. He admonishes her not to reject love without trying it. She says that there is no turning back once one has entered the court of love.

He then describes to her the palace of love. There, the god of love uses the eastern portal; the other three portals are used by three types of women. The southern group of ladies stand in the doorway; the western ones wander outside; the northern ladies huddle inside closed doors. That is, he explains, the southern ladies discriminate and choose worthy lovers; the western women give in to any man; the northern ones refuse to love. The noblewoman snaps that she feels quite safe within the northern portal.

Then, he tells his dream. More familiar than its context, this sequence is summarized in detail by C. S. Lewis.[20] Lewis describes it as one of Andreas's new imaginative contributions to the religion of love.

Having fallen asleep in the woods, the nobleman says, he sees three groups of women ride by, like the three in the palace – discriminating, undiscriminating, and aloof. He follows them to the underworld, where discriminating lovers enjoy eternal bliss, promiscuous ladies remain in limbo, and ladies who had refused all suitors suffer gruesome tortures for all eternity. Approaching the god of love, the dreamer receives twelve precepts of love, and a crystal rod as his means of returning home. At the moment the crystal rod disappears, he wakes up in a flow of water.

After hearing of this dream, the noblewoman decides after all to dwell among discriminating lovers. He then assures her that he is a worthy lover, even though she may not have heard about all his good deeds.

As I discuss this dialogue, I will sometimes refer to three specialized dictionaries of erotic Latin terminology, those compiled by Pierrugues, Forberg, and Blondeau.[21] Andreas, I thus suggest, was writing in a clerical tradition of Latin wordplay, and from a knowledge of at least Ovid, who is very often the author cited to define a term in these dictionaries. A translation of *De amore* must take into account the probability that Andreas understood Ovid's use of common erotic metaphors, such as *cognoscere* for sexual intercourse.

Andreas's nobleman begins the fifth dialogue with one in a long series of plays on most of the inflected forms of *poena*, "punishment," which sound and are sometimes spelled like penis. Leonard C. Hector says that "from about 1150 . . . diphthong *ae* (*oe*) is merged indistinguishably with *e*."[22] And this spelling occurs in some manuscripts of *De amore*: "De meritis et penis amantium et non amantium" (p. 91, n. 12).

Parry's rendering of *poena* throughout as "pain" is common in neither classical Latin nor medieval.[23] A late classical use for torment, and medieval uses for infernal tortures, still implied the primary meaning of punishment in retribution. But Andreas's nobleman has done nothing to warrant punishment, nothing except to have seen his lady's treasure in his heart's eye: "Illum thesaurum, circa quem mea versatur intentio, cordis me facit oculis semper aspicere poenasque mihi affert et solatia multa" (p. 81).

The vision of her treasure brings forth both *poenas* and *solatia multa*. Both terms imply relief. The play on *poenas* is clarified by the use of *adferre*, "bring forward," rather than *ferre*. Lewis and Short cite a typically physical use from the Vulgate: "Adfer manum tuam," reach out your hand (s.v. *affero*). Thus the sentence suggests that the vision of the lady's treasure brings forward the man's penis, and much relief.

The nobleman looks forward to sleep, when he can see her image in the air and find release. "Sed quousque mihi affuerit licet vita poenalis, levis potest aura imbrem mihi liberationis infundere et rorem svavitatis inducere" (p. 83). Parry translates *poenalis* as "even though it may be a painful one" (p. 69). But Lewis and Short cite its only recorded use – of punishment, penal. The latter comes close to rendering the pun in English: "But as long as penal life is in me," he says, "a pleasant air [her image in his dream[24]] can pour out for me a shower of release and bring on sweet drops of dew."

The nobleman's last sentence before the woman's reply is particularly laden with double entendres: "Credo . . . quod tam nobilis tantaeque femina probitatis non diu permittet, me poenis subiacere tam gravibus, sed a cunctis me relevabit angustiis" (p. 83). Such a noblewoman, he hopes, "will not long permit me to endure such heavy pains, but will raise me up out of all my difficulties" (Parry, p. 69). The untranslatable wordplay involves syntax as well as sound. For the French audience of *De amore*, the possessive precedes the noun in the vernacular, making *me poenis* sound like "my penis." *Cunctus* of course means all. But its similarity to *cunnus* and French *con*, as well as its link to the oft-repeated *poenis*, would here perhaps make it a bad pun on *cunnus*. Mingling, also, French and Latin meanings of *a*, the phrase *a cunctis angustiis* takes on an over-tone of "with or by means of a tight, narrow vagina." *Relevare* does mean raise up etymologically; more commonly, it means lighten, relieve, or assuage. Besides its grammatical statement, then, the sentence suggests that such an upright woman would not long permit his penis to be sub-ject to such burdens, but would with her narrow *cunnus* raise him up and relieve him.

The noblewoman replies that she is grateful for his thoughts, that she will think of him in his absence, and that he may serve and see her more often. But the man is far from satisfied at her proper "courtly love" response to his apparent requests. He wants more.

Andreas's gentleman again speaks of showers and dewdrops to declare that such mild favors might prolong his life, but that he would rather die at once than after a tormented life of false hope. Andreas, like writers in other centuries, may imply sexual intercourse or ejaculation when he speaks of death. A Latin *comedia* of Andreas's milieu, *Alda*, elaborately describes the sex act as a scholastic paradox – one dies yet still lives.[25]

In a suggestive comment leading into a blunter one, the nobleman then says that "it is worse to do without what we have been given some hope of attaining than what the wish alone prompts us to hope for" (Parry, p. 70). In that last phrase, "quam quod nuda voluntate speratur" (p. 85), he refers to his naked wishes directly, and indirectly to her naked willing-ness.

He then asks her to open up the untried road to all good *peragenda*: "Ad omnia peragenda bona viam aperire incognitam, an hoc denegando cunctorum bonorum praecludere viam et mortis semitam aperire" (p. 85). Besides accomplishment, *peragere* is a verb for intercourse (Pierrugues, Blondeau); specifically, to *peragere* someone is to exhaust him or her sexually. And *cognoscere* is used for intercourse in both Ovid and the Vulgate Bible (Pierrugues, Blondeau), two precedents that Andreas cer-tainly knew. For example, in Gen. 24.16, the virgin Rebecca is an *incognita viro*. Thus, to Andreas's audience the *viam incognitam* would suggest a pathway that is unknown in a sexual sense.

The man offers her an apparent alternative. If she refuses to open that wide road of all goodness (*viam cunctorum bonorum*, another possible bad pun on *cunnus*), then she should open the narrow pathway, *semita*, of death. *Semita* and *via* are frequently contrasted terms for narrow and wide roads. Pierrugues adds that *semita* is used "saepe in obscenis" to mean penetration, especially of a virgin. The suitor offers her no alternative, then, just an insulting insinuation: Have sex, or have sex. Either open up your wide road, which is still sexually unknown to me, or else open up your narrow road in which I will be able to die, or ejaculate.

Parry's gentleman seems not to wonder why the woman – instead of, perhaps, inquiring what good deeds he wishes to do – snaps that she has promised him as much as she intends to. She is firmly resolved never to serve Venus nor "amantium me poenis subiicere," subject herself to lovers' *poenis*. Andeas is not one to let an overworked pun rest. Nor is he concerned with characterization: Andreas puts double entendres into the words of the protesting woman as readily as into the seducer's. Her next comments keep on with *angustiis, cognoscere,* and "poenis atque languoribus exponuntur," "[lovers] are exposed to so many punishments and weariness." Besides that *poenis* pun again, *exponere,* "expose," is primarily a physical word in both classical and medieval Latin; and *languor* names the state of post-coital exhaustion (Pierrugues).

After more comments about trying his fortunes in the narrow pathways of love, the wooer tells the woman that she should not reject love without trying it first: "Nihil enim, quid sit vel quale, aperta potest veritate cognosci, nisi primitus illud experientiae probaverit usus" (p. 86). *Cognosci* again suggests the biblical term for intercourse. And the adjective in *aperta veritate,* as in *nuda voluntate* earlier, implies the female role in intercourse.

The woman replies that it is easy to contrive entrance to love's court, but on account of lovers' *imminentes poenas* it is difficult to stay: "In amoris curiam facillimus est inventus ingressus, sed propter imminentes amantium poenas ibi est perseverare difficile" (p. 86). But, she promptly contradicts herself, it is very difficult to escape from the court, on account of the desirable acts of love: "Ex ea vero propter appetibiles actus amoris impossibilis deprehenditur exitus atque durissimus" (p. 86). Which does she mean? Is it hard to stay in love's court, or hard to leave?

The difficulty of exit appears for example in the troubadour Guiraut de Calanso: "To her palace, where she abides, there are five gates; and he who can open two of them easily passes through the three [others], but hard is it for him to come out again."[26] The woman's second assertion uses this commonplace. But her contradictory first statement seems explicitly phallic. "Propter imminentes amantium poenas" could indeed mean Parry's "because of the pains that threaten lovers" (p. 71). But only two minims away, twelve instead of ten little lines in the manuscript, lurks the pun "propter imminuentes amantium poenas," because of lovers' diminishing penises.

She compares the court of love to the door, *porta*, of hell; anyone can enter but no one can leave. *Porta* occurs frequently in Ovid and elsewhere as a term for vagina, especially of a prostitute (Pierrugues).

The man again argues that all good comes from love, and the woman again says she has resolved never to serve love. Then he changes his assertions, saying not only that she ought to try love before rejecting it, but also that if she does reject love she will be subjected to punishments. To give her one more chance, before he tells about the punishments, he describes love's palace.

The god of love uses the eastern doorway; which of the other three doorways will this lady choose? "Et dominae portae meridianae ianuis semper morantur apertis et ostii semper reperiuntur in limine, sicut et dominae occidentalis portae, sed ipsae extra ipsius limina portae semper reperiuntur vagantes. Quae vero septentrionalis meruerunt portae custodiam, semper clausis morantur ianuis et extra palatii terminos nihil aspiciunt" (p. 89). Parry translates: "The ladies at the southern gate always linger around the open door, and you can always find them at the entrance. The ladies at the western gate do the same, except that you can always find them roaming around outside the entrance. But those who have been assigned to the care of the northern gate always keep the door shut and never look at anything outside the palace walls" (p. 73).

Parry must manipulate grammar in order to fit all these orifices into the walls of the building. In each of the three descriptions occurs several words for doorway. *Porta* (Pierrugues) and *ostium* (Forberg) both refer to the vagina in classical erotica; Andreas here plays also with *ianua*. Referring to the south, Parry translates *ianuis apertis* as ablative singular, even though it is plural in the earlier seven manuscripts. In the west, Parry simply eliminates one door. And for the north gate, in all twelve manuscripts, the phrase which Parry translates as "door shut" is in fact plural, *ianuis clausis*.

It is hardly possible to render the exact innuendos of the Latin ablative case into the preposition-bound English language. And certainly, the implied sexuality of all these doors peeks through Parry's translation. But a literal translation here could suggest sexuality to us in the same degree as it was suggested to Andreas's audience. Those northern women keep their doors shut.

The noblewoman asks him to explain his obscure, allegorical words. The man praises the first group, those ladies who wait on the threshold at the open door. When anyone begs entry, these ladies first inquire carefully about his uprightness, then admit the worthy and reject the unworthy. Specifically, a lady should find out whether a potential lover can *probitatem retineat* (p. 90). What good would he be as a lover, after all, if he had trouble maintaining his uprightness?

With no recorded precedents in classical erotica, I suggest, Andreas here seems to pick up on an implied physicality in the abstract term *probitas* – on an overtone, as in English straightforwardness or uprightness, that can make *probitas* suggest an erection. In addition, *retinere* means maintain or keep (Lewis and Short, Du Cange); to its root *tenere*, "have," it adds a potentiality of loss. A man might have an abstract moral *probitas*, indeed, but how could a lady's discreet inquiries ascertain whether he was able to keep it? Again, Andreas seems to have contrived an immediate context as a vehicle for his double entendre.

The nobleman continues to interpret his allegory. The women at the western door "sunt illae mulieres communes" (p. 90). Not surprisingly, *mulier* and *communis* can both refer to harlots or prostitutes (Pierrugues). They admit everyone and are exposed to the pleasures of everyone, "universorum sunt expositae voluptati" (p. 90). *Exponere*, again, usually refers to physical exposure. And *voluptas* means not only pleasurable passions but also, according to Lewis and Short, semen.

The women of the north, he goes on, open to no one who knocks, but deny everyone entrance to love's palace. "Illae feminae, quae nemini pulsanti aperiunt, sed denegant ad amoris palatium cunctis ingressum" (p. 90). The verb *pulsare*, "knock" can refer to sexual attack (Pierrugues). And the grouping "ad amoris palatium cunctis ingressum" could suggest "entrance to the *cunnus*, love's palace."

Now, as the nobleman tells why each group deserves its compass direction, Andreas creates a rather elaborate image from a double entendre that even translates into English. His metaphor *radius*, like English "beam," derives the meaning ray of light from its primary use as rod or staff. Blondeau adds that *radius* can indeed mean penis. Andreas pictures the god of love rising in the east, like the sun – but only one beam is rising.

Andreas writes that the properly compliant southern ladies deserve their place because "ab ipsius in oriente habitantis amoris meruerunt radio coruscari. Occidentales vero sunt meretrices . . . et merito, quia, quum in occidente ipsarum reperiatur habitatio sita, igneus amoris radius ab oriente ad illas usque pervenire non potest. Septentrionales vero sunt illae mulieres, quae amare recusant . . . et merito, quia in sinistra positas deus non respicit ipsas, quia sunt maledictae" (pp. 90–1). The women in the south, Parry translates, "are worthy to be illumined by a ray from Love himself who lives in the east. Those of the west are loose women . . . this is proper because, since their dwelling is in the west, the fiery ray of Love cannot reach to them from the east. Those of the north are those who refuse to love . . . and this is proper, too, since the god has no consideration for those placed upon his left hand, because they are cursed" (pp. 73–4).

Referring to the southern ladies, Parry's "to be illumined" is an unlikely rendering of *coruscari*. Du Cange cites a twelfth-century definition of *coruscare* in which it refers to lightning flashes as opposed to steady solar illumination: "Sol radiat, mucroque micat, fulgorque coruscat." The passive voice of Andreas's verb suggests that the ladies are butted at, brandished at, set trembling by love's lightninglike beam. In their description, also, occurs another superfluous *cunctae*.

The western women are harlots, *meretrices*, and they deserve the west because there the fiery beam of love cannot reach them. *Igneus amoris radius* suggests that love's beam is aflame with sexual passion (Lewis and Short, s.v. *igneus*), while still making sense with the rising-sun image.

The chaste women of the north deserve their place: Because they are cursed, they are at the deity's left hand. Since they are in the north and he the east, the god of love seems to have turned his back, facing out his doorway, so that north is to his left. Presumably Andreas did not consider problematical such convolutions in the details of his imagery. Having proposed on rather shaky grounds an eternal damnation for women who remain celibate, Andreas now intends to describe that damnation.

Because the woman declares herself "esse securam, non maledictam" (p. 91) inside the northern gate, the nobleman proceeds to tell his dream of the afterlife of lovers. On a ride through a forest, he lies down to sleep in a pleasant grove. Going off in search of his horse, he comes upon a vast throng of women who, he learns, form the army of the dead, being led to their rewards and punishments by the god of love. Andreas here shifts from obscene wordplay to a series of harsh and explicit images. As befits a dream, this Freudian imagery might seem the subconscious outpourings of an embittered priest's lifetime of repression were it not set in its context, one of an intricate manipulation of words to purposely emphasize the obscene, nonspiritual aspects of sexuality.

Riding first in line are the discriminating ladies, elegantly dressed and mounted and attended. Second come the harlots, accompanied by a clamoring mob. And third are the celibate ladies – now, after death, they are sweltering in fox fur in the heat of summer, covered with dust, unattended, and riding improperly upon gaunt, rough-gaited, unsaddled horses: "Indecentes indecenter equitabant caballos scilicet macilentos valde et graviter trottantes et neque frena neque sellas habentes et claudicantibus pedibus incedentes" (p. 94). I would tend to picture a woman riding *indecenter*, "improperly," as one riding astride, astride and bareback on the skinny, limping horse. If so, that jutting and jolting backbone prefigures the punishment that each rider will suffer for eternity.

A woman of the third group hails the nobleman, explains the scene as they ride along, and tells of her deep regret that she refused all suitors. Let living women beware, she sighs. They approach the underworld itself, which is divided into three concentric regions: Amoenitas at the center, then Humiditas, the Ariditas around the outside. As the less blessed troops of ladies drop off in their destined places of eternal abode, their leader, the god of love, penetrates toward Amoenitas.

There, at the center of Amoenitas, stands a tree bearing every sort of fruit, with a fountain bursting from beneath its roots. Gershon Legman says, "The vagina as a fountain and the penis as a tree . . . are among the commonest of symbols in folktales, myths, dreams, and even in the older and less expurgated genealogical charts."[27] Under the tree sits the queen of love, holding a golden staff; the king when he enters takes up a crystal one. Each staff is a *virga* (pp. 100, 102), a common term for penis (Lewis and Short, Forberg; Pierrugues as *virgula*). The fountain's sweet water, full of little fishes, spreads out in rivulets throughout Amoenitas. All around are richly decorated *tori* (p. 100). *Torus*, "bridal bed," is also used "saepissime pro concubitu" (Pierrugues). Andreas leaves no question as to what eternal bliss consists of: Each blessed woman has a *torus* prepared especially for her, then each soldier of love chooses his lady.

As the rivulets from the fountain cross into Humiditas, they overflow their banks. The fruitful tree's branches are no longer overhead; the sun beats down but the swampy water has turned icy cold. This linking of extreme heat and excessive cold water, as an image for promiscuity, appears elsewhere. For instance, in some accounts of the Last Judgment, on one of the fifteen days the oceans turn to fire as a punishment for lust.

In Ariditas the streams dry up, and the hot sun bakes the ground. The torture prepared for celibate women is thoroughly sadistic. For each woman awaits a long pole bundled about with thorns, held by two strong men. As punishment for her celibacy she must spend eternity seated astride the pole, her bare feet just touching the burning ground, as the two men twist and grind the thorny bundle.

The dreamer's companion goes to her thorn-wrapped pole, begging him to plead mercy for her when he goes to the god of love's throne to ask a return home for himself. He approaches the king with formalities. The king replies that the dreamer has seen this vision so that he can reveal love's glory to the unknowing, and so that he can provide opportunity for the salvation of many women, "ut tua praesens visio sit multarum dominarum salutis occasio" (p. 105). Parry's translation of *salus* as "salvation" captures Andreas's sacrilegious attitude. More specifically, in Du Cange, *salus* is the usual term for Christian baptism. Its overtones perhaps imply that the man should anoint many women with holy water.

The king then gives the dreamer twelve brief precepts of love. Parry expands each one until its terse language sounds biblical and its ambiguous content sounds appropriate to a "courtly lover." The first precept well represents this potential for ambiguity: "Avaritiam sicut nocivam pestem effugias et eius contrarium amplectaris" (p. 106), literally "Flee avarice like the plague and embrace its opposite." What is its opposite? One of the twelve manuscripts adds "scilicet largitatem." Perhaps. But Morton Bloomfield emphasizes "the great difficulty medieval writers

faced when . . . they attempted to oppose the virtues and vices . . .
The chief sins were in flux; the authorities disagreed."[28] Lewis and Short
(s.v. *castitas*) find evidence that chastity, not generosity, may be opposed
to avarice. And chastity seems an appropriate virtue for a lover to embrace, particularly when considered with *amplector* – yet another term
for sexual intercourse, particularly if adulterous (Pierrugues). Moreover,
the mention of plague perhaps suggests venereal disease.

Precept II then begins with chastity. "Castitatem servare debes amanti"
(p. 106) or "You must preserve chastity for a lover." Parry's elegant
"Thou shalt keep thyself chaste for the sake of her whom thou lovest"
(p. 81) represents one possible interpretation. But perhaps one keeps
one's chastity, of necessity, until one can find a lover. Or perhaps *servare*
works as a pun on *servir*, and a man should be of service to his lady's
chastity – by embracing her, as the first rule has instructed.

The other precepts are equally terse and ambiguous, in Latin. These
twelve precepts, along with the later thirty-one rules of love (pp. 310–12
in Trojel, pp. 184–6 in Parry), are a source for the vague generalizations
often believed about "courtly love" – that love must be adulterous, secret,
bad for the health, and so on. These precepts should not be taken out of
context, nor at the face value of Parry's interpretations.[29]

The god of love then gives the dreamer a means to return home:
"Accipias ergo hunc crystallinum baculum et cum nostra recedas gratia;
in priori autem fluvio, quem inveneris, eum proiicias" (p. 107). Parry
translates, "Take now this crystalline staff, and with our grace depart;
but throw the staff into the first stream you find" (p. 82).

Several problems would arise from an asexual interpretation of this
passage. Amoenitas and Humiditas both run with streams; why does the
dreamer not find one until after he says goodbye to the now somewhat
less tortured woman in Ariditas? And why such a strange order at all,
from the god of love? Historical kings did not dismiss visitors by handing
out disposable crystal rods; no literary tradition suggests the idea; and it
appears in no recorded folklore tradition.[30] But the image makes sense
in phallic terms.

A crystal scepter had symbolized the god of love's power, though here
baculum rather than the more commonly phallic *virga* is used. And
proiicere has a variety of uses, most of which do not imply letting go. As
legitimately as Parry's "throw," *proiicere* means extend or thrust.

Thus, the king commands that the dreamer take this crystal rod and
thrust it into the first river he finds.[31] After revisiting his companion in
Ariditas, the man mounts his own horse and finds that he has obeyed the
king's order, instantaneously and effortlessly: "Post haec autem equum
ascendi proprium et in momento oculi circa fluenta sum deductus
aquarum. Ibi crystallina virga dimissa illaesus ad propria remeavi" (pp.
107–8). Parry translates: "I mounted my own horse, and in the twinkling

of an eye I was led through the waters that surrounded the place. Into them I threw the crystalline staff and returned unharmed to my own home" (p. 82).

To avoid the explicitness of the wet dream, Parry expands the single word *circa* into "that surrounded the place," even though the elaborate geographical description had not told of surrounding waters. He likewise expands *ad propria* into "into my own home," even though the dreamer fell asleep in a forest clearing. Parry presumes a first-person subject for the ever-ambiguous ablative absolute of *crystallina virga dimissa*. He translates *deducere* as if it were *perducere*, thus leaving it unclear just who leads him out, and how that amorphous leader gets the dreamer from one place to another in the twinkling of an eye. A literal translation of Andreas's sentence might be: "After this I mounted my own horse; and in the flash of an eye, I was drawn out, surrounded by a flowing of waters. There, the crystal rod having been given up, I returned to myself unhurt." [32]

After this climax, Andreas's imagination peters out. In the rest of the fifth dialogue, the seducer repeats the same double entendres he had been using earlier. But a new pun occurs in the words of the lady, who now agrees to serve love wisely – although she is not yet convinced that this nobleman has sufficient *probitas* to be a worthy lover. She says, "ab amoris nolo militia exsistere aliena, sed eius affecto consortio copulari" (p. 109), which Parry translates as, "I do not wish to be a stranger to Love's service; but I would be reckoned among his fellowship" (p. 83). But in fact *copulare* means join, not reckon; and *copulare* is cited as the usual verb for sexual intercourse in Pierrugues, Forberg, Blondeau, Du Cange, and Lewis and Short.

Past critical controversy about *De amore* has often resulted from attempts to stuff the entire work into the context of one or another of its patchwork components – church dogma, love-poetry commonplaces, misogyny, "Ovid misunderstood." But the treatise's most immediate context, as an imitation of Ovid's *Ars amatoria* and *Remedia amoris*, has been ignored. Peter Dronke, denying the applicability of Andreas's work to troubadour lyrics, adds:

Popular as it was, it is only one of a large number of treatises *De Amore*, both Latin and vernacular, in the twelfth and thirteenth centuries. There is also a tradition of *tensos* and *jeux-partis* on questions of love from Marcabru onwards. Many of the treatises were once ably discussed by Egidio Gorra in "La teorica dell'amore" (*Fra drammi e poemi*, Milano, 1900), which does not seem to have been read – it is in no bibliography. To see Andreas's work in its true perspective, interpreting it in terms of the genre in which he wrote, would demand a full-length study.[33]

Dronke's suggestion is excellent. Michael Curschmann suggests in addition a study of *De amore*'s progeny, "a detailed comparison with medieval vernacular translations besides Drouart's. The Italian versions and Hartlieb's German rendering in particular should prove rewarding as examples of a medieval understanding of the text."[34]

No generalizations should be made about the meaning of *De amore* until these and similar studies have revealed more about its immediate context. I would suggest only that the obscene wordplay and harsh sexual fantasies that I have pointed out go to support Coghill's and Halverson's senses of Andreas's near-perverted psychological makeup, and go to oppose readings of *De amore*'s content as historically accurate.

And my evidence goes to support, as well, those commentators who have felt that Andreas is joking about something not quite clear. E. Talbot Donaldson says, "I think that Andreas meant to be funny; my sense of humor is insufficiently robust for me to agree with Robertson and Drouart . . . that he succeeded." Hermann J. Weigand believes that Andreas "wrote every line . . . tongue in cheek," parodying the Christian world view. John C. Moore calls *De amore* a satire, which the urbane and sophisticated Andreas wrote to amuse his fellow clerics. To Charles Muscatine, Andreas seems "an ironist or a nasty fool." Peter Dronke sees him as an "amusing, vulgar, gossiping little *clerc*." Peter Nykrog emphasizes that by contradicting himself Andreas "*joue* avec les institutions courtoises."[35]

These scholars share my sense that Andreas's frivolous tone permeates the treatise. But, have I discussed a particularly obscene chapter, or one typical of the whole work? I can spot suggestive wordplay elsewhere in *De amore*, other lumps in the veneer of Parry's translation. For example, regarding persons fit for love, Andreas says that "a blind man cannot see anything upon which his mind can reflect immoderately, and so love cannot arise in him" (p. 33). Or again, a middle-class woman declares that she guards the gate to love's palace; after long consultation and careful deliberation she will admit only the man who gets in on the strength of his own *probitas*. The nobleman protests that such deliberations might be pleasant "if there weren't a snake here hidden in the grass" (p. 67). It is clear that scholars who wish to use any part of *De amore* as evidence should read it in Latin, not in Parry's innuendo-free interpretation.

The puns in *De amore*, thick in the fifth dialogue and at least scattered elsewhere, constitute textual evidence for the jocular tone that many modern critics have sensed in Andreas's work. But, as Dronke and Curschmann suggest, much more work must be done before we can generalize outward from *De amore*. Does Andreas's wordplay represent a common clerical pastime? Or, at the other extreme, does it show him to be a man driven neurotic by the sexless system?

Like the thrusting tree and bursting fountain in Amoenitas, perhaps this one harshly erotic dialogue stands solidly inside concentric circles of obscene contexts – within this treatise, within a neglected genre of

Ovidian imitations, within a seldom-studied tradition of clerical games and incidental obscenity. Further studies of this scholastic context could focus on Latin wordplay in this and other genres, erotic fantasies, dialectical-debate games, literary parody,[36] the passion for Ovid, and other elements that bear as much impact on the interpretation of *De amore* as does either church doctrine or troubadour lyrics.

Such studies might come to show, instead, that this chapter of *De amore* is an aberration. Like Andreas's dreamer, frightened by the unknown world after sex and death, perhaps Andreas is an intruder who wishes he could have stayed home in a safe context of scholastic writing that does avoid sexual matters, that sees punishments where Andreas compulsively sees penises. In that case, perhaps *De amore*'s survival in twelve manuscripts attests to its power to release subconscious tensions, unarticulated.

Further studies will show neither extreme to be true, certainly. The tone of this passage is not unique; but neither will most scholastic writing be revealed as bristling with hitherto-undetected obscene wordplay. Somewhere along the spectrum of medieval literature is a place for *De amore*. We must ask where along this spectrum Andreas's treatise fits, how typical its content, how typical its tone, how fitting its sentiments. We must ask why it was popular. And only then can we begin to generalize, to ask what *De amore* might have meant in the medieval minds of the clerics who copied it in late-twelfth-century France.

NOTES

1. Andreas Capellanus (André le Chapelain), *The Art of Courtly Love*, trans. J. J. Parry (1941; reprint ed., New York: Frederick Ungar Publishing Co., 1959). Page numbers in text refer to this volume and not, please note, to the abridgment of it by F. W. Locke, in Ungar's Milestones in Western Thought series (New York, 1957).
2. *Allegory of Love* (1936; reprint ed., New York: Oxford University Press, 1958), p. 42.
3. "Courtly Love in Perspective," *Traditio* 24 (1968): 136.
4. Most specifically in "The Subject of the *De amore* of Andreas Capellanus," *Modern Philology* 50 (1953): 145–61. See also "The Doctrine of Charity in Medieval Literary Gardens," *Speculum* 26 (1951): 36–9; and *Preface to Chaucer* (Princeton: Princeton University Press, 1962), pp. 393–448. An earlier attempted proof of Andreas's orthodoxy is Alexander J. Denomy's *The Heresy of Courtly Love* (New York: D. X. McMullen and Co., 1947).
5. Robertson, "Subject of the *De amore*," p. 161.
6. Andreas Capellanus (André le Chapelain), *De amore libri tres*, ed. E. Trojel (Copenhagen: Libraria Gadiana, 1892). Page numbers for Latin quotations in my text refer to this edition.
7. Historical readings include those by Parry, introducing *Art of Courtly Love*; Paul Zumthor, "Notes en marge du traité de l'amour de André le Chapelain," *Zeitschrift für romanische Philologie* 63 (1943): 178–91;

W. T. H. Jackson, "The *De amore* of Andreas Capellanus and the Practice of Love at Court," *Romanic Review* 49 (1958): 243–51; Felix Schlösser, *Andreas Capellanus: seine Minnelehre und das christliche Weltbild um 1200* (Bonn: H. Bouvier, 1960); Aldo Scaglione, *Nature and Love in the Late Middle Ages* (Berkeley and Los Angeles: University of California Press, 1963); and Claude Buridant, introducing his translation of Andreas's work, *Traité de l'amour courtois* (Paris: Klincksieck, 1974). All are careful to limit the practice of "courtly love" to certain social circles. Opposed stand those who object to Andreas's historicity: John F. Benton, "The Court of Champagne as a Literary Center," *Speculum* 36 (1961): 578–82, and also "Clio and Venus: An Historical View of Medieval Love," in *The Meaning of Courtly Love*, ed. F. X. Newman (Albany: State University of New York Press, 1968), pp. 19–42; Bartina H. Wind, reviewing Schlösser, *Cahiers de civilisation médiévale* 7 (1964): 346–50; and Gustavo Vinay, "Il 'De amore' di Andrea Capellano . . . del secolo XII," *Studi medievali*, n.s. 17 (1951): 203–76. See also Francis L. Utley, "Must We Abandon the Concept of Courtly Love?" *Medievalia et Humanistica*, No. 3, 1972, pp. 299–324.

8. Melvin W. Askew, "Courtly Love: Neurosis as Institution," *Psychoanalytic Review* 52 (1965): 19–29; and R. A. Koenigsberg, "Culture and Unconscious Fantasy: Observations on Courtly Love," *Psychoanalytic Review* 54 (1967): 36–50.

9. "Amour and Eros in the Middle Ages," *Psychoanalytic Review* 57 (1970): 246.

10. "Love and 'Foul delight,' " in *Patterns of Love and Courtesy*, ed. John Lawlor (London: Edward Arnold, 1966), p. 142.

11. See A. J. Denomy, "The *De amore* of Andreas Capellanus and the Condemnation of 1277," *Medieval Studies* 8 (1946): 107–49; and Martin Grabmann, "Das Werk *De amore* . . . vom 7. März 1277," *Speculum* 7 (1932): 75–9.

12. *Li livres d'amours de Drouart la Vache*, ed. Robert Bossuat (Paris: Librairie Ancienne Honoré Champion, 1926), p. 2. Translation provided by Joseph Duggan.

13. *Ibid.*, p. 217.

14. *European Literature and the Latin Middle Ages*, trans. Willard R. Trask (New York: Pantheon Books, 1953), p. 320.

15. Kelly, "Courtly Love in Perspective," p. 123.

16. "The Myth of Courtly Love," *Ventures* 5 (Fall 1965): 16–23.

17. *Drouart la Vache: traducteur d'André le Chapelain* (Paris: Librairie Ancienne Honoré Champion, 1926), pp. 33–65.

18. By the eighth dialogue, Andreas has run out of social ranks but has some additional arguments in mind, so he has the same woman argue from the point of view of a widow (p. 172 of Trojel, p. 117 of Parry), then a virgin (p. 181 of Trojel, p. 121 of Parry), then a fiancée of another man (p. 195 of Trojel, p. 129 of Parry).

19. Close analogues to *De amore* come from a surviving group of fifteen *comediae*, edited and translated by Gustave Cohen and his students as *La "comédie" latine en France au XIIe siècle*, 2 vols. (Paris: Société d'édition "Les belles-lettres," 1931). These lively narratives in Latin elegiacs, which show evidence of origin and use in the schools of the Loire Valley during the late twelfth and early thirteenth centuries, resemble *De amore* in their Ovidian heritage, scholastic pomposity, dialectical argumentation, and explicit sexuality including obscene puns. See also Edmond Faral, "Le fabliau

latin au moyen age," *Romania* 50 (1924): 321–85; and Frederic J. E. Raby, *A History of Secular Latin Poetry in the Middle Ages*, 2d ed., 2 vols. (Oxford: At the Clarendon Press, 1957), 2:54–69.

20. Lewis, *Allegory of Love*, pp. 37–9.

21. Pierre-Emanuel Pierrugues, *Glossarium eroticum linguae Latinae*, rev. ed. (Berlin: Hermann Barsdorf Verlag, 1908); Frederick Charles Forberg, *Manual of Classical Erotology*, 2 vols. (1844; facsimile ed., New York: Grove Press, 1966); Nicolas Blondeau and François Noël, *Dictionnaire erotique latin-français* (Paris: Isidore Liseux, 1885). Gershon Legman presents a bibliography of the five erotic Latin dictionaries ever compiled, including pseudonyms and plagiarisms, in his introduction to *Dictionary of Slang and its Analogues*, ed. John S. Farmer and William E. Henley, rev. ed., 7 vols. (1903; reprint ed., New Hyde Park, N.Y.: University Books, 1966), 1:li–liv. The most complete dictionary alphabetizes its own words along with all terms from three of the other dictionaries, giving page references and sometimes additional citations: it is the twelfth volume of the journal Κρυπτάδια (Kryptadia), *recueil de documents pour servir à l'étude des traditions populaires*, 12 vols. (Paris and Heilbronn: H. Welter, et al., 1883–1911). With Legmanian zeal, let me warn of the difficulty of finding these dictionaries in libraries. To this day they may remain hidden or misleadingly filed, presumably in order to prevent the mental corruption of Latin scholars.

22. *The Handwriting of English Documents*, 2d ed. (London: Edward Arnold, 1966), p. 24.

23. I will refer to Lewis and Short for classical Latin, and Du Cange for medieval. The former is Charlton T. Lewis and Charles Short, *A Latin Dictionary*, rev. ed. (1879; reprint ed., Oxford: At the Clarendon Press, 1962). The latter is Charles du Fresne, Dominus du Cange, *Glossarium mediae et infimae Latinitatis*, 10 vols. (Niort: Léopold Favre, 1883–7); this edition is one of the most recent since 1679 of this standard work.

24. He has just told of her image transmitted through the air to him, "solus ad aera transmissus aspectus efficacia mihi praestat fomenta vivendi" (p. 82).

25. Cohen, *"Comédie" latine*, 1:130–51.

26. Trans. after W. Ernst, *RF* 44:340, as quoted by Curtius, *European Literature*, p. 513.

27. *The Horn Book* (New Hyde Park, N.Y.: University Books, 1964), p. 190.

28. *The Seven Deadly Sins* (1952; reprint ed., East Lansing: Michigan State University Press, 1967), pp. 67 and 78.

29. We would do better on the matter to follow the cautions of Ibn Hazm, the eleventh-century Arabic scholar whose treatise on love Parry describes in his introduction, pp. 8–12. "Such themes . . . as the poet's exaggerated description of the lover's wasting," explains Ibn Hazm, "are all without reality . . . Wasting may sometimes become very serious; but if it proceeded to the point which poets allege, the lover would shrink to the stature of an ant or less." Trans. A. J. Arberry, as *The Ring of the Dove* (London: Luzac and Co., 1953), p. 280.

30. See Stith Thompson, *Motif-Index of Folk-Literature*, rev. ed., 6 vols. (Bloomington: Indiana University Press, 1955–8).

31. Andreas's description of Humiditas had already linked rivers with female sexuality. This psychological association is further evidenced by the Thompson motif-index, for example, and by D. H. Lawrence and *Finnegans Wake*.

32. Michael Curschmann, member of the editorial board of *Medievalia et*

Humanistica, points out "the totally innocuous way in which, e.g., Johannes Hartlieb, who was, incidentally, a physician by profession," translates this passage: "Darnach sas ich auf mein pfärd. Do kam ich in ainem augenplick zw dem fliessenden wasser, da warf ich ein mein cristallen stab vnd kam vnuersert haym." That is, "after that I mounted my own horse, and in the flash of an eye reached the running water. Into this I threw my crystal wand and returned home unharmed."

33. *Medieval Latin and the Rise of the European Love Lyric,* 2d ed., 2 vols. (Oxford: At the Clarendon Press, 1968), 1:85.
34. Private communication, 2 June 1976.
35. Donaldson, "Myth of Courtly Love," p. 20; Weigand, *Three Chapters on Courtly Love in Arthurian France and Germany* (Chapel Hill: University of North Carolina Press, 1956), p. 24; Moore, *Love in Twelfth-Century France* (Philadelphia: University of Pennsylvania Press, 1972), pp. 122–9; Muscatine, *Chaucer and the French Tradition* (Berkeley and Los Angeles: University of California Press, 1957), p. 39; Dronke, reviewing Schlösser, *Medium aevum* 32 (1963): 60; and Nykrog, *Les fabliaux* (Copenhagen: E. Munksgaard, 1957), p. 205.
36. Peter Dale Scott suggests that Andreas may be directly parodying biblical language by giving it sexual overtones. For example, when the wooer speaks of the women in the northern portal who open up to no one who knocks, "nemini pulsanti aperiunt" (p. 90), he is echoing Matt. 7.7–8: "Pulsate, et aperietur vobis . . . pulsanti aperietur." Private communication, 5 April 1976.

Langland's Trinitarian Analogies as Key to Meaning and Structure

LAWRENCE M. CLOPPER

At the end of the fifth vision of *Piers Plowman*, the Samaritan likens the Persons of the Trinity to the fist, fingers, and palm of a hand and to the wax, wick, and flame of a taper. It is appropriate that these analogies should appear at the end of a vision that has been preoccupied with trinitarian images; more important, the analogies conclude one movement in the poem, the progress from the world (*Visio*) into the mind (*Vita de Dowel*) and thence into the soul (*Vita de Dobet*) where is to be found, according to Augustine, the image most closely analogous to the Trinity.[1] The presence in the poem of the concrete hand and taper analogies, the Faith, Hope, and Charity analogy, and Augustine's psychological analogies all suggest that Langland used trinitarian analogies in constructing major sections of his poem and as models for key concepts such as Dowel, Dobet, and Dobest. This essay will make a study of these analogies in order to resolve three problems which have puzzled critics of the poem: the sources of the hand and taper analogies; the meaning of the terms Dowel, Dobet, and Dobest; and the relationship between the *Visio* and the *Vita*.

First, it is necessary to establish the main points of orthodoxy on the relations which obtain between the Persons of the Trinity and on the appropriated attributes, Power, Wisdom, and Goodness. An understanding of these relations and attributes is essential to the discussion of Langland's analogies because the language of his descriptions reveals his debt to the language of Trinitarian discussions.

The paradox which must be explained in any discussion of the Trinity is that God is three Persons but one God.[2] The commentator must avoid suggesting that the persons are three gods (Tritheism) or emanations (Manichaeism and related Neoplatonisms); in addition, he must avoid suggesting that the Persons are only nominal distinctions (Sabellianism). The Church worked out a formula whereby it argued that the Persons of the Trinity were real relations within the deity but that these relations did not imply a division in the essence of the deity.[3] There are two kinds of relations in the Trinity. The first is that which obtains between the Father and the Son, paternal and filial, and that which obtains between both the Father and the Son and the Holy Spirit. This latter relation is more difficult to describe because it is similar to but not identical with the relationship of the Son to the Father. It can be better expressed in the second set of relations: the Father is ingenerate, the Son is generated from the Father (generation, filiation), and the Holy Spirit proceeds from the Father and the Son (procession, spiration). The relation between the Holy Spirit and the other two Persons of the Trinity is unlike that of the Son to the Father insofar as the Holy Spirit proceeds from both the other Persons whereas the Son is generated only from the Father. These two distinctions are real; they state that the Father is not the Son nor the Holy Spirit and that the Father and the Son are not the Holy Spirit. Nevertheless, the Persons are not distinct from the Essence: they are neither species of the genus, Essence, nor does the Essence in any way form a quaternity. The patristic period formulated the statement of the mystery thus: the Father is God, the Son is God, the Holy Spirit is God, the Father is in the Son but is not the Son, the Father is in the Holy Spirit but is not the Holy Spirit, and so forth for each of the Persons.[4] The formula is that there are three Persons but one God or three subsistences (Gk. *hypostases;* L. *personae*) and one essence (Gk. *ousia;* L. *essentia*).[5]

In addition to these two relations, many Fathers of the patristic period as well as later medieval theologians associated particular attributes with each of the Persons, the most common being those of power (*potestas*) with the Father, wisdom (*sapientia, scientia*) with the Son, and goodness (*benignitas, caritas*) with the Holy Spirit.[6] These "appropriated attributes" denote logical or mental, not real, distinctions, for, if they were real, they would seem to deny the power of the Father to the Son and the Holy Spirit and so forth. Commentators excused the usage on the grounds that these were the names by which men might better know the Persons of the Trinity; consequently, it is common to find an association of each of these appropriated attributes with one of the Persons. But since the association could also suggest an unorthodox third set of relations, the careful commentator might note that the distinction was mental and that power was not only in the Father but also in the Son and the Holy Spirit.[7] In his *De trinitate*, Augustine summarizes thus: "So each are in each, and all in each, and each in all, and all in all, and all are one."[8]

Since the concept of the Trinity was regarded as one of the most sacred – and most baffling – of mysteries, commentators approached the subject with some trepidation and considerable apology; nevertheless, since it was also a key doctrine which distinguished the Christians from the pagans, the Jews, and the Gnostics, it was necessary not only to expound the doctrine but to find ways of illustrating it. Even while the early church was developing a technical vocabulary it was thought desirable to develop analogies which would help believers and non-believers alike understand the special relationships which existed between the Persons.[9]

The earliest analogies tended to be ones which used visible objects or material things and which were sanctioned by scriptural language; for example, the Father was likened to a fountain or source (*fons; Jer* 2:13; *Baruch* 3:10–12) and the Son to the river from it (*fluvius; Psa* 65:9); the Father was like the sun (*sol; John* 1:5) and the Son the ray or radiance from it (*solis radium: Heb* 1:3).[10] In response to the Arian threat in the fourth century, when the doctrine of the Trinity was fully elaborated, these analogies of the generation of the Son were simply extended: Thus, the Holy Spirit was analogous to the radiance which proceeded from the sun, the Father, and its light, the Son; or it was likened to a stream from the river, the Son, and fountain or source, the Father.[11]

The principal difficulty with concrete analogies of this type is that they often emphasize the separateness of the Persons over the Unity of the deity. For example, Tatian and Justin Martyr proposed that the generation of the Son was like that of a fire from which another fire or torch had been lit.[12] The analogy was intended to show that there could be two distinct manifestations (Persons) of one essence without any consequent reduction of the parent manifestion, and the analogy was fairly successful in making this distinction. It was less successful in illustrating the unity of substance because the analogy ended with two torches rather than one; consequently, Athanasius rejected the formulation on the grounds that the analogy suggested Ditheism, and developed the trinity of sun/light/radiance, an analogy, he argued, that the Nicene Fathers had in mind when they incorporated the phrase *lumen de lumine* into the Nicene Creed.[13]

Analogies of torches and of sun/light/radiance are, therefore, some of the oldest trinitarian analogies in Christianity and they continued to be employed up into Langland's day.[14] Langland's analogy of the taper ultimately derives from this tradition, yet it must be stressed that his analogy is not simply a recapitulation of an older one but a unique synthesis out of his own insights into the tradition and out of other materials. For example, Skeat noted a general similarity between the taper analogy and Augustine's trinitarian analogy *ignis/splendor/calor* and pointed to a closer analogue in Bartholomeus Anglicus' chapter on the torch (*cereus*) in which Bartholomeus distinguishes three parts of the torch, the wax, wick, and fire.[15] Yet it is obvious that neither of these can be said to provide a *source* for Langland's analogy, for Augustine does not mention a torch at all and Bartholomeus makes no association between his torch and the Trinity.

No one, by contrast, has even suggested, at least to my knowledge, a source of any kind for Langland's hand analogy,[16] but it may have derived ultimately from Isaiah 40:12:

> quis mensus est pugillo aquas et coelos palmo ponderavit
> quis appendit tribus digitis molem terrae et libravit in
> pondere montes et colles in statera.[17]

The passage is the only one in the Vulgate which combines the references to the fist, finger, and palm; furthermore, medieval commentators frequently singled out the reference to the three fingers as an image of the Trinity, and the context suggests the involvement of the Trinity in the acts of creation, another trinitarian commonplace. No commentator elaborates the passage as Langland has; those references to the passage that I have located either emphasize the rhetorical nature of the questions and thereby associate the acts described with God's incomprehensible magnitude and power, or they single out the three fingers as an image of the Trinity.[18]

Langland's analogy of the hand succeeds at the very point where most concrete and material analogies fail, for it emphasizes the unity of essence – the fist, fingers, and palm *are* the hand – at the same time that it denotes the parts of the hand and their relationships to each other:

> The fader was first as a fust wiþ o fynger foldynge
> Til hym [likede] and liste to vnlosen his fynger,
> And profre[d] it forþ as *with* a pawme to what place it sholde.
> (17.141–43; cf. C. 20.111–15)[19]

The Father was manifested before the Advent of the Son, both of whom preceded the advent of the Holy Spirit; thus, their appearance in history imitates their relations in the Trinity.

In lines 144–68, Langland goes on to present the argument that the Trinity is a Unity and that, therefore, there is no temporal distinction between the Persons in eternity. In addition, Langland is meticulous in demonstrating that the Father is in the Son and in the Holy Spirit, and so forth. Although he attributes "miȝt" to the Father (line 171), "Science" to the Son (line 174), and "*grace*" to the Holy Spirit (line 205), he adds that the Father's "miȝt" resides in the Son (line 175) and in the Holy Spirit (lines 176–81). Moreover, Langland develops his concept of divine power in two other places in the poem in order to demonstrate its existence in the Godhead as well as in the Incarnation: Abraham's Trinity is made up of the Power, the Medium of Power, and Suffering (16.191–3), which he associates with the Father, the Son, and the Holy Spirit, respectively. Conscience later identifies these as three "degrees" of Christ's Incarnation, Knight, King, and Conqueror (19.26–62). The effect of these repetitions with variations is to demonstrate that the Power is attributed to the Father yet also belongs to the Son and the Holy Spirit, and that the distinctions can be expressed either in temporal or more abstractly formal relationships.

The hand analogy recalls, therefore, but does not simply iterate, the appropriated attributes of the Trinity, Power, Wisdom, and Goodness; however, instead of merely associating each of these qualities with one Person, Langland explores and modifies them. For example, the fist is an appropriate symbol for the Father because it suggests his might or power and his awesomeness which men should fear, yet the outstretched palm is appropriate for the Holy Spirit because it suggests the act of giving, the gift of grace. Rather than denoting the Son as *sapientia*, Langland calls Him "Science," a specialized sense of Wisdom which connotes knowledge that is applied; hence, the Son is described as the fingers which are used to "portreye or peynten," for "Keruynge and compasynge [i]s craft of þe fyngres" (lines 172–3).[20] This description of the Son links the analogy to the acts of creation implied in the *Isaiah* passage.

Langland alters the trinity Power/Wisdom/Goodness not only in order to emphasize the creation of man through the Son but also to focus on the salvation of man through the Grace of the Holy Spirit. He insists that the fist is a complete hand (line 169) and that the fingers are a complete hand (line 172), that is, that the Father is God and the Son is God. The palm, he says, is also a complete hand and has power in itself to put out the fingers and open the fist when it feels the will of the fist and the fingers (lines 176–81); thereby, Langland denotes the Deity's unity of will and the Holy Spirit's cooperation in the act of creation. However, in an extended passage (lines 187–203), Langland stresses that the Holy Spirit/palm is essential to man's salvation. The Samaritan says that a man who is injured in the thumb and fingers but not in the palm might still help himself, but that the man who injures his palm is totally incapacitated. This difference he understands as evidence that anyone who sins against the Holy Spirit will not be forgiven (*Mark* 3:29), for he wounds that with which God grips and thereby quenches God's grace. This passage, which might seem to teeter on orthodoxy (part of it is excised from the C-test), explains that the man must show charity toward God if he expects to have grace in return.[21]

Though there is a tradition of associating light with the Persons of the Trinity, neither this image, nor the torch analogy, which in any case had been rejected by some Fathers, could have provided the source for Langland's taper analogy. The symbol closest to Langland's is that of the Paschal candle which typically was understood to represent Christ's divine spirit (the flame) wrapped in his humanity (the wax).[22] It is possible that Langland developed his analogy out of this symbolism, Bartholomeus' analysis of the three properties of candles, the old light analogies, and the association of the Holy Spirit with the fire at Pentecost. The Samaritan's exposition of the taper analogy emphasizes the role of the Holy Spirit and thus is a continuation of the commentary which appears at the end of that of the hand analogy. The entire passage stresses the necessity of the Holy Spirit and of "lele loue," or charity, in man's salvation. The Samaritan arrives at this conclusion by showing that a quenched taper, the embers of a fire, the wax of a candle alone, and the wick and the fire alone may solace men, gain them mercy and forgiveness, but that they do not enlighten or enflame men. Without charity, or "lele loue," he says, there is no fire and no salvation, and thus, in effect, Faith and Hope without Charity are to no avail.

Langland begins his taper analogy with a statement of the unity of the Father and the Son and the procession of the Spirit from them both:

> [For] to a torche or a tapur þe Trinite is likned,
> As wex and a weke were twyned togideres,
> And þanne a fir flawmynge forþ out of boþe.
> (lines 206–8)

He describes the unity of will and action:

> And as wex and weke and [warm] fir togideres
> Fostren forþ a flawmbe and a fair leye
>
> .   .   .
>
> So dooþ þe Sire and þe sone and also *spiritus sanctus*
> [Fostren forþ amonges folk loue and bileue]
> That alle kynne cristene clenseþ of synnes.
> (lines 209–14)

In all of the examples which follow, those of the smoking torch, the glowing embers, and so forth, the Samaritan iterates that the Holy Spirit/fire is a necessary element in the process of salvation which requires a union of the divine will:

> Til þe holy goost gynne to glowe and to blase,
>
> .   .   .
>
> And þanne flawmeþ he as fir on fader and on *filius*
> And melteþ hire myȝt into mercy, as men may se in wyntre
> Ysekeles in euesynges þoruȝ hete of þe sonne
> Melte in a Mynut while to myst and to watre.[23]
> So *grace* of þe holy goost þe grete myȝt of þe Trinite
> Melteþ to mercy, to merciable and to [noon] oþere.
> (lines 226–34)

In this passage the Samaritan shows that grace or mercy resides in the Holy Spirit (*benignitas, caritas*) and that power ("myȝt") resides in the Father *and* the Son, but that mercy also resides in the Father (238–9) and in the Son (243–7). He adds that the Holy Spirit is "god and grace wiþouten mercy" to those who are uncharitable (252–3). At the end of the passage (252–98), the Samaritan returns to the question of sins against the Holy Spirit, and, as at the end of the hand analogy, argues that these cannot be forgiven:

Thus "vengeaunce, vengeaunce!" verrey charite askeþ.
And siþ holy chirche and charite chargeþ þis so soore
Leue I neu*er*e þat oure lord [at þe laste ende]
Wol loue [þat lif] þat [lakkeþ charite],
Ne haue pite for any preiere þer þat he pleyneþ.

(lines 294–8)

The Holy Spirit is emphasized, apparently, not because It is more important than the other Persons of the Trinity and not because Christ is less important to man, but because at Langland's stage in history, in purely temporal terms, the Holy Spirit is the intermediary between man and God: Christ has become distant in time and the Father even more distant, an idea expressed in the sequential appearance of Abraham-Faith, Moses-Hope, and Samaritan-Charity.[24]

The hand and torch analogies are neither developed without plan, nor are they ordered one after the other without cause. In the first analogy Langland focuses on the involvement of each of the Persons in creation; and in the second analogy he focuses on man's ultimate end and elaborates the idea that the fire of the Holy Spirit is necessary to man's salvation. In worldly terms, therefore, he stresses that the Holy Spirit is the link to the Father by way of Christ and he iterates that Charity is essential to salvation. By placing these images at the end of the trinitarian section of the poem, and within the context of the Faith/Hope/Charity trinity that is developed earlier in the vision, Langland makes clear the distinction implied in Paul's statement about Faith, Hope, and Charity: The Pauline statement first suggests an equality among the three ("faith, hope, love abide, these three"), but then suggests a hierarchy ("but the greatest of these is love"). Langland, in fact, uses this dual construct of equality and hierarchy, as we shall see later, throughout the poem in order to demonstrate that these are two relations but one essence.

Augustine's *De trinitate* was the culmination of the process in the West of defining the doctrine of the Trinity; moreover, its psychological analogies inform all later discussions of the Trinity. Augustine's work does not dismiss concrete analogies, nor does it restrict itself to producing just one analogy; instead, it, like his *Confessions*, describes the quest for an understanding of the Trinity which begins with concrete analogies in the world, proceeds into those of the mind and thence into that of the soul, the trinity of Memory, Intellect, and Will. The analogy of the three faculties united in their essence, the rational soul, was rejected like all of his other analogies as inadequate, but it was deemed better than the others because it expressed the Unity as well as the Trinity of the Godhead. Augustine's principal analogy, however, is not a simple one: The three faculties are elements in a whole series of motions of the soul by which man remembers and comes to understand and to love first himself and then God. For Augustine and later theologians the shift from visual or concrete analogies to psychological ones had significant consequences: Not only could the analogy illustrate the concept of the Trinity but it could also provide a guide for the soul's approach to God.

By the late Middle Ages the three theological virtues, Faith, Hope, and Charity, were associated with the Persons of the Trinity; in addition, they described the individual's way to God and suggested the three ages of the world in each of which one of the Persons had manifested Himself.[25] Langland took these relationships and twined them together in order to suggest the parallel between the history of mankind's redemption, the individual's road to God, and the means whereby man achieved salvation. Joachim of Fiore, St. Bonaventure and St. Edmund of Abingdon associated each of the Persons with one of the theological virtues.[26] Since St. Edmund's *Mirror* had wide currency in northern England in the fourteenth century, I shall use one of the vernacular versions of his tract to illustrate the point:

Be-leeue ordeyneþ vs to God þe Fader, to whom is a-titlet strengþe; **Hope** to God þe Sone, to whom is a-tytlet cynnynge; Loue to God þe Holygost to whom is a-tytlet godnesse. And þerfore, Be-leeue makeþ vs haue knowyng of God; and þat knowiŋge seiþ to vs þat he is wonderliche corteis þat in such manere and so largeliche ʒiueþ vs of his godes: and of þat be-leeue comeþ Hope; and of þat knowynge þat he is god, comeþ þe þridde vertue, þat is Loue, ffor whi? eueri þing loueþ kyndeliche þe goode.[27]

The passage is significant because it links the Persons of the Trinity with the appropriated attributes, Power, Wisdom, and Goodness, and with the virtues, Faith, Hope, and Charity; moreover, the latter part of the statement links these with the way to God.

Similarly, St. Bonaventure associates the three virtues with the way to God:

As man, in the first creation, resembled God through a trinity of powers with unity of essence, so in the recreation, he resembles God through a trinity of habits with unity of grace. Through these, the soul is carried straight up to the supreme Trinity in a way corresponding to the appropriated attributes of the three Persons: faith, through belief and assent, leads to the supreme Truth; hope, through trust and expectation to the loftiest Height; charity, through desire and love, to the greatest good.[28]

Although Joachim of Fiore's association of the Persons with the three ages of the world may have influenced Langland, it is clear that Joachim regarded the age of the Holy Spirit as a manifestation of some future time whereas Langland conceives of the age of the Holy Spirit as having begun with the descent of the Spirit at Pentecost.[29] Langland's three ages seem to correspond more closely to another division in which history was designated as being *ante legem, sub lege,* and *in gratia.* These ages were figured forth in Abraham, Moses, and Christ, respectively. Bishop Wimbledon's sermon (c. 1388) makes the common distinction: He says that God calls men in diverse ages of the world and that he called Abel, Enoch, Noah, and Abraham according to the "lawe of kynde," and Moses, David, Isaiah, and Jeremiah in the "tyme of þe olde lawe," and the apostles, martyrs, confessors, and virgins in the "tyme of grace." [30] But the idea is an old one and is linked by Augustine with the way to God.[31]

To associate each of the Persons of the Trinity with one of the three ages in history might seem to emphasize the distinctions of the Persons over the Unity of essence. It is to avoid this problem that many of Joachim of Fiore's *figuræ* and his discussions of the three ages emphasize that the three overlap; further, he and other commentators insist that we are to understand these as manifestations in history rather than as statements descriptive of the divine essence.[32] Hence, the Father manifests himself to Adam, Abraham, and Moses before the coming of Christ; and Christ, through the Incarnation, manifests himself to the apostles; after Christ's Ascension, the Holy Spirit manifests himself at Pentecost and continues to manifest himself by leading men back to the Father by means of the Son.

Similarly, Langland tries to avoid simplistic associations of the Persons with periods in history lest he suggest that the Persons are a series of emanations. It is true that Langland associates the Persons with the redemptive process in time when he has Piers identify them with the three props of the Tree of Charity; however, he later avoids explicit links between the Persons and the three ages by substituting for them the *figuræ* of Abraham-Faith, Moses-Hope, and Samaritan-Charity. Moreover, it is the omission of the middle terms, the Persons of the Trinity, which has obscured Langland's rationale for linking Abraham to Faith, Moses to Hope, and Samaritan to Charity. The association of Abraham and Moses with the first two ages, those *ante legem* and *sub lege*, might have suggested a rationale for their inclusion, but will not account for the association of the third age with the Samaritan rather than Christ; similarly, while Abraham and Samaritan might readily illustrate Faith and Charity, respectively, it is difficult to understand the basis of the connection between Moses and Hope.[33]

The usual figural interpretation of Moses is that he represents the first Covenant and Christ the second. This point is clearly expressed in Moses' expounding of the two great commandments rather than the Decalogue (17.11–16). But he is linked with Hope because Christ is usually linked with Hope in those passages which link the theological virtues with the Persons of the Trinity. Furthermore, the Moses-Hope figure suggests the peculiar relationship which obtains between the Son, who is the image of the Father but who is not the Father.[34] Moses reflects Abraham and the Old Law or Faith, but is conceived as the Son who brings the New Law.

Samaritan-Charity resolves for the Dreamer the apparently contradictory claims of the two figures (lines 127–40) and uses the hand and taper analogies which immediately follow as illustrations of how one may believe in three Persons and one Truth.[35]

The criticism on the poem has thus far failed to produce a consensus on the meaning of Dowel, Dobet, and Dobest because the definitions attributed to these terms change as the poem progresses; yet each of the definitions can be seen to express the kinds of relationships which exist among the Persons in the Trinity. Many definitions of the Do's have been too exclusive or simplistic; for example, they have depended on hierarchical structures (plowman/priest/bishop; active/contemplative/prelatical) or degrees of sanctity (Active/Contemplative/Mixed Lives; Purgative/Illuminative/Unitive; degrees of perfection).[36] In the last twenty years, however, critics have tended to soften these distinctions; thus, Professor Bloomfield also notes that rank is less important than fulfilling one's assigned role in society; Professor Frank thinks that the Do's do not possess individual meanings but are divisions of the generic term Dowel; and Professor Kirk implies that the various definitions are manifestations of the same essence.[37] Both Frank and Kirk come close to seeing the trinitarian conception of the Do's, but Frank, while he discusses the dominance of one of the Persons in each of the *Vitae*, chooses not to "become involved in the doctrinal complexities of the Trinity" because the "poet uses it in a fairly simple fashion," and Kirk says that the Do's are superseded in Passus XV by other triads.[38]

Although he sometimes recalls one of the specific relations in the Trinity, for example, the procession of the Holy Spirit from the Father and Son, Langland seems to have developed most of the definitions out of the models suggested by the appropriated attributes, Power, Wisdom, and Goodness, and by the three theological virtues, Faith, Hope, and Charity. In addition, some of the sets of definitions have been modified by exchanging some of the terms in these two models or by shifting the attribute of one of the Persons to another Person. The shifting of the terms of the definitions, analogous to the weave in trinitarian discussions, permits Langland to enunciate that the Do's, like the Persons, are distinct from each other yet of the same essence.

If we recall St. Edmund's exposition of the way to God, then we can see not only how the three theological virtues express a progression from believing to loving, but also how the progression describes the individual response to the three appropriated attributes: obedience and submission to, even dread of, God's power and might; coming to know and to communicate God's wisdom, which leads to hope rather than despair; and coming to know God's love, which must result in returning that love.[39] This pattern and variations of this pattern are evident in a number of the definitions of the Do's. For example, Patience defines Dowel, Dobet, and Dobest as learning, teaching, and loving, respectively (13.136-9), or acceptance of faith (knowing), and knowing and teaching (wisdom), and loving, respectively. Even the Doctor of Divinity, who chews on the Trinity and dissects his God, has a vestigial knowledge of the trinitarian configuration of the Do's:

> "Dowel," quod þis doctour, "do as clerkes techeþ.
> [That trauailleþ to teche oþere I holde it for a dobet].
> And dobest doþ hymself so as he seiþ and precheþ:
> *Qui facit & docuerit magnus vocabitur in regno celorum.*"
>   (13.116-19)

The Doctor's definition echoes earlier ones which describe doing well as believing, being obedient, and doing better as teaching, being a priest, and doing best, as doing both, being a bishop.[40] For example, Thought describes Dowel as a laborer who is meek, simple in speech, truthful and moderate in diet (8.78-84). Dobet does well but much more, for, though he is meek as a lamb, he also helps those who are in need (lines 85-95); and Dobest is a bishop whose higher position imposes on him the burden of protecting Dowel (lines 96-9). The definition suggests a hierarchical pattern in which the laborer is at the base and the bishop or king is at the top; moreover, it suggests various degrees of perfection in which it is sufficient that the laborer believe but demands that others in the hierarchy believe and teach.

Clergy's definition modifies the Faith, Hope, and Charity formula by making it conform to Patience's trinity of learning, teaching or doing, and loving. Clergy says that doing well is believing on the holy church with all the articles of faith, among which is the belief that there are three persons and one God: "þus it bilongeþ to bileue to lewed þat willen dowel" (10.238-57). Dobet is to suffer holy church's teaching and to do in deeds what one says in words (lines 258-63); thus, Dobet is faith, or Dowel, as well as good deeds, acts of charity, or Dobest. Dobest is to blame the guilty, but to beware lest one be guilty of that for which he blames others (lines 264-72). This definition of Dobest appears to have no relation to the other two unless one recognizes that it is a variant of the injunction to judge not lest one be judged and thus it is a definition of Charity which implies the special responsibilities of the magistrate, bishop, or king. In Clergy's definition we see vestiges of Faith, Hope – Faith and Charity are the ground of Hope – and Charity, the explicit teaching of the doctrine of the Trinity under the first, the suffering of the Son under the second, and the Charity of the Holy Spirit under the third.

Basic to the concept of the Trinity are the beliefs that the Persons are distinct yet One and that each inheres in the other. These concepts are basic to the definitions of the Do's as well; therefore, there is only an

apparent contradiction between the Friars' statement that Dowel is
Charity (8.44–5) and Imaginatyf's that Charity is Dobest (12.28–31).[41]
In fact, both Dame Study and Piers insist that all the Do's are love. Dame
Study represents the conservative reluctance to probe mysteries and the
basic tenets of the faith. She chastises Will for wishing to divide up
Dowel from Dobet and from Dobest and thereby suggests the contemporary reaction against the dissections of the Trinity (10.52–64); she
tells Will that all three are of "loves kynne" (10.134–9, 192–3), that is,
that they are One. When Clergy is asked to give his definition, he first
passes on Piers':

> For oon Piers þe Plowman haþ impugned vs alle,
> And set alle sciences at a sop saue loue one;
> And no text ne takeþ to mayntene his cause
> But *Dilige deum* and *Domine quis habitabit;*
> And [demeþ] þat dowel and dobet arn two Infinites,
> Whiche Infinites wiþ a feiþ fynden out dobest,
> Which shal saue mannes soule; þus seiþ Piers þe Plowman.
>
> (13.124–30)

Piers' definition suggests that the three are one in two different ways;
first, like Dame Study, he emphasizes that all knowledge is useless except
love; and secondly, he implies that the first two terms are "infinities"
which discover the third. Professor Anne Middleton has argued that "Infinite" is a grammatical term which refers to words which are completed
by a third or another term.[42] This is certainly possible and would suggest
the idea of progression latent in the concept of the Do's. Nevertheless, the
terms may be intended as vestiges of the Trinity and thus assert the reality
of the Persons – each is infinite – and their Unity – all are infinite. Finally,
it should be noted that the third Infinite is discovered by "feiþ," not by
reason or even scriptural testimony.

To illustrate that each state of perfection inheres in the other, Langland has Imaginatyf tell the Dreamer that Faith, Hope, and Charity are
all Dowel. When Will awakes from the inner dream, he says, perhaps sar-
donically, that to do well is "To se moche and suffre more" (11.398–429),
but Imaginatyf rebukes him and tells him that if he had suffered, he would
have known better what clergy knows and what reason conceives Dowel
to be:

> Feiþ, hope and Charite, and alle ben good,
> And sauen men sondry tymes, ac noon so soone as Charite.
> For he dooþ wel, wiþouten doute, þat dooþ as lewte techeþ.
>
> (12.30–2)

Then follows a long commentary on Dowel alone in which Imaginatyf
uses illustrations of the three estates of marriage, religious celibacy, and
maidenly abstinence to describe the concept of obedience, of bowing oneself to the Law, to Faith. Thus the passage anticipates the similar trinitarian

discussion in the *Vita de Dobet* (16.67–72) by utilizing the concept of the three grades of perfection and by linking the three theological virtues with the definition of the Do's; it differs from the *Dobet* passages by stressing that the three are one (Dowel) whereas the Dobet passage emphasizes their threeness. In any event, Imaginatyf's Dowel, basically defined as obedience, is shown to contain Dobet and Dobest. The reverse of this concept is shown later in Christ who is Dobest but who manifests himself as Dowel, Dobet, and Dobest (19.106–98), and by the single sacrament of Penance which contains Contrition, Confession and Satisfaction, three parts of one essence (14.16–24).

Many of the definitions imply the relations which exist between the Persons of the Trinity; for example, it is common to find that Dobet is Dowel and something else – that is, that the Son is the image of the Father but not the Father – and that Dobest contains both Dowel and Dobet – that is, that the Holy Spirit proceeds from both the Father and the Son. Thus, Piers' statement that Dowel and Dobet are two infinites which "fynden out dobest" suggests the procession of the Holy Spirit from the Father and the Son. Wit's second definition is similar:

> [Thanne is dowel] to drede, and dobet to suffre,
> And so comeþ dobest [aboute] and bryngeþ adoun mody . . .
> (9.207–08)

Thought's discussion of the Do's suggests both of the above and anticipates the Samaritan's emphasis on the necessity of the Holy Spirit to man's salvation:

> And [as] dowel and dobet [dide] hem [to vnderstonde],
> [Thei han] crowne[d a] kyng to [kepen] hem [alle],
> That if dowel [and] dobet dide ayein dobest
> [And were vnbuxum at his biddyng, and bold to don ille],
> Thanne [sholde] þe kyng come and casten hem in [prison,
> And putten hem þer in penaunce wiþoute pite or grace],
> But dobest bede for hem [abide] þer for euere.
> Thus dowel and dobet and dobest þe þridde
> Crouned oon to be kyng, [and by hir counseil werchen],
> And rule þe Reme by [rede of hem alle],
> And ooþer wise [and ellis noȝt] but as þei þre assent[e].
> (8.100–10)

Thought's statement, the first extended discussion of the Do's in the poem, not only recalls the action of the *Visio* in which the King governs with the aid of Reason and Conscience, but also anticipates most of the terms in the definitions which follow as well as the Samaritan's central thesis. The passage suggests that Dobest proceeds from Dowel and Dobet (lines 100–1): Dowel and Dobet crown one to be king to rule all three with one will. If any commit sins against Dobest, then this king shall come to put them into prison or hell, where he will command them to remain

without pity or grace forever. The last four lines imply that there is a
hierarchical relationship between the Do's at the same time that they are
said to be equal and unified in will.

The definitions of Dowel, Dobet, and Dobest can be grouped into two
sets of categories: those conceived hierarchically to suggest the estates and
their functions or degrees of perfection (for example, the layman who
works and believes, the priest who teaches, and the bishop who does
both),[43] and those conceived as progressions to denote the successive
stages in the individual's development in moral perfection and his way to
God (for example to fear God, to love God and one's fellowman, to per-
form acts of charity). The first category might suggest the Persons of the
Trinity insofar as it manifests the Trinity in three different persons or
ranks or functions, whereas the second might suggest the Trinity's Unity
insofar as it manifests itself in one individual. It is also clear that the progressions which might be performed successively by individuals are parallel to the estates and their functions; the latter, therefore, might also
describe the worldly progress of an individual from layman to priest to
bishop.[44] Thus the parallels between the hierarchies, which suggest the
Persons, and the progressions, which suggest the states of the individual,
reveal the Trinity in its Threeness and Oneness.

Both the hierarchies and progressions are recalled in the Trinitarian
images of the *Vita de Dobet;* for example, there are the three states of
matrimony, widowhood, and virginity in the Tree of Charity (16.67–72),
and there is the progression from Abraham-Faith to Moses-Hope and to
Samaritan-Charity, which is conceived as an allegorization of the manifestation of the three Persons in time as well as of the individual's progress
toward God. In addition, Christ's life is later defined (19.26–198) both
hierarchically and progressively when Conscience shows how Christ manifested himself as Knight, King, and Conqueror and as Jesus (Dowel),
Jesus, the Son of David (Dobet), and the risen Christ (Dobest). The individual's progress toward God, therefore, is described as a linear, temporal progression which is synonymous with the vertical ascent through
hierarchical states, that is, through the Holy Spirit to the Father by means
of the Son.[45]

Furthermore, Langland repeatedly uses this nexus of constructs which
suggest hierarchy and progression to describe the paradox of salvation:
that to do well, if one is a plowman, is to do best. The paradox is often
expressed ironically in the pilgrimage images: In the *Visio* the Palmer who
has journeyed through space and time has been unable to find Truth, yet
Piers, who has remained at home, knows the way – expressed as a journey
through the landscape of the Ten Commandments – because the way is
within, the journey to Truth begins with the plowing of the half acre.
Similarly, Will repeatedly and mistakenly assumes that Dowel is located
in some place that he can journey to, but he finds that the pilgrimage is

one into his soul when Conscience forces him to confront Haukyn, another manifestation of the Palmer of the *Visio,* a man who thinks he can
save his soul by a physical journey. Will is forced to recognize his own
sins in Haukyn and to see that his search for the Do's in any physical
sense is a false pilgrimage. It is then that Will turns from his geographical
quest within his mind and discovers the Do's in the image of the Trinity
in his heart; the pilgrimage to God, as Piers iterates in this scene, is within.
Lastly, the Dreamer never comprehends his vision of Truth as long as he
is engaged in wandering through the countryside; it is when he sits down
to hear Mass at home that he has his visions of Unity.

Once the Dreamer and Will see that time and space are merely earthly
attributes, not essences, then they have a vision of the cosmos in its Unity;
and it is in order to underline this point that Langland makes the temporal
and spatial schemes begin to converge. The climax of the liturgical year,
Easter and Pentecost, are made to converge with the climax of Will's life,
and these are made parallel with the climax of the world's history.[46]
Everyman's death, Langland implies, is his own individual millennium
which imitates the general day of doom.[47] The building of the Barn of
Unity not only occurs in Langland's England but parallels the building of
Holy Church; its collapse parallels Will's weakening body and mind with
the weakening of the body of Christ, the Church, from within by the
friars. And it is the friars who weaken Unity because they are the ones in
this poem who divide up the Unity of God with their speculations on the
Trinity and with their improper offering of the sacrament of penance.[48]
However, Will, who has finally begun to make his life conform to the
image of God within him, has become the besieged Castle of Unity and
feels himself, his vision, faltering; invaded by speculations and doubts,
teetering on the brink of death, he sends Conscience for the Priest, Piers,
before he awakens to eternity. This convergence of time and space rids
the poem of its emphasis on hierarchies and on progression through time;
it suggests the sweeping away of such distinctions in eternity and in the
essence of God and thus, for a moment, attempts to reveal all of human
history as it exists in the mind of God.

It is not possible in this essay to give a detailed analysis of the *Vita de
Dobest* or to summarize adequately the way that Langland's use of the
Trinity accounts for the development of the poem as a whole, but I think
that the trinitarian emphasis in the first sections of the poem argues for
a different kind of significance for the last section than has heretofore been
offered. The critical assumption has been that the *Visio* forms some kind
of prologue or introduction to the remainder of the poem and that the
Vita de Dowel, Dobet, and Dobest is an ungainly elaboration of the *Visio.*
Furthermore, though the poem's critics have recognized parallel incidents
and scenes in the *Visio* and the *Vita de Dobest,* there seems to be little

consensus on the significance of these parallels or of the relationship of the two sections to the bewildering middle sections of the poem. Yet it is clear that Langland divided his poem into four sections and that each of these sections contains two paired visions.[49]

I think that Langland intended the four-part structure to dominate rather than the division between the *Visio* and the *Vita*, and that the *Visio* is devoted to the image of the Father and the instruction in the Faith, the *Vita de Dowel* to the Son and the attainment of Wisdom whereby one abandons despair for Hope, and the *Vita de Dobet* to the Holy Spirit by whose grace Will is instructed in Charity and allowed to see the Trinity in his soul, and the *Vita de Dobest* to the Unity of the Godhead wherein Will perceives the reality of God which he had formerly seen as in a glass darkly.[50] In addition, Langland has overlapped the three Persons on the last sections of the poem so that the Father, Son, and Holy Spirit play dominant roles in the *Dowel, Dobet,* and *Dobest,* respectively. This pattern suggests that the assistance of the Holy Spirit is required in order to do best and that to do best is to perceive not just the Threeness of God but His Oneness.

The *Visio, Dowel,* and *Dobet* describe the pathway to salvation at the same time that they are linked to the theological virtues, Faith, Hope, and Charity; the virtues, in turn, are associated in the *Vita de Dobet* with the manifestations of each of the Persons in salvation history, a cosmic history which is imitated in Will's individual progress. The dominant images in the *Visio* are of Dame Holy Church, who insists that the Dreamer need only know the basic tenets of the church in order to be saved, and of Piers, who intuitively knows the way to truth (the Pater Noster, the Ten Commandments, and so forth), and yet who may be saved by remaining at home to plow his half acre (Dowel). The pardon is taken from the Pseudo-Athanasian Creed and echoes the teachings of Dame Holy Church; it constitutes all that the plowman need to know for his salvation – to do well is to be saved (*Et qui bona egerunt ibunt in vitam eternam*). The *Vita de Dowel* is less clearly devoted to a study of Hope than to its opposite, Despair; yet each of the persons Will meets, all of whom are exemplars of Dobet, holds out the possibility for learning truth, the hope of salvation. Will can willingly accept their teachings or willfully contradict them, and his perversity of will deters him from understanding either Dowel or Dobet until he is reproved by Imaginatyf. Once he has been awakened from the inner dream, the fantasy which his life has become, he can choose between a life of Hope and one of Despair, a choice personified in a meeting with Haukyn. The *Dobet* section is dominated by the images of the Tree of Charity and the Good Samaritan, each symbols of Dobest. In other words, the instructors in each section of the poem – Piers in the *Visio,* the teachers in *Dowel,* and the Samaritan in *Dobet* – are manifestations of the succeeding sections, that is, Piers is Dowel, the teachers are Dobet, and the Samaritan is Dobest. Moreover, the *Vita de Dobet* is the pivotal point of the poem, for unless one understands and practices Charity, one cannot see God who is manifested as three (Father/Faith/ Dowel, Son/Hope/Dobet, and Holy Spirit/Charity/Dobest) but who is one (God/Charity/Essence or Unity).

The *Visio*, the *Vita de Dowel,* and the *Vita de Dobet* are not only linked, respectively, to the three theological virtues, Faith, Hope, and Charity, but also to three progressive stages in the life of the Dreamer. In the *Visio* we see him in his innocence; indeed, he is a child who is learning his ABC's at the knee of his first teacher, Dame Holy Church. His naive perceptions of the world – what is good? what is false? – remain throughout the *Visio* until his simple world view is rent asunder like the pardon at the end of his second dream. In the *Vita de Dowel* he goes off to school; first his thought is awakened, then he is sent to discipline it, and then, like a student who would know without troubling to undergo the process of learning, he leaps to wrong conclusions and petulantly rejects his faith. His middle life, the first inner dream, is abandoned to fruitless journeyings to and fro until he matures intellectually and is led to the vision in his own soul. The final visions occur in his old age.

These stages in the individual life are linked to the stages in human history, for just as Will undergoes instruction in the three phases of Faith, Hope, and Charity, so the world passed through the Age of Faith, dominated by the Father and the Old Law, the Age of Hope, dominated by the Son and the New Covenant, and resides in the Age of Charity, dominated by the Holy Spirit and Grace: *ante legem, sub lege, in gratia.*

It is clear, therefore, that each of these stages is evidence, a vestige, of the very trinitarian God revealed in the *Vita de Dobet;* furthermore, Will is moving toward a state of perfection in which all phases of his life conform to the pattern of the archetype. Thus the poem moves toward Unity, which is perfect, being One. But before Will can achieve that Unity, he must understand that the Trinity is not three Persons but that it is three Persons and They are One. The trinitarian analogies in the *Vita de Dobet* explain that the Three are One and thereby resolve the conflict which had kept Will from understanding what Dowel, Dobet, and Dobest are.

Up until the *Vita de Dobet*, it is the spatial, temporal and hierarchical distinctions which impede Will's understanding that all ways are one way, that Dowel is Dobest; moreover, even in the *Vita de Dobet*, the analogies and images are expressed in worldly terms which suggest the appearance in time of the Persons of the Trinity and the relative hierarchical relationship of the Persons at the time of the Dreamer's vision. Since the *Vita de Dobet* stresses that the hierarchies and progressions are manifestations of one essence, it provides the transition to the final two visions in which Will comes closest to understanding that all that he has formerly seen fragmented in time are, in eternity, One.

Langland, however, has gone further than simply emphasizing one of the Persons in each of the three sections and their Unity in the last, for if he had made these simple associations, then he would have undermined the very sense of trinity that he had worked so hard to achieve. In fact, he seems to have overlapped the Persons on the four-part structure of the poem as a whole in order to stress that Each is in Each:

1	Father	Son	Holy Spirit	Unity
2	*Visio*	*Dowel*	*Dobet*	*Dobest*
3	Truth	Father	Son	Holy Spirit

First, we should note that Truth is a unity; thus, the poem ends where it begins. The relationships between lines 2) and 3) bring out points established by the discussion of the Do's: to do well is to conform oneself to one's superiors and teachers, an act of the will which Will perversely fails to do until he learns Patience, accepts poverty, and sees himself in the tattered figure of Haukyn. To do better is to love one's friends and foes and this action is best symbolized in the Samaritan's caring for the man who had fallen among thieves, an image of the Christ who mercifully descended to care for fallen man. To do best is to do both of these for faith without charity is to no avail, and without the aid of the Holy Spirit, it is impossible to know God or to be saved.

It is significant that Will's last dreams occur during the mass at the season of Pentecost, for, although it might at first seem that the Dreamer's falling asleep is indicative of inattention and idleness, in fact, it is an action whereby his inner eyes are opened and he passes from the world of illusion and symbols into the world of reality itself. Indeed, I suspect that Langland's four-part structure may recall Augustine's theory of vision.[51] The external sight, the seeing of things outside the body, seems to correspond to the *Visio* – hence its title. The second stage involves the first stage of internal sight, the remembrance of external objects; and since memory is the first term of Augustine's principal trinitarian analogy and synonymous in *Piers* with Dowel and the Father, it may be that Langland has modeled *Dowel* on this type of vision. Further, Augustine says that "Whatsoever ideas are in the mind of the faithful man from this faith . . . when they are contained in the memory, and are looked at by recollection, and please the will, set forth a kind of trinity of its own sort."[52] This stage suggests the action which follows in *Dobet*. But the Trinity is not to be found in the fact that the mind remembers, understands and loves itself; it is only when the mind loves God that it loves itself rightly. And so the image of God is to be found in the fact that the mind remembers, understands and loves God.[53] This unified vision corresponds to *Dobest*.

Will's penetration into the mystery of his self wherein is revealed the image of the Trinity results in a transformation of his perception of the world. As Will begins to conform his image to the image of God within him, he begins to see, as God sees, things in their essence. In the *Vita de Dobest* Langland reveals the significance of the events of the *Visio*: The plowing of the half acre is replaced by Piers' plowing of the world with the Gospels. Thus, when the poet calls the plowman, "Piers, *id est Christus*," he tells us that Piers is Piers, a plowman, Dowel, but that insofar as he fulfills his function as plowman, he is Christ, Dobest. This is the same Piers who could direct the pilgrims to Truth by means of the Old Law or simple faith which now is revealed as the New Law; and it is the same Piers who knew then as now that the journey to Truth is within, that to do well, if one is a plowman, is to do best.

NOTES

1. *De trinitate* 10.12.19; 14.4.6. See also Barbara Raw, "Piers and the Image of God in Man," in *Piers Plowman: Critical Approaches*, ed. S. S. Hussey (London, 1969), pp. 143–79, and Joseph S. Wittig, "'Piers Plowman' B, Passus IX–XII: Elements in the Design of the Inward Journey," *Traditio*, vol. 38, 1972, pp. 211–15.
2. The points of orthodoxy discussed below can be found in the Lombard's *Sentences*, e.g., I, d.2, c.1–2; d.5; d.9, c. 3; d.11, c.1, et passim. Langland's statements on the Trinity are thoroughly orthodox; see the speeches by Clergy (B.X.238–48), Piers (XVI.25–52), Abraham (XVI.181–230), and the Samaritan (XVII.140–356). All B-text citations are from George Kane and E. Talbot Donaldson, eds., *Piers Plowman: The B Version* (London, 1975); the C-text readings are from W. W. Skeat, ed., *The Vision of William concerning Piers the Plowman*, EETS no. 54 (London, 1873).
3. See Augustine, *De trin.* 5.5.6, 10.11, 16.17; Boethius, *De trinitate* 5, in *Theological Tractates*, ed. and trans. H. F. Stewart and E. K. Rand (Cambridge, Mass., 1936), pp. 25, 28–9; and Harry Austryn Wolfson, *The Philosophy of the Church Fathers*, 3rd ed. rev., vol. 1 (Cambridge, Mass., 1970), p. 310.
4. Pseudo-Athanasian Creed, in Heinrich Denzinger, ed., *Enchiridion Symbolorum* (Freiburg, 1962), pp. 16–17; Boethius, *De trin.* 3.
5. Wolfson, *Church Fathers*, pp. 332–3; Roy W. Battenhouse, ed., *A Companion to the Study of St. Augustine* (New York, 1955), pp. 237–8; and Jaroslav Pelikan, *The Christian Tradition*, 2 vols. to date (Chicago, 1971–), 1:219–20.
6. For example, Hugh of St. Victor, *De Sacramentis* 1.3.26–7; Bonaventure, *Breviloquium* 1.6.1; Aquinas, *Summa contra gentiles* 4.12.4–5, 20.2–3, 21.1–11; Rupert Morris, ed., *Dan Michel's Ayenbite of Inwit*, EETS no. 23 (London, 1866), pp. 120–1; Wyclif, Tract 26, in *English Works*, ed. F. D. Matthew, EETS no. 74a (London, 1902), p. 362. Aquinas summarizes the patristic and medieval tradition to his day in *Summa Theologiae* 1.39.7–8.
7. Augustine, *De trin.* 6.1.2–2.3; 7.1.2–2.3; Bonaventure, *Brevil.* 1.6.1. Both Abelard and William of Conches were accused of asserting that these mental distinctions were real. See Abelard's statements in *Theologia christiana* (PL 178:1131, 1288–9; cited by Edmund J. Fortman, *The Triune God* [London, 1972], p. 179). See also A. Victor Murray, *Abelard and St Bernard* (Manchester, 1967), pp. 58–9, 70. William of St. Thierry quotes William's errors in *De erroribus Guillelmi de Conchis* (PL 180:333) and equates them with Abelard's (c. 334).

8. 6.10.12.
9. Commentators are insistent that the Trinity is an article of Faith and that analogies are aids to understanding which are imperfect because they are material. See Athanasius, *Letters*, trans. C. R. B. Shapland (New York, 1951), pp. 113–16; Hilary of Poitiers, *De trinitate* 1.19; 3.1; 7.28–9; Augustine, *De trin.* 8.2.3.
10. Origen, *De Principiis* 1.2.4; Hippolytus, *Adversus Noetum* 11; Lactantius, *Divinae institutiones* 2.9; 4.29; Tertullian, *Adversus Praxeam* 8, 22.
11. Athanasius, *Letters*, p. 109; Irenaeus, *Adversus haereses* 3.18.3.
12. Tatian, *Ad Graecos* 5; Justin Martyr, *Dialogus cum Tryphone Judaeo* 61, 128.
13. *Epistola de Nicaenis decretis* 23 (PG 25:455, 458). See also Hilary, *De trin.* 6.12.
14. See, for example, the light and sun analogies in Rupert Morris, ed., *Cursor Mundi*, EETS no. 57 (London, 1874), lines 289–308; "A Disputisoun Bytwene a Cristenemon and a Jew," in *Minor Poems of the Vernon MS, Part II*, ed. F. J. Furnivall, EETS no. 117 (London, 1901), lines 117–48.
15. *The Vision of William concerning Piers the Plowman in Three Parallel Texts*, 2 vols. (Oxford, 1886), 2:245.
16. The only analogy based on the hand that I have been able to locate is that which Irenaeus developed to replace the torch analogy of Tatian and Justin Martyr: "Now man is a mixed organization of soul and flesh, who was formed after the likeness of God, and moulded by His hands, that is, by the Son and Holy Spirit, to whom also He said, 'Let Us make man.'" *Adv. haer.* 4.Pref.4; trans. from *Ante-Nicene Fathers*, ed. Rev. Alexander Roberts and James Donaldson, vol. 1 (Buffalo, 1888). The analogy is significant because it preserves the unity of the deity (the body) at the same time that it differentiates the persons of the deity (through the distinction between the body and the parts that make up the body); in addition, it links the three Persons in creation. There is no evidence that Langland was aware of this analogy; in any event, his hand analogy is considerably different.
17. Skeat, *Vision* (Oxford, 1886), 2:244, pointed out that Langland included the phrase, *Mundum pugillus continens*, at the beginning of the C-text version of the analogy and that the line was quoted from the Latin hymn, *Quem terra, pontus, sidera*, which is included in the Roman Breviary at Matins in the Office of the Blessed Virgin. He also noted that the line ultimately derived from *Isaiah*, but he either did not look at the biblical passage or failed to note the connection between it and the terms of Langland's analogy.
    It should be noted that *pugillus* does not literally mean "fist"; instead, it means "that which can be held in the hand or fist" (DuCange), but it is often translated as "hand" (see *Douai*). From the fact that Langland quoted a part of the line, it is clear that he regarded *pugillus* as referring to the fist itself and we can find support for this in the gloss on the passage: *Pugillus, contractis digitis pugnus, palmanus a pollice usque ad minimum digitum extenta manus* (*Glossa ordinaria*, PL 113:1281).
18. A typical commentary might be that found in Haymo of Halberstadt's *Commentary on Isaiah* (PL 116:911). Haymo says that the similitude of the hand expresses God's omnipotence, the three fingers the Trinity, and the "consiliarius" of the next verse the Holy Spirit who assists in the creation. Other typical references are to God's omnipotence (Gregory, *Homiliæ in Ezechielem*, PL 76:991; Irenaeus, *Adv. haer.* 4.19.2–3), or to the Trinity (Isidore, *De fide catholica*, PL 83:459; Novatian, *De trinitate*,

CCSL 4:30.44–5; Cassiodorus, *Expositio Psalmorum, CCSL* 98:*Psa.* 135.6.123; 143.1.49). Raban Maur says that by the *Quis* the verse indicates the Deity's single substance and by the *tres* the unity of the Persons (*Allegoriæ in sacram scriptorum, PL* 112:910). The passage is also quoted in St. Edmund's *Speculum,* a tract that had wide circulation in Latin and English in northern England in the fourteenth century: *Ipse enim supra omnia est, infra omnia, intra omnia, et extra omnia. Supra omnia gubernans; infra omnia supportans; intra omnia implens; extra omnia circumdans, et quasi pugillo concludens et continens universa. Huiusmodi contemplacio generat in corde firmam fidem et securam devocionem* (Helen Forshaw, ed., *Speculum Religiosorum and Speculum Ecclesie,* Auctores Britannici Medii Aevi, vol. 3 [Oxford, 1973], p. 131).

19. There is a later passage in both texts which parallels this one, but the C-version, lines 130–4, expresses the concept of the Father's "priority" to the Son and the Holy Spirit better than does B169–71:

> And as þe fust is ful hand yfolde to-gederes,
> So is þe fader a ful god þe furste of hem alle.
> And as my fust is furst er ich my fyngers shewe,
> So is he fader an former þe furste of alle þynges;
> > *Tu fabricator omnium;*
> And alle þe myghte with hym is was, and worth euere.

The fist, Langland says, is a complete hand and is the Father, the "furste" of them all; He is "furste" on the same principal as that of the fist which exists prior to its showing its fingers. There is also a pun on "former" (i.e., "prior to," "first," and "shaper," "maker"); the emphasis, then, is on God's existence from the beginning and through eternity as well as on his creation (formation) of the world.

20. While the C-text, 20.135–9, also describes the Son's creative functions, it does not call him the "Science" of the Father; instead, Langland says that the fingers are a complete hand, for if they lacked a thumb they could do no work. Conversely, the Son did not fail the Father "be ne myghte." The implication is that since the Son performed the work of creation, He is complete and co-equal with the Father, i.e., He does not lack a thumb. The focus on the thumb, rather than on the abstract "Science," helps convey the sense that the Son's relationship to the Divine Essence is one of specialized function. Augustine differentiates between *scientia* and *sapientia* in *De trin.* 12.14.22; see also F. Holthausen, ed., *Vices and Virtues,* EETS no. 89 (London, 1888), pp. 65, 85, 91.

21. The commentary on sins against the Holy Spirit is fairly commonplace (e.g., Bonaventure, *Brevil.* 3.11), but the deficiency of the analogy is that the Holy Spirit/palm seems to be given greater power in the Trinity than the other two Persons. Langland may have deleted B189b–92a from the C-text in order to avoid any conflict with the emphasis on the equality of the Persons elsewhere in the passage. Thus where B takes up the example of the hurt palm and compares it to the maimed fingers in order to suggest that the former is worse than the latter, in C, Langland simply proceeds from the hurt palm to the explanation: "If my palm were without injury I might help myself in many ways even if all my fingers ached." Langland also changes B198's "skile" to "simile" in order to emphasize that his illustration is an analogy and not a rational exposition.

22. Sicard of Cremona, *Mitrale* (*PL* 213:323, 329). See also Belethus, *Rationale*

divinorum officiorum (PL 202:110–12), and Rupert of Deutz, *De divinis officiis* (PL 170:171).

23. John Myrc uses a related analogy in his *Instructions for Parish Priests*, EETS no. 31 (London, 1902), p. 15, and in his *Festial*, EETS, ES no. 96 (London, 1905), p. 166.

24. Thus Bonaventure says, *Brevil.* 2.12.3, that a creature "cannot have God as an infused Gift unless it conforms to Him through the threefold dowry of faith, hope, and love. The first conformity is distant, the second close, and the third most intimate. That is why the first is called a 'trace' of the Trinity, the second an 'image,' and the third a 'likeness' " (trans. José de Vinck, *Works*, vol. 2 [Paterson, N.J., 1963]). Augustine calls these traces "vestigia"; see *De trin.* 10.8.11.

25. Bonaventure, *Itinerarium mentis* 3.2; 4.6.

26. Marjorie Reeves and Beatrice Hirsch-Reich, The Figuræ *of Joachim of Fiore* (Oxford, 1973), pp. 55, 71–2, 204 et passim; Bonaventure, *Brevil.* 2.12.3, 5.4.4; St. Edmund, *Spec. Relig.*, pp. 11, 29.

27. C. Horstmann, ed., *Yorkshire Writers*, 2 vols. (London, 1895), 1:249. It should be noted that Horstmann altered the MS readings when he printed the Vernon MS version of the text and associated the Son with Faith and the Father with Hope. The Thornton MS version, Horstmann, pp. 219–40, can be identified with the Latin Bodley MS 54 recension (see *Spec. Relig.*, pp. 17–20), as can the poetic versions in the Vernon MS, "Hou a man schal lyue parfytly," lines 857–912, and "Þe Spore of Loue," lines 461–75; C. Horstmann, ed., *The Minor Poems of the Vernon MS*, Part I, EETS no. 98 (London, 1892), pp. 221–51, 268–97, respectively.

28. *Brevil.* 5.4.4.

29. Morton Bloomfield, *Piers Plowman as a Fourteenth-Century Apocalypse* (New Brunswick, 1962), pp. 65–7 et passim; Reeves and Hirsch-Reich, *Figuræ*, pp. 153–9 et passim.

30. Ione Kemp Knight, ed., *Wimbledon's Sermon*, Duquesne Studies, Philological Series, vol. 9 (Pittsburgh, 1967), p. 62.

31. *Enchiridion* 118. See also Professor Raw's discussion, pp. 154–6 (cited above, n. 1).

32. *Figuræ*, pp. 164–5, 249–61 et passim.

33. Bloomfield, *Piers*, p. 216, note 69, says that the identification of Moses with Hope "is rare or unknown." Abraham is frequently cited as a figure for the Father, but I think that Langland may also have chosen Abraham because it was to him that the three angels appeared, the first indisputable testimony to the Trinity, according to Augustine, in the Old Testament.

34. Several analogies were developed – and some like Abelard's brass seal declared heretical – to explain how the Son could be the image of the Father and yet be distinct from the Father. See Didymus, *De spiritu sancto* 22 (PG 39:1052–3); Hilary of Poitiers, *De trin.* 7.28; 8.44; and, for Abelard, Murray, *Abelard*, pp. 103–6.

35. It is important to note the pattern here because it repeats that of some of the definitions of the Do's, as we shall see below: Moses-Hope is Abraham-Faith (Dowel, 17.115–17) and something more (the common definition of Dobet; compare 8.84–93 with 17.118–22), and Samaritan-Charity subsumes both of these (Dobest; compare 8.94–106 and 9.202–6 with 17.118–26).

36. Nevill K. Coghill, "The Character of Piers Plowman Considered from the B Text," in *Interpretations of Piers Plowman*, ed. Edward Vasta (Notre Dame, 1968), pp. 54–86; D. W. Robertson, Jr., and Bernard Huppé, *Piers Plowman and Scriptural Tradition* (Princeton, 1951), pp. 236–7; Henry W.

Wells, "The Construction of *Piers Plowman*," in Vasta, pp. 1–21; Howard Meroney, "The Life and Death of Longe Wille," *ELH*, vol. 17, 1950, pp. 8–12; and Morton Bloomfield, *Piers*, pp. 116–18, respectively.

37. Bloomfield, *Piers*, pp. 49, 102; Robert W. Frank, Jr., Piers Plowman *and the Scheme of Salvation* (Yale, 1957), pp. 12, 38–44; Elizabeth Kirk, *The Dream Thought of* Piers Plowman (Yale, 1972), pp. 160–8.

38. Frank, p. 16; Kirk, pp. 167–8. Professor Kirk never uses "trinity" to describe the Do's; instead, she uses "triads," "trios," or "trilogies." It must be stressed that the poem did not drop the Do's from the poem after Passus 15; they are used to define the stages of Christ's life in 19.108–98 and, therefore, the last definition of the Do's is an archetypal one in which the three states are shown to be manifested in the one Person of Christ.

39. See also Augustine, *De trin.* 13.4.6; 9.12.18; Bonaventure, *Brevil.* 5.4.4; St. Edmund, *Mirror*, in Horstmann, *Yorkshire Writers*, 1.259–60.

40. See Wit's description of the Castle of Kynde, 9.1–24.

41. Augustine makes a similar point (*De trin.* 8.4) when he says that Faith enables man to love that which he does not know in order that he may come to know and love it; hence, love is both first and last.

42. "Two Infinites: Grammatical Metaphor in *Piers Plowman*," *ELH*, vol. 39, 1972, pp. 171–3, 178.

43. The three estates are associated with the Persons of the Trinity in the Wycliffite tract, "The clergy may not hold property," *English Works*, p. 362.

44. Conscience makes this point (19.26–7) when he imagines Christ to be knight, king, and conqueror.

45. The latter is commonplace; see, for example, Irenaeus *Adv. haer.* 4.20.4–6; 5.36.2; St. Basil's commentary on *I Cor* 12:4–6 in *De spiritu sancto* 37 (*PG* 32:134). Bonaventure imagines the recovery of the knowledge of God to combine progression and ascent; see *Brevil.* 2.12.1–3 and *Itin. mentis* 4.6.

46. Bloomfield, *Piers*, p. 185, note 44, and Frank, *Scheme*, p. 98, associate the climax of the poem with Pentecost; Kirk, *Dream Thought*, pp. 183–7, says that Langland's use of the liturgical year provides one of the poem's unities.

47. Wimbledon, *Sermon*, p. 99, says that men are called to the individual judgment by sickness, old age ("elde"), and death: "þe first warneþ; þe secunde þreteneþ; *and* þe þridde takiþ." These correspond to the three "callers" to the general judgment: "þe worldlis sykenesse," i.e., "charites acoldyng," its "feblenesse," which shall be known by signs, and its end, which will be marked by the coming of the Antichrist (p. 109).

48. We should recall that one of the definitions of the Do's is the trinity, contrition, confession, and satisfaction; the frustration of any one of these, therefore, destroys the essence of the sacrament of penance.

49. Raw, "Image," p. 154; Frank, *Scheme*, pp. 16–7.

50. Critics who have discussed the trinitarian associations with the poem have not satisfactorily accounted for the four parts of the poem, I think, because they imagine the Trinity to involve three things (Persons) when, in fact, it involves four (three Persons, One God). Thus, Frank devotes a chapter to the dominance of each of the Persons in one of the *Vitae* without accounting for the role of the *Visio* in this pattern. Professor Raw sees several patterns: Piers is associated with the Father, Son and Holy Spirit in the *Visio*, *Dobet*, and *Dobest*, respectively, pp. 163–8; and, the *Visio* represents the Old Testament, and the "*Dowel, Dobet, Dobest* triad . . . corresponds to the three persons of the Trinity and to three periods of time" (p. 154). I do not wish to dispute Professor Raw's analysis, and it

should be stressed that she is conscious of the overlapping of several different kinds of patterns; however, she usually omits one section of the poem when she seeks out her triad.

51. *De trin.* 11.2.2–5, 3.6, 4.7. Compare Hugh of St. Victor's discussion of triple vision in his *De Sacramentis* 1.10.2 (cited by Bonaventure in his *Brevil.* 2.12.5).

52. *De trin.* 13.20.6; A. W. Haddan, trans., *Select Library of Nicene and Post-Nicene Fathers*, ed. Philip Schaff, vol. 3 (Grand Rapids, Mich., 1956).

53. *De trin.* 14.12.15; 15.14.18; Battenhouse, *Augustine*, pp. 252–3.

Theology and Politics in the Towneley Play of the Talents

THERESA COLETTI

The Towneley *Play of the Talents* exhibits a number of qualities that have vexed even the most sympathetic readers of the Middle English religious drama. Its provenance has been disputed, and its name bears no relation to its subject, the dicing for Christ's seamless garment.[1] Its tone, a mixture of the ribald and homiletic, seems strongly out of keeping with the solemnity of its position between the *Crucifixion* and the *Deliverance of Souls*. The play itself appears to be redundant, for it treats an episode dramatized earlier in the cycle during the Crucifixion, the moment at which the canonical gospels all records the soldiers' dice game at the foot of the cross.[2] None of the other English mystery cycles makes this brief scriptural reference the occasion for an entire play. Furthermore the *Play of the Talents* assigns to Pilate a large and complex role in its central action. In this respect it contributes to the Towneley cycle's unique and consistent characterization of Christ's judge as a ruthless and evil tyrant.[3]

These anomalies perhaps can account for the minimal attention that the play has received from commentators. The *Talents* has been briefly praised and just as briefly dismissed; and although many scholars argue that the play is good drama, a detailed investigation of the *Play of the Talents* has yet to be offered.[4] Even Rosemary Woolf, whose provocative speculations on the play's subject will be considered below, finds the *Talents* "an ambitious attempt at a *tour de force* which was not quite successful."[5] This essay argues that the *Play of the Talents* is at once thematically appropriate to its position in the Towneley cycle and integrally related to the religious and dramatic significance of the Corpus Christi play.

The *Play of the Talents* does present a strange conflation of elements. Around the framework supplied by the scriptural text, the *Talents* weaves a drama that draws upon homiletic and exegetical tradition and apocryphal and popular legend. As a play ostensibly concerned with Christ's seamless robe, the *Talents* invokes the authority of the exegetical tradition that glossed the garment in several ways. Secondly, in its unequivocally evil Pilate, the play presents a portrait of the corruption of civil law in the person of a ruthless tyrant. That portrait, moreover, shows the influence of a widespread popular tradition that had assigned to Pilate a vicious and sinful life and a horrible death. The *Talents* also provides the occasion for homiletic moralizations upon the evils of gambling, a subject treated frequently in contemporary sermons. Because the play's casting of lots involves notions of gaming, it suggests in turn the medieval understanding of the vagaries of Fortune. Finally, all of these aspects of the play contribute to the larger design of the Corpus Christi cycle drama, the mimesis of Christian history.

Christ's seamless garment provides the center of dramatic attention in the *Talents*. The three torturers rush into the scene fresh from the Crucifixion, and each proclaims his desire to possess the garment. They anticipate, however, that Pilate will want the robe for himself. When these fears are realized, they squabble with Pilate over the garment and attempt to resolve the conflict through a game of dice. Though Pilate loses the game, he is nevertheless able to gain the robe from its winner by threatening him. By focusing on Christ's seamless coat the *Talents* follows the gospel account in John 19:23-4, which distinguishes between the soldiers' division of Christ's clothing (23) and the casting of lots for his seamless coat (24). The synoptic gospels make no such distinction, recording simply that the soldiers divided Christ's garments by casting lots.[6]

The twofold division of Christ's clothing described in John 19:23-4 might in fact be related to the apparent redundancy of the *Play of the Talents*. In the Crucifixion play directly preceding it, one of the torturers remarks: "we will departe his clothynge tyte" (23.499).[7] Then they recognize there is one garment they are "lothe" to divide, and instead they cast lots for it. As soon as the winner of the seamless coat takes possession of it, one of his companions offers to buy it from him. The offer goes unanswered because at this moment the torturers notice Pilate's inscription on the cross. A reviser of the Towneley cycle might have seen in this suspended action the opportunity for a more extensive treatment of the casting of lots for Christ's robe, an opportunity that he developed in the *Play of the Talents*. Medieval commentators had devoted considerable attention to the *tunica inconsutilis* mentioned in John 19:23-4, and it is neither surprising nor insignificant that this theologically resonant scriptural reference was recognized as good dramatic material. The *Play of the Talents* is far from being repetitive; rather, it is expansive. It elaborates the meaning of the much sought after seamless coat within a context appropriate to it, the moment after the death of Christ.

Scriptural exegesis furnishes glosses for Christ's seamless robe that illuminate the central action of the *Play of the Talents*. The episode narrated in John's gospel was interpreted in several ways, and together these meanings form an important and coherent theological idea. Commentators regularly interpreted the division of Christ's garments among the soldiers as a figure of the church, which is spread equally over the four quarters of the world. The *tunica inconsutilis* signified the unity of all the parts of the church through the bond of love, which no one can divide. In the casting of lots exegetes saw a figure of the grace of God.[8] Perhaps even more important than those glosses that identified Christ's seamless robe with the indivisible unity of the church, His mystical body, were those that interpreted the *tunica inconsutilis* as *corpus Christi:*

The seamless garment denotes the body of Christ, which is woven from above: for the Holy Spirit came upon the Virgin, and the power of the highest over-shadowed her. This holy body of Christ then is indivisible: for although it be distributed for everyone, sanctifying the soul and body of each one individually, yet it subsists in all wholly and indivisibly.[9]

Christ's seamless garment signifies His body, both His physical body, which He assumed through the Virgin in order to redeem man, and the mystical body of His church, which is the union of all the faithful who become one with that body through His human sacrifice.

Biblical commentary thus provides a foundation for viewing the *Play of the Talents* in a new and significant light. When the three torturers and Pilate conduct their unsuccessful search for a seam along which they might cut the *tunica inconsutilis* (24.274–82), they are in effect trying to divide what cannot be divided. Their abortive attempt to divide the seamless robe mimics the Crucifixion, an equally ineffectual effort to rend the body of Christ once and for all. It also anticipates the next two plays: In the *Deliverance of Souls* Satan tries to stop the action of God's *caritas* by fortifying the gates of Hell, and in the *Resurrection* Pilate and his minions think they can keep Christ's body from rising by placing a careful guard around His tomb. When glossing the *tunica inconsutilis* of John 19:23–4, biblical commentators frequently emphasized the indivisible unity of *corpus Christi* by referring to those heretics who profane both Scripture and the sacraments and yet cannot disturb the bond of charity that Christ's body in its oneness represents.[10] Thus although the actions of Pilate and the torturers appear humorous because they are bound to fail, they also point to the inevitable flimsiness of all attempts to threaten the essential unity of *corpus Christi*. The *Play of the Talents*, like the entire story of the Passion, presents the frustrated efforts of those who fail to understand the providential design of Christian history.

In her brief discussion of the *Talents* play Rosemary Woolf alludes to some of these meanings as possible explanations for what she calls an "otherwise almost inexplicable invention."[11] Although she acknowledges that the dramatist who shaped the *Play of the Talents* probably had in mind the implications of the *tunica inconsutilis*, she is reluctant to view the play as a carefully elaborated dramatic formulation of an important theological idea. The remainder of this essay suggests that the *Play of the Talents* does in fact explore the meaning of the *tunica inconsutilis* on several levels. As a figure for *corpus Christi*, and hence for the ultimate oneness of God's love and the community of believers that it binds together, the seamless robe can be contrasted to the fragmented and illusory law that Pilate constructs and manipulates. His repeated attempts to assert the supremacy of his law, which relies on his creation of self-serving appearances, act as a foil for the supreme law that, according to medieval exegetes, the *tunica inconsutilis* represents.

There is ample evidence to suggest that the meaning of Christ's seamless robe would have been present in the mind of the dramatic audience. F. P. Pickering observes that the *tunica inconsutilis* appears regularly in Passion narratives as a garment that the Virgin made for Christ.[12] Furthermore, the garment that the Virgin wove for her son was identified with the human flesh she gave Him in her womb.[13] The Towneley manuscript itself supports this association of Christ's garment with His flesh, and hence His body, for in the cycle's *Crucifixion* play the Virgin laments at the foot of the cross:

> To deth my dere is dryffen
> his robe is all to-ryffen
> That of me was hym gyffen,
> And shapen with my sydys.
> (23.386–9)

Similarly, in the *Parliament of Heaven* play in the N-Town cycle, the Son refers to the Incarnation as the taking on of a garment: "lete me se how I may were þat wede."[14]

The dramatic evidence reinforcing the association of Christ's garment with His body also helps to explain the seemingly problematic position of the *Talents* play in the Towneley cycle. The play would focus the audience's attention on a symbol of *corpus Christi* immediately after it had witnessed the death and deposition of that body in the preceding play. The solemn closing of the *Crucifixion* play is enhanced rather than disturbed by the action of the *Play of the Talents*, for the unsuccessful attempt to divide the *tunica inconsutilis* affirms a fundamental Christian truth that the medieval play-goer would surely have in mind. Without the knowledge that the body of Christ remains one in spite of His death, the ending of the *Crucifixion* is potentially horrifying. The dramatic audience would know the joyous outcome of the Christian story; but the *Play of the Talents* serves to remind it of that outcome, and thus it acts as a bridge between the tragic action of the Passion and its comic resolution in the Harrowing of Hell and Resurrection.

In the *Talents* play the identification of Christ's garment with His body seems to have undergone an interesting transformation in which the seamless robe emerges as a magical garment capable of protecting its owner. When the three torturers in the play first appear with the *tunica inconsutilis*, they attribute special properties to it (24.105–8; 140–4); Pilate's concerted efforts to win the garment by any means also suggest its unique value. Indeed, in the evil Pilate legends upon which the Towneley cycle consistently draws, Pilate is saved from the Emperor's anger over his un-just condemnation of Christ only through the agency of the seamless robe, which Pilate wears when he meets his superior. When Pilate is stripped of the coat, he becomes defenseless.[15]

The salutary effects of the *tunica inconsutilis,* presented in both the *Talents* play and the evil Pilate legends, seem to manifest a more popular understanding of its theological implications.[16] Because the garment sig-nifies the body of Christ, it points to the ultimate protection of salvation that the participation in that body assures. To make that garment the ob-ject of a raucous and discordant game, as occurs in the *Play of the Talents,* suggests that the game and its players are involved in actions that have larger meanings. The dice game in which Pilate and the torturers engage provides more than a simple opportunity for moralization on the dangers of gambling, though the relationship of the dramatic action to sermon themes is clear.[17] Rather, the dicing juxtaposes an image of the workings of Fortune against that which transcends her worldly instability, the unity of God's love represented in the seamless robe. In the *Talents* play it would seem that theological meanings become all the more resonant be-cause of their presentation in a timely context. The geographic and tem-poral distance between the gambling table and the foot of the cross is not so great.

The evil characterization of Pilate dominates the *Play of the Talents.* His opening and closing speeches frame the main action, and apart from the scene in which the torturers enter, he provides the focal point of dra-matic interest. As I noted previously, popular legends of an evil Pilate told how Christ's judge used the seamless garment to save his own skin; on the literal level, then, the *Play of the Talents* gives some backbone to popular tradition by showing how Pilate became the owner of that garment. Ar-nold Williams argues that the purpose of the *Talents* play is the rounding out of the cycle's consistently villainous characterization of Pilate, who emerges as the central antagonist of Christ.[18] Although the portrait of Pilate in the *Talents* play has attracted considerable interest, its relation-ship to the thematic elements outlined above remains largely unexamined.

The *Play of the Talents* departs substantially from traditional accounts of the Passion to give Pilate a direct involvement in the dicing for Christ's garment. In doing so it emphasizes the absolute conflict of good and evil apparent throughout the Towneley Passion sequence by focusing on Pi-late's participation in a number of more specific struggles: the power of love against the blindness of power, willing subjection against forced obedience, divine truth against man-made fictions, the incarnate Word against silence.

As a figure of self-conscious evil, Pilate is the culmination of the Towne-ley cycle's line of villains, which reaches back to Lucifer and includes Pharaoh, Caesar Augustus, and Herod. Walter Meyers sees in this series of wicked temporal rulers a "diabolical typology" that contrasts with the line of patriarchs and prophets united in their love for God.[19] The members of this satanic genealogy all attempt to use guile to thwart divinely ordained events and ultimately contribute to their own demise. In their shared dedication to Mahomet, the god of illusion and perpetrator of the belief in an earthly kingdom, these rulers presume an absolute temporal authority that depends largely upon artifice.[20] But although the demise of Lucifer, Pharaoh, Caesar Augustus, and Herod is swift and clear, the Towneley cycle reveals Pilate's fall from power subtly and deliberately. It is orchestrated over a series of plays extending from the *Conspiracy* to the *Resurrection*, a group of plays in which the *Talents* serves a crucial function. In presenting Pilate at the height of his duplicity, the *Play of the Talents* also suggests the degree of his vulnerability, and its exposure of his weakness is most clearly expressed through the dice game he plays to win Christ's seamless coat.

Throughout the plays of Christ's Passion, Pilate presents himself as supreme lord of the secular kingdom. In his first appearance in the *Conspiracy* play he flatters himself that there "was neuer kyng with crowne / More worthy" (20.13–14). Intimately connected to Pilate's notion of kingship, which depends upon a consent exacted by force, is his understanding of the law. In the Towneley Passion sequence Pilate, Annas, and Caiaphas repeatedly assert that they seek to destroy Christ because he threatens their "law." The law that they represent, however, is slippery at best. First of all it seems to be a tool that Pilate uses to his own practical advantage:

> ffor I am he that may / make or mar a man;
> My self if I it say / as men of cowrte now can;
> Supporte a man to day / to-morn agans hym than,
> On both parties thus I play / And fenys me to ordan
>   The right;
> Bot all fals indytars,
> Quest mangers and Iurers
> And all thise fals out rydars
>   Ar welcom to my sight.
>
>   (20.19–27)

In addition, Pilate's law has its foundation not in any stable and abiding truth, but rather in the force of public opinion, as Annas suggests: "for if oure lawes were thus-gatys lorne, / men wold say it were lake of lare" (20.84–5). The law Pilate defends is also a projection of his deluded notion of truth, which can be understood as that which serves his own self-interest. Thus, for Pilate, Christ is simply the spreader of "talys," a "fature fals" who gets in the way of the "law" and the exercise of his power.

Pilate seeks to kill Christ because He threatens his game of power, which depends upon his ability to maintain the illusion of absolute strength. His desire to crucify Jesus manifests both his faith in the power of illusion to achieve his end and the measure of his own insecurity. As the Passion sequence progresses and especially in the *Play of the Talents*, this insecurity grows as Pilate's efforts to win sovereignty by falsehood are directly and indirectly undermined. Not until the *Resurrection* play does Pilate realize that his fiction of power must bow to the power of the lord of truth just as the devils in Hell must recognize their own impotence as Jesus leads their prisoners out of the infernal domain.

The perverse intent with which Pilate exercises his claims to lordship and the fundamental insubstantiality of these claims are reflected in the discord that characterizes Pilate's relationship with his subordinates. An index to the kind of social bond that exists under illusory claims to power, the interaction of Pilate and his men stands in sharp contrast to the simplicity and concord that characterizes the behavior of Christ's followers. This discord is evident throughout the Towneley Passion sequence, which shows a world governed by cross purposes, suspicion, jealousy, and harassment.[21] In every instance Pilate relates to his minions through threats, insults, and false promises. Pilate wields language to gain obedience, just as he waves his burning brand, but eventually he is made to realize that his own weapons can be turned against him.

This emphasis on kingship, law, and master-servant relationships bears directly on the thematic preoccupation of the *Play of the Talents* and the historical design of the cycle play. Jerome Taylor observes that the Corpus Christi play commemorates "the history of God's wonders, that is, of his responses, specifically, to man's defections from the divine Monarchy and Law and to man's consequent social, familial, and personal disintegrity."[22] Through its mimesis of the divine kingship the Corpus Christi play reflects the theological principles that informed the medieval understanding of the governance of human society:

in all centuries of the Middle Age[,] Christendom, which in destiny is identical with Mankind, is set before us as a single, universal Community, founded and governed by God Himself. Mankind is one "mystical body"; it is one single and internally connected "people" or "folk"; it is an all embracing corporation (*universitas*), which constitutes the Universal Realm, spiritual and temporal, which may be called the Universal Church (*ecclesia universalis*), or with equal propriety, the Commonwealth of the Human Race (*respublica generis humani*). Therefore that it may attain its one purpose, it needs One Law (*lex*), and One Government (*unicus principatus*).[23]

The proper governance of the human community thus depends upon its accord with God's eternal law and Word, which is Christ. All relationships of power and authority are subsumed within the greater unity that His mystical body represents.

The Towneley cycle's portrayal of earthly tyranny in the figure of Pilate reflects the corruption that ensues when the community of men departs from the authority of divine law.[24] Pilate's rule substitutes fragmentation and forced servitude for the order and willing obedience that should characterize relationships among the members of Christ's mystical body, which is at once the unity of mankind under divine rule and the reflection of that unity as it is mirrored in the political state. In the Towneley cycle Pilate's perversion of the authority and law entrusted to the earthly ruler finds a most concrete expression in the action of the *Play of the Talents*. For the *Talents* shows the nature and consequences of temporal power that governs according to its own self-serving law (at the beginning of the play Pilate calls himself "fownder of all lay" [24.22]). Moreover, the play juxtaposes its image of misguided earthly authority with the symbol of that which provides the ultimate sanction for all authority. The *tunica inconsutilis* represents Christ's physical body, which Pilate has already attempted to rend apart by crucifying Him. It also symbolizes the unity of His mystical body – His church and His law – which Pilate continually challenges in his capacity as a temporal ruler. The *Play of the Talents* thus reflects the theological meanings present in the religious and historical design of the Corpus Christi play.

Pilate's rant at the beginning of the *Talents* play defines the absolute opposition between corrupt earthly power and the divine kingship founded upon love. Calling himself "dominus dominorum," Pilate utters his claims to majesty to an audience that has just seen the true king silently suffer death. The Towneley *Crucifixion* draws to a close as Joseph of Arimathaea and Nicodemus acquire Christ's body and prepare it for burial. Although the cycle does not include a play dealing with the entombment, the closing lines of the *Crucifixion* play suggest that the action might nevertheless have occurred on stage (23.655–66). The entombment could have taken place directly before or perhaps even during Pilate's opening tirade in the *Talents*, thereby sharpening the contrast between earthly and divine kingship and prefiguring the defeat of Pilate's self-conscious evil through Christ's death on the cross.[25]

The speech of Pilate that opens the *Talents* play indicates the way he employs language as a principal weapon. His image of himself and the image he projects to others are verbal constructs through which he perpetuates his fiction of absolute authority. For Pilate, language is power, and the proper response to authority is silence:

> And talke not a worde;
> ffor who so styrres or any dyn makys,
> deply in my daunger he rakys
> That as soferan me not takys
> And as his awne lorde.
>
> (24.60–4)

Pilate wants to silence all voices because any utterance that impinges on his protective web of words poses a threat to his illusory sovereignty. In the medieval cycle drama rulers commonly command silence, but the Towneley characterization of Pilate puts this convention to a dramatic purpose as well. Pilate emerges as one whose fear as well as strength is closely connected to the spoken word. This emphasis on language and silence suggests the implicit contrast between those individual human utterances that Pilate can control and God's utterance, Christ, the incarnate Word that cannot be silenced and whose seamless coat cannot be divided.

The irony inherent in Pilate's use of language to assert his power is apparent early in the *Talents* play, when the tyrant's behavior belies the force of his words. Pilate's strength requires pampering, and he luxuriates in physical comfort.

> he has myster of nyghtys rest that nappys not in noynyng!
> boy, lay me downe softly and hap me well from cold.
>
> (24.65–6)
>
> Bewshere, I byd the vp thou take me,
> And in my sete softly loke that thou se me sett.
>
> (24.196–7)

A tyrant being tucked under his covers loses some of his overweening self-possession. In addition Pilate's concern for his physical well-being calls to mind the horrifying physical abuse that Christ suffers throughout the Towneley Passion plays. Whereas Pilate must command persons to minister to his pleasures, Christ quietly subjects Himself to the violent punishments exacted by false temporal authority because He is the Word of God. Ironic too is Caiaphas's attempt to make Christ speak in the *Buffeting* play (21.127ff.); the Savior can be silent because His law is spoken for eternity.

The *Play of the Talents* demonstrates several of Pilate's efforts to silence the divine Word. When the three torturers return from Calvary, they engage Pilate's counselor to communicate the news of Christ's death to Pilate. As he does so, he adds his own comment upon Pilate's role in the event:

> The cause of my callyng is of that boy bold,
> ffor it is saide sothely now this same day,
> That he shuld dulfully be dede,
>   Certayn;
> Then may youre cares be full cold
> If he thus sakles be slayn.
>
> (24.203–8)

The counselor insinuates that the matter of the Crucifixion may not be at an end for Pilate. His speech, with its hint that greater threats are in store for his superior, suggests that conclusion of the evil Pilate legends in which the Roman governor is finally condemned for his false judgment of Christ – legends with which the audience would have been familiar. Pilate, in any case, is sensitive to the counselor's insinuation, and his response evinces both his fear and his urge to preserve his facade of control:

> ffare and softly, sir, and say not to far;
> Sett the with sorow, then semys thou the les,
> And of the law that thou leggys be wytty and war,
>   lest I greue the greatly with dyntys expres;
> ffals fatur, in fayth I shall slay the!
>   Thy reson vnrad I red the redres,
> Or els of thise maters loke thou nomore mell the.
>
>   (24.209–15)

The counselor perceives at this point that Pilate's threats are only words, and he continues to provoke his lord:

> Why shuld I not mell of those maters that
>   I haue you taght?
> Thoug ye be prynce peerles withoutt any pere,
>   were not my wyse wysdom youre wyttys were in waght;
> And that is seen expresse and playnly right here,
>   And done in dede.
>
>   (24.216–20)

Pilate, now made to squirm for the first time in the Passion sequence, queries: "Why, boy, bot has thou sayde?" (221), recognizing that challenges to his power are indeed possible; his verbal authority is susceptible to verbal threat. Appropriately, Pilate recovers from the challenge not through another threat, but by cursing and changing the subject: "ye knaw not the comon cowrs that longys to a kyng" (225).

This encounter between Pilate and his counselor in a sense prepares for the battle of words and wits that is about to take place between the governor of the Jews and the torturers. Pilate has shown himself vulnerable to efforts to undermine his power, and he is on guard. It is no surprise, then, that his first exchange with the torturers displays his desire that they remain silent about the Crucifixion. When the torturers proudly announce that they have fulfilled his command, Pilate tells them to keep quiet about it:

> lefe syrs, let be youre laytt and loke that ye layn;
> ffor nothyng that may be nevyn ye it noght.
>   (24.238–9)

Pilate's desire to silence the news of the Crucifixion can be interpreted in several ways. First of all, it indicates that he wishes to hide all trace of his involvement in the affair, cognizant perhaps of the possibility of personal danger. Moreover, it is a measure of his own ludicrous blindness to the truth of the Word that he has helped to crucify that he thinks he can silence it. His impotence becomes patently clear in the *Resurrection* play, when he reprimands the Centurion for mentioning the death of Christ: "sese of sich saw" (26.92).[26] The Centurion exposes the flimsiness of Pilate's falsehood when he says:

> To maytene trowth is well worthy;
> I saide when I sagh hym dy,

That it was godys son almyghty,
    That hang thore;
So say I yit and abydys therby,
    ffor euermore.

                (26.98–103)

Truth will out, whether Pilate acknowledges it or not. And though Pilate may try stoutly to defy the Centurion's words of Christ by commanding that "he shall not ryse" (26.187), the truth of Christ's victory is final. Pilate's last appearance in the Towneley cycle will show him still engaged in efforts to silence this truth, but now without any pretense for claims to his own power. He responds to the news of the Resurrection with a brief and incredulous question: "whi, bot rose he bi hym self alone?" (26.518), and then must acknowledge: "Alas, then ar oure lawes forlorne / ffor euer more!" (524–5). Pilate, however, must still maintain the fiction in which he once rested secure, and he promises a reward to the soldiers who guarded the tomb if they will keep silent about the Resurrection (26.544–56).

Recognizing the *Talents* play's subtle elaboration of ideas of falsehood and truth, silence and the Word, sensitizes us to the entry speech of the first torturer. Bearing the seamless garment, he announces: "hedir haue I broght his clethyng now, / To try the trowthe before you" (24.98–9). Occurring in the middle of Pilate's own game of power, the game of dice that the torturers play with their master does indeed become a test of truth. For the object of their game is a symbol of truth itself, Christ's seamless robe, His body, the Word of God. The fundamental irony of the dicing in the *Play of the Talents* is that it makes eternal truth the object of a game of chance, the most unstable of human endeavors. The relation of the *Talents'* dice game to homiletic condemnations of gambling was noted previously; it is worthwhile to point out, however, that dicing came under attack from the pulpit because games of chance are within the province of Fortune. Those who participate in such games display an overly zealous faith in the power of Fortune to bring happiness and temporal reward. But the gifts that Fortune bestows are at best as transitory and illusory as Pilate's power, and the defeat he experiences when he tries a hand at her game serves as a comment on the insubstantiality of earthly authority that relies on the manipulation of appearances.

By revealing themselves as quarrelsome gamesters who compete with Pilate for Christ's robe, the torturers acknowledge their devotion to Fortune and her arbitrary methods for distributing rewards. But they also forswear their game at the end of the *Talents* and imply that their efforts at "winning" have been sadly misplaced. The remarks of the second torturer are especially telling:

Bot fare well, thryfte!
Is ther none other skyfte

Bot syfte, lady, syfte?
Thise dysars thay dote.
(24.391–4)

"Is there something besides Fortune's trickery?" he asks. The answer to his question is implicit in the object that he sought to win; the alternative to Fortune, illusion, and the discord they cause is the power present in Christ's seamless garment. The third torturer's speech reinforces this reading:

I red leyf sich vayn thyng / and serue god herafter,
 ffor heuens blys;
That lord is most myghty,
And gentyllyst of Iury,
 we helde to hym holy;
  how thynk ye by this?

(24.398–403)

Commentators have had difficulties with the conclusion to the *Talents'* dice game. John Gardner, for example, remarks that Pilate's threats undermine the forswearing of gambling and that the third torturer "comes for wrong reasons to a right conclusion. . . ."[27] But if we recall that the casting of lots was glossed as the action of God's grace, the torturers' resolution to embrace the lord who is "most myghty" and "gentyllyst of Iury" suggests that they do move to a new insight, an insight which rejects Pilate's brand of lordship and makes his forced possession of the *tunica inconsutilis* irrelevant. Owning the symbol of *corpus Christi* does not necessarily make one a member of that body, as the conclusion to the evil Pilate legends clearly demonstrates. Rather, participation in Christ's body requires simply that one acknowledge the bond of love that the seamless robe represents.

Perhaps it is difficult to accept such a hasty dramatic turnabout on the part of the torturers, considering the energy with which they are able to indulge in the game of Fortune they play with Pilate. But the strength of their claims to amendment is bolstered by comparing their conclusion to the game with Pilate's. For Pilate tries his hand at Fortune's game and sees that he can lose. The thirteen he throws with the dice is not the fifteen that wins the garment for the third torturer. Once again reminded of his capacity to be the victim instead of the one who victimizes, he tries to overcome Fortune's decision by a display of force; he is able to gain the much sought after robe only by threatening the life of its new owner. He seems to have scored another victory, temporary though it may be, but the second torturer offers an admonition that can be understood as a gloss on that victory:

As fortune assyse / men wyll she make;
 hir maners ar nyse / she can downe and vptake;
  And rych

> She turnes vp-so-downe,
> And vnder aboue,
> Most chefe of renowne
> She castys in the dyche.
>
> (24.379–85)

The torturer's speech is in fact prophetic. The fate that he forecasts for Fortune's victims is corroborated by the evil Pilate legends that tell how the body of Christ's judge found its resting place in a pit in the hills.[28] Though Pilate, "most chefe of renowne," may think that he can manipulate worldly circumstances, at the Resurrection he experiences the ultimate defeat of his false authority as he witnesses the triumph of the true law of Christ.

The Towneley *Play of the Talents* is not the anomaly that some of its readers have judged it to be. In its thematic intricacy it is a remarkable piece of tightly constructed drama, and in its skillful treatment of language and character it holds a close relationship with the plays that surround it in the Towneley grouping. More importantly, the *Talents*, in a sense, crystallizes the theological design of the Corpus Christi play, which dramatizes the power of divine kingship and the history of salvation through the sacrifice of Christ's body. As a play about misguided attempts to rend that body and hollow challenges to the supremacy of that kingship, the Towneley *Play of the Talents* affirms the meaning of *corpus Christi*.[29]

NOTES

1. Mendall Frampton has argued that the Towneley *Play of the Talents* is a lost play from the York cycle; "The Processus Talentorum," *PMLA*, vol. 59, 1944, pp. 646–54. This theory is refuted by Martin Stevens in "The Composition of the Towneley *Talents* Play: A Linguistic Examination," *Journal of English and Germanic Philology*, vol. 58, 1959, pp. 423–33. The name *Processus Talentorum* means the "play about coins or money." Noting the inappropriateness of this rubric, Rosemary Woolf suggests that for *talentorum* one should read *talorum*, or dice; *English Mystery Plays* (Berkeley and Los Angeles, 1972), p. 403, n. 63.
2. Matt. 27:35; Mark 15:24; Luke 23:34; John 19:23–4.
3. Pilate is associated with Christ's seamless coat in only one other surviving medieval play, the fifteenth-century German Passion Play *Donaueschingen*, in which one of Christ's executioners gives Pilate the seamless coat as a gift; Woolf, *op. cit.*, pp. 266–7. The portrait of Pilate in the Towneley cycle has been fully treated by Arnold Williams, *The Characterization of Pilate in the Towneley Plays* (East Lansing, 1950).
4. See Martial Rose, *The Wakefield Mystery Plays* (Garden City, 1962), p. 543; Williams, *ibid.*, pp. 26–7, and his *The Drama of Medieval England* (East Lansing, 1961), p. 128; Stevens, "The Composition of the Towneley *Talents* Play," p. 423. John Gardner, however, remarks that the play needs "no detailed discussion"; *The Construction of the Wakefield Cycle* (Carbondale, 1974), p. 116. Upon completing this essay, Robert Brawer's article,

"Dramatic Craftsmanship in the Towneley *Play of the Talents*," *Educational Theatre Journal*, vol. 28, 1976, pp. 79–84, came to my attention. While Mr. Brawer and I arrive at some of the same conclusions, our approaches are distinctly different. Brawer argues that theological tradition has "little direct bearing on the play," and that we do little justice to the *Talents* "by searching outside the play for its meaning," p. 80. My essay suggests that, on the contrary, the *Play of the Talents* is subtly informed by a theological tradition that helped shape its dramatic and symbolic action. See also Jeanne S. Martin, "History and Paradigm in the Towneley Cycle," *Medievalia et Humanistica*, No. 8, 1977, pp. 125–45.

5. Woolf, *English Mystery Plays*, p. 268.

6. The Chester cycle explicitly observes the twofold division of Christ's clothing; *The Chester Mystery Cycle*, R. M. Lumiansky and David Mills, eds., EETS, s.s. 3 (London, 1974), Play 16a, lines 72–148. In the York cycle the soldiers draw lots for the coat in a brief episode at the end of the *Crucifixion* play; *York Plays*, Lucy Toulmin-Smith, ed. (New York, 1885, rpt. 1963), Play 35, lines 289–300. The N-Town cycle refers to the action only in a stage direction; *Ludus Coventriae, or The Plaie Called Corpus Christi*, K. S. Block, ed., EETS, e.s. 120 (London, 1922, rpt. 1960), p. 268.

7. *The Towneley Plays*, George England and Alfred W. Pollard, eds., EETS, e.s. 71 (London, 1897, rpt. 1925). All quotations, cited by play and line numbers, refer to this edition.

8. See, for example, Rabanus Maurus, *Allegoriae in sacram Scripturam* (PL 112:1069); Hildebert, *Sermones de diversis*, 29 *Ad monachos* (PL 171: 874–5); St. Bernard, *Epistolae*, 334 *Ad Guidonem Pisanum* (PL 182:538–9); Peter Lombard, *Commentarium in Psalmos*, Psal. 21 (PL 191:235); *Glossa Ordinaria* (PL 113:875; 114:174, 238, 347, 421–2).

9. Thomas Aquinas quotes this passage from Theophylactus in his commentary on John 19:23–4 in the *Catena Aurea in Quatuor Evangelia* (Parma, 1861), vol. 2, p. 448. Cf. Eucherius, who glosses Christ's garments as His flesh; *Liber formularum spiritualis intelligentiae* (PL 50:733); Rabanus Maurus, *ibid.*

10. Peter Lombard, *Commentarium in Psalmos* (PL 191:235); St. Bernard, *Ad Guidonem Pisanum* (PL 182:538–9); Cassiodorus, *Expositio in Psalterium*, Psal. 36 (PL 70:270). Cf. Hildebert, "Hanc unitatem in corpore suo tunica sua designavit"; *Ad monachos* (PL 171:875).

11. Woolf, *English Mystery Plays*, pp. 267–8.

12. F. P. Pickering, *Literature and Art in the Middle Ages* (Coral Gables, Florida, 1970), pp. 314–18. See also *A Stanzaic Life of Christ*, Frances A. Foster, ed., EETS, o.s. 166 (London, 1926), lines 6697–700; 6729–30. For a discussion of the seamless tunic in a fuller context, see Gail McMurray Gibson, "Swaddling Cloth and Shroud: The Symbolic Garment of the Incarnation in Medieval Art and Literature," M.A. Duke University, 1972.

13. Woolf, *English Mystery Plays*, p. 267.

14. *Ludus Coventriae*, p. 103, line 178.

15. See Williams's summary of the evil Pilate legends in *The Characterization of Pilate*, pp. 7–9. Referring to the magical qualities of the seamless coat in the *Talents* play, John Gardner calls it an "exegetical joke: in the radiant apparel of God (in the New Jerusalem) one has everything." Gardner, however, does not explain how the use of the garment in the play might be a parody of its exegetical meaning; *The Construction of the Wakefield Cycle*, p. 117.

16. The seamless robe was itself the object of popular devotion in the late Mid-

dle Ages. It was reputed to exist in at least several cities, and it became the object of devotional pilgrimages; Louis Réau, *Iconographie de l'art chrétien* (Paris, 1955–9), vol. 2, pt. 2, p. 15. The robe also figured as one of the "Arma Christi," the instruments of the Passion so widely venerated in pictorial art and vernacular lyrics. See Douglas Gray, *Themes and Images in the Medieval English Religious Lyric* (London, 1972), pp. 132–3 and Plate 6; Rosemary Woolf, *The English Religious Lyric in the Middle Ages* (Oxford, 1968), pp. 207–8.

17. On the influence of the pulpit in the Towneley cycle and especially the *Talents* play, see G. R. Owst, *Literature and Pulpit in Medieval England*, 2nd. ed. (Oxford, 1961), pp. 487, 491, 511.

18. Williams notes that the Towneley cycle's omission of certain episodes common to the other cycles and its addition to others, e.g., *Play of the Talents*, form a purposeful design that establishes Pilate as a figure of absolute evil; *The Characterization of Pilate*, pp. 22–7.

19. Walter Meyers, *A Figure Given: Typology in the Wakefield Plays* (Pittsburgh, 1970), Ch. 3, "Diabolical Typology."

20. For an excellent discussion of the relationship of Mahomet to "diabolical typology" see Michael Paull, "The Figure of Mahomet in the Towneley Cycle," *Comparative Drama*, vol. 6, 1972–3, pp. 187–204. Paull notes the similarities between Pilate and Mahomet, a comparison that is particularly illuminating in view of Pilate's consistent efforts to subvert Christ's truth by maintaining his own illusory power.

21. Robert A. Brawer, "The Dramatic Function of the Ministry Group in the Towneley Cycle," *Comparative Drama*, vol. 4, 1970–1, pp. 173–4.

22. Jerome Taylor, "The Dramatic Structure of the Middle English Corpus Christi, or Cycle, Plays," *Literature and Society*, Bernice Slote, ed. (Lincoln, 1964), reprinted in *Medieval English Drama*, Jerome Taylor and Alan Nelson, eds. (Chicago, 1972), pp. 151, 156.

23. Otto Gierke, *Political Theories of the Middle Age*, F. W. Maitland, trans. (Boston, 1958), quoted by Taylor, *ibid.*, pp. 152–3. For an exhaustive discussion of the *corpus mysticum* as the prototype for the foundation and organization of the medieval political state, see Ernst H. Kantorowicz, *The King's Two Bodies: A Study in Medieval Political Theology* (Princeton, 1957), especially the section entitled *"Corpus Ecclesiae mysticum,"* pp. 194–206.

24. Several scholars have seen in the Towneley portrait of Pilate a strong social comment on corrupt judicial officials; see Owst, *Literature and Pulpit*, pp. 343–4, 495–6; Williams, *The Characterization of Pilate*, Ch. 3, "The Towneley Pilate as Social Satire." Bennett A. Brockman, however, has examined the implications of judicial satire in the Towneley *Mactatio Abel*, concluding that the play transmutes "social satire into theological statement" by showing "a secular society which has forgotten or chosen to ignore its spiritual foundation." Brockman's observation is applicable to the Towneley cycle's treatment of Pilate as well; "The Law of Man and the Peace of God: Judicial Process as Satiric Theme in the Wakefield *Mactatio Abel*," *Speculum*, vol. 49, 1974, pp. 699–707.

25. The importance of staging should be emphasized here. In a production of the *Play of the Talents* by the Poculi Ludique Societas of the University of Toronto in February, 1974, the Entombment of Christ was enacted in a tableau as Pilate prepared for his officious harangue at the opposite end of the stage. The effect was extraordinary.

26. Pilate's attempts to silence the divine Word are related to yet another ma-

nipulation of language and truth. When Pilate, Annas, and Caiaphas hear the centurion describe the response of the earth and the heavens to Christ's death, they humorously offer their own explanations, renaming divinely controlled phenomena. Thus the darkness of the sun, moon, and stars becomes what "clerkys the clyppys it call" (26.124), and the stirring of dead men from the earth is merely a demonstration of "socery" (129). For an illuminating discussion of language in the Towneley cycle see Martin Stevens, "Language as Theme in the Wakefield Plays," *Speculum*, vol. 52, 1977, pp. 100–17.

27. Gardner, *The Construction of the Wakefield Cycle*, p. 118.
28. Williams, *The Characterization of Pilate*, p. 9.
29. The author wishes to thank the Graduate School of the University of Maryland for a General Research Board Award that helped support research for this paper and the editorial board of *Medievalia et Humanistica* for helpful advice.

Christine de Pizan's Epistre Othea:

An Experiment in Literary Form

MARY ANN IGNATIUS

Scholars concerned with Christine de Pizan are agreed that the *Epistre Othea*, probably composed in 1399 or 1400,[1] represents the poet's first attempt at a work of serious content and scope, but are seemingly baffled when it comes to evaluating the literary merit of the work. Most scholars have concurred with Rigaud's opinion that the *Othea* shows up the poet's worst faults ("ses plus insupportables défauts") as a writer;[2] the work is *singulier, curieux,* and even *bizarre* according to M.-J. Pinet;[3] its content repetitious, entirely unoriginal and frequently deformed by Christine as she pillaged half understood sources, in the opinion of P. G. C. Campbell.[4] For Campbell, the worst fault (among very many) lies in the rigidity of its form.[5] Pinet is at least willing to credit Christine with her structural novelty, although she finds the poet guilty of an "ignorance totale de la beauté formelle."[6] Even a very recently published work joins this unfortunate tradition in stating that, despite its immense popularity during the fifteenth and sixteenth centuries, the *Othea* is "one of the least palatable of Christine's works" to the modern reader.[7]

How do these critics explain the extraordinary success of the *Othea,* which was Christine's "best seller" (the work is preserved in at least forty-three manuscripts,[8] was translated into English three times within a hundred years,[9] and was one of the very few French literary works deemed worthy of printing in the fifteenth century, an honor whose significance is often overlooked or underestimated by manuscript-oriented medievalists)? Some writers simply blame this incomprehensible literary fortune on the uncritical taste of the times: "Singulier ouvrage que cette *Epître d'Othéa,*" writes Robineau, "et bien conforme au goût encore barbare de cette époque."[10] Pinet expresses a similar opinion.[11] Campbell lists several factors which might have contributed to the success of the book: the many illustrations gave it wide appeal; its didacticism was suited to the taste of the times; the fact that the book was written by a woman gave it a certain freak value; finally, and most of all, Christine provides detailed accounts of stories that were only alluded to elsewhere, so that the book served as a kind of handbook of classical mythology for the general public.

It is certainly true that many readers of the later Middle Ages were interested in didactic works; it is also true that the illustrations, which in one manuscript represent "the first and best cycle of illustrations of ancient history and mythology,"[12] markedly enhance the value of the book. We must hasten to point out, however, that not all the manuscripts were as completely and beautifully illustrated as those presented to such clients as Jean de Berry or the Queen of France. It is more difficult for us to assess the degree of sensationalism that may have been aroused by the sex of the author. Christine herself suggests that certain princes received her early works ". . . plus comme ie tiens pour la chose non usagee que femme escripse comme pieca ne avenist / que pour dignete qui y soit."[13] She later complained that some members of her public refused to believe that she really wrote the books that appeared under her name. Scrope's dedication of his translation of the *Othea* to Sir John Fastolf contains a passage that may give an indication of public attitude: "This seyde boke, at the instaince and praers of a fukle wyse gentylwomen of Frawnce called Dame Cristine, was compiled and grounded by the famous doctours of the most excellent in clerge the nobyl Universyte off Paris . . ."[14]

That the *Othea* should owe its success to its usefulness as a handbook of classical mythology is an overly simplified statement, but probably comes closest to the truth, although the treatment of mythology in the *Othea* is too unsystematic for it to have been intended as an actual handbook, and there were available in the fifteenth century far more complete treatments of ancient myth. Christine was not relating entire stories, as R. Tuve pointed out, but rather selecting "story-moments" as illustrations of something else.[15] We know, however, that medieval culture was never without an awareness of and interest in its classical origins, and in a period when humanism was spreading from clerical into secular milieux, a work such as the *Othea*, particularly in its most fully illustrated versions, must have fed an intense hunger for culture in circles to which the more massive or more scholarly works such as the *Ovide Moralisé* or the *Genealogia Deorum* were not accessible. J. Seznec shows how a synthesis of classical and medieval cultures was pervasive in other art forms of the early fifteenth century, particularly in monumental art;[16] in the context of his observations, the *Othea* would appear to be highly representative or even in the vanguard of its cultural milieu

Generally, we must conclude that neither Campbell nor the other Christine scholars we have mentioned understood the significance of the *Othea* or successfully explained its wide popularity. These scholars' attempts to define the *Othea*, to assign it to some literary genre, have been similarly diverse and unsuccessful; all seem to reflect poorly on Christine. Tuve points out that "as always, much criticism at [Christine's] expense derives from expecting her to do what she is not doing."[17] It is essential to clarify our understanding of the author's own conception of the *Othea* before we can attempt to criticize her. A briew review of the various opinions held prior to Tuve will illustrate the problem.

The first printed edition of the *Othea*, that of Pigouchet in 1490, may have initiated the controversy by publishing the work under a title never used by Christine, *Les Cent histoires de Troye*. In his edition of a Middle English translation of the *Othea*, J. D. Gordon concluded that the work should *not* be considered a collection of Troy stories since two-thirds of the episodes recounted by the Goddess of Wisdom to Hector are unrelated to the legend of Troy.[18] Misled perhaps by the subtitle given to the Babyngton translation, Gordon went on to state that the book is "primarily a book of knighthood as is seen in the large bulk of material it has in common with such works"; the work contains "a body of teaching by which the young gentleman may become a perfect knight."[19] Campbell had already rejected this notion, since the *Othea* is entirely silent on the practical aspects of knighthood, with which Christine was not unfamiliar. We can be sure that the author of the *Faits d'armes et de chevalerie* or of the *Ditté de Jeanne d'Arc* had both a political and technical appreciation of the military functions of knighthood. Pinet refers to the *Othea* as an "ouvrage de pédagogie allégorique, préoccupé de la formation morale du jeune chevalier,"[20] in agreement with Campbell, who writes that, whereas the public considered the book primarily as a mythology manual, Christine's own goal was to "esquisser les qualités qu'elle juge nécessaires dans un prince ou un gentilhomme de son époque."[21] Campbell is disturbed, however, by some of the content, which he find unsuited to the moral edification of a young man.

Rosemond Tuve, in approaching Christine as a master of allegorical form, provides the first really penetrating treatment of the *Othea*. Because Christine "tells us outright how she expects to be read," she provides us with an "invincible authority" on "what distinguished allegory from other ways of reading, to mediaeval and Renaissance readers."[22] Thus Tuve considers that in the *Othea*, Christine exemplifies the definition of the form she employs. With Tuve we are quite far from Campbell's unelaborated remark that Christine's use of allegory does not correspond to the "real" meaning of the term.[23] In the Foreword to *Allegorical Imagery*, Tuve describes her approach: "I tried in each case to give the works their head, to follow where I was led rather than impose judgment or ask questions, to read works of art as though that were the one status that counted." It is not surprising that such a sympathetic respect for the text should have led to a much better understanding of the *Othea* than is found in earlier studies. Indeed, Tuve shows how much unjustified criticism of Christine is prompted by an incomplete understanding both of allegorical relationships and of Christine's literary intentions. In direct opposition to Campbell, she emphasizes the structural design of the *Othea,* and shows how "the formlessness of mere casual didacticism is removed from Christine's list of demerits."[24]

The one thing that students of the *Othea* prior to Tuve have in common, and the cause of their inability even to give the work a sympathetic reading, not to speak of a fair literary assessment, is their preoccupation with content over form. The carefully designed structure of the *Othea* simply eluded them as they focused on the content of the stories (or "story-moments" as Tuve preferred to call them) and on a linear development from story through gloss to allegory. The stories were, of course, found to be incomplete, repetitious, incoherent. Critics reproached Christine with a lack of historical perspective, the inability to distinguish between fact and fable, as though that were her goal. The absurdity of the farfetched connection between the stories and the allegories drawn from them was mocked while no attempt was made to understand the nature of allegorical relationships as they appeared to Christine and her contemporaries. Tuve can well wonder why ". . . nothing has ever been made of the fact that the structural design related Christine's book to one of the commonest kinds of earlier medieval works," the *Summa.*[25] The fact is that earlier critics were unable to perceive the overall structural design. That there were patterns or sets running through the allegories was noticed but what the earlier critics, even Gordon, failed to see was that the structure of the entire work was determined by the sets of allegories and not by the content of the stories. Thus, the *Othea,* when it was read at all, was consistently misread. We think, though, that there is more to blame than lack of familiarity with allegory as a mode of investigation and presentation. It has to do even more with our ingrained reading habits, backed by centuries of tradition, and with our very concept of the book, quite different from that of Christine's contemporaries.

Histories of the book focus on the beginnings of printed books with, usually, an introductory chapter on the production of manuscript books prior to printing. In *The Gutenberg Galaxy,*[26] Marshall McLuhan gives considerable attention to the passage from "manuscript culture" to "print culture" but does not develop the question of how books were considered by their owners in these early days of the non-scholarly private library, the kind of library for which the *Othea* was created. William Ivins, in *Prints and Communication,* is discussing precisely the period just prior to the invention of printing, but he takes for granted a content-oriented concept of the book: "A book, so far as it contains a text, is a container of exactly repeatable word symbols arranged in exactly repeatable order."[27] Obviously, this notion of the book as *container* does apply to many late medieval books, especially to university texts. But we are dealing with "art editions" produced for private libraries, with the kind of books collected by such extraordinary bibliophiles as Jean de Berry. It has often been suggested that, while the Duke clearly loved to look at his beautiful books, it is not so certain to what extent he actually read them. For him as for most of Christine's patrons, the physical form of a book was at least as important as its content and textual structure, and if the book is a container, it is in much the same sense as were the magnificent jeweled reliquaries produced throughout the Middle Ages. For Christine's clients, the book was an art object, like a tapestry, like a statue, like a painting. We would not think of using narrative content as the primary focus in a critical treatment of, say, the Apocalypse tapestries of Angers or the sculptural program of a church, although such works do have narrative meaning. The fact that a book contains the additional dimension of a verbal text is obviously important but does not justify an exclusive emphasis on textual content.

"The student of literature and philosophy is prone to be concerned with book 'content' and to ignore its form," writes Marshall McLuhan. "This failure is peculiar to phonetic literacy in which the visual code always has the 'content' that is the speech recreated by the person engaged in reading. No Chinese scribe or reader could make the mistake of ignoring the form of writing itself, because his written character does not separate speech and visual code in our way. But in a world of phonetic literacy this compulsion to split form and content is universal, and affects non-literary people as much as the scholar."[28] Perhaps McLuhan's supposition about Chinese readers could be applied to French readers of the fifteenth century. The paleographer E. A. Lowe observed that: "The Gothic script is difficult to read. It has the serious faults of ambiguity, artificiality, and overloading. It is the child of an age that was not bent on achieving the practical, the age of St. Louis and St. Francis. It is as if the written page was made to be looked at and not read. Instead of legibility its objective seems to be a certain effect of art and beauty, which it accomplishes by loving care bestowed upon each stroke and by the unerring consistency of its style."[29]

Campbell did mention the importance of the illustrations in the success of the book, and both Gordon and Pinet went on to say that the full significance of the *Othea* could only be appreciated in its most beautifully illuminated manuscripts such as Harley 4431 of the British Museum, or ms. fr. 606 of the Bibliothèque Nationale. But neither scholar attempted to relate these important considerations of external form to the internal form, or structure of the text.

There is no doubt that Christine herself supervised the production of the illuminations for ms. fr. 606, and that some of the credit for their success is hers. Meiss seems to feel that the book was designed by her in part as a vehicle for the cycle of illuminations, and says that "the combination of the attentive, learned authoress and the imaginative painter produced an exceptional result. No comparable text was written elsewhere in Europe . . ."[30] It would be an exaggeration to see the text as no more than a pretext for the illustrations, but Meiss lends emphatic support to the idea that the miniatures are an integral part of the book and not simply decorations of it.

That Christine composed poetry for the eye rather than the ear is well known. There is no evidence of her having collaborated with musicians, and criticism of her "lack of musical talent"[31] are simply irrelevant. Her collaboration with miniaturists, however, was more extensive than that of any poet before her.[32] It is as though she has transferred the embellishment of the musical accompaniment to the visual realm. Furthermore, her experiments in versification could only be appreciated by a reader holding the text before his eyes. We can be certain that the visual impact of the *Othea* was an integral part of Christine's esthetic intent. The non-textual formal properties of the manuscripts are related to the structure of the work, as we shall see, and can also help show the way in which Christine expected the work to be read.

Until quite recently, the Western reader has been accustomed to read essentially chronologically arranged narratives which are developed in linear fashion. We expect a certain logical progression to unfold from one narrative unit to the next. The *Othea* is, of course, not a continuous narrative but consists of 100 sections, each subdivided into *texte, glose,* and *allegorie.* This tripartite structure is grounded in medieval traditions of religious exegesis, as Tuve has shown,[33] yet is at the same time highly original. "[Christine] was acquainted with the common habit of providing a texte with a glose, texte . . . glose, texte . . . glose, in her own adaptation of the pseudo-Seneca-Four Virtues-Treatise; it was the ordinary procedure there as in the glossed *City of God,* the glossed Boethius. Many explanations of Christine's method have been given; and even the best students of the *Othea* do not make the connection between it and the ancient distinctions of religious exegesis."[34] What Tuve does not point out is that a gloss is usually provided by a scholar for a text written by someone else.

In emphasizing the linear relationship between *texte* and *glose,* Tuve misses an important insight into the structure of the *Othea.* There were two common ways of presenting a glossed text. The text might be interrupted where necessary and the expository glosses inserted as appropriate. Although the text would be distinguished from the gloss by ink color and/or lettering style, the reader would be confronted with a piece of text followed by the relevant commentary; in this arrangement, the text and its glosses might be perceived as an organic whole, developed in linear fashion. The older tradition, however, maintains the integrity of the text by presenting it without interruption, the glosses being written in the wide margin left for that purpose; only very short glosses (etymologies, synonyms, and the like) could be inserted between the lines of the continuous text. Needless to say, these two formats encourage us to perceive the relationship between text and gloss in different ways. Certainly the latter format emphasizes a certain separateness of text and gloss when the two are juxtaposed as for contemplation, rather than positioned in linear fashion as though one were a logical outgrowth, a natural appendage of the other.

Nearly all the manuscripts of the *Othea* present text-gloss-allegory in that order. This naturally encourages the reader to put most of the stress on the narrative portions further emphasized by the accompanying miniature and to see the allegories as more or less decorative appendages. A few of the manuscripts, however, and most notably ms. fr. 848 of the Bibliothèque Nationale, have a format similar to that of the marginally glossed medieval religious or legal texts. In ms. fr. 848, the *textes* occupy the center of the page, with the glosses on their left and the allegories, in the position of honor, on the right. Since the glosses are generally the longest of the three parts, and vary considerably in number of lines, they take up the most space on the page, occupying not only the entire left side, but frequently extending well beyond the center above and below the section reserved for the *textes*. The allegories, which are shorter and somewhat more uniform in length, are written in very small characters in a slender column. The texts, usually written three together, appear surrounded by their commentaries. Mombello describes the disposition of the text in this manuscript as capricious,[35] but this is true only if we assume a linear relationship among the three parts of the work. The format of ms. fr. 848 (which Mombello considers to be the oldest extant manuscript of the *Othea,* perhaps even the first, because of its excellent reading, the fact that it was not part of a larger codex, and because of apparent uncertainties in the writing, as though the scribe were experimenting with the format for the first time)[36] very clearly guides us away from such a linear reading. The *texte* (and not the *glose,* which contains the narrative sections and is considered by most of the critics to be the core of the book) is literally central, while the glosses and allegories are set off so that their independence is more apparent, and they invite reading for their own sake. Since the narrative portions, thus visibly decentralized, can no longer be considered as structurally central to the work, it appears incorrect to continue designating each set of *texte-glose-allegorie* as a *story.* (Mombello uses the French word *histoire,* as did Campbell, but he writes it in quotation marks to suggest he is aware of the ineptness of the term). Perhaps chapters or lessons would be more appropriate.

The disposition of the text of the *Othea* in ms. fr. 848, as well, interestingly, as in the Pigouchet edition, invites a non-linear, contemplative style of reading. Nothing directs us to read first a text, followed by a gloss, followed by an allegory, and so forth. We conclude that Christine intended her book more as an object of contemplation than a container of information. This is consistent with the emphasis on stunning visual effect in the magnificently illuminated presentation copies.

A comparison of the miniatures in ms. fr. 848 with those in ms. fr. 606

and Harl. 4431 offers an insight into other non-textual aspects of the *Othea*. In the latter two manuscripts, presumed to have been prepared under Christine's supervision, we find, in addition to the usual presentation scene, a miniature preceding each *texte* and illustrating some aspect of the ensuing chapter. Aware that her public does not necessarily have a clerical education, Christine provides us with some iconographic explanations to aid us in interpreting certain of the pictures. In these explanations, she attempts to relate the literal meaning of the image with its higher, allegorical meaning. Here is the text of the first such explanatory rubric in the ms. fr. 606 (fol. 1 v.):

Affin que ceulx qui ne sont mie clers pouetes puissent entendre en brief la significacion des hystoires de ce livre est assavoir que par tout ou les ymages sont en nues, c'est a entendre que ce sont les figures des dieux ou deesses de quoy la lettre ensivant ou livre parle selon la maniere de parler des anciens pouetes. Et pource que deitté est chose esperituele et eslevée de terre, sont les ymages figurés en nues; et ceste premiere est la deesse de sapience.

A similar passage explains why Attrempance is portrayed with a clock, and there is a series to explain the iconography and astrological properties of each of the seven planets. After the astrological series (chapters six through twelve), we find only five more explanatory rubrics (chapters fourteen through eighteen) and these are presumably abandoned as superfluous, since the glosses provide all the information necessary to understand the images. The explanatory rubrics are really necessary only where the miniature represents a purely allegorical figure that is not a character in a narrative, as in chapter one (Othea = Prudence or Sapience), chapter two (Attrempance), and the seven chapters dealing with the zodiac figures.

The *Othea* illuminations have been described and commented on by several art historians, most recently by Millard Meiss, who emphasizes their originality and importance in the history of Western iconography.[37] Except for the specific examples mentioned above, the miniatures all represent some portion of the literal narrative, never the allegorical significance. They are generally uncluttered, clearly focused and consistent with the succinct style favored by Christine in the *Othea*. To illustrate the Pyramus and Thisbe episode in a manuscript of the far more prolix *Ovide Moralisé* (ms. 5069 of the Bibliothèque de l'Arsenal) there are no fewer than eleven often repetitious miniatures; the single miniature representing the same subject in the *Othea* (ms. fr. 606) manages to show without any confusion the city that the lovers have fled and the fountain where they were to meet, the lion vomiting the entrails of its recent prey onto the veil of Thisbe, the bleeding body of Pyramus, the suicide of Thisbe, shown in the act of falling, onto her lover's sword, and the metamorphosed mulberry tree.

The far less spectacular ms. fr. 848 has not received the attention of art historians, for whom it offers little intrinsic interest. We have already shown how the layout of this manuscript suggests a different relationship among the parts of Christine's triple discourse than has generally been perceived. The illustrations also reflect what we take to be Christine's experimental intent better than those of the more famous manuscripts. The miniatures unfortunately number only six; graceful line drawings, they do not have the splendid impact of their colorful and justly more famous counterparts. What distinguishes them is that they attempt to illustrate *simultaneously* the textual and allegorical significance of the narrative contained in the glosses, thus stressing the unity implicit in Christine's trinitarian form. In the above-mentioned manuscript of the *Ovide Moralisé* both literal and allegorical meanings are illustrated, but never simultaneously. The reader is suddenly confronted with some familiar religious scene: a Crucifixion, a Resurrection, a Descent into Hell, or the like, that bears no visible relationship to the myth being interpreted. Christine's allegorized illustrations are more successful, because her imposed allegories are never so forced as those of the *Ovide Moralisé*, but they do not succeed on image alone. The first pair of illustrations following the presentation scene are placed directly beneath the incipit on fol. 2 r. First we see Othea presenting her epistle to Hector against a background of eight crowned, enthroned and sword-bearing lions, which Mombello identifies as the eight *preux* (Hector himself is the ninth).[38] Hector's name is inscribed above his head, while Othea is designated twice, by her proper name and by her allegorical significance, *Prudence*. In the adjoining panel, we see Othea's sister, Attrempance, adjusting her clock, her name also printed above her head. Being an allegorical character to begin with, she does not require two names. On fol. 2 v., we find two more miniatures side by side. The first is a judgment scene in which the judge is identified literally as Le Roy Minos and allegorically as *Justice*. Hercules, in the following miniature, bears the designation *Force* along with his literal name. Finally, on f. 3 r., we see Andromeda, so identified, about to be devoured by a toothy whale, as "Parceus" flies to her rescue astride the winged steed that bears its literal name, Pegasus, on its flank, while its allegorical identity, *Renommée*, is inscribed above the wings.

It is not clear why the remaining chapters were not similarly illustrated in ms. fr. 848. Christine's daring formal experimentation seems to have encountered practical obstacles. Only the first five chapters are illustrated. Because of the peculiar disposition of the text in this manuscript and the irregular length of these early chapters, the miniatures could not be placed adjacent to the relevant text. For the remaining chapters, whose *textes* are all quatrains, the scribe adopted the practice of writing three chapters to a page, however long the glosses. This layout required a very tiny hand, particularly for the allegories, which are relegated to a narrow column, and simply did not allow space for three miniatures on the same page.

Christine may have been too uncertain of the success of this experimental work to dare risk the expense of allowing an entire page per chapter with a costly illustration on each page. Or perhaps, by grouping the chapters three by three, she preferred to underscore her triple form. In preparing later manuscripts, Christine must have accepted with some regret that the linear format was not only more accessible to the uninitiated reader, but far more practical to produce. Certainly the linear arrangement of miniature-text-gloss-allegory is clearer to the eye, if a less satisfactory reflection of the structure of the work.

Before concluding we must give some consideration to the intended public of the *Othea*, and its relationship to Christine's esthetic aim. The identity of our poet's wealthy clients is well known; although she was much concerned with her reputation in a wider posterity, her immediate public was more limited.[39] Indeed, certain of her books, written on command, might be said to have been composed for an audience of one, such as the biography of Charles V or the *Corps de Policie*, for the young dauphin. Assuming that "Othea" represents Christine herself, every student of the *Othea* has wondered about the identity of "Hector de Troye quant il estoit en l'aage de quinze ans," to whom the Epistle is addressed. The assumption that Hector must correspond to some adolescent Prince, son of one of Christine's patrons, lay behind the earliest attempts to date the *Othea*. Campbell realized the fruitlessness of such efforts, which assigned dates either far too early or too late for the possible composition of the work. He did discover, though, that the most probable date was approximately coincident with the fifteenth birthday and journey to England of Christine's own son, whom he then identifies with the young Hector. Pinet dismisses all the arguments about the identity of "Hector" as irrelevant; in any case, Pinet cannot imagine Christine teaching her son by means of such licentious stories. If the author did have her son in mind at all, "ce n'est que très indirectement qu'il fut le sujet de l'*Epistre*, très secondairement qu'elle lui fut destinée."[40] Mombello is willing to accept as reasonable Campbell's unproved working hypothesis that Hector was Jean du Castel. Tuve too is interested in Hector's identity: ". . . the book was ostensibly written for a boy of fifteen, possibly Christine's son, possibly the young Prince; and were it not a mediaeval work, we would attend more to these facts of audience and narrator."[41] Tuve does not develop her point about the relationship between audience and narrator, nor is it clear in what direction she would have developed it had she chosen to. It would be helpful here to return to her initial commitment to "read works of art as if that were the one status that counted." Speculation about the "real life" identities of literary characters can often prove valuable, but in this case it seems to have been leading away from the work rather than toward it. Assuming that the *Othea* is a work of art, and without trying to classify it as a pedagogical treatise or whatever, must we necessarily assume that it was literally written for a youth of fifteen? No minimally sophisticated reader of a modern work with artistic pretensions assumes that statements made by the narrator, whether about the purpose of the book, the nature of the characters or the meaning of the narrative, are necessarily to be taken at face value. Why should this be any less true of a medieval work, and most particularly of one that is essentially metaphorical in both structure and content? We would prefer to assume that the fifteen-year-old youth and even the didactic nature of much of the content are simply pretexts to a loftier ambition.

In trying to penetrate Christine's esthetic intentions, there are two more factors we must keep in mind. The first concerns the concept of the book in the early fifteenth century. H. J. Chaytor, in *From Script to Print*, speaks of medieval literature as though everything before the invention of printing had been composed for oral performance: "Authors of 1150 wrote works intended primarily for recitation; those of 1500 wrote for a public that could read as well as listen."[42] The statement is correct, but says nothing about an author of 1400. We are dealing with that transitional period before the invention of printing when private reading, at least for a privileged elite, has already begun to replace public performance as the principal mode of literary consumption. The secular, non-scholarly book as a personal possession is something fairly new in France; attitudes toward its purpose and assumptions about its nature have not yet been fixed. Authors were obviously aware that the new eye-oriented medium invited the development of literary forms that could not be conveyed in an oral medium. Like any transitional period, this was naturally one of experimentation.

The second factor is that Christine wrote the *Othea* early in her career; it was apparently her first attempt to go beyond the courtly genres on which she had built her reputation but which she also considered frivolous. In her *Avision*, Christine refers to a concept of poetry that is akin to theology and philosophy. She writes that "les premiers en Grece renommez de science fussent appellez pouetes theologizans, car de ce qu'il disoient ilz formoient dittiez et parloient saintement theologisans aussi qu'ilz parloient des dieux et des choses divines."[43] The function of this kind of poetry is to describe truth "par maniere de ficcions et de paroles transsumptives."[44] It was through the study of such serious poets that Christine finally discovered "le stile a moy naturel, me delittant en leurs soubtilles couvertures et belles matieres mucees soubz fictions delictables et morales."[45] In the *Epistre Othea* Christine is experimenting not only with a concept of what a book should be, but with an attempt to develop a literary form that might adapt itself to this particularly lofty concept of poetry toward which her serious muse urged her to turn.

Just as the format of ms. fr. 848 indicates some experimentation on the part of the scribe,[46] the text of the *Othea* gives some indication of initial hesitation on the part of the author: it is only with the sixth chapter that she settles on the four-line *texte* that she will maintain for the remaining 94 chapters; the first five *textes* vary in length from eight to fifty-eight lines. As for other formal considerations, such as her use of the gloss, we must remember that the autodidact Christine did not have the systematic clerical education of the University; this fact may have been responsible for lacunae in her erudition but it also left her free of some assumptions or prejudices that might have prevented an ordinary scholar from making the literary innovations she made. A more learned cleric, for instance, might have thought it absurd to "gloss" a text of his own composition.[47] Christine was sufficiently removed from the assumptions of academic tradition to recognize the possibility of a purely formal use of the gloss in a non-scholarly context. One is reminded of Vladimir Nabokov's witty use of academic forms in his novel *Pale Fire*,[48] which poses as a critical edition of a set of poems, complete with scholarly apparatus: a Foreword including a critical discussion of the relevant manuscripts, followed by the text, with notes and index.

Christine, who had already read and admired Dante, was trying to produce a work of art, an object of contemplation, and not a didactic treatise. Her subject is the highest aim of allegory, the portrayal of "things in their essence, beautiful to contemplate."[49] Christine's understanding of allegory in this *visually* contemplative sense is explicitly stated at the end of *Lavision-Christine*, where the author gives a metaphorical description of her method, in which the three levels of discourse are likened to three stones, each with its individually precious properties:

la premiere est en forme de dyament lequel est dur et poingnant. Et tout soit il cler hors oeuvre, quant il est relié et mis en l'or, il semble estre obscur et brun, et toutefois ne rement sa vertu, qui est moult grande. La seconde est le kamayeu, en qui pluseurs visages et figures diverses sont empraintes; et est son siege brun et l'empreinte est blanche. La tierce au rubis precieux, cler et resplandissant et sans nue obscure, qui a proprieté *de tant plus plaire comme plus on le regarde.*[50]

Each of these stones, the diamond, the cameo, and the ruby, gives its own reflection of reality. Christine had inherited from her cultural tradition a concept of reality as a closed and formally perfect system, containing many levels of truth, all of which reflect the same ultimate Truth. Within this vast edifice of reality, seemingly irreconcilable forms of truth can be elucidated and reconciled. Like the Gothic cathedral, the ideal work of art should aim for the synthetic totality of the scholastic *summa*, whose formal perfection it emulates.[51] The humanist in Christine would make her work man-centered (hence its appearance as a compendium of advice) without sacrificing its universality. What Christine has attempted in the *Othea* is a global synthesis of reality as her culture perceived it, a single universal reality reflected in various modes of investigating or expressing truth: classical literary tradition, poetry, art, science, the social ethic of chivalry, the consoling discipline of philosophy, and the all-encompassing revealed truth of the Church. These modalities of truth are addressed to man on different levels of his being: through myth, poetry, and the art of the illuminator, Christine touches our esthetic sense; our intellect through science and philosophy; our moral and social being through exploration of historical roots and in the ethic of chivalry; and finally our spiritual being, our soul, through her use of allegory. Only a complex multiple structure could convey the author's synthetic vision of interrelated levels of truth, all subordinated to ultimate metaphysical reality. Christine has often been accused of prolixity; we cannot help but admire in the *Othea* how her use of multiple structure has allowed her to be so universally inclusive within such a miniature form.

Christine has created in the *Othea* a tiny mirror of the medieval world view, by means of which young "Hector" may be initiated into the totality of his extraordinary cultural heritage: from its ancient origins to its artistic, scientific, and social thought, from its personal and social ethic to its eschatology, its total vision of human destiny. In this context, Hector may be identified with Christine herself, a relative newcomer to the "chemin de long estude," having just devoted the recent years of her life to a courageous attempt to assimilate all the intellectual riches her civilization had to offer.

Had Christine written a generation or so earlier, when courtly literature was still what McLuhan would call "tribal" in nature, she would have had her poetic works set to music. For the generation of Machaut, "Les formes de l'écriture sont, par le nombre et le rythme, par la mélodie même qui doit les soutenir, expressives de la réalité métaphysique du monde . . . Pour [Machaut] l'écriture n'est qu'un des éléments d'un travail qui tend à construire l'édifice savant de la chanson polyphonique. Dans un tel ensemble la parole . . . peut n'être qu'un ornement superficiel de la réalité rythmique et mélodique, ou une sorte de vise, de légende, que précise le sens symbolique de la composition numérale."[52] These observations of Daniel Poirion could, *mutatis mutandis,* be applied to the text of the *Othea.* Christine has substituted a kind of textual and *visual* polyphony to support the complex structure of her expression of universal reality. In this sense, the miniatures can be considered not as illustrations of the text but as a fourth level of the text.

Indeed, Christine's structure is only superficially tripartite: if we include the miniatures and analyze the components of the glosses and allegories, we actually find a structure based on *seven* levels: image, poetic text, narrative or gloss, philosophical text, allegory, patristic text, and finally scriptural text. It is not necessary to insist on the relationship of this sevenfold structure with the sets of seven which appear throughout the *Othea* as throughout the medieval consciousness: days of the week, planets, metals, virtues, vices, deadly sins, gifts of the Holy Spirit, sacraments, and so forth.

It is by concentrating on the formal structure of the Othea that we can begin to appreciate the importance of Christine's esthetic intentions, and understand the appeal of the work to readers of the fifteenth and sixteenth centuries, without disparaging either the book or its readers. We can assess the worth of the *Othea*, and the originality of its author more generously, assigning to the book a more appropriate place in literary history, not only as a very important transmitter of medieval culture and its classical origins, but as a remarkable experiment in literary form. Its flaws, hesitations, and uncertainties are those of any pioneering effort: Christine's effort occurs at a point in her career where she is casting about for a new and more authentic mode of serious personal expression, and coincides with the emergence of the popular book, whose nature and impact are not yet fully realized. She developed for the *Othea* an original and sophisticated structure intended to reflect and communicate a personal and cultural experience of the structure of reality. The book is *poetic* rather than didactic: Christine does not claim to impose a definitive interpretation of the metaphors through which she investigates reality, but tries rather to suggest, to open the eyes of her readers to the myriad secret relationships that exist.

NOTES

1. For a recent summary of efforts to date the *Othea*, see G. Mombello, "Per un'edizione critica dell'*Epistre Othea* di Christine de Pizan," *Studi Francesi*, vol. 24, 1964, pp. 411–12. Since concise summaries of the *Epistre Othea* are available in several sources, we will not provide one here.
2. R. Rigaud, *Les Idées féministes de Christine de Pisan* (Neuchâtel, 1911), p. 21.
3. M.-J. Pinet, *Christine de Pisan* (Paris, 1927), p. 280.
4. P. G. C. Campbell, *L'Epître d'Othéa: Etude sur les sources de Christine de Pisan* (Paris, 1924), passim. Hereafter cited as *Sources*.
5. *Ibid.*, p. 50.
6. *Christine de Pisan*, p. 407.
7. E. McLeod, *The Order of the Rose, The Life and Ideas of Christine de Pizan* (Totowa, N.J., 1976), p. 51.
8. G. Mombello, *La Tradizione Manoscritta dell'Epistre Othea di Christine de Pizan* (Torino, 1967).
9. C. F. Bühler, *The Epistle of Othea Translated from the French Text of Christine de Pisan by Stephen Scrope* (London, 1970), p. xiii.
10. E. M. D. Robineau, *Christine de Pisan, sa vie, ses oeuvres* (Saint-Omer, 1882), p. 89.
11. *Christine de Pisan*, p. 277.
12. M. Meiss, *French Painting in the Time of Jean de Berry: The Limbourgs and their Contemporaries* (London, 1974), p. 62.
13. M. L. Towner, ed., *Lavision-Christine* (Washington, D.C., 1932), p. 165.
14. Cited by P. G. C. Campbell, "Christine de Pisan en Angleterre," *Revue de Littérature Comparée*, vol. 5, 1925, p. 669.

15. R. Tuve, *Allegorical Imagery: Some Mediaeval Books and their Posterity* (Princeton, 1966), p. 34.

16. J. Seznec, *The Survival of the Pagan Gods*, B. F. Sessions, tr. (Princeton, 1953), p. 125.

17. *Allegorical Imagery*, p. 293.

18. J. D. Gordon, *The Epistle of Othea to Hector, a "Lytil bibell of knighthood"* (Philadelphia, 1942).

19. *Ibid.*, p. xxv and p. xvi.

20. *Christine de Pisan*, p. 20.

21. *Sources*, p. 158.

22. *Allegorical Imagery*, p. 34.

23. *Sources*, p. 39.

24. *Allegorical Imagery*, p. 39.

25. *Ibid.*, p. 39.

26. (Toronto, 1962). See also C. F. Bühler, *The Fifteenth Century Book* (Philadelphia, 1960).

27. (Cambridge, Mass., 1953), p. 2.

28. *Gutenberg Galaxy*, p. 77.

29. "Handwriting," G. C. Crump and E. F. Jacobs, eds., *The Legacy of the Middle Ages* (Oxford, 1962), p. 223.

30. *French Painting*, p. 37.

31. J. C. Schilperoort, *Guillaume de Machaut et Christine de Pisan; Etude comparative* (The Hague, 1936).

32. C. C. Willard has even suggested that Christine may have been associated as a copyist with a Parisian atelier of book production, in "An Autograph Manuscript of Christine de Pisan?" *Studi Francesi*, vol. 9, 1965, pp. 452–57.

33. See also H. R. Jauss, "La Transformation de la forme allégorique," *L'Humanisme médiéval dans les littératures romanes du XIIe au XIVe siècle* (Paris, 1964), pp. 108–46.

34. *Allegorical Imagery*, p. 293. We should add another source that might have been familiar to Christine: the glossed law texts produced at the University of Bologna during her father's tenure there. There were many of these in Paris to which Christine could have had access.

35. *Tradizione Manoscritta*, p. 23.

36. *Ibid.*, pp. 28–9.

37. *French Painting*, pp. 23–41. Other studies of the *Othea* illuminations are to be found in: M. Meiss, "Atropos-Mors: Observations on a Rare Early Humanist Image," Rowe and Stockdale, eds., *Florilegium Historiale: Essays Presented to Wallace K. Ferguson* (Toronto, 1971), pp. 151–9; idem, "The Exhibition of French Manuscripts of the XII–XVI Centuries at the Bibliothèque Nationale," *The Art Bulletin*, 1956; J. Porcher, *L'Enluminure française* (Paris, 1959), p. 56; idem, *Manuscrits à peintures en France du XIIe au XVIe siècle* (Paris, 1955); L. Schaefer, "Die Illustrationen zu den Handschriften der Christine de Pisan," *Marburger Jahrbuch für Kunstwissenschaft*, vol. 10, 1939, pp. 119–208. See also C. C. Willard, "Christine de Pisan's Clock of Temperance," *L'Esprit Créateur*, vol. 2, 1962, pp. 149–54.

38. *Tradizione Manoscritta*, p. 24.

39. C. C. Willard has pointed out, in "The Manuscript Tradition of the *Livre des Trois Vertus* and Christine de Pizan's Audience," *Journal of the History of Ideas*, vol. 27, 1966, pp. 433–44, that the existence of a number of paper manuscripts of the *Othea* indicates that its appeal was not limited to wealthy aristocrats.

40. *Christine de Pisan*, p. 89.

41. *Allegorical Imagery*, p. 286.

42. (Cambridge, 1945), p. 80.
43. *Lavision*, pp. 119–20.
44. *Ibid.*, p. 120.
45. *Ibid.*, p. 163.
46. See Mombello, *Tradizione Manoscritta*, p. 24, n. 1.
47. Boccaccio did write glosses to accompany his *Teseide*, but they are explanatory in nature, somewhat like the modern footnote, and are not systematically incorporated into the structure of the text. These glosses were discussed by S. Noakes in a paper, "The Function of Boccaccio's Gloss for his *Teseide*," presented at the Twelfth Conference on Medieval Studies (Kalamazoo, 1977).
48. (New York, 1962).
49. *Allegorical Imagery*, p. 289.
50. *Lavision*, pp. 192–93. Emphasis added.
51. Cf. E. Panofsky, *Gothic Architecture and Scholasticism* (New York, 1957). J. Seznec treated representations of the universalism of medieval culture in various art forms in *The Survival of the Pagan Gods;* see particularly chapter IV.
52. D. Poirion, *Le Moyen Age, II: 1300–1480* (Paris, 1971), p. 60.

Gesture in Chaucer

BARRY WINDEATT

For wel sit it . . . A woful wight to han a drery feere,
And to a sorwful tale, a sory chere (*TC*, I, 12–14).[1]

Chaucer feels the point worth making, and throughout his work is interested both in the significance and appropriateness of gesture.[2] – Gesture is here taken in its most inclusive sense of "all physical motions or positions of the body which have a meaning but do not serve a practical purpose."[3] – The present study aims to isolate instances of Chaucer's introduction of gestures into his retelling of received narratives and to trace the patterns of interest and emphasis these reveal in Chaucer. To do this it concentrates largely on those of Chaucer's works for which there is a known literary source in order to provide some check on what are Chaucer's own innovations. Innovation in description of human gesture must have natural limits, and in all writers' use of the same gesture will be a common core of similar observation: moreover, a network of previous usages may have endowed some gestures with archetypal associations. But in Chaucer the significance of the gestures he adds when translating lies not only in their commonness but also in the effect they have of altering, of intensifying, the emphases conveyed by the characterization of the sources. The concentration of this study on certain areas of gesture has been determined because those gestures emerge strongly as those to which Chaucer consistently recurs when reshaping source material. They are those gestures by which Chaucer can suggest the inner life of his characters.

Chaucer's most persistent interest in gesture, revealed by divergences from his sources, centers on the eyes and faces of his characters and their acts of looking, which are expressive outwardly of the inner life – not necessarily of a cognitive self-analytical activity, but often of a force of feeling or a strength of will, a capacity to appreciate the full difficulty of their situation.

Chaucer's concern with facial expression emerges most directly when he chooses to mention the face in narratives where his sources do not explicitly refer to it. Chaucer himself "sees" the face when he sees the scene in his mind's eye, and he makes sure that his audience will also visualize the faces of his actors. When battle is over in *KnT* Chaucer, not Boccaccio, mentions that Arcite takes off his helmet in order to reveal his face (*CT* I, 2676; cf. *Teseida* 8.130),[4] and in his description of Arcite's funeral so soon afterwards only Chaucer troubles to visualize the detail that Arcite lay on the bier with his face bare and exposed (2877; cf. *Tes* 11.15). Chaucer's Hypermnestra weeps on her sleeping husband's face (*LGW* 2706), rather than generally on his body as in Ovid (*Heroides* XIV, 68). It occurs to Chaucer, not to Ovid, to describe a series of moonless nights as the moon hiding her face (*LGW* 2504; cf. *Her* II, 5), and it is Chaucer (in one of the few changes in that closely translated text) who visualizes the circumspection of a fugitive in *SecNT*, poking his head forth Piers Plowman-like into the world to look about (VIII, 312; cf. *SA* 674).[5] Before the Theban lady tells Theseus her story it is Chaucer who mentions her deadly cheer (913; cf. *Tes* 2.26). Thisbe's deadly cheer is also Chaucer's touch (*LGW* 869; cf. *Metamorphoses* IV, 137), as is Theseus's "sad" visage before beginning his last speech (2985; cf. *Tes* 12.5). At the denouement of her story Petrarch's Griselda bedews her children generally with her tears (*SA* 328/55ff.), while Chaucer's heroine bathes with her tears her children's faces and hair (IV, 1085). Such instances widely scattered in his work reveal Chaucer's interest in the expressive power of the face.[6] These details are no major departures from the sense of the original; rather, Chaucer is seeking to make more through gesture of the potential expressiveness of his sources.

Intrigued by the sensitivity of the face, Chaucer shows by his visualizings of situations suggested in the sources his concern with the importance of outward changes in faces, particularly with paleness and the indications this gives of inward developments of distress and reflectiveness. The clearest single instance of such interest is Chaucer's simple substitution of pallor for redness of face as a sign of distress at one important moment: whereas at the handing over of Criseyde, Boccaccio imagines Troilo to be "tutto tinto nel viso" (*Filostrato* 5.13),[7] Chaucer instead conceives his hero "with face pale" (*TC* V, 86). In *PrT* Chaucer describes the little clergeoun's mother in her desperate search for her child as "pale of drede and bisy thought" (VII, 589), and this makes explicit what emerges elsewhere from the contexts of Chaucer's added gestures of growing pale: that pallor indicates in his characters not simply recognition of distress but inward reflective response to the cause of that distress, the suggestion of a continual appraising which goes together with sensitivity to the course of events. Constance is described as turning pale at the various climacterics of her life (III, 265; 822), and these are Chaucer's own visualizations of the gestures of those scenes (cf. *SA* 166; 175). Paleness is grave and serious, and this is why Saturn in *KnT* is described as pale (2443), and why the father in *PhysT* is as pale as ash (209) as he prepares to tell his daughter her destiny. He is pale not simply with distress, but with remorseful, reflective distress, just as Hypermnestra turns pale according to Chaucer when receiving her father's terrible commands, and also trembles (2648–9), a gesture that Chaucer often goes out of his way to mention when his characters come upon fearful intelligence. On hearing of the covered rocks, Dorigen too turns bloodlessly pale (1340), and when she proceeds to soliloquize, an equivalent of mental activity, Chaucer notes that she is pale (1353). Griselda turns pale with wonder in Chaucer's account of Walter's arrival at her father's house (340; cf. *SA* 304/48, 305/57), and in rendering *KnT* from *Teseida* Chaucer adds three instances when Palamoun grows pale (1082, 1302, 1578; cf. *Tes* 3.17; 5.3, 33ff.) to convey his distress. Constance's paleness is compared to the pallor of a condemned man led through a crowd to a death from which he is conscious that there is no escape (645ff.; cf. *SA* 171). Such a concentration on the thoughts and feelings behind one pale face in a sea of faces is a characteristically Chaucerian awareness of the individual's feelings as they may be perceived by noticing the face.

It is in the extent to which he stresses and confirms the proper facial expression that Chaucer is conspicuous, however common in itself the expression. A network of many added observations together indicates a concern to emphasize by means of facial detail his characters' greater ability to respond, and this is most acutely seen in Griselda, in whom Chaucer emphasizes both the face and its unchangingness. When Walter arrives at Janicula's house Chaucer's Griselda is described as greeting him "with sad contenance" and "with reverence, in humble cheere" (293/8). With these added details Chaucer brings out through facial expression that humility of the heroine mentioned by the sources (*SA* 304/37-8; 305/42-3). This very unchangingness of Griselda's expression, in accord with her undertaking and despite her feelings, becomes thematic in the tale (". . . that she hadde suffred this with sad visage," 693), and the gap between outward expression and apparent truth becomes a matter of poignancy ("How kynde / Ye semed by youre speche and youre visage," 852-3). For to Chaucer it seems instinctive to look out for the face of a character, and he imagines society supporting this attachment to the face by such added familiar ideas that Griselda (413), Constance (532) and Troilus (I, 1078) each became beloved by all who looked upon their faces (cf. *SA* 308/83-4; 169). The sources for *ClT* tell of the beauty of the brother of Walter's supposed new bride (*SA* 326/19; 327/89), but it is in Chaucer that the people notice that he "so fair was of visage" (992), while with a similar attention to faces in *MLT* Chaucer expresses the bravery of David against Goliath by stressing the traditional ability to look the enemy in the face (937).

It is this stress upon understanding another person's nature through examining his face that explains Chaucer's fascination with eyes, for in mention of the eyes is expressed something of the inner life of Chaucer's characters. This is so natural and fundamental to observation of behavior as not to be noticed, if the check provided by Chaucer's sources did not expose his persistent taste for introducing such observation of the eyes. Although some of Chaucer's usages may retain something of more formulaic poetry's simple emphasis on the bodily agents (". . . with eyen tweyne," etc.), when Chaucer's Theseus at the end of an inward meditation "gan to looken up with eyen lighte" (1783), the added detail suggests the exhilaration of understanding. When *Teseida*'s vague mention of general weeping at Arcite's fate (11.38) is replaced by Chaucer's note that all the mourners rode out with red and wet eyes (2901) the specific emphasis on the disorder of the eyes contributes to the consciousness of extreme grief. But it is with the gestures accompanying Constance's second embarkation in *MLT* that one sees Chaucer transforming and intensifying a brief scene from Trivet with a concentration of added references to looking (cf. *SA* 175). To comfort her weeping baby Chaucer's Constance takes the coverchief from her head "and over his litel eyen she it leyde . . . And into hevene hire eyen up she caste" (838/40), while Constance's subsequent prayer to the Virgin repeatedly appeals to her as another mother who saw her child suffer with her own eyes ("Thy blisful eyen sawe al his torment . . . Thow sawe thy child yslayn bifore thyne yen," 845/8). In a final added touch Chaucer sees his heroine casting her gaze back at the retreating coast ("Therwith she looked bakward to the londe / And seyde, 'Farewel, housbonde routhelees!' " 862–3). In this scene Chaucer is perhaps putting Constance's suffering into juxtaposition with some of the archetypal gestures of the Virgin's sorrowing gaze at her son on the cross, familiar from many lyrics.[8] But whatever analogous uses of gesture may contribute here, the sheer density of ideas of looking introduced into this scene confirms Chaucer's awareness of the emotional potency of the actions of the eyes, for this powerful development of pathetic but dignified motherly distress is conceived and advances as narrative through Chaucer's added emphasis on the role of the eyes.

Eyes fascinate Chaucer because of the part played by looking – as confessors and preachers would naturally stress – in the formation and the revelation of motives and intentions. Just as Langland's Will imagines himself waylaid by *Concupiscencia carnis* and "Coueitise of ei3es,"[9] so in his retelling of Livy's material in *PhysT* we see Chaucer adding precisely an act of looking to precede the development of the judge's lust. For Chaucer, looking is here made to express the crucial moment of motivation that initiates the tale. Livy had referred summarily to the judge's evil intentions towards Virginia (Livy, III, xliv; *SA* 402). But it is Chaucer who chooses to bring within his narrative a visualization of an earlier occasion when the judge – through *seeing* the maiden – succumbs to an infatuation ("And so bifel this juge his eyen caste / Upon this mayde avysynge hym ful faste / As she cam forby ther as this juge stood. / Anon his herte chaunged . . ." VI 123–6). What happens is that Chaucer's interest in the origin of the intention leads him to invent a moment of looking to "explain" it, and later in this tale Virginius's amazement at the corrupt verdict ("Virginius gan upon the cherl biholde," 191) and his solemn decision about his daughter's fate ("Upon hir humble face he gan biholde," 210) are both again added aspects of Chaucer's handling of his source that use the steadfast gaze as a token of inner consideration.

For Chaucer, looking is bound up with his way of representing intention and he will introduce it in the closest weave of his translations. Since the *Heroides* account refers only obliquely to the occasion when Hypermnestra received her dreadful instructions, it is Chaucer who introduces a look, here of a parent's evil intent, when he visualizes the scene where the father orders her to commit murder (*LGW* 2626). Again, whereas Ovid had briefly noted that Lucretia when she fell dying took care that her skirts were so arranged as to avoid impropriety (*Fasti* II, 833-4), Chaucer characteristically declares that as Lucrece fell "she kaste hir lok / And of hir clothes yet she hede tok" (*LGW* 1856-7).

To Chaucer the steady fixed gaze offers a way of representing through gesture a focusing of attention. For Chaucer is concerned with every possibility of perceiving in his major characters, and so in the case of Theseus Chaucer introduces looks as tokens of his understanding and of his attempts to better his hasty nature. The tale's events cost Theseus some impatience and chagrin before he is able to resume that composed expression he has at the opening of the tale. At least, it is only Chaucer who specifies that he casts his look to one side from concentrating on his own triumph to behold the intrusive spectacle of the Theban women (896; cf. *Tes* 2.25), and when Theseus starts his concluding speech it is only Chaucer who, in an added gesture for his eyes to represent inner resolution, describes Theseus as "setting" them again ("His eyen sette he ther as was his lest," 2984; *Tes* 12.5). With these added gestures of Theseus, Chaucer is using variations on the settled gaze to represent the achievement of inward concentration.

The effect of mentioning gestures suggestive of the inner life, in contexts where the sources do not articulate this, gives the impression of a markedly deliberating reflectiveness in Chaucer's characters – sometimes a stylizing separation of our attention to incident and response – which may prompt in readers a correspondingly contemplative approach to the scenes Chaucer is visualizing. The averted look and the lowered gaze – that very attitude for which Chaucer the pilgrim is twitted by the Host (VII, 697) – are gestures widely introduced into Chaucer's recastings of various sources as a sign of inner activity, often indicating the intense inward concentration that comes with great grief: Alcyone hangs her head overcome with sadness after her prayer to understand her husband's fate, and the Black Knight hangs his head in grieving contemplation (*BD* 122; 461). On the cliffs Dorigen looks down because she is starting to think, rather than because she is seeking to look at the rocks (V, 857-61).

These come to her notice, but her downcast eyes denote inward consid-eration, as when Hypermnestra hears from her father his plan for her hus-band's murder, Chaucer imagines her first response in some added lines as a downcast look while she takes in the horror of her position (*LGW* 2647). It is Chaucer who evokes Hypermnestra's reflectiveness by visualiz-ing her as staring at her hands before making the exclamation suggested by Ovid (*Her* XIV, 53ff.) that they will be bloody (2688). The slow-motion effect of staring before speaking may suggest naivety to later read-ers, but for Chaucer the carefully deliberate approach suggests the capac-ity to reflect upon an action and to be moved. While Chaucer's sources for *ClT* see Walter simply responding with a troubled visage to his wife's constancy in her second test (*SA* 316/27; 317/5), Chaucer has his Walter lower his gaze on hearing his wife's affirmation that "Deth may noght make no comparisoun / Unto youre love" (666–7). Later, when Walter grants his wife a smock, Chaucer's sources see Walter turning his face aside to hide his tears (*SA* 322/36–7; 323/51). Here Chaucer simply has Walter unable to speak for pity (892). For Chaucer, the suggestion of embarrassment in the avoided look indicates Walter's possession of rather more moral awareness than the original character, whose averted look is a face-saving concealment of tears. The comparison with the source re-veals not simply that Chaucer has appreciated and borrowed the idea of an avoided look, but that he has moved the gesture to a context where he can make more of it to suggest the inner life of his characters.

These instances, with Hypermnestra and Walter, of Chaucer's interfer-ence in his source account to introduce averted looks of reflection and embarrassment are part of a persistent concern in Chaucer's translations with the deliberating "one-sided" gazing and the exchanged mutual gaze between two characters, both gestures expressing strong emotion and ap-plication. These gestures derive their effect from an awareness in Chau-cer's works of the significance of being looked at. It is through adapting from his sources the embarrassability or otherwise of his protagonists that Chaucer uses gesture to comment on their strength and sincerity of char-acter, on how through gesture the differences between the inner and out-ward life may be revealed or concealed.

In his use of steady gazes Chaucer values the isolating specialness of that conception of the moment of perceiving, which becomes an experi-ence conspicuous in itself, as a comment on characters in whose ability to feel intensely Chaucer is interested. While Chaucer's interest in stylized moments of looking may be seen against a background of the formalized accounts in much romance of the moment of falling in love,[10] his own interest covers a wide range of emotional contexts. The Italian lover's gaz-ing at Emilia from the tower in *Teseida* grows rather more gradually into passion than Chaucer's conception of his Palamoun being transfixed by an arrow of sight. Chaucer prefers a heightened instant of looking which implants in his character an unalterable resolve (1077; cf. *Tes* 3.11ff.). Similarly, Chaucer diverges from Boccaccio in emphasizing the element of looking in Troilus's falling in love. Boccaccio – more interested in effects than causes – remarks that Troilo was unaware it was he "il quale Amor trafisse" (*Fil* 1.25). But Chaucer, concerned to present the inward movement of Troilus, heightens the stylized transfixing moment of his first perception of Criseyde (I, 204–10), and then enlarges on the process where Troilus meditates and "wax therwith astoned / And gan hir bet biholde in thrifty wise" (274–5). From the beginning, this deliberateness of serious gazing by Chaucer's characters associates their love with the greater force of their inner feelings. This same emphatic looking marks the visits to Troilus by Criseyde and by Pandarus. When Troilus first asks Criseyde's favor in his "sick-room" he formulates this as a wish that she occasionally look at him in a friendly way (III, 130). To this Criseyde's response is that of most Chaucerian thinking characters confronted with a serious situation: she looks at Troilus. Chaucer stresses that she looks slowly, relaxedly. Her deliberate looking betokens reflection on the case presented to her (155ff.), an opportunity for reflection stemming from awareness of her own advantage in being able to look coolly at her lover with his lowered gaze and abashed manner. This whole first interview with its gestures of looking is Chaucer's own invention, but the same interest in a concentrated gaze by one person at another to betoken inner reflection and consideration distinguishes Chaucer's modifications of the scene from *Filostrato* (4.43) where Pandarus visits the sorrowing Troilus in Book IV. When Pandarus enters the bedchamber it is only the English character who is made to stand still for a moment, in a pause in the action created by Chaucer, taking in the spectacle of misery before him. It is also Chaucer who at this point adds that Pandarus stands with his arms folded (359), a gesture still linked for the Elizabethans with melancholy.[11] It is Chaucer who specifically notes that Pandarus directs his gaze to that area that most acutely evinces distress: "He stood this woful Troilus byforn / And on his pitous face he gan byholden" (IV, 360–61).

While at the end of *MLT* the pathetic scene where Constance's son stands gazing at his father's face until recognized (1013ff.) is substantially from Trivet (*SA* 179), it is Chaucer (with his characteristic taste for a deliberateness about important actions) who intensifies the gesture by having the boy's mother tell him to stand still and look, instead of looking while moving around serving as in Trivet. If for Chaucer an emphasis on a deliberating gaze by one character expresses the seriousness of his or her response to the situation described, then an exchange of looks, a meeting of eyes, is a correspondingly powerful gesture of mutual feeling and understanding. It is one which he himself introduces sparingly at important moments, but even when he finds such an idea in his source, as in *MLT*, it is noticeable that Chaucer augments the stylized deliberateness of the moment where he wants to bring out a sense of an emotional occasion. In *FranklT* it is the returning of a gaze that Chaucer uses to express the moment when both parties understand their situation. A sign of Aurelius's fixation is his gazing at Dorigen's face ("It may wel be he looked on hir face / In swich a wise as man that asketh grace," V, 957–8). Of this Dorigen remains unaware until Aurelius declares himself, whereupon Chaucer expresses Dorigen's shocked realization through a stare ("She gan to looke upon Aurelius," 979). In *TC* Chaucer conveys his lovers' moments of understanding and fellow-feeling by added gestures of mutual looking, especially in the aftermath of the scene where Criseyde's faint nearly causes Troilus's suicide. First, in his account of Criseyde's recovery Chaucer shows his usual sensitivity to what his characters' eyes are doing in a scene. In *Filostrato* Criseida simply sees the sword on waking and asks why it is drawn (4.125). But Chaucer introduces the idea that perception of the sword impinges more gradually on Criseyde: she does not look directly at it, but catches sight of the drawn weapon in a glance aside ("As that hire eye glente / Asyde anon she gan his swerd espie," IV, 1223–4). By suggesting through this added hesitant gesture a slower onset of understanding that reveals Criseyde's fearful, inexperienced nature, Chaucer prepares for the more intense distress his lovers feel at their danger, which is expressed in looks. When Troilus admits he was near suicide, Criseyde's response – before she says anything – is to look once more at Troilus ("For which Criseyde upon hym gan biholde, / And gan hym in hire armes faste folde," IV, 1229–30). The release of tension in an impulsive embrace is also Chaucer's touch, and when the lovers shortly afterwards retire to bed Chaucer again adds an exchange of looks to convey the lovers' awareness of their altered circumstances ("For pitously ech other gan byholde, / As they that hadden al hire blisse ylorn," 1249–50). Chaucer's additions to this scene of mutual gazing suggest the force of the characters' horrified realization that they have been near to death.

Such moments of oneness of feeling are powerful but relatively fleeting in Chaucer's narratives. All too aware of the elusiveness of understanding others, Chaucer is concerned with what looks and a consciousness of being looked at can reveal of a character; in some cases he actually removes the mutual attention between characters that he finds in his sources to bring out his own interpretation of the material. While her two admirers fight for her, Chaucer's Emelye remains an idealized courtly lady, the object of high-minded aspiration but unknown in her particular nature. Chaucer completely excises those occasions during the story in *Teseida* where there is some indirect communication between lady and lovers because Emilia is conscious of being looked at. When Palamoun and Arcite are gazing at Emelye from their prison, Chaucer removes Boccaccio's idea that Emilia, although pretending otherwise, is aware of being looked at and plays up to the situation (*Tes* 3.19). Chaucer's Emelye remains unaware of being looked at and thus detached. Later, when the lovers are discovered fighting, Boccaccio describes how Emilia looks bashfully at the wounds caused for her sake, while her lovers gazing back take comfort in looking at her (*Tes* 5.101). But Chaucer entirely removes any such personal interchange of looks among the three: Emelye's feelings are merged in the general compassion of the ladies (1748ff.). Yet when the problems are apparently resolved by Arcite's victory, it is Chaucer who chooses to visualize Boccaccio's account (*Tes* 8.124) of Emilia's inwardly setting her heart on Arcite by describing a mutual gazing between lover and lady ("He priketh endelong the large place / Lokynge upward upon this Emelye, / And she agayn hym caste a freendlich ye," (2678–80). Because to Chaucer the reciprocated look is a sign of inner understanding, an earlier returning of looks would have betokened the all-too-human attractions in *Teseida*. Chaucer wants his protagonists held apart to endure the tension of an unreciprocated passion.

In *Troilus* Chaucer also removes instances from *Filostrato* of gestures of mutual regard between the lovers, but here to suggest by hints of a one-sidedness of looking the unequal foundations upon which the relationship is built. When Boccaccio's lovers come together in Book III they gaze at each other so much that they cannot turn their looks away, and they kiss each other asking if it be true that each is really there with the other (3.35). But for Chaucer the gazing is not mutual, or at least, only Chaucer chooses to say that it was Troilus who could not turn his gaze from his lady, and Troilus who wonders if he is really there (III, 1345ff.). Criseyde is not described as returning the gaze, although she reassures Troilus with a kiss. Similarly at the leave-taking outside Troy, the Italian lovers gaze at each other and take each other's hand (5.12), whereas in *Troilus* it is Troilus alone who gazes at Criseyde, and only Troilus who takes the initiative in taking Criseyde's hand (V, 79/81).

This inequality in the lovers' feelings is brought out in those uses of gesture by which Chaucer differentiates his lovers in their attitude to being looked at. These changes reveal Chaucer's wide interest in gesture as a gauge of sincerity. He is concerned with how far the whole range of outward gestures other than those of the eyes can be taken as a reflection of the inner state of the character. In *Troilus* he makes significant distinctions between the lovers in the strengths and weaknesses which arise from their embarrassability, and by what he adds and amplifies from *Filostrato* Chaucer is more sustainedly interested in blushing and the downcast looks of embarrassment in *TC* than in his other work. When Criseyde enters Troilus's sick-room and when Troilus is brought to Criseyde's bedside – both scenes conceived by Chaucer – in each case the character in bed is seized with such a sudden blushing in the presence of the other that Chaucer remarks that the blushing partner could not speak a word, even if his or her head were to be cut off (III, 81; 957). This thought of beheading appears equivalent to the modern wish to "fall through the floor," to escape from all consciousness of being looked at. Chaucer's introduction of these blushes emphasizes strongly his lovers' ability to appreciate the delicacy of their situation, as do the averted looks that Chaucer includes. Criseyde's hiding her face on seeing Pandarus (IV, 821) is from *Filostrato*, but it is Chaucer who adds her hiding her face under the sheets for shame at her uncle's visit (III, 1569), and for sorrow at the thought of Troilus's jealousy (III, 1056). Urged by Criseyde to explain that jealousy, Troilus hangs his head in the shame of feeling false (III, 1079), just as in their first talk about Troilus Chaucer had shown both Pandarus and Criseyde comparably anxious to avoid each other's eyes. Pandarus begins his persuasions here with a cough (II, 254); he is Chaucer's only character to cough outside the characters of the fabliaux. As she listens to her uncle, Criseyde is described as looking downwards (253), and when Pandarus has finished his exhortation he too hangs his head and looks down (407). In the averted looks Chaucer catches that embarrassed thoughtfulness and sense of awkwardness in over-solemn talk between relatives, but Criseyde's embarrassment seems social – she feels the awkwardness of her position – while the embarrassment of Chaucer's Troilus stems more from some moral sense.

The quality of Criseyde's embarrassment is revealed by her responses when Troilus twice rides past her window. On the one occasion he passes in *Filostrato* Criseida stares steadily over her shoulder at Troilo, who walks by below staring up at her. Neither character is embarrassable (2.82). But on both occasions in *Troilus* both lovers are deeply and variously embarrassed. They are both aware of each other the second time, and a briefly exchanged look between them causes blushes on both sides (II, 1256–8). The earlier occasion (II, 645–58) is more revealing of Criseyde's sense of the difference between her inner feelings and outward appearance. Here Troilus is unaware of Criseyde's watching him as he rides past, although still embarrassed by the praise of the bystanders. Chaucer shows Criseyde able to watch her lover feeling awkward without feeling herself involved, enjoying that sense of advantage she is to experience when visiting her lover in his sickbed. But Criseyde's detached observation soon gives way to such embarrassment at the thought of her power over Troilus that she quickly pulls her head in from the window. Chaucer's inclusion of this strikingly impulsive gesture serves to reveal Criseyde's extreme sensitivity to the pressures of outward appearances. The gesture suggests that, although none of the crowd are looking at her nor could understand her embarrassment, as soon as Criseyde herself sees her behavior in its true light she imagines that everybody else will see through her too unless she avoids their looks. At such moments Chaucer brings out through gesture the weakness of Criseyde's sense of individuality to stand against the social pressures of embarrassment.

In contrast to this, a change in a gesture of Troilus reveals Chaucer's interest in some moral sensitivity in his hero, although Chaucer has elsewhere allowed some of the moral cynicism of Troilo to stand in his own translation (e.g. *TC* III, 407–13; cf. *Fil* 3.18). Translating the scene of Troilo's confession of his lady's identity to Pandaro (2.12ff.), Chaucer adapts the context of Troilo's blushing and so alters its cause. Pandaro urges Troilo to trust him with his secret, but at this Troilo blushingly confesses he loves a relative of Pandaro and hides his face weeping; Pandaro urges him to get up, asking if she is in Pandaro's house, for then they will speed the better; on hearing this Troilo turns away even more, but at last confesses Criseida's identity with tears. The main point of difference in *TC* is that Chaucer omits Troilo's early blushing admission that he loves a relation of Pandaro. Instead, Chaucer has his hero blush in response to Pandarus's direct challenge "Knowe ich hire aught?" (I, 864). This characteristic Chaucerian delaying of the gesture makes the confession of his lady's close relatedness to his friend much more of a climactic moment of embarrassment for Troilus, because much more of a moral issue for the English hero. The comically semi-violent gesture of Pandarus's shaking Troilus and crying "Thef, thow shalt hyre name telle!" (870) is a piece of Chaucerian "business" which draws attention to the outrage of family even as it comments on Pandarus's ability to make light of things, in marked contrast to the English Troilus, who instead of weeping trembles with fear and apprehension born of a greater awareness of his predicament (871). No wonder the English Pandarus urges his friend not to get up but to look up (862).

Here Chaucer is using the gestures of blushing and the avoided look in the characterization of Troilus to suggest his hero's capacity to feel moral uneasiness. The nature of Diomede, so strongly contrasted with Troilus, is correspondingly brought out by an added ability to look Criseyde quite confidently in the eye despite his intentions. To an otherwise closely translated passage expressing the apparent embarrassment of this new lover in Criseyde's presence, Chaucer adds the idea that Diomede is nonetheless still able to look "sobreliche" at the lady with a deliberateness that belies his seeming awkwardness (V, 929; cf. *Fil* 6.23). In Chaucer's adaptations of Ovid's gestures in the Philomela story a similar interest emerges in this capacity to contrive gesture, but it is also clear that Chaucer intervenes to rehabilitate gestures in Ovid's account which for the English poet have powerful associations. In Ovid (*Met* VI, 424ff.) Pandion weeps as his daughter Philomela sails away with Tereus, whereas Chaucer brings the tears forward so that his Pandion weeps when Tereus asks to take Philomela away with him (*LGW* 2279). Chaucer redeploys what in Ovid is a gesture of simple pathos in order to convey the emotionally difficult moment of apprehension and decision by the father. Ovid's Tereus so burns with lust for Philomela that he weeps in his entreaties to Pandion. Chaucer instead gives the tears of entreaty to his heroine, whom Ovid does not mention as weeping, and makes his Tereus kneel to Pandion. Because Chaucer – unlike Ovid – has stressed that the father is extremely aged and thus venerable, it is not surprising that Chaucer omits the firm manly handshakes as between equals, with which the classical poet's Pandion and Tereus greet each other at the beginning and end of the son-in-law's visit. But such changes are full of implications about Chaucer's own preferences in gesture. Chaucer's removal of the tears from the insincere villain to the innocent heroine indicates his concern for the genuineness of weeping as an outward gesture of the inner life. Chaucer's substitution of kneeling for weeping shows his sense of the evidently plausible use of such ceremonial outward gestures to disguise real feelings. This possibility of deception through contrived gesture is one part of Chaucer's interest in gesture as a sign of the inner life, but it is a qualification contained within what is his more preponderant overall impulse: to endow human feelings with gesture which intensifies the emotion but often surrounds it with an aura of dignity.

If we scrutinize those instances in his work where Chaucer adds and changes such gestures as weeping and kneeling, which interest him in *Philomela* – together with such other strong outward signs of emotion as swooning and embracing – patterns of emphasis are exposed in Chaucer's approach to his sources which sustain and extend the interests suggested by his concern with looking. For the gestures to which Chaucer returns sufficiently to form patterns in his poems are those by which, in intensifying the emotions of many of his characters and evoking their capacity to feel, Chaucer suggests their inner life. But this added and augmented vehemence of feeling among many characters goes in parallel with an added solemnity, an almost ceremonial deliberateness about the order and the pace with which the gestures of the emotional life are expressed. These two strands of vehemence and order in Chaucer's gestures are not contradictory but complementary, for both patterns of interest in gesture stem from the same fundamental concern in Chaucer with the importance of the inner life of the character. The sense of the value of feeling demands expression which both reveals its force and range and acknowledges its seriousness.

In losing consciousness, in fainting, is perhaps the most uncontrivedly spontaneous and forceful manifestation of inner activity. Griselda shows no embarrassment at the humiliations she endures but she is embarrassed, Chaucer tells us, to find she has fainted for joy at discovering her children (1108). Since Chaucer has himself added this faint he is very much in control of the implications of gesture here. Almost despite herself, Griselda's faint has the effect of revealing in public the true strength of her feelings. It is Chaucer who makes the eldest Theban lady faint before addressing Theseus, as part of the heightened pathos of his visualization of that meeting of lord and suppliants, a gesture which by intensifying the distress enhances the importance of Theseus's compassion (913; cf. *Tes* 2.26). Emelye's faint is moved after Ancite's death, part of that pattern of intensification of responses at important emotional moments (2819; cf. *Tes* 10.84, 11.4). For his more long-suffering heroines Chaucer resorts to the hyperbole of a double faint. In this he shows his distinctive emphasis on the inner life, for the added gesture of a double faint pushes the emotions of his characters to extremity, and yet the pace of response that allows two faints suggests a sustainment of grief that has implicit dignity. It is Chaucer's Griselda who faints on discovering her children alive and again on embracing them, a pattern of repetition that by prolonging and distinguishing the responses intensifies the reported experience (1079–99; cf. *SA* 329/20–1). Virginia's two faints before her father slays her are Chaucer's added gestures and stress his sense of the sincerity of fainting. For Chaucer's handling of pathos here resembles that juxtaposition of pious resolution with touching fearfulness which he may have seen "upon a scaffold hye" in the mystery-dramatists' presentation of the Isaac Story. After her first faint when she hears her doom, Virginia rises up crying "Blissed be God that I shal dye a mayde!" (248), but after these resolute words she begs her father to "smyte softe" and, fainting again, is beheaded while unconscious. Whereas in Livy Virginia is suddenly stabbed by her desperate father (*SA* 406) and the *Roman* gives a summary account of her beheading by her father (*SA* 401), Chaucer's introduction of these gestures of fainting both intensifies and much draws out the heroine's distress. Through the added swoons Chaucer contrasts the fearfulness of Virginia's inward emotions with her voiced determination, and in the extremes of both Virginia acquires an awful dignity. Similarly, it is Chaucer's Constance who faints twice on meeting Alla again in Rome, where Trivet's Constance swooned once on hearing he had arrived there. Chaucer stresses that "Twyes she swowned in his owene sighte" (1058). He intensifies yet slows the pace of the heroine's response by doubling her faint and adds the solemnity of having her husband witness her grief. Because the feelings are more intense and the forgiveness slower than in Trivet, the achievement of reconciliation is greater, and this has its own sense of completeness and dignity.

The significance of this balance held between extreme feeling and slowed pace of response can be seen by contrast with Troilus's faint in the bedroom (III, 1092), reproved by Pandarus and Criseyde as undignified and unmasculine, although elsewhere Chaucer adds a faint for the virile character of Arcite (1572; cf. *Tes* 4.88). Chaucer has borrowed the swoon from its original place as Troilo's response in parliament to Criseida's exchange (*Fil* 4.18) and, like Arcite's faint in the grove, Troilus's collapse so becomes a relatively private response. But Chaucer is using the gesture to show the quality of the hero's inner life at the expense of his dignity. Troilo's faint is simple distress at losing his mistress: Troilus's faint expresses a crisis born of some moral sense, for he faints out of embarrassment, overcome by the distress of shame at having deceived his lady with the trumped-up story of jealousy. The humorous aspect of his naiveté should not blind us to that very force of inner feeling expressed by the faint that causes him to relinquish dignity. In these revealing strains between inner life and outward behavior the *Franklin's Tale* reaches its emotional climax: when Arveragus commands his wife to keep a commitment that must run counter to all his inward instincts, Chaucer conveys the unbearable strain of his position, breaking out in the tears which gush obtrusively just as he is expressing his highest principle (1480).

The transfer of the gesture of weeping from Tereus to Philomela is symptomatic of that respect Chaucer shows throughout his work for the sincerity and emotional force of *tears*. The *MLT* represents a concentration of added gestures of weeping that not only augment Constance's sense of grief but construct a social milieu where good people show their goodness by weeping and by being susceptible to the tears of others. The kindness of the constable and his wife who find Constance (529), and the compassionate nature of Alla on hearing of his wife's supposedly monstrous child (768), are indicated by added tears (cf. *SA* 168; 173), and Chaucer's Constance converts Hermengyld by her tears (537; cf. *SA* 169). Chaucer's use of tears tends not merely towards augmented emotiveness per se but tends to endow the serious moments of life with a sense of solemnity and a kind of order. It is Chaucer's Troilus who gives his responses over the fainted Criseyde a ceremonial orderliness ("His hondes wrong and seyd that was to seye, / And with his teeris salt hire brest byreyned," IV, 1171–2). His reactions are expressed in gestures which by their combination of emotional force and solemn deliberateness give a ritualistic impression, and it is noticeable how Chaucer uses tears to create such a sense of climactic moments. Both *MLT* and *ClT* are brought to their climaxes in tears, and one recalls the tableau effects of a churchful of weeping people at the end of *PrT* or of the two weeping sisters at the close of *Philomela*, by which Chaucer replaces the bacchantic violence in Ovid (*Met* VI, 609ff.). In both *MLT* and *ClT* Chaucer is sparing with some gestures in the course of the narrative, as if saving up effects to dignify especially solemn moments. To avoid associating the gesture of weeping with insincerity Chaucer omits any mention of Walter's tears (cf. *SA* 322/35–6; 323/50), but he adds the tears of Griselda's father as he comes out with the too-small coat (914; cf. *SA* 322/48–50; 323/61). When Alla meets Constance again, Chaucer stresses twice that he wept (1052/9), until Constance relents and they melt into mutual sobs of reconciliation (cf. *SA* 179).

From the patterns of changes and additions it emerges that for Chaucer the gestures of kissing and embracing are also important in contributing to this solemnizing of emotionally important scenes. Although in the sources Walter embraces his wife when throwing aside his pretense, it is Chaucer who explicitly adds that he kissed her (1057; cf. *SA* 328/49; 329/10). Kissing is linked with the solemnifying of an agreement, just as one notes Chaucer tending to mention the formal movements or position of the hands to accompany serious moments. Only Chaucer mentions Arcite's hands in their white gloves on his bier (2874; cf. *Tes* 11.16), or the reassuring gestures of the hands at moments in *TC* (II, 1671; III, 72; 1128). In Virginia's response to her fate Chaucer visualizes not only her weeping but the twining of her arms imploringly around her father's neck (232–3). For Chaucer, embracing at serious moments betokens a conscious sense of commitment, as a change from a source hints. When Hypermnestra and her husband are in bed the Ovidian husband, more than half asleep, makes an instinctive attempt to embrace his wife just before she wakes him to warn him to escape (*Her* XIV, 69). But Chaucer instead imagines his heroine – all too conscious of the grave situation – waking her husband by embracing him (2707). This reversal of responsibility for the embrace suggests the conscious dignity Chaucer associates with the proper tenderness of embraces. From the source differences one notices how Chaucer sometimes delays gestures of this kind to achieve emotional climaxes. Chaucer omits Petrarch's note that the ladies embraced Griselda as they came to attire her for her wedding (*SA* 306/69). The English poet prefers to postpone the solemn overtones he associates with embracing until the tale's matter is resolved, where he then puts much greater emphasis on the fervor of Griselda's embrace of her children; only Chaucer envisages the children grasped so that they can scarcely be extricated from the arms of their fainted mother (1100ff.). Similarly, when Alla and Constance are reunited in Trivet, the king immediately embraces and kisses his wife when he recognizes her (*SA* 179). It is Chaucer who holds this gesture back until the couple are truly reconciled, whereupon they kiss in Chaucer a hundred times (1074).

This greater sense of force and dignity in the gestures made by Chaucer's characters implies an ideal of order behind human actions which expresses itself in a wish to surround human living with ceremony and restraint. Theseus's wish to control and contain the disorder of human passions within the created pattern of the lists is one theme of *KnT*, and a comparable sense of a need to assert order underlies some patterns of movement and stillness in Chaucer's own visualizings of actions. It is Chaucer who imagines Virginius's way of breaking his news to Virginia: he first seats himself in his hall and then has his daughter summoned to him (207–8). It is Chaucer who reverses the idea of movement in his sources to emphasize the dignity and the strength of Griselda's feelings: the original Griselda rushes to embrace her children, but Chaucer's heroine remains still after her faint and calls the children over to her (1081; *SA* 328/57).

In both cases Chaucer chooses to emphasize the central authority of parents by giving them the dignity of stillness. There is no doubt of the force of the mother's feelings (which indeed has been much augmented by Chaucer), but in such moments Chaucer invests his characters' actions with a dignified sense of fundamental order.

The rehandling of these scenes implies a concern to order experience, in which Chaucer is also interested in his attention to kneeling, a gesture which he shows being used to ritualize both private and public life. Kneeling is a formal and conscious gesture which may convey great earnest. The devil is impressed that the old woman in *FrT* means the literal truth of the oath she makes solemnly on her knees (III, 1625). Chaucer's use of kneeling suggests its serious overtones stemmed for him mainly from devotional contexts: he goes out of his way to mention that characters kneel and pray. He also introduces the gesture to express the devotion of children to their parents in three added instances in *MLT* (383, 1104, 1153; cf. *SA* 167, 180–1). There are also three added instances of kneeling in *ClT*, and Chaucer introduces kneeling into contexts where it comments on the kneeling characters' feelings and conception of how they should behave. Walter's subjects (*ClT* 187; cf. *SA* 298/25ff.) and the unmarried Griselda (292; cf. *SA* 304/31ff.) kneel to the marquis with proper respect. But when Griselda is summoned back to organize her successor's reception, Chaucer adds that she kneels to her husband, and this added gesture stresses the extreme humility of Griselda's conception of her role (951; cf. *SA* 324/4).

In *Troilus*, Chaucer's introduction of kneeling within some intimate contexts is a gesture used to express the strength of the characters' feelings, however misguided those may be, and their desire to formalize experience. On the one hand, some of Chaucer's additions confirm the formal associations of kneeling: although in a mock prayer, Pandarus's kneeling to Cupid implicitly stresses the gesture's devotional overtones (III, 183–4). Pandarus mocks Chaucer's Troilus who kneels in courtesy on entering Criseyde's bedroom (III, 953), but Pandarus himself embarrasses his niece by kneeling to her (II, 1202), a gesture excessive in the context of his visit. It is Chaucer's Troilus who falls to his knees with feelings of shame and remorse at Criseyde's embarrassing questions (III, 1080), and in the meetings between Troilus and Pandarus it is noticeable how Chaucer introduces the gesture of kneeling and often omits embraces between the men. When Pandarus visits the anguished Troilus, Chaucer omits Boccaccio's action where Troilo runs to embrace his friend (4.44), preferring a solemnly static meeting without embraces where Troilus stays still in his bed (IV, 365ff.). When Pandaro reports success with Criseida, Troilo embraces and kisses him a thousand times (2.81), but Chaucer replaces this with the more formalized gesture: "And to Pandare he held up both his hondes" (II, 974). Chaucer suggests the less relaxed approach and greater formality with which the English characters treat their expressions of feeling. In both scenes where Troilus kneels to Pandarus – in gratitude when Pandarus takes on the affair, and after the consummation (I, 1044; III, 1592) – the two Italian friends simply kiss and embrace (*Fil* 2.33; 3.56). Chaucer's conception of these scenes reveals Troilus's submissiveness, but also his conscious wish to formalize his feelings.

It is in Chaucer's handling of gestures at two important moments of decision in *KnT* that a number of patterns of gesture observable in his work can be seen coming together to suggest the refinement of the inner life. The contexts are the two occasions when Theseus is influenced by petitions from kneeling ladies. Whereas the Theban ladies who interrupt Theseus in *Teseida* are in frenzied disorder, beating their breasts, Chaucer instead has them kneeling two by two at the roadside (898; cf. *Tes* 2.26). But whereas Teseo listens from his chariot, it is Chaucer who conveys Theseus's inner movement of compassion by having his hero get down from his horse to embrace the ladies in his arms, in an important putting aside of that rightful static position of authority which Virginia's father had consciously assumed. Chaucer has transformed Boccaccio's scene by using those gestures that recurrently have force for him: the ladies' plea is given more dignity, while the force of Theseus's response is conveyed by his impulsive movement and by his use of embraces to affirm his feelings. Again, in the scene where Theseus finds the lovers fighting in the grove, the gestures of petition and forgiveness are Chaucer's, to convey the inner movement to compassion in Theseus. It is Chaucer who makes very much more of Theseus's initial anger (cf. *Tes* 5.88) and then himself invents the scene where the weeping ladies go down "on hir bare knees" to Theseus to have pity and would even have "kist his feet ther as he stood" (1758-9). So powerful are these gestures that Theseus is persuaded, even though Chaucer stresses he was trembling with rage (1762). Chaucer's changes have followed his pattern: he has much increased the emotional intensity of Theseus's first feelings and then shown how those feelings are shaped and controlled by courtly gestures. Because the feelings are stronger, the voluntary achievement of restraint and dignity has more value, and Chaucer so suggests more range and depth in Theseus's inner life. Moreover, the introduction of this incident by Chaucer is part of the pattern in his use of gesture, in that the change in this second scene puts it into close parallel with the earlier scene with the Theban ladies, and so introduces that characteristic Chaucerian deliberateness of repeated emotion and resolution into the experience of Theseus which was not explicit in *Teseida*.

A project to record all the gestures Chaucer introduces when translating would produce a list as interestingly diverse but as essentially unconnected as the variety of narrative situations in which they occur. It would include the numerous instances of lively incidental observation in narrative. Some patterns of limited occurrence intriguing in their implications could also be traced, such as Chaucer's attitude to smiling,[12] or the range of his use of vocal gesture, from the one occasion he has a character hum (to express Criseyde's awkwardness when asked if she likes her lover's letter, II, 1199) to his increasing from *Filostrato* the mention of sighing in *TC* to suggest reflectiveness. But within a narrative poet's usages there will be more scattered instances of gesture than can be taken to support particular patterns. The present study reflects those gestures which Chaucer has most recurrently chosen to add when translating and which, by contributing to the distinctively tender yet dignified internalization of his characters, contribute significantly to that process of interpreting the meaning of his materials which is almost inseparable from Chaucer's work as a translator.

NOTES

1. Chaucer quotations are from F. N. Robinson, ed., *The Works of Geoffrey Chaucer*, 2nd ed. (London, 1957).
2. For general historical and literary developments – beyond the present study's particular scope – in the use of gesture, cf. Andrea de Jorio, *La mimica degli antichi nel gestire napoletano* (Naples, 1832); Carl Sittl, *Die Gebärden der Griecher und Römer* (Leipzig, 1890); L. Beszard, "Les larmes dans l'épopée," *Zeitschrift für romanische Philologie*, XXVII (1903), pp. 385–413, 513–49, 641–74; L. Gougaud, *Devotional and Ascetic Practices in the Middle Ages* (London, 1927); A. Delatte, "Le baiser, l'agenouillement et le prosternement de l'adoration chez les Grecs," *Académie royale de Belgique, Bulletin de la Classe des Lettres et des Sciences Morales et Politiques*, 5th Ser., XXXVII (1951), pp. 423–50; W. Habicht, *Die Gebärde in englischen Dichtungen des Mittelalters*, Bayerische Akademie der Wissenschaften, Philosophisch-Historische Klasse, Abhandlungen, Neue Folge, XLVI (1959); P. Ménard, *Le rire et le sourire dans le roman courtois en France au moyen âge (1150–1250)* (Geneva, 1969).
3. Habicht, *Die Gebärde*, p. 8. *CT* V, 103–4 suggests Chaucer knew the advice on gesture offered by some rhetorical handbooks, cf. Geoffrey of Vinsauf, *Poetria Nova*, ll.370–5; 2036–65 (E. Faral, *Les arts poétiques du XIIᵉ et du XIIIᵉ siècle* (Paris, 1924), pp. 208, 260); cf. also: Ernest Gallo, *The Poetria Nova and Its Sources in Early Rhetorical Doctrine* (The Hague, 1971), pp. 222–3, 231. On Chaucer's interest in physiognomy, cf. Jill Mann, *Chaucer and Medieval Estates Satire* (Cambridge, 1973), esp. pp. 128ff.
4. References are to *Teseida delle nozze d'Emilia*, A. Roncaglia, ed., *Giovanni Boccaccio: Opere 3, Scrittori d'Italia* no. 185 (Bari, 1941).
5. Page and line references are to W. F. Bryan and G. Dempster, eds., *Sources and Analogues of Chaucer's Canterbury Tales* (Chicago, 1941; repr. New York, 1958), hereafter named *SA*.
6. Chaucer's sensitivity to the face has parallels in contemporary visual art. Margaret Rickert (*Painting in Britain: The Middle Ages* [Harmondsworth, 1954]) describes a psalter illuminated in the 14th-century East Anglian Style: "The facial types too have a delicate charm and variety which is typically English" (p. 141). In another MS are noted "delicately modelled

faces" (p. 143) and that "untinted outline drawing of exquisite delicacy is always used by this artist for the faces" (p. 148).

7. References are to *Il Filostrato*, V. Pernicone, ed., *Giovanni Boccaccio: Opere 2, Scrittori d'Italia*, no. 165 (Bari, 1937).

8. Cf. Carleton Brown, ed., *English Lyrics of the XIIIth Century* (Oxford, 1932), 24.90; 49.13–18; 54.51–4.

9. Cf. G. Kane and E. Talbot Donaldson, eds., *Piers Plowman: The B Version* (London, 1975), XI, 13–14.

10. Cf. A. Micha, ed., *Cligés*, CFMA (Paris, 1975), ll.687ff.

11. Cf. *The Tempest*, I, 2.224. On relations between rhetorical and dramatic gesture, cf. B. L. Joseph, *Elizabethan Acting* (Oxford, 1964), ch. I and ch. III.

12. Smiling is often associated with the superiority of unshared knowledge, cf. *TC* I, 194 (from "laugh" in *Fil*); I, 329; II, 1639; V, 1457. Describing Hate in the *Romaunt*, Chaucer adds that she was "grennyng for dispitous rage" (156).

Chaucer and Leigh Hunt

PAUL M. CLOGAN

Criticism of Chaucer in the early part of the nineteenth century is very different from that of the last one-third of the century. The aims of the Romantic critics of Chaucer were far different from the scholarly pursuits of such men as ten Brink, Child, Furnivall, and Skeat. The last one-third of the nineteenth century may be characterized as an age of professional English studies. The efforts of the above-mentioned scholars and the Chaucer Society (founded by Furnivall in 1868) were focused on such matters as purification of the Chaucer canon, establishment of an accurate text of the poet's works, and factual determination of the events and chronology of the poet's life. The period was chiefly one of scientific philology – not of evaluation and criticism of the literary value of a work.

On the other hand, the first one-half of the century was not characterized by scholarly concerns, but by popular revival of Chaucer's poetry. There were no courses on Chaucer in the universities. Indeed, English studies were not introduced into the universities until well into the Victorian era. Criticism and commentary on Chaucer came from the pens of reviewers and men of letters – not from scholars and antiquaries. These men were interested chiefly in gaining for Chaucer a reading public, and such anthologies as Hazlitt's *Select British Poets* (1824), Hunt's "Characteristic Specimens of the English Poets" (1835) and *Wit and Humour* (1846), and Southey's *Select Works of the British Poets* (1831) were instrumental in presenting the works of Chaucer to a general audience.

Of the Romantic essayists who commented on Chaucer and his works, none was more devoted and enthusiastic than James Henry Leigh Hunt. Indeed, as Caroline Spurgeon has noted, Hunt was perhaps the "most constant and enthusiastic lover of Chaucer in the early nineteenth century."[1] References to Chaucer abound in his works, and they range from lines of poetry cited in an essay to illustrate some point to lengthy and extensive critical comments on the poetry of Chaucer. An accomplished translator of Italian, Greek, Latin, and, to a lesser extent, French, Hunt also turned his attention to translations of Chaucer's work – from a few lines to entire tales. His translations range from paraphrase to modernization and are of mixed quality. Hunt's overall performance, however, was quite good and he preserved more of the original than other translators.[2]

Educated at Christ's Hospital, Hunt was a fighting liberal journalist, poet, translator, editor, critic, and prolific essayist. He recognized and championed Shelley and Keats, for a short time influenced Keats's style, and seems to have introduced him to Chaucer's works. Clarence Thorpe has suggested that Hunt's fame should probably rest on his criticism. Apart from his poetry, Hunt ought to be seen as

one of the half-dozen greater literary men of his time: standing for his total performance in criticism, if not as a prose-writer in general, next to Coleridge and Hazlitt, and above Lamb, De Quincey, and Carlyle.[3]

In his copious and astute critical comments on Chaucer, Hunt initiated a kind of technical analysis of Chaucer's writings. He is one of the first to attempt an analysis of irony, humor and narrative techniques, and to associate poetry with the idea of music. Hunt's critical comments are characterized by close attention to the text at hand, as his many references to a single line illustrate. This is especially apparent in his comments on Chaucer, for in many of them he seems to be as concerned with the music and imagery of a single line or passage as with the texture of the entire work.

One of Hunt's earliest references to Chaucer can be found in the 1814 essay "On Washer-women." In that essay Hunt voices his desire that writers might more frequently concern themselves with picture-making, rendering manners through descriptive sketches of men and things. Although Steele and Shenstone are seen as masters of the detached portrait, it is Chaucer, in his portraits of the Canterbury Pilgrims, who attained "unrivalled perfection." Subsequent writers "can only dilate and vary upon his principle."[4] In the following year in his sonnet "The Poets," published in *The Examiner* on 24 December 1815, Hunt again expresses his admiration for Chaucer's descriptive portraits. Naming the poets dearest to him, he includes Chaucer "for manners and close, silent eye."[5] Hunt particularly admired the sketch of the Shipman in the "General Prologue" to the *Canterbury Tales*. In an 1820 essay, "Seamen on Shore," he commented on the resemblance of Chaucer's Shipman to the nineteenth-century sailor:

There is the very dirk, the complexion, the jollity, the experience, and the bad horsemanship. The plain unaffected ending of the description has the air of a sailor's own speech; while the line about the beard is exceedingly picturesque, poetical, and comprehensive.[6]

With "close, silent eye," Chaucer portrayed the manners of a sailor. The fact that the modern sailor is of the same cast as the Shipman is indication to Hunt that Chaucer's portraits possess enduring and unrivaled value.

Just as he admires the skill with which Chaucer created individual portraits and rendered manners, so too he admires Chaucer's descriptions of nature. The *Flower and the Leaf* is called "a beautiful poem," and it is applauded for its pictures of the laurel and the daisy.[7] The description of the cave of Morpheus in the *Book of the Duchess* is another passage which Hunt praises. Nothing has "a more deep and sullen effect" than Chaucer's cliffs and running waters: "It seems as real as an actual solitude, or some quaint old picture in a book on travels in Tartary."[8] In "May-Day," published in 1820, Hunt comments on Chaucer's description of morning pleasures, especially those passages in the "Knight's Tale" which describe Emily's and Arcite's solitary observances of May. The descriptions, according to Hunt, are "exquisite" and sparkle through the antiquity of the language. Comparing Chaucer's "Knight's Tale" to Dryden's translation, Hunt insists that Dryden's is inferior – even in versification. Chaucer's tale is "delicate" and has a "finer sense of music." Dryden's version is commonplace:

Dryden's genius, for the most part, wanted faith in nature. It was too gross and sophisticate. There was as much difference between him and his original, as between a hot noon in perukes at St. James's, and one of Chaucer's lounges on the grass, of a May-morning.[9]

It is through Chaucer's descriptions of nature that Hunt comes to regard him as a lively, delicate, and animated poet. In "Fine Days in January and February" (1828), Hunt confesses that in those months he cannot help but hear the singing of Chaunticleer and the "strenuous music" of the poetry of Chaucer, adding that it is an "old fancy" of his "to associate the ideas of Chaucer with that of any early and vigorous manifestation of light and pleasure."[10] It is readily apparent that, in most of his observances, Hunt emphasized the lighter side of Chaucer's work. As one critic has noted, Hunt was chiefly attracted by literature "that delights and entertains through sensuous appeal or charm of wit, humor, or narrative."[11] However, he appreciated the serious and weighty, as well, and in his lengthier and more extensive essays he discussed many dimensions of Chaucer's poetry.

One rather lengthy discussion of Chaucer may be found in "Specimens of Chaucer," which was included in Hunt's "Characteristic Specimens of the English Poets," which appeared in the *London Journal* in 1835. Hunt begins his essay with a brief biographical sketch of Chaucer, which incorporates much of the legend that Godwin had filled out in such detail in his *Life of Geoffrey Chaucer*. He accepts the story of the poet's period of difficulties, including his supposed exile and imprisonment. He further accepts the tale of Chaucer's confession and betrayal of his confederates, calling it "a blot on the memory of this great poet, an apparently otherwise amiable and excellent man."[12] The "blot" on Chaucer's memory, however, cannot have caused too much concern for Hunt, for elsewhere he calls Chaucer the greatest of individuals. Chaucer is to be considered one of the four great English poets (with Spenser, Shakespeare, and Milton), as well as the "Father of English Poetry." To Hunt, Chaucer is not an "old poet," but a "young" one, with consistent maturity of mind. Because this essay and the accompanying "specimens" were part of an anthology of extracts from the best English poetry, Hunt takes great pains to describe the general nature and attractiveness of Chaucer's poetry for the reader who is not familiar with the poet's works. Chaucer, Hunt states,

combines an epic power of grand, comprehensive, and primitive imagery, with that of being contented with the smallest matter of fact near him, and of luxuriating in pure vague animal spirits, like a dozer in a field. His gayety is equal to his gravity, and his sincerity to both.[13]

The poet's excellences are pathos, humor, satire, character, and description, while his faults are coarseness and occasional tediousness. The coarseness is to be attributed to the age in which Chaucer lived.

The selections which Hunt includes are modernized in spelling and are taken from Charles Cowden Clarke's *Riches of Chaucer*. Although Hunt elsewhere insisted that Chaucer's works were not difficult to read in Middle English, the desire to make Chaucer known to a general audience was stronger than Hunt's attachment to the language of the original. He adds, however, that even in a modernized state, Chaucer's versification can be seen to be smooth, powerful, and various. The first specimens exhibited are extracts from the "General Prologue" to the *Canterbury Tales*, partial descriptions of the Knight, Squire, Prioress, Monk, Clerk, Shipman, and Parson. The Wife of Bath, Miller, Reeve, Summoner, and Pardoner are conspicuous by their absence.

The second group of specimens is prefaced by a brief discussion of Chaucer's debts to other works. Hunt notes that some of Chaucer's best poems are translations from Italian and French. They are translations, however, of a very high order, "of so exquisite a kind, so improved in character, so enlivened with fresh natural touches" that they really may be considered originals.[14] Especially praiseworthy in this regard is the "Knight's Tale," from which Hunt has gathered the second group of extracts. Hunt is particularly impressed by the descriptions of Lygurge and Emetreus, the warrior kings of Thrace and Inde, and with the poet's ability to present both the particular and the general in their descriptions.

The third group of specimens exhibit Chaucer's pathos, a pathos which is direct and true to nature. The death of Arcite in the "Knight's Tale" and the woes of Custance adrift in the "Man of Law's Tale" are passages which Hunt feels exhibit the deepest pathos. The fourth group of extracts is also presented to illustrate Chaucer's pathos. These extracts are taken from the "Clerk's Tale." Hunt notes that the story of Griselda, always immensely popular, is really not believable. The story is unnatural and horrifying – yet it is effective, principally because the "sense of duty" predominates. It is set up in the story above all other considerations. That principle of duty, "once believed in by a good and humble nature is exalted by it, in consequence of its very torments, above all torment and weakness."[15] The pathos in this tale has a heightened effect, for the reader not only pities Griselda, but holds her in awe.

Another group of specimens is provided to illustrate Chaucer's humor and satire. In this section, Hunt focuses most of his attention on Chaucer as a reformer. Chaucer took pleasure, says Hunt, in exposing abuses in the Church, "but because his very good-nature, and love of truth, made him more dislike the abuses of the best things in the most reverend places."[16] Included are specimens of Chaucer's satire in the Pardoner's manner of preaching and the Wife of Bath's version of the disappearance of the fairies. The last specimens provided are a miscellaneous collection exhibiting Chaucer's powers of description, portrait-painting, and fine sense. The "Specimens of Chaucer" may not be notable for extraordinary depth of analysis, but as extracts designed to entice the general audience to read Chaucer's poetry, they are an attractive, varied, and well-chosen collection.

Imagination and Fancy, published in 1844, is something of a manifesto of Leigh Hunt's principles of literary criticism. The object of that work was threefold: to present passages of the finest English poetry; to provide an account of the nature and requirements of poetry; and to indicate, in Hunt's words,

what sort of poetry is to be considered *as poetry of the most poetical kind*, or such as exhibits the imagination and fancy in a state of predominance, undisputed by interests of another sort.[17]

Hunt's efforts may be judged successful on all counts, but it is his discussion of the nature of imagination and fancy which sheds the most light on Hunt's appreciation of Chaucer.

A primary requisite of both imagination and fancy is the poet's perception of truth. Truth of every kind belongs to the poet, "provided it can bud into any kind of beauty, or is capable of being illustrated and impressed by the poetic faculty."[18] One of the greatest proofs of a poet's genius consists in the simplicity of truth being allowed to stand alone, infused by an imaginative economy. A simple passage may have the most considerable and complete effect if only, through the workings of imagination, truth is reflected. What, then, is imagination, that quality by which truth is conferred and which is essential in poetry of the highest order? In Hunt's words, imagination is all feeling, "the feeling of the subtlest and most affecting analogies; the perception of sympathies in the natures of things, or in their popular attributes."[19] Fancy, on the other hand, "is a sporting with their resemblance, real or supposed, and with airy and fantastical creations."[20] Fancy lacks the weight of thought and feeling of imagination. "Imagination belongs to Tragedy, or the serious muse; Fancy to the comic."[21] The last statement should not rest without some modification, however, for Hunt is quick to point out that imagination and fancy may sometimes dwell together and that the serious and the comic muses may often share a common sympathy. Indeed, Hunt insists that in the greatest poets both imagination and fancy are to be found. To better illustrate his point, Hunt assesses the degree to which imagination and fancy are to be found in certain poets. His scale is rather revealing. Shakespeare, he maintains, was the only poet who possessed both imagination and fancy in equal perfection. Spenser had both imagination and fancy, but more of the latter. In Milton, too, both are to be found, but in that poet imagination was dominant. Pope was seen to have hardly any imagination, but a great deal of fancy, while Coleridge had little fancy, but imagination "exquisite." Finally, both fancy and imagination were possessed by Chaucer, who was seen to have "the strongest imagination of real life, beyond any writers but Homer, Dante, and Shakespeare," and was "in comic painting inferior to none."[22]

Hunt's conception of the imagination is very much like that of Coleridge, for both see the imagination as a unifying, shaping, and conferring power. It is the necessary element of the greatest poetry. It is evident that Hunt's standards were quite high and that his praise of Chaucer as a poet of great imagination is not to be taken lightly. For Hunt, Chaucer was not a poet of thoughtless mirth or of facile seriousness. His serious and tragic poetry reflects that Chaucer was "one of the profoundest masters of pathos that ever lived."[23] His work is informed by the greatest in "primeval intensity" – an intensity of conception and expression. His narratives are infused with action and character, so much so that Hunt believes Chaucer to be the greatest narrative poet, for Chaucer dwells in the universal and profoundly simple. The depth of his imagination enabled Chaucer to go beyond the resemblances with which fancy sports, to penetrate the reality that lies beneath appearance.

Imagination and Fancy was followed, in 1846, by *Wit and Humour*, in which Hunt once more turned his attention to the lighter vein in literature. Hunt begins by defining both wit and humor. He realizes, of course, that there are many definitions for *wit*, but he is applying the term chiefly in its relation to humor. He defines wit as

the Arbitrary juxtaposition of Dissimilar Ideas, for some lively purpose of Assimilation or Contrast, generally of both. It is fancy in its most wilful, and strictly speaking, its least poetical state; that is to say, Wit does not contemplate its ideas for their own sakes in any light apart from their ordinary practical one, but solely for the purpose of producing an effect by their combination.[24]

Humor, on the other hand, is

a tendency of the mind to run in particular directions of thought or feeling more amusing than accountable. . . . . It deals in incongruities of character and circumstance, as Wit does in those of arbitrary ideas. The more the incongruities the better, provided they are all in nature; but two, at any rate, are as necessary to Humor, as the two ideas are to Wit; and the more strikingly they differ yet harmonize, the more amusing the result. Such is the melting together of the propensities to love and war in the person of exquisite Uncle Toby; of the gullible and the manly in Parson Adams; of the professional and individual, or the accidental and the permanent, in the Canterbury Pilgrims.[25]

The tendency of wit and humor, of course, is to coalesce, and it is by this combination that the richest effect is produced. Hunt then proceeds to illustrate the coalescence of wit and humor in selections from the works of Chaucer, Shakespeare, Jonson, Dryden, Pope, Swift, and Goldsmith, among others.

The selections from the poetry of Chaucer may be something of a disappointment for the modern reader. Because the nature of *Wit and Humour* was to provide an anthology of selections for a wide and varied audience, Hunt felt constrained to omit any passages which might be determined offensive by scrupulous readers. He states that he would like to have included more than one comic story, "but the change of manners renders it difficult at any time, and impossible in a book like the present."[26] There are five selections from the poetry of Chaucer. The first includes extracts from the "General Prologue," including the portraits of the Knight, Squire, Yeoman, Prioress, Monk, Clerk, Friar, Sergeant of the Law, and Shipman. The second selection is the "Friar's Tale," minus the words of the Host, Summoner, and Friar and the Friar's final words against the Summoner. The other selections are brief extracts which describe the Pardoner's manner of preaching, the Merchant's opinion of wives, and the Wife of Bath's explanation for the disappearance of the fairies.

By far the most interesting part of the section on Chaucer, however, are Hunt's prefatory remarks to the selections of poetry. In those remarks the characteristics of Chaucer's comic genius are discussed. Calling Chaucer's humor "entertaining, profound, and good-natured," Hunt comments on the nature of the Canterbury Pilgrims as artistic creations:

Classes must of course be drawn, more or less, from the individuals composing them; but the unprofessional particulars added by Chaucer to his characters (such as the Merchant's uneasy marriage, and the Franklin's prodigal son), are only such as render the portraits more true, by including them in the general category of human kind.[27]

Hunt's insistence that the Canterbury Pilgrims were more than simple stereotypes of certain classes of people is a rare remark in early nineteenth-century criticism of Chaucer. While other commentators saw the Pilgrims as perfect representatives of fourteenth-century society, Hunt perceived them as complex, masterfully delineated individuals, each having a distinctive personality.

Hunt's discrimination is further evidenced by his selection of the three qualities which he finds characteristic of Chaucer's humor. The first is "a certain tranquil detection of particulars, expressive of generals." This aspect is reflected in the Cook's infirmities, the Prioress's knowledge of French, and the lawyer who seemed busier than he was. The second characteristic is the poet's manner of describing the spiritual through the material. Hunt very aptly observes that the Miller is "as hardy and as coarse-grained as his conscience," and the Reeve "shaves his beard as closely as he reckons with his master's tenants."[28] The last of the characteristics is the poet's sense of fair play, his insidiousness without malice. Justice is accorded to good and bad, but even the worst characters "have some little saving grace of good-nature, or at least of joviality and candor."[29] Thus, the Pardoner is made to acknowledge his hypocrisy and the Clerk is shown to be somewhat stuffy and pedantic. Hunt also admires what he calls Chaucer's self-knowledge, the fact that the poet does not spare even himself in his description of the Pilgrims, but describes himself as fat and has the Host interrupt his tale. Though the prefatory comments are brief and to the point, they reflect an extraordinarily acute and discriminating appreciation of Chaucer's humor. Hunt's remarks reveal an understanding of Chaucer which may not have been exceeded by any other essayist of the period and which certainly was not so well illustrated.

The Preface to *Stories in Verse* (1855) contains the distillation of many of Hunt's observations on Chaucer and his poetry. It also contains, I think, some of Hunt's best criticism and a further indication of the depth of his admiration for Chaucer. He begins by recommending Chaucer to those who are not familiar with him, insisting that the difficulty of Chaucer's language can be overcome with a little study and can be as easily understood as most provincial dialects. Once again, Hunt calls Chaucer the greatest narrative poet in the language, adding that he is the very greatest in many things:

He is greatest in every respect, and in the most opposite qualifications; greatest in pathos; greatest in pleasantry, greatest in character, greatest in plot, greatest even in versification.[30]

Again, too, Hunt feels obliged to apologize for a distasteful and offensive element in Chaucer's poetry, passages which persons of thorough delicacy "will never read twice; for they were compliances with the licence" of the age. The great majority of his works, however, were characterized by "delicacies of every kind, of the noblest sentiment, of the purest, most various, and most profound entertainment."[31]

As in other instances, Hunt defends Chaucer's versification against the charge that it was ragged and that it was not harmonious. He maintains that Chaucer's verse is most harmonious and musical, that Chaucer studied French, Latin, and Italian meter, and that, indeed, Chaucer was a master of versification. Most interesting is Hunt's discussion of the musical nature of versification. Maintaining that proportions hold together, he insists that the poet who is "wanting in musical feeling where music is required, is in danger of being discordant and disproportionate in sentiment, of not perceiving the difference between thoughts worthy and unworthy of utterance."[32] His emphasis on the unity of sound and sense is reflected in his appreciation of Chaucer's verse. Throughout, he stresses the analogy between musical and poetical composition, adding that Chaucer would very much have liked Coleridge's "Christabel." An example Hunt provides to illustrate the unity of sound and sense is line 880 of the "Clerk's Tale," Griselda's plea, "Let me not like a worm go by the way." Calling it "one of the most imploring and affecting lines that ever were written," Hunt says that the line is "beautifully modulated," although not in the fashion of the "smooth couplet." Though it is not a short, lyric measure, it is highly musical. Particularly impressive to Hunt are the "masterly accents" and the emphasis on "worm."[33]

"Sense," to Hunt, should not be the only thing in poetry, the all in all. The best poetry combines passion, imagination, simple speaking, music, animal spirits, and "the true thinking which all sound feeling implies."[34] He adds that only Chaucer and Shakespeare have combined all of those qualities. An example of this combination of qualities is line 2273 of the "Knight's Tale," "Uprose the sun, and uprose Emily." By working his imagination upon these two simultaneously occurring matters of fact, Chaucer was able to create a line of "pure morning freshness, enthusiasm, and music." Hunt's habit of close reading is nowhere so well demonstrated, I think, as in his discussion of that single line. He observes that by implication the line contains both simile and analogy, but with a remarkable economy. Chaucer saw "the brightest of material creatures, and the beautifulest of human creatures" rise at the same time, and he was able to do justice to both by "repeating the accent on a repeated syllable, and dividing the *rhythm* into two equal parts, in order to leave nothing undone to show the merit on both sides."[35] In stressing the musical nature of poetry, Hunt was able to underscore the conception of the poet as singer and maker, calling the essence of poetry "geniality, singing." As the singer in whom imagination predominates, Chaucer is a poet of the highest order.

In the last year of his life, Hunt's attention was turned to a far less stylistic and theoretical consideration of Chaucer's poetry. In "English Poetry versus Cardinal Wiseman,"[36] an essay published posthumously in 1859, Hunt set about to defend the poetry of Chaucer and Spenser from charges made by Nicholas Patrick Stephen Cardinal Wiseman in "On the Perception of Natural Beauty," a lecture which had been delivered in 1855. Cardinal Wiseman had suggested in that lecture that the descriptions of natural beauty in the poetry of Chaucer and Spenser, especially in that of Spenser, were connected with wantonness, voluptuousness, and debauchery. Hunt, of course, felt that the charges were unfounded, and he proceeded to refute them with careful and well-chosen references to the poets' works.

To refute the charge against Chaucer, Hunt cites the two poems which were most admired in the early nineteenth century for their descriptions of nature – the *Flower and the Leaf* and the *Cuckoo and the Nightingale*. To be sure, they are both rich in description, but they have since been rejected from the Chaucer canon. The *Flower and the Leaf*, Hunt maintains, is "eminently chaste and reserved, and its moral is the triumph of manly and womanly virtue over idle dissipation."[37] The *Cuckoo and the Nightingale* is characterized by the same "spotless treatment, as well as sentiment."[38] The *Legend of Good Women*, the *Book of the Duchess*, and the "Knight's Tale" are similarly acquitted of wantonness, voluptuousness, and debauchery.

Hunt then proceeds to refute the spirit of the Cardinal's objections in other works of Chaucer. As he has done in other essays, Hunt concedes that there are passages, and in some cases entire poems, in Chaucer's poetry which are characterized by grossness and license, passages which "give pain to the most devoted of Chaucer's admirers, and are never re-perused by them but for some purpose of criticism by which they cannot be overlooked."[39] These Hunt once again attributes to the grossness of the age in which the poet lived, adding in this instance that the poet was of so uncircumscribed a nature as not to be intolerant of any social phase of his fellow creatures. It was not the poet's nature, he continues, to side with the coarse, the selfish, and the degrading, but to make them appear repulsive. Virtue is held in high regard and vice made to look ridiculous and disgusting. The reader of Hunt's essay is struck not only by that critic's broadmindedness, but by his awareness of Chaucer's moral vision, as well. Too many critics have been struck only by the licentiousness of a certain passage or work and have failed to perceive the poet's intent.

It is Hunt's belief that the Cardinal was less interested in attacking the wantonness of Chaucer's and Spenser's descriptive passages than insinuating Catholic associations and interests into the minds of the public. Certainly Hunt is unfair and unreasonably harsh in that judgment, but in his attempts to counter what he thinks to be the Cardinal's purpose, Hunt does make some astute observations on Chaucer's less attractive ecclesiastical figures. He comments on the Prioress's brooch, which bears the motto *Amor vincit omnia*, insisting that the motto may be taken in its ordinary rather than in its religious sense. The Monk's worldliness and contempt for canon law are illustrated. The Friar's wanton nature is remarked, as is his greed. The Summoner and Pardoner are noted as being covetous, and the Pardoner's duplicity is highlighted. Hunt's views, if anything, seem harsher than the poet's:

Money-making and love-making, the gurgling of decanters, the smell of good dishes, jollity of person, after-dinner tendencies of discourse, and other indications of "wantonness, voluptuousness, and debauchery," attend the clergy in Chaucer, wherever they appear, almost without exception.[40]

Hunt makes no mention here of the Parson, whose goodness is beyond question. A striking example of the best of the clergy would not have suited his refutation of Cardinal Wiseman. One may surely insist that this, Hunt's last essay, is marred by the author's attempts to discredit the Cardinal and the Roman Catholic Church. Had the author limited himself to literary criticism, his readers might have been more pleased. It seems a pity that perhaps the best of the early nineteenth-century critics on Chaucer should conclude on a defensive and rather belligerent note his commentary on the poet he so greatly admired.

In his copious and astute critical comments on Chaucer, Hunt initiated a kind of technical analysis of Chaucer's writings. He was one of the first to attempt an analysis of irony, humor and narrative techniques, and to associate poetry with the idea of music. His admiration of Chaucer is seen in his appreciation of the poet's comic skills, satire of ecclesiastical abuses and subtle strokes of irony and in his realization that Chaucer excelled in serious and tragic poetry as well. Hunt's literary criticism of Chaucer contributed to the Romantic conception of Chaucer the poet and in a wider sense provides a valuable insight into the history of medievalism in the nineteenth century.

NOTES

1. Caroline F. E. Spurgeon, *Five Hundred Years of Chaucer Criticism and Allusion, 1357–1900*, 3 vols. (Cambridge, 1925), I, p. lxv. It is not the purpose of this article to collect or revise allusions to Chaucer, a task already superbly, though inevitably selectively, performed by Miss Spurgeon. See also William L. Anderson and Arnold C. Henderson, *Chaucer and Augustan Scholarship* (Berkeley: University of California Press, 1970). On the significance of Chaucer's apocryphal works in the Romantic era, see Francis W. Bonner, "Chaucer's Reputation During the Romantic Period," *Furman Studies*, 34 (1951), pp. 1–21. In the preparation and submission of this article, I am indebted to J. Davis for information and help.
2. For an extensive study of Hunt's translations of Chaucer, see Minotte McIntosh Chatfield, "Chaucer Translation in the Romantic Era" (unpublished Ph.D. dissertation, Lehigh University, 1961), pp. 500–82.
3. "Leigh Hunt as a Man of Letters," in *Leigh Hunt's Literary Criticism*, eds. Lawrence Huston Houtchens and Carolyn Washburn Houtchens (New York, 1956), p. 14.
4. *The Seer*, 2 vols. (Boston, 1864), II, p. 160.
5. *The Poetical Works of Leigh Hunt*, ed. H. S. Milford (Oxford University Press, 1923), p. 269.
6. *The Indicator*, 2 vols. (New York, 1845), I, p. 169.
7. "Spring and Daisies," in *The Indicator*, I, p. 192.
8. "A Few Thoughts on Sleep," in *The Indicator*, I, pp. 119–20.
9. *The Indicator*, I, p. 204.
10. *The Essays of Leigh Hunt*, ed. Arthur Symons (New York, 1903), p. 138.
11. Thorpe, "Hunt as Man of Letters," p. 23.
12. "Specimens of Chaucer," in *The Seer*, I, p. 11.

13. *Ibid.*, pp. 212–13.
14. *Ibid.*, p. 220.
15. *Ibid.*, p. 233.
16. *Ibid.*, p. 243.
17. *Imagination and Fancy* (New York, 1845), p. viii.
18. *Ibid.*, p. 4.
19. *Ibid.*, p. 20.
20. *Ibid.*
21. *Ibid.*, pp. 21–22.
22. *Ibid.*, p. 23.
23. *Ibid.*, p. 11.
24. *Wit and Humour, Selected from the English Poets* (New York, 1847), p. 6.
25. *Ibid.*, p. 8.
26. *Ibid.*, p. 50.
27. *Ibid.*, p. 51.
28. *Ibid.*, p. 52.
29. *Ibid.*
30. Preface to *Stories in Verse*, in *Leigh Hunt's Literary Criticism*, p. 587.
31. *Ibid.*, p. 588.
32. *Ibid.*, p. 591.
33. *Ibid.*, p. 594.
34. *Ibid.*, p. 596.
35. *Ibid.*, p. 598.
36. *Fraser's Magazine*, LX (December, 1859), 747–66.
37. *Ibid.*, 750.
38. *Ibid.*
39. *Ibid.*, 751.
40. *Ibid.*, 761.

Malory's "Tale of Sir Tristram":

Source and Setting Reconsidered

DHIRA B. MAHONEY

Scholarly opinion has long been severe on the section of Malory's *Morte Darthur* which has been known since Eugène Vinaver's edition of the Winchester MS as Book 5 or the "Tale of Sir Tristram."[1] Critical attitudes range from a benign neglect of the Tale, as if in tacit agreement that it is only a rather tiresome digression from the main Arthurian story – "largely irrelevant," as E. K. Chambers put it[2] – to outright condemnation. Thomas C. Rumble introduces his chapter on the Tale in *Malory's Originality* with an impressive array of such indictments, which he proceeds to refute; but his study and Donald G. Schueler's article on the "Tristram" (both of which I shall discuss later) have, until recently, been the only serious reconsiderations of the Tale as a whole.[3] Now further remedy has been provided by Larry D. Benson in his recent book on the *Morte Darthur*, which counters criticisms of the Tale's disorganized prolixity by demonstrating its "solidly coherent, even elegant, thematic structure."[4]

Benson is not interested, however, in studying in detail Malory's source for the Tale or his treatment of it, for his chief purpose is to put Malory back into the context of fifteenth-century culture and English romance tradition (p. viii). Many critics have suggested that the faults of the "Tristram" were really due to its source; as Chambers said, "the prose *Tristan* was the worst of models."[5] Benson recognizes that Malory might have been attracted to the history of Tristan for "the image of chivalry embodied in his career" (p. 115), and asserts that the principal theme of the "Tale of Sir Tristram" is Trystram's "attainment of full knighthood as one of the four best knights in the world" (p. 116). I do not quarrel with the essence of Benson's statements, but find them incomplete: the theme of the "Tristram" is not just the attainment of knighthood but the pursuit of "worship" gained by fighting, and the bond of fellowship that develops among those who achieve it. In his earlier discussion of Malory Benson suggested that the English knight's method of handling his sources was dictated by his desire to " 'anglicize' them, to adapt them to the forms and conventions he admired in English romance,"[6] and in his recent study Benson demonstrates those conventions convincingly. However, he is, I believe, ignoring a vital dimension of that "anglicizing" process – the heritage of the alliterative revival. One of those admired English romances is the alliterative *Morte Arthure*, which Malory used as his source for Book 2, the "Tale of Arthur and Lucius." The alliterative *Morte* differs from the other English romances Malory might have known by its demonstrably heroic spirit, which is transmitted, slightly diluted but still characteristic, into Malory's Book 2, from where it subtly pervades the whole work. Vinaver points out that Malory's familiarity with this native epic may well have shaped and colored his concept of Arthurian knighthood as a whole (*Works*, p. lvii). It is certainly in the light of this heroic spirit that his choice of the *Tristan* as a source and his consistent modifications of it are best illuminated; this paper will consider some of these modifications in that light, and, as a corollary, the function of the Tale in the *Morte Darthur* as a whole.[7]

The term "heroic" may need further definition. Malory departs most obviously from his source when he ends the "Tristram" on a note of harmony and joy with the welcome of Palomydes into the Round Table, while the news of Trystram's death is suppressed for nearly two whole Tales. It might seem inappropriate to call such a conclusion "heroic." However, the heroic spirit is a coin with two faces: the joy and cohesiveness of the "Conclusion" of the "Tristram" is but the positive and celebratory face; the reverse has tragic potential which is only fully realized in the last Tale of the *Morte Darthur*. Benson characterizes the final movement of the work as an "interweaving" of two kinds of narrative, the historical tragic narrative and the thematic "comic" one (p. 209); I prefer to describe it as a modulation to the tragic which has always been implicit in the heroic mode. In the "Tristram" both comic and tragic potentialities co-exist.

Malory's source, the Second Version of the prose *Tristan*, was not part of the great early-thirteenth-century cycle called the Vulgate, which provided the sources for four other Tales, but dated probably from the second half of the century.[8] This version of the Tristan legend was far removed from the bittersweet, delicate narrative of the original poetic form as in Béroul or Eilhart, or even the more courtly versions of Thomas and Gottfried von Strassburg. In the prose romance the center of interest had shifted from the moral complexities of the love affair to Tristan's progress as a "chevalier errant," the first climax of which is reached when he is solemnly received at the court of Artus and made a knight of the Table Ronde. Whereas in the poems the death of the lovers is an inevitable result of their unlawful love,[9] in most versions of the prose romance Tristan's death is caused by the treachery of Marc, who stabs him from behind while he is harping to Yseult, and the context of his death is predominantly chivalric. Yseult is called to his deathbed, but before she dies in his death embrace, Tristan kisses his sword and arms and entrusts them to Saigremor, taking a formal leave of chivalry: "desormais comant a Deu toute chevalerie. Ormés preing je a lui conjé; molt l'aime et honore. . . ." When the news is brought to Artus, the court is plunged into terrible despair: Lancelot laments, "puis que li bons Tristan est mort, toute chevalerie est morte."[10]

Such a chivalric atmosphere must clearly have attracted Malory. Sir Walter Scott suggested a further source of attraction when he commented on "those eternal combats, to which, perhaps, the work owed its original popularity."[11] It was certainly popular, as witnessed by seventy-eight extant MSS and fragments in French, translations and adaptations in Italian, Spanish, Portuguese, Danish, German, and Russian, and nine printings between 1489 and 1533.[12] It was probably a close rival to the *Lancelot* in later medieval times. The combats must also have been to Malory's taste, for, though his version is some six times shorter and a great deal more simplified than his source (*Works*, p. 1443), it is still remarkably full of them; indeed, the Tale resounds with the joy of fighting. A cursory survey alone reveals three major tournaments, nine smaller tournaments or jousts, individual quests, fights in fulfillment of a vow, and single combats for judicial or political reasons. There are also four individual combats of thematic importance, which I shall discuss later, and any number of chance encounters, challenges in the forest, fights with and rescues from the ubiquitous sir Brewnys Saunz Pité, fights undertaken by both Trystram and Launcelot in their madness, and fights during the establishment of the Sangreal. They are essential to the texture of the Tale.

In his treatment of the combats, however, Malory shows a different emphasis from his source. As Maria Rosa Lida de Malkiel has shown, the pursuit of glory was a theme common to the greater part of medieval romances of chivalry: "la renommée est ressentie comme la fin première et naturelle de la chevalerie."[13] The prose *Tristan* was no exception. However, in the French courtly romances "chevalerie" is inseparable from "cortoisie," and "cortoisie" is as much an attribute of love as of fighting. In this aspect Malory is less interested. Take, for instance, his treatment of the great battle between Tristan and Lancelot. In the *Suite du Merlin*, a romance which dates from before the Second Version of the prose *Tristan*,[14] Merlin inscribes on the tomb of Launceor and Columbe: "en ceste place assambleront a bataille li dui plus loial amant que a lour tans soient" (*Works*, pp. 1308–9). The two most loyal lovers are Tristan and Lancelot, and the prophecy is fulfilled in the *Tristan* when they meet in battle by mistake. Though on this occasion the prophecy itself is not repeated, the tradition is clearly recalled: the stone where they meet is called the "perron merlyn" (B.N. 334, f. 298b), and when the two knights finally discover each other's identity they embrace and sit down to discourse on love (*Works*, p. 1484).

Malory's focus is subtly but fundamentally different. The *Suite du Merlin* is his source for Book 1, the "Tale of King Arthur," and his Merlyne renders the prophecy thus:

"Here shall be," seyde Merlion, "in this same place the grettist bateyle betwyxte two knyghtes that ever was or ever shall be, and the trewyst lovers; and yette none of hem shall slee other."

(72.5–8)

And in the "Tristram," before the event itself, the narrator recalls the prophecy:

And at that tyme Merlyon profecied that in that same place sholde fyght two the beste knyghtes that ever were in kynge Arthurs dayes, and two of the beste lovers.

(568.18–20)

Thus, where the French tradition designated the two knights as lovers, Malory has shifted the emphasis to their prowess as fighters: it is here that their source of fascination lies.

Even more revealing is his treatment of another incident in the *Tristan*. During the tournament of Lonezep Launcelot and Arthur ride out in disguise to catch a glimpse of Isode, who is accompanied by Trystram and Palomydes. Arthur, who has not seen Isode before, is struck by her beauty and gazes at her so long that Palomydes takes offense and knocks him off his horse. Launcelot is then in a dilemma: his duty is to avenge Arthur and unhorse Palomydes, but this will bring him into conflict with Trystram, his friend. He knocks down Palomydes, but calls out to Trystram:

. . . I am lothe to have ado wyth you and I myght chose, for I woll that ye wyte that I muste revenge my speciall lorde and my moste bedrad frynde that was unhorsed unwarely and unknyghtly. And therefore, sir, thoughe I revenge that falle, take ye no displesure, for he is to me suche a frynde that I may nat se hym shamed.

(744.23–9)

Not only is this speech subtly different from the source, where Lancelot explains his attack on Palamedes thus: "se je labaty fait lancelot ce ne fu mie sans raison Car il abaty par son oultrage un mien chier amy qui icy est" (B.N. 99, f. 479d), but terms equivalent to "moste bedrad frynde" could not be found in a French courtly romance. (Significantly, Caxton also excises the phrase in his edition, just as he tones down the heroic flavor of Book 2.) The position of Malory's Arthur in relation to his followers is closer in spirit to that of the "seigneur" of *chanson de geste* or the "wine-dryhten" of Anglo-Saxon poetry than the more formal, technical, feudal relationship of the French. Indeed, in Book 1 he is called a "chyfftayne" (54.19); his knights owe him a direct and personal obligation.

Whereas the French Lancelot has been concerned more with his own honor, fearing that if he failed to avenge Artus "len ly pourroit atourner a grant honte et a trahison et a trop grant laschete de cuer" (f. 479c), Malory's Launcelot is torn between his friendship with Trystram and his unstated obligation to Arthur (744.6–11). The French Tristan ponders on the phrase "un mien chier amy," but does not guess Artus's identity; and he asks Palamedes solicitously how he is, for in his view there is nothing reprehensible in defending the Queen of Cornwall from impudent knights. Malory's Trystram guesses the truth from Launcelot's hint and proceeds to rebuke Palomydes severely for his unknightly deed against "my lorde kynge Arthure, for all knyghtes may lerne to be a knyght of hym" (745.28–9). The essentially courtly episode of the source has been given a different *sen* by the alteration of a few details.

There is, indeed, a fundamental difference in outlook between Malory's work and his sources. Where in the French an old knight releases Tristan, his prisoner, less for love of him than "pour l'onneur de chevalerie mettre en avant" (*Works*, p. 1481), the corresponding character in Malory acts because he has appreciated that Trystram could not have helped killing two of his sons at a tournament: " 'All thys I consider,' seyde sir Darras, 'that all that ye ded was by fors of knyghthode' " (552.24–5). "Fors of knyghthode" is Malory's own singular phrase, and Trystram's compulsion to act by it his own concept. In the prose *Tristan* characters may expound on "cortoisie," "frankise," "onneur," make vows to or take action for the sake of "chevalerie," and so on; but these are abstract concepts, existing outside and independent of the knights who may exemplify them from time to time. The desire for fame that impels Malory's knights is more urgent, tense and personal. It is the individual knight's own reputation that concerns him, his "worshyp." "Worshyp" is an old word: the *OED* records "weorðscipe" as first occurring in Alfred's translation of Boethius, c. 888, and the Old English form shows its meaning more clearly. To gloss it as "honor" is inadequate; it is, rather, worth-ship, a man's total self-concept, measured by what is said and known about him, publicly recognized.

Mark Lambert in his recent study, and D. S. Brewer before him, have demonstrated the importance of public recognition of worth in the *Morte Darthur*. Indeed, Lambert shows that Launcelot's behavior in the last two Tales makes sense when he is viewed as acting within a shame system rather than a guilt system: "in the imagined world of Sir Lancelot, where one's official, social identity is one's real identity, shame is more significant."[15] In the Malorian world it is the public concept of self that directs action; values are externally apprehended. Public identity is defined in "name," a term equivalent to "worshyp" in the Malorian vocabulary, as demonstrated by Arthur's rallying cry in Book 2: "Fayre lordys, loke youre name be nat loste! Lese nat youre worshyp for yondir bare-legged knavys" (221.4–6). I need hardly repeat that the source for Book 2, the "Tale of Arthur and Lucius," is the alliterative *Morte Arthure:* it is predominantly from the heroic alliterative tradition that Malory's terminology comes. The chivalric preoccupations derived from his French sources were tempered by his long familiarity with native alliterative poetry[16] and the elements of Germanic heroic tradition still retained by it. In this context Thomas Greene's remarks in his paper "The Norms of Epic" are illuminating:

> A man's name is very important in heroic poetry; it becomes equal to the sum of his accomplishments. It is always assumed that a man's action is knowable and is known, and is known to be *his*. . . . It is important that every combatant who is killed in the *Iliad* have a name, for the name is an index to the victor's accomplishment. A hero wears his victims' names like scalps and his own name is aggrandized by theirs.[17]

Thus the distinction between "name" as identity and "name" as reputation becomes so fine as to be almost nonexistent. A knight's name is not only the formula that identifies himself and his lineage, but the formula that conjures up for the hearer all his known achievements. As Vinaver has shown from the first, one of Malory's chief divergences from his French sources is his practice of naming characters left anonymous in the French, or refusing to delay their identification.[18]

The desire for worship is the desire for a name, and the knight's life is devoted to informing that name with meaning: "hit ys oure kynde to haunte armys and noble dedys," says young Percyvale when his mother begs him to stay at home (810.6–7, not in *F*). Similarly, witnesses to those noble deeds are necessary. Throughout the early Tales defeated or rescued knights come to "bear recorde" to the exploits of the hero of their respective adventures (e.g., 286.25–36); indeed, Malory sends them to court when his source does not (104.16–17, 175.5–8, 178.31–3). Worship cannot exist in isolation; name has meaning only in the context of one's peers. It is measured by what they say: "tyll men speke of me ryght grete worship" (132.11–12); "I pray you . . . force yourselff there, that men may speke you worshyp" (1103.19–20); "I woll never se that courte tylle men speke more worshyp of me than ever they ded of ony of them bothe" (814.24–6). It is precarious, fragile; and it needs constantly to be maintained, as Isode recognizes when she objects to Trystram staying away for her sake from the great feast and tournament at Pentecost: "ye that ar called one of the nobelyste knyghtys of the worlde and a knyght of the Rounde Table, how may ye be myssed at that feste?" (839.31–3).

We confirm that the concept of self expressed in Malory's work owes much to his heroic alliterative source when we recognize that the "boste" or "avaunte" in the *Morte Darthur* is more than merely swagger or self-advertisement. In Book 2, the "Tale of Arthur and Lucius," when Gawayne is accused of not being able to back up his "boste," his answer is to cut off his taunter's head, even though the Arthurian party is totally outnumbered in an enemy camp (207.20–7). The incident recalls an OE "beot." Though ME *boste* and OE *beot* do not seem to be etymologically related, they are both clearly used in the same way,[19] and it is instructive to turn to OE scholarship to explain the concept. The warrior who makes a *beot* is making an oath, dedicating himself to some promised action. In his study of the covenant in Anglo-Saxon thought, Father Zacharias Thundyil has demonstrated that such an oath in the ancient world implied a self-imprecation, a curse of self, if the promised action were not fulfilled.[20] The result would be shame, not only to the self, but to kin also; the man who was dishonored dragged his race down with him. Later in Book 2 Arthur rebukes Launcelot for having persevered in battle when heavily outnumbered, and is in turn rebuked by Launcelot:

"Not so," sayde sir Launcelot, "the shame sholde ever have bene oures."
"That is trouthe," seyde sir Clegis and sir Bors, "for knyghtes ons shamed recoverys hit never."

(217.28–218.2)

Whereas the incident of Gawayne's embassage is closely translated from the *Morte Arthure*, the quotation above is original to Malory. Not only does he transmit, but he accentuates the heroic flavor of his source.

Father Thundyil has shown that the covenant state or relationship did not only exist among kinsmen, but was "a kind of brotherhood which was an extension of blood-brotherhood or natural kinship" (p. 3). In Germanic society the health of such a brotherhood depended on internal love and harmony, of *friỡ*, and mutual fidelity, or *triuwe* (see pp. 55–66). In Malory's work the *comitatus* of Germanic literary tradition has become a more fluid kind of brotherhood, but one whose roots are still recognizable. The rules by which the state of harmony is maintained in the Arthurian brotherhood may never be verbalized, yet all know when they are transgressed. To break that state of harmony is treachery, and "traytoure" is one of the most frequent terms of abuse in the *Morte Darthur*, surfacing in the last Tale as a formal charge that must be answered in public combat (1215.7–1216.6). Similarly, the loyalty which held the *comitatus* together has been transmuted into an emotion equally forceful, if less restricted, a bond which may even override the most fundamental tie, the tie of blood, as we see in the love of Gareth for Launcelot, who made him knight. The most evocative word in the *Morte Darthur* is "felyshyp": it denotes the compelling attraction between great knights, the centripetal pull which draws the great together and the less toward the great in admiration. The chief center of attraction is naturally the place where the great can "infelyshyp," the glorious Arthurian court, which draws all to it like a beacon. When Arthur hears of a particularly noble knight, he longs to make him a knight of the Round Table, for his glory is increased by theirs, and they glow as jewels in his crown.

The strength of this centripetal pull between the great names of the Arthurian world is revealed in the public occasions, the great tournaments.

There are three major tournaments in the "Tale of Sir Tristram," contests which last for several days, and for which the contestants may come from far afield. The atmosphere of excitement that is generated before one of them is like that of the Olympic Games: much of the interest lies in getting a sense of who has come, identifying the great names. On the day before the tournament opens at the Castle of Maidens, for example, Trystram and Persydes stand before a bay window, watching the knights riding to and fro. When Trystram hears that one of them, Palomydes, has smitten down thirty knights, he cannot bear to miss the action: "Now, fayre brother . . . lat us caste on us lyght clokys, and lat us go se that play" (515.5–7).

Similarly, before Lonezep, many days elapse as kings and knights and nobles gather from many realms. Trystram, Palomydes, Dynadan, and Gareth ride together toward the castle and marvel at the great "ordynaunce" of four hundred tents and pavilions; but, characteristically, the conversation reminds them of previous tournaments, and those who won worship at them (698.3–18). The great contests of the past are remembered and create resonances through the Tale.

It is minor events, however, that show most clearly how Malory's source modifications consistently emphasize the cohesive aspects of fellowship, particularly in certain details that have escaped Vinaver's otherwise extensive commentary. In the "Tristram" the extension of the field of action beyond the Round Table proper displays the centripetal bond of attraction between great knights in its most fluid, yet powerful state. When Trystram, the young Cornish knight, having returned from his first visit to Ireland, goes out to rescue Segwarydes's wife after her abduction from king Mark's court, he encounters two "lykly" knights of the Round Table, sir Sagramoure le Desyrous and sir Dodynas le Savyayge (398.6–10). Governayle warns him that they are both proved knights, but Trystram is eager for a fight: "As for that . . . have ye no doute but I woll have ado with them bothe to encrece my worshyp, for hit is many day sytthen I dud any armys" (398.14–16). His challenge is accepted, and the two proved knights are defeated by the young Cornish knight whom they had mocked. But when they learn his name they are delighted: "Than were they two knyghtes fayne that they had mette with sir Trystrames, and so they prayde hym to abyde in their felyshyp" (399.28–30).

Though the incident is minor, it is useful, for comparison with the source episode shows differences which Vinaver does not note. In B.N. 103, Tristan does not mention that he is spoiling for a fight, but is more tactical:

Maitre dit tristan . se ils sont preudommes tant vault mieulx Et se ilz sont tielz comme vous dictes ilz ne masaudront pas tous ensemble mais chascun par soy . Et puis quil nen vendra que lun corps a corps contre moy le mencheviray bien.

(f. 47d; Curtis, § 383)

After the fight, when Saigremor learns that he and his companion have been defeated by one of the despised Cornish knights, his reaction is not delight but chagrin. He declares that he will never be able to carry arms after the court has learned the truth, and that rather than be deprived of them by a judgment of the court, he will forswear them himself (f. 48b; Curtis, § 385).

Two other battles further demonstrate the strength of mutual knightly attraction. First is the chance encounter between Trystram and Lameroke in the Forest Perilous. In the source, B.N. 103, Tristan and Lamourat, having fought for some time, pause for breath, and, following chivalric etiquette, ask each other's name. Hearing that he has been fighting the knight who sent the magic horn to Marc's court to dishonor Yseult, Tristan challenges Lamourat to further combat, and Lamourat defies him to do his worst. However, their "cortoisie" prevents them from actually fighting again; Lamourat agrees to surrender to Tristan, and Tristan admits that he had challenged Lamourat the second time only to test his "orgeuil" (f. 109a,b). Malory's version of the encounter has a significant alteration. When Trystram and Lameroke challenge each other to further battle, the challenge is taken up and they fight till they are weary of each other:

> Than sir Trystrams seyde unto sir Lamorak,
> "In all my lyff mette I never with such a knyght that was so bygge and so well-brethed. Therefore," sayde sir Trystramys, "hit were pité that ony of us bothe sholde here be myscheved."
> "Sir," seyde sir Lamerok, "for youre renowne and your name I woll that ye have the worship. . . ."

> (483.14–20)

Vinaver's note here is confusing, for he implies that the knights' dialogue is "interrupted" by their "laysshing" at each other (*Works*, p. 1469), whereas in fact the dialogue has led to a second and sourceless combat. Though the scene ends with the same sense of reconciliation, Malory has changed its central motivation. His knights swear friendship like their French counterparts, but it is admiration for each other's fighting prowess, not their "cortoisie," which has prompted it.

The second battle takes place later in the Tale. Palomydes and Dynadan have decided to fight the knights of Morgan's castle because of their shameful "custom," but are forestalled by a strange knight with a red shield who asks their leave to take on the task. When this stranger has overcome three knights in succession, Palomydes offers to help, but is rejected. The stranger overcomes two more opponents, and again Palomydes begs to joust, suggesting that the red knight needs rest. The latter takes this as an aspersion on his stamina, and challenges Palomydes, unhorsing both him and Dynadan before returning to his task to defeat another seven of the castle knights. Narrative comment is always sparse in Malory, but reference to the source confirms the suggestion of his text that Palomydes is motivated not only by a genuine desire to help a brave knight, but also by annoyance that the stranger is hogging all the fighting. He accepts the red knight's challenge eagerly, and when unhorsed is so angry that he follows the stranger to demand a return battle in spite of the latter's weariness. They fight mightily on foot, until Palomydes grows faint from his earlier wound, and requires his opponent's name, as they have "assayed ayther other passyngly well" (602.12); when he hears that it is Lameroke, for so it is, he is overcome at his unknightly behavior in forcing a further fight on a weary man. He begs Lameroke's pardon, and they swear a lasting friendship. The account is much compressed from the source, but Malory's most important change is in leaving out the French Dinadan's mockery at these sudden changes of the combatants' moods: "voirement font il tout ausint comme les enfanz . qui legierement se couroucent et legierement se racordent" (B.N. 334, f. 326c). As Vinaver has pointed out, Malory frequently draws Dinadan's sting by deleting or shortening his antichivalric speeches (*Works*, pp. 1447–8). In Malory's work the battles and friendships are neither arbitrary nor motiveless. The compulsion of his Arthurian knight is always to test himself against his peers, and when he has met a worthy opponent, to forge a bond of brotherhood. As the King with a Hundred Knights comments on the tournament field, "evermore o good knyght woll favoure another, and lyke woll draw to lyke" (527.5–7).

To decide on the function of the "Tale of Sir Tristram" in the *Morte Darthur* as a whole requires, first, a definition of its major theme. Subtitling his study of the Tale "Development by Analogy," Thomas Rumble was the first critic to recognize a significance in the parallel between the stories of Trystram and Launcelot: "these similarities of incident and episode reinforce each other" (p. 182). However, what they emphasize is, in his view, the adulterous nature of both knights' love affairs; thus the relationship between Trystram and Isode becomes "symbolic of the moral degeneration to which the potentially perfect world of Arthur's realm is so inevitably being brought" (p. 181). But Malory does not stress the adultery. In fact, he cuts almost all of the stratagems which the French lovers Tristan and Yseult employ in order to meet or to escape discovery (Löseth, §§ 48–51). Far from exploiting it as a moral omen, he seems to have forgotten it altogether by the end of the Tale, representing his lovers living in comfortable domesticity in Joyous Garde.

Rumble's contention has been attacked by Vinaver (*Works*, p. 1446), and, more recently, by Donald G. Schueler, who argues that the parallel between Trystram and Launcelot serves rather to emphasize the difference between them, and Trystram's independence from Arthur's court: "Tristram has no significance larger than himself; he is ever the aimlessly wandering knight-errant of chivalry in its decline. Lancelot, on the other hand, is the archetype of Arthur's ideal fellowship, the heroic right arm of a heroic king" (pp. 65–6). Schueler's contention does not allow, though, for the extent to which Trystram and Launcelot are balanced in worship throughout the Tale, their names almost interchangeable as measures of greatness (e.g., 388.29–32, 487.16–17). Whereas the source, on the whole, presents Tristan as the better knight (see *Works*, p. 1486, n. to 578.4), Malory will never allow it: he goes out of his way to establish the equality of their prowess, even interrupting the account of a combat to do it:

(Than was sir Trystrames called the strengyst knyght of the worlde, for he was called bygger than sir Launcelotte, but sir Launcelot was bettir brethid.)

(415.31–3)

During Lonezep Malory inserts a whole narrative passage of praise for Launcelot and Trystram (742.23–33), where in the source all the members of the house of Artus are praising Palamedes: "tout le loz et tout le pris donnent a palamedes . ilz ne parlent fors de luy" (B.N. 99, f. 478c). Similarly Ector's speech urging Launcelot to return to court after his exile as Le Shyvalere Mafete has even less authority from the source:

. . . ye muste remembir the grete worshyp and renowne that ye be off, how that ye have bene more spokyn of than ony othir knyght that ys now lyvynge; for there ys none that beryth the name now but ye and sir Trystram.

(831.26–30)

In B.N. 99, f. 546a, b, Hector merely assures Lancelot that the Queen desires his return.[21]

Therefore, although his interpretation of the purpose of the analogy is misguided, Rumble's stress on the similarity between the two knights seems to be more faithful to Malory's text. The French romance operates against a vaster, more populated canvas; by excising many rival knights and reducing the roles of others,[22] Malory narrows the focus to Trystram and Launcelot. Indeed, the events of the Tale are balanced around these twin presiding genii, though Vinaver's sometimes arbitrary narrative divisions slightly obscure the architecture.[23] The long section that establishes Trystram's fame is counterweighted by the long section of Launcelot and Elayne, and the love madness of one knight echoes the other's, even to the extent of the addition by Malory of a sourceless scene when Trystram is recognized in the garden by his hound, paralleling Launcelot's recognition by Elayne (*Works*, p. 1473, and *Malory*, pp. 40–1). The three great tournaments are also carefully distinguished: at the Castle of Maidens Trystram wins the *gre* on two days, though his wound prevents his winning on the third; at Surluse (while Trystram is in Cornwall), Gwenyver presides, and Launcelot and Lameroke win the *gre;* at Lonezep Isode presides, for Gwenyver is ill, and Palomydes wins the first day, Trystram the second, and Trystram and Launcelot share the prize for the third day. Even the minor characters revolve in association with one or the other, drawing the almost independent stories of La Cote Male Tayle and Alysaundir le Orphelyne into the pattern.

Benson's recent study has shown that the parallel between Trystram and Launcelot is thematically essential, informing the entire Tale (p. 122), and he examines its "elegant structure" with perception and insight. Each quest of a subordinate knight, he points out, "by parallel or contrast helps define the quest in which Tristram is engaged and, by the very multiplicity of perspectives, helps us to recognize that the real subject of this book is not Tristram's quest but knighthood itself" (p. 133). The explanation of the process is brilliant, but the conclusion drawn from it needs qualification. The subject of the Tale is not knighthood in a chivalric context, as Benson assumes, but rather knighthood in a heroic one. Benson demonstrates convincingly that fifteenth-century aristocratic preoccupations with chivalry explain why Malory chose to write a chivalric work (Chs. 7 and 8), but it does not necessarily follow that the concerns of Malory's work are therefore identical with those of his real life contemporaries. No king of Malory's day was likely to be called a "chyfftayne," as Arthur is (54.19). Throughout his work Malory looks back to an earlier day, "at that tyme" (287.24), "in tho dayes" (1055.12). His Arthurian world is a fictional construct, a heroic world in which cohesiveness and harmony depend on the achievement of "name" and the recognition and reward of loyalty. A brief scrutiny of the first six sections of the Tale, for instance, will demonstrate that Trystram builds up his "name" in a traditional heroic manner before he can be welcomed into Arthur's court.

Trystram's first victory, over Marhalte, gives him the right to wear his opponent's shield (383.7–10, not in *F*). His second victory is over Palomydes at the Irish tournament, and by the time he returns to Cornwall both triumphs are part of his "name":

"Truly," seyde sir Bleoberys, "I am ryght glad of you, for ye ar he that slewe Marhalte the knyght honde for honde in the ilonde for the trwayge of Cornwayle. Also ye overcom sir Palomydes, the good knyght, at the turnemente in Irelonde where he bete sir Gawayne and his nine felowys."

(401.5–9)

Similarly, when Trystram fights on behalf of king Anguyssh at his treason trial, the judges and spectators are equally delighted with his "name" (408.13–19), whereas in the source episode Tristan is still incognito.[24] When Trystram is caught in bed with Isode, and delivered to his judgment by Andret, the victory over Marhalte is still a vital element of his "name." Trystram appeals to the Cornish lords to remember what he has done for their country, and Andret's answer, "For all thy boste thou shalt dye this day" (431.24–5), confirms that a "boste" in Malory's Arthurian world is still a *beot*, an account of past deeds and worth-ship.

Stages in Trystram's early career are marked by such metaphorical signposts, as he sums up his past exploits and dedicates himself to a new task. Shipwrecked on the Ile of Servayge, for instance, he is told of the perils of the valley, and answers:

Wete you well, fayre lady . . . that I slewe sir Marhalte and delyverde Cornwayle frome the trewage of Irelonde. And I am he that delyverde the kynge of Irelonde frome sir Blamoure de Ganys, and I am he that bete sir Palomydes, and wete you welle that I am sir Trystrames de Lyones that by the grace of God shall delyver this wofull Ile of Servage.

(442.17-23)

It is Malory who has turned this speech and the one answered by Andret into *beots:* in the source both are delivered by other speakers (*Works*, pp. 1464-5).[25] The most elaborate *beot* is that made by Trystram when exiled from Cornwall for ten years by Mark and his barons: the short speech of justification in the source (*Works*, p. 1475) is expanded and elaborated into a long, formal, reproachful lament, enumerating all the exploits done and dangers endured for Mark and his country, building up on a refrain to its climax: "And at that tyme kynge Marke seyde afore all hys barownes I sholde have bene bettir rewarded" (503.25-504.15).

Once in the realm of Logres the need for self-justification seems to disappear. However, as Trystram's reputation mounts, so does king Arthur's desire to draw him into the Round Table fellowship, and, at the same time, Launcelot's desire to meet him. Trystram and Launcelot were first excited to admiration by accounts of each other's exploits, and long before they meet they express that admiration in loving terms (e.g., 418.9-11, 435.14-16). One of the main narrative threads in the first six sections of the Tale is this compulsion of Trystram and Launcelot to "infelyshyp," and suspense is created by their repeated failures. When on the second day of the Castle of Maidens tournament Trystram and his friends slip away unseen, Launcelot rides here and there "as wode as a lyon that faughted hys fylle, because he had loste sir Trystram" (527.19-20). "Mad as a hungry lion": the vivid image captures the undercurrent of rivalry in the attraction which marks this stage of the relationship, the urge to test themselves on each other as opponents worthy of their mettle.

On the third day of the tournament they do meet, and Launcelot mistakenly wounds Trystram in the side. Arthur's comment on the incident points up the paradox of the heroic ethic: "whan two noble men encountir, nedis muste the tone have the worse, lyke as God wyll suffir at that tyme" (535.13-15). If the heroic code is taken to its logical extreme, one man must die. On most occasions the Round Table knights are aware of the wastefulness of the principle, and their respect for prowess prevents their fighting to the "outrance" when they face a really good opponent. The encounter between Trystram and Lameroke in the Forest Perilous and between Palomydes and Lameroke outside Morgan's castle are both occasions when potentially fatal combats turn into sworn friendships. As long as the strong centripetal pull of attraction, the love of worship, operates, fatal possibilities are avoided; but they remain latent, ready to rise to the surface. The tension and fragility of the bond are always apparent.

The element of danger, then, is present in the desire of Trystram and Launcelot to "infelyshyp," but the love of worship triumphs. Vinaver has shown how Malory has altered his source to set the two knights out on separate quests which will eventually come to fruition together. After the Castle of Maidens tournament Launcelot and his fellows swear an oath to bring Trystram to court (537.23–31) – whereas in the source he embarks on a quest simply to identify the Knight with a Black Shield (*Works*, p. 1477). Later Trystram sets out to find the white knight with a covered shield who served him and Palomydes so summarily at the fountain, and who is finally revealed as sir Launcelot, quite without authority from the source (*Works*, p. 1484). Meanwhile rivalry with Palomydes intervenes, so that when the white knight with the covered shield appears at the appointed meeting place, Merlyne's stone, Trystram assumes it is Palomydes. Thus the long-delayed, yet half-expected encounter takes place, a meeting not in love but in combat. The battle lasts for four hours while the two squires stand by and weep, and only when the combatants pause to require each other's name do they discover what they have done. This is the signal to yield to each other, to take off their helmets in order to cool themselves, and to kiss each other a hundred times (569.32–570.2). The suspense which leads up to the fight and the importance of the fight itself are not, of course, original to Malory: in B.N. 334 the description of the fight fills three and a half columns (ff. 298c–299b). But the emphasis of the French event is on the meeting of the two greatest Arthurian lovers. In Malory, as the two knights take their horses and ride toward Camelot, they are met in turn by Gawayne and Gaherys, Arthur, and finally the Queen and her ladies, in a crescendo of joy and welcome which owes nothing to the source in effect (*Works*, p. 1485). Trystram had concealed his identity when he arrived in Logres, but had begun to reveal it in his own quest; now he is fully known. The movement from disguise to discovery is deeply revelatory here: as in the source, Trystram's name is found written on Marhalte's seat, but unlike the source, what follows is a narrative recapitulation of the fight with Marhalte, the first adventure which gave him "name" (572.17–25).[26]

In developing the theme of the pursuit of worship Malory has altered his source to focus on Trystram's acquisition of "name" and his development through the Tale as a twin hero to Launcelot. It is in the function of the lesser knights Palomydes and Lameroke, however, that his most striking alterations appear. Palomydes and Lameroke represent the two faces of the coin, the two potential modulations of the heroic mode. There is no space in this paper to discuss in detail the role of Palomydes; that will have to wait for a later article. Suffice it to say that, whereas the French Palamedes is a melancholy, noble figure whose chief function is to be Tristan's unsuccessful rival for the love of Yseult, Malory's Palomydes is Trystram's rival as much in worship as in love, and, furthermore, a disciple as much as a rival. His relationship with Trystram is a complex mixture of jealousy at Trystram's possession of Isode and admiration for his prowess and nobility:

"What wolde ye do," seyde sir Trystram, "and ye had sir Trystram?"
"I wolde fyght with hym," seyde sir Palomydes, "and ease my harte uppon hym. And yet, to say the sothe, sir Trystram ys the jantyllyste knyght in thys worlde lyvynge."

(529.12–16)

As Benson also shows, the development of this rivalry is one of the narrative patterns that structures the Tale (pp. 117–18). Two abortive attempts at a rendezvous are resolved in the "Conclusion" of the Tale, when Trystram, riding without his armor to court for the feast of Pentecost, meets Palomydes in the forest. He challenges Palomydes, who refuses to fight an unarmed man; but when Trystram learns that their battle is all that remains for Palomydes to fulfill his vow, he borrows some armor from a wounded knight, and a magnificent two-hour battle follows, till Palomydes appeals for an end to the combat:

. . . I have no grete luste to fyght no more, and for thys cause . . . myne offence ys to you nat so grete but that we may be fryendys, for all that I have offended ys and was for the love of La Beall Isode.

(844.20–4)

They make peace, and Palomydes is baptized at Carlisle and then welcomed with joy at the court. In the French episode, after Palamedes's courteous refusal to fight, there is no further combat (see Sommer, pp. 56–60). Vinaver points out Malory's originality in providing a reconciliation: "Dans le roman français, il n'est point question de l'amitié entre Tristan et Palamède" (*Le Roman de Tristan*, p. 206, n. 2); but he suggests that this final battle must have been in the immediate source: "It would be contrary to *M*'s practice to replace a friendly conversation between two knights . . . by a fight" (*Works*, p. 1532). But we have seen that, unremarked by Vinaver, Malory did precisely that in the Trystram-Lameroke encounter (483.12–14); and how could the rivalry between Palomydes and Trystram be satisfactorily resolved except by a splendid final battle ending in a bond of love? The French Palamedes is not baptized or sworn into the company of the Table Ronde until much later, and his reconciliation with Tristan in this scene is only temporary. In Malory, the bond is permanent: after Trystram's death, Palomydes becomes a follower of Launcelot (1109.2–4; 1170.22; 1205.15–16).

If Malory had continued with a "rehersall of the thirde booke" (845.31) of the prose *Tristan,* he would have embarked on a version of the Quest which included as questers Tristan, Palamedes, Erec, and many others. He chose not to; thus his Tale ends on a note of reconciliation, acceptance, and joy. Yet we are never to see Trystram alive again. Even in joyful, cohesive moments of the heroic life we may be made aware of its tragic potential. It is the career of Lameroke that strikes this note most poignantly, providing, as Benson puts it, "a dark, ironic undertone" (p. 127) to this Tale of positive achievement.

Few scholars have failed to recognize the importance of Lameroke. Rumble, for instance, has devoted some pages to Malory's heightening of his role from the source (pp. 172–6), and Charles Moorman describes the murder of Lameroke as a "focal point" in the Tale.[27] Both scholars, however, judge the event in terms of plot structure, seeing it as the turning point of the Lot-Pellynor feud which is, in their view, one of the chief causes of the failure of chivalry in Arthur's kingdom. But, as Vinaver has shown in *The Rise of Romance,*[28] and Benson in his book on Malory (pp. 51–64), concepts which belong to naturalistic fiction or organic structure are irrelevant to medieval romance, which depends for its organizing impulses on principles of design, such as repetition and reversal, amplification and ornament. Lameroke's career functions as a contrast to that of Palomydes and creates important resonances in the *Morte Darthur* as a whole.

Though Lameroke appears as third in the roll of honor in the "Tale of Sir Gareth" (e.g., 316.23–6), we have no sense of his character till the "Tristram," where we first see him at the jousts held by king Mark beside the river at Tintagel. Lameroke and his brother sir Dryaunte defeat thirty Cornish knights, arousing Mark's ire. Mark orders Trystram to encounter Lameroke, which Trystram does only reluctantly, lecturing Mark on the unknightly behavior of a fresh man and horse attacking a weary one (428.5–12, 16–23). He gives Lameroke a fall, but refuses to continue the fight on foot, which Lameroke takes as a personal insult. The whole episode emphasizes the contrast between Trystram, the exponent of "jantyllnesse," and the young knight burning to make his name against proved fighters. As Lameroke's reputation increases, Arthur wishes he would come to court; and at the same time Lameroke's meetings with Trystram in the Forest Perilous and with Palomydes outside Morgan's castle lead, in both cases, to sworn brotherhood. As Trystram comments after hearing of this second battle, "there is no knyght in the worlde excepte sir Launcelot that I wolde ded so well as sir Lamerok" (606.11–12).

Benson states that Lameroke's "doleful career" provides an analogy with Trystram's (p. 126). It does indeed, but the effect Malory creates is due less to structure than to tonality and emotion. In the quick succession of events that develop before the tournament of Surluse, relationships take form, and incidents that are present in the source are given new emphasis by Malory's juxtapositions. Lameroke's arrival at court is welcomed by all except sir Gawayne and his brethren (608.1–24). They plot against him, and Gaherys murders their mother after catching her in bed with Lameroke. Meanwhile Arthur has reconciled Trystram and Mark, and the two have left for Cornwall, with the court "wrothe and hevy" (609.19) at Trystram's departure. Now Lameroke rides away from court in shame and sorrow, and Launcelot, who warned Arthur that Mark's "accorde" with Trystram would not last, warns him that treason may also rob them of Lameroke (613.15–17). Dynadan encounters Aggravayne and Mordrede, whose hatred is roused against him although he has just rescued them from sir Brewnys Saunz Pité. Vinaver explains this ungrateful response by referring to the source, where the brethren's friend Dalan turns them against Dinadan because of a previous grudge of his own (*Works*, p. 1494). However, Malory has given the incident a new motivation. Mordrede and Aggravayne hate Dynadan "bycause of sir Lameroke":

> For sir Dynadan had suche a custom that he loved all good knyghtes that were valyaunte, and he hated all tho that were destroyers of good knyghtes. And there was none that hated sir Dynadan but tho that ever were called murtherers.
> (614.27–31)

By cutting the French Dinadan's antichivalric mockery during the scene (*Works*, p. 1494, n. to 614.21), Malory has turned the episode into a wholly serious one, which leads naturally into the prophecy of Dynadan's murder (615.5–8), retained from the source (Löseth, § 258). Thus the characters begin to fall naturally into two groups, those who love and foster worship, like Trystram, Launcelot, Lameroke, and Dynadan, and those who envy it to the point of destruction, like Gawayne and his brethren (excluding, always, Gareth). The ominous notes build up the theme of future treason and loss.

Lameroke's reputation is at its highest peak at the tournament of Surluse, in which, again, Malory has diverged from the source, as the French account makes it Lancelot's occasion. Lameroke outdoes Palomydes, and there is much sourceless admiration and congratulation at his exploits on the fourth day, at the end of which he wins the prize.[29] The fifth day shifts to Arthur's rival tournament beside Surluse, where Lameroke revenges the defeat of Gawayne and his brethren for Arthur's sake. Arthur urges him to join his fellowship, promising to curb his nephews, but Lameroke refuses; this conversation, as Vinaver shows in *Le Roman de Tristan* (pp. 193–5), is not found in any *Tristan* MS. Again, at the end of the contest of Surluse proper, Launcelot repeats Arthur's invitation, and again Lameroke refuses, saying he will never trust the brethren. "Than sir Lameroke departed frome sir Launcelot and all the felyship, and aythir of them wepte at her departynge" (670.26–7). P. J. C. Field has commented on Malory's use of the word "depart" in tragic contexts;[30] this is no exception, for we never see Lameroke again.

It is not until the next section of the Tale, when a casual discussion on worship leads into it, that we learn that Lameroke is dead. Palomydes tells Ector that there was a third knight besides Trystram and Launcelot who had bested him:

. . . and he myght have lyved tyll he had bene more of ayge, an hardyer man there lyvith nat than he wolde have bene, and his name was sir Lamorak de Galys. And as he had justed at a turnemente, there he overthrewe me and thirty knyghtes mo, and there he wan the gre. And at his departynge there mette hym sir Gawayne and his bretherne, and wyth grete payne they slewe hym felounsly, unto all good knyghtes grete damage!

(688.3–10)

The news is as much a shock to us as it is to Lameroke's brother Percyvale, who falls over his horse's mane, swooning. He laments:

Alas, my good and noble brother, sir Lamorak, now shall we never mete! And I trowe in all the wyde worlde may nat a man fynde suche a knyght as he was of his ayge. And hit is to muche to suffir the deth of oure fadir kynge Pellynor, and now the deth of oure good brother sir Lamorak!

(688.15–19)

Lamourat's murder certainly occurs in the prose *Tristan*, but most of the MSS only report it in a brief statement, and those that provide a description follow that of B.N. 99, which is Vinaver's "source" for this section. Here the brethren kill Lamourat's brother Drian, and when Lamourat, already badly wounded, follows them to avenge his brother, they set on him and bring him near to death. Gauvain taunts Lamourat with the information that it was he who killed Lamourat's father, Pellinor, and then beheads him. A nearby hermit inters the brothers' bodies and sends Lamourat's head to the court of Artus with an accusing message about his relatives (ff. 532b–533a). One MS, however, B.N. 103, gives an account somewhat similar to Malory's version in 688.1–10 and 699.14–27. It is close enough to suggest that Malory's actual source resembled it (*Works*, p. 1511), and one of its repeated phrases, "ce fut grant dommage a toute chevalerie" (f. 298a, c), becomes Palomydes's lament, "unto all good knyghtes grete damage" (688.10).

The Old French "dommage" meant "harm, injury or loss,"[31] and this meaning was preponderant in Middle English also, but a secondary meaning had developed, of "a matter of regret, a misfortune, a pity" (*OED*, 3b). Malory is using both senses simultaneously: such murders are both a source of lament and an injury to all good knights. His retentive ear has also caught another near-formulaic verbal motif which had been used frequently in connection with Lamourat in the prose *Tristan*: "il est bon chevalier de son aage, et croy quil sera preudome sil vit longuement." It is found in all three of Vinaver's "source" MSS.[32] Used by Malory only in the context of lament, it becomes deeply poignant: Lameroke might have been the best knight of the world if he had lived, "suche a knyght as he was of his ayge."

This conversation between Palomydes, Percyvale, and Ector, which is our first report of Lameroke's death, is not present in the "source" MS, B.N. 99, but a conversation of similar form is found in other similar MSS (e.g., B.N. fr. 772, B.M. Add. 5474, etc. [see Löseth, § 359]) and is therefore likely to have been present in Malory's immediate source. Yet in these MSS the dialogue concerns only Palamedes expressing his admiration of Lamourat and Perceval his grief: there is no description of the murder, nor is it Perceval's first intimation of his brother's death. Furthermore, the account of the murder in B.N. 103 is narrative, not dialogue. It is a brilliant and bold stroke on Malory's part to combine the narrative account and the conversational form to give readers and knights alike such dramatic and startling news of Lameroke's death. The manner in which he develops the theme is even more original.

Palomydes becomes the chief spokesman of Lameroke's death, and as the theme is repeated it causes ripples and eddies that widen and swell; each time, it gains a formidable accretion of anger, sorrow, and loss, becoming ultimately a steady undercurrent of lament. Trystram reproaches the brethren angrily, crying, "I wolde I had bene by hym at hys deth day" (691.33-4), and when he, Dynadan, Gareth, and Palomydes are together outside Lonezep the cry is repeated:

". . . wolde God I had bene besyde sir Gawayne whan that moste noble knyght sir Lamorake was slayne!"

"Now, as Jesu be my helpe," seyde sir Trystram, "hit is passyngly well sayde of you, for I had lever," sayde sir Trystrams, "than all the golde betwyxte this and Rome I had bene there."

"Iwysse," seyde sir Palomydes, "so wolde I . . . ."

. . .

"Now fye uppon treson!" seyde sir Trystram, "for hit sleyth myne harte to hyre this tale."

"And so hit dothe myne," seyde sir Gareth, "bretherne as they be myne."

"Now speke we of othir dedis," seyde sir Palomydes, "and let hym be, for his lyff ye may nat gete agayne."

(699.7-14, 28-33)

The lament has become a refrain, the keynotes of which are treason and loss. Palomydes meets Hermynde on his quest in the Red City, and finds himself telling yet another kinsman of the murder: "For as for sir Lamorak, hym shall ye never se in this worlde" (716.2-3). Percyvale, taking leave of his mother, is reminded by her of the loss; she too links it, as he did, with the murder of her husband, king Pellynor:

And alas! my dere sonnes, thys ys a pyteuous complaynte for me off youre fadyrs dethe, conciderynge also the dethe of sir Lamorak that of knyghthod had but feaw fealowys.

(810.13-16)

All these laments are original to Malory. D. S. Brewer has commented that Malory's narrative sequence "weaves patterns whose effects come from events which are held in memory by the reader, and which thus interact as it were out of time" (p. 21). Events are held in memory by Malory's characters also, and the narrative progression is not only linear, but cumulative, so that each time the event is recalled it is weighted more heavily with emotional significance. The phrases which characterize the lament for Lameroke are repeated in different situations, and in the last two Tales of the *Morte Darthur* they recur in association with Trystram also. As with Lameroke, we are given little warning of Trystram's death. The narrator slips in the briefest of allusions, coupling his name with Lameroke's (1112.10–11), and then we hear:

> Also that traytoure kynge slew the noble knyght sir Trystram as he sate harpynge afore hys lady, La Beall Isode, with a trenchaunte glayve, for whos dethe was the moste waylynge of ony knyght that ever was in kynge Arthurs dayes, for there was never none so bewayled as was sir Trystram and sir Lamerok, for they were with treson slayne. . . .
>
> (1149.28–33)

Launcelot recalls Trystram's death when speaking to Bors: "for all the worlde may nat fynde such another knyght" (1173.20), just as he recalls Lameroke when facing Gawayne: "he was one of the beste knyghtes crystynde of his ayge. And hit was grete pité of hys deth!" (1190.8–10). Percyvale's and Palomydes's phrases are echoing again.

It is significant that, although Malory's source is likely to have contained long, tear-bestrewn death scenes for both Lamourat and Tristan, he chose in both cases to eschew them. It is loss rather than death which is emphasized. Lameroke is more important in memory than in life, for it is in memory that his "name" is purest. He has become the permanent symbol of knighthood cut off in its prime, the formula "the beste knyght of his ayge" ringing like a knell. When those elegiac phrases are associated with Trystram, he too becomes, like Lameroke, pure "name," atemporal, frozen in memory. Death of a hero in this heroic mode has nothing of the flavor of late medieval religious convention, an affair of bodily corruption and earthly vanity. To the heroic mind death simply makes fame permanent: "He was a man, take him for all in all / I shall not look upon his like again" (*Hamlet*, I.ii.187–8). Poignancy lies in the fact that the moment of death is both the moment of greatest flowering, when "name" is purest, and simultaneously the moment when the living realize most clearly what they have lost. Elegy rises naturally out of the heroic mode.[33]

Let me repeat, however, that Malory obviously did not intend the elegiac note to predominate in the "Tale of Sir Tristram." It was to be reserved for the final Tale, where the mourning is not for the loss of one knight, but for the dissolution of a kingdom, the passing of a way of life. Thus the death of Trystram is not recounted either in the "Tale of Sir Tristram," which ends on a romance note of reconciliation and achievement, nor in the following Tale, the "Quest of the Holy Grail," Malory having chosen to return to the Vulgate version for his source. The absence of Trystram from Malory's Quest indicates that for the English writer he was associated more purely with the heroic world whose values were to be disturbed and questioned during the search for the Grail. Launcelot had to be retained, for the Grail Quest is defined in his failure or partial success; but the achievement is on a different plane, and needs no distraction from Trystram's world. That world returns in the last two Tales, when the memories of Trystram and Lameroke underscore Launcelot's magnificent final *beot* before exile; indeed, a deliberate parallel is evoked with Trystram's *beot* at his own exile (see 503.25–504.15; 1198.1–1199.4). The most stirring passage occurs when, with no way to avoid open breach with Arthur, Launcelot and his kinsmen call on old fellowships:

Than there felle to them, what of Northe Walys and of Cornwayle, for sir Lamorakes sake and for sir Trystrames sake, to the numbir of a seven score knyghtes.

(1170.26–9)

The centripetal attractions that operated when these knights were alive do not die out with their deaths. Old loyalties are still honored and the past is always alive. The heroic vision is imprisoned, encapsulated in the past; this is the source of both its strength and its despair. The essence of the "Tale of Sir Tristram" has been its portrayal of the heroic world, with all its energy and tension, joy of brotherhood and rich memories; yet implicit in its ethic are its severely limited responses, its narrow inevitability of action. When the fragility of all earthly institutions is evoked, Malory's own voice tells us that worship and the love of worship provide the only stability, the only cohesion: "Lo ye all Englysshemen, se ye nat what a myschyff here was?" (1229.6–14). It is the "Tale of Sir Tristram" that displays worship in action and in memory. Far from being "irrelevant," it is the center of the *Morte Darthur*, the heart of the work.

NOTES

1. Quotations from or references to the text and Vinaver's Commentary are taken from *The Works of Sir Thomas Malory*, 2nd ed., 3 vols. (Oxford, 1967), hereafter cited as *Works*. To avoid confusion I have employed "Tale" rather than "Book" as the title of the "Tristram" section, and to facilitate comparison with the French I have spelled proper names such as Trystram, Launcelot, etc., in the form in which they most frequently appear in the text rather than in the customary form.
2. *English Literature at the Close of the Middle Ages* (Oxford, 1945), p. 191.
3. Thomas C. Rumble, " 'The Tale of Tristram': Development by Analogy," *Malory's Originality: A Critical Study of "Le Morte Darthur,"* ed. R. M. Lumiansky (Baltimore, 1964), pp. 118–83; Donald G. Schueler, "The Tris-

tram Section of Malory's *Morte Darthur*," *Studies in Philology* 65 (1968): 51–66.

4. *Malory's "Morte Darthur"* (Cambridge, Mass., 1976), p. 109. Benson's work was published after the bulk of this paper was written; it will be apparent that I agree with his study of the "Tristram" in essentials, but approach the material from a different perspective.

5. *Sir Thomas Malory*, English Association Pamphlet no. 51 (London, 1922), p. 5.

6. Larry D. Benson, "Sir Thomas Malory's *Le Morte Darthur*," *Critical Approaches to Six Major English Works: "Beowulf" through "Paradise Lost*," ed. R. M. Lumiansky and H. Baker (Philadelphia, 1968), p. 111.

7. The exact text of the prose *Tristan* used by Malory is unfortunately unidentified and probably nonextant. Vinaver reconstructs it from its best and closest representatives, MSS Paris, Bibliothèque Nationale f. fr. 103, 334, and 99, corresponding to *Works*, pp. 371–513, 513–619, 619–846, respectively; he also uses Chantilly 646, Pierpont Morgan Library fr. 41, Leningrad fr. F. v. XV, 2, and Sommer's selections from British Museum Add. 5474 (see end of note), among others. As a supplement to Vinaver's Commentary I have consulted the first three MSS, hereafter cited as B.N. 103, 334, and 99, all transcriptions from these MSS in my text being my own unless otherwise attributed. However, B.N. 103 is abridged, and it and 99 belong to the fifteenth century; only 334 is definitely earlier than Malory's work, and it is incomplete (see note 12). Thus the originality of episodes, motifs, or striking verbal patterns in Malory's work cannot be assumed only by comparison with the appropriate "source" MS; a wider base of comparison must be employed. No complete edition of the romance exists, but the first 130 folios of MS Carpentras 404, chosen as the best representative of the oldest family of *Tristan* MSS, have been edited by Renée L. Curtis, *Le Roman de Tristan en prose*, Vol. 1 (Munich, 1963), Vol. 2 (Leiden, 1976), hereafter cited as Curtis. I have checked significant passages against this edition (providing the relevant transcriptions in my text with cross references to paragraph numbers in Curtis) and also against the following comparative analyses and partial editions: Eilert Löseth, *Le Roman en prose de Tristan, le roman de Palamède, et la compilation de Rusticien de Pise: Analyse critique d'après les Manuscrits de Paris* (Paris, 1891), cited as Löseth, *Le Tristan et le Palamède des Manuscrits français du British Museum* (Kristiania, 1905), *Le Tristan et le Palamède des Manuscrits de Rome et Florence* (Kristiania, 1924); Eugène Vinaver, *Le Roman de Tristan et Iseut dans l'œuvre de Thomas Malory* (Paris, 1925), cited as *Le Roman de Tristan*; C. E. Pickford, ed., *Alixandre l'Orphelin: A Prose Tale of the Fifteenth Century* (Manchester, 1951), from Pierpont Morgan fr. 41; H. O. Sommer, ed., "Galahad and Perceval," *Modern Philology* 5 (1907–8): 55–84, 181–200, 291–341, selections from B.M. Add. 5474, cited as Sommer. Source study under such conditions cannot be conclusive, but can be extremely suggestive.

8. Eugène Vinaver, *Etudes sur le Tristan en prose* (Paris, 1925), pp. 22–33, and "The prose *Tristan*," *Arthurian Literature in the Middle Ages: A Collaborative History*, ed. R. S. Loomis (Oxford, 1959), hereafter cited as *ALMA*, p. 339. Vinaver's simple distinction between the First and Second Versions has, however, been challenged: see the exhaustive discussion by E. Baumgartner, *Le "Tristan en prose": Essai d'interprétation d'un Roman médiéval* (Geneva, 1975), pp. 18–62. Malory's source was clearly a late version, either Version IV or derived from it (see pp. 71–87).

9. See W. H. T. Jackson, "Gottfried von Strassburg," *ALMA*, pp. 153–5, and Vinaver, *Le Roman de Tristan*, pp. 127–9.
10. "The Death of Tristan, from Douce MS 189," ed. E. S. Murell, *PMLA* 43 (1928): 374 and 383.
11. Ed., *Sir Tristrem* (Edinburgh, 1819), pp. lxxii–iii, quoted by Vinaver, *Etudes*, pp. 83–4.
12. For a classification of the MSS and the printings, see Curtis, 1:12–17, 2:12–15; for more detailed discussion of the MS tradition see Curtis, 2:15–52 and her *Tristan Studies* (Munich, 1969), pp. 66–7 (*re* Part 1), also Baumgartner, pp. 18–87, summed up in pp. 85–7; for versions in other languages, see Vinaver, *ALMA*, p. 346, n. 4.
13. *L'Idée de la Gloire dans la Tradition occidentale* (Paris, 1968, trans. from Madrid, 1952), pp. 163–4; Dr. Malkiel is specifically discussing the *Libro de Alixandre* by Juan Lorenzo de Astorga.
14. See Fanni Bogdanow, "The *Suite du Merlin* and the Post-Vulgate *Roman du Graal*," *ALMA*, pp. 334–5.
15. D. S. Brewer, ed., *The Morte Darthur, Parts Seven and Eight* (London and Evanston, 1968), Intro., pp. 23–35; Mark Lambert, *Malory: Style and Vision in "Le Morte Darthur"* (New Haven, 1975), p. 179. Lambert's whole section on the function of public values in the final catastrophe, "Shame and Noise" (pp. 176–94), is excellent.
16. See William Matthews, *The Ill-Framed Knight: A Skeptical Inquiry into the Identity of Sir Thomas Malory* (Berkeley, 1966), pp. 100–3.
17. *Comparative Literature* 13 (1961): 198–9.
18. *Malory* (Oxford, 1970, reprint of 1929), pp. 34–8.
19. Both are used in similar constructions, and both have been glossed as L. *jactantia*: see *beot*, III, *An Anglo-Saxon Dictionary*, ed. Bosworth and Toller; *bost*, I (a), and (b), *The Middle English Dictionary*, ed. H. Kurath; *boast*, 3 and 4, *OED*.
20. *Covenant in Anglo-Saxon Thought* (Madras: The Macmillan Co. of India, Ltd., 1972), pp. 13–14. This is the published form of the author's Ph.D. dissertation for Notre Dame, 1969.
21. Malory has altered the end of the Tristan-Brunor fight (415.29–35, cf. B.N. 103, f. 60c, d; Curtis, § 463), as Vinaver has implied but not clarified; Vinaver does not note the originality of 742.23–33; thirdly, Vinaver comments on Ector's notorious "twenty thousand pounds" (831.32–3) but does not make clear that the whole speech is considerably expanded from the source.
22. E.g., two important narrative threads in the French romance are the friendship between Galeholt le hault prince and Lancelot, and the rivalry between Tristan and Brunor (La Cote Mal Taillée).
23. E.g., there are no breaks in the Winchester MS between Vinaver's Sections I and II, or V and VI.
24. Vinaver does not note the originality of either passage: in B.N. 103, f. 49b (Curtis, § 392), Blioberis does not mention these specific victories, simply Tristan's fame in general; for the King of Ireland's treason trial see B.N. 103, f. 53c (Curtis, § 418).
25. However, in the Ile of Servage speech Malory is clearly recalling Tristan's slightly earlier speech designed to bolster up his own courage and that of the despondent Segurades (B.N. 103, f. 86b; Curtis, § 595) – yet another example of retained *matière* but altered *sen*.
26. Benson also comments on Malory's thematic recapitulation of the Marhalte fight (p. 117).

27. *The Book of Kyng Arthur: The Unity of Malory's "Morte Darthur"* (Lexington, Ky., 1965), p. 58.
28. Oxford, 1971, pp. 85–92, on the French Arthurian romances. Vinaver sees Malory as attempting a more modern *novella* structure, but Benson shows that Malory belongs firmly in the medieval tradition.
29. Cf. B.N. 99, ff. 390d–391b (Löseth, § 282.d). Vinaver notes only that 662.16–18 is original, and not that Malory has altered the whole episode (661.24–662.22) by bringing Lameroke into Galahalte's party and having Launcelot rescue rather than defeat him.
30. *Romance and Chronicle: A Study of Malory's Prose Style* (London, 1971), p. 82.
31. F. Godefroy, *Dictionnaire de l'ancienne Langue française*, s.v. *damage*.
32. The quotation is from B.N. 103, f. 72b; see also B.N. 99, ff. 119d, 529a, b, 533a, B.N. 334, ff. 328c, 330c, and Löseth, §§ 246, 250.
33. See Stanley B. Greenfield, *"Beowulf* and Epic Tragedy," *Studies in Old English Literature in honor of Arthur G. Brodeur*, ed. S. B. Greenfield (Eugene, Ore., 1963), pp. 91–105, an article to which I am greatly indebted.

The Monastic Achievement and More's Utopian Dream

WALTER M. GORDON

Most histories of utopian literature skip the Middle Ages and pass from Plato's *Republic* and its satellites to Thomas More's *Utopia*.[1] One historian explains this gap by pointing out the medieval habit of projecting their ideal communities into the next world either "in the mystic and philosophic manner of St. Augustine's *De Civitate Dei*, or in the poetical and naive fashion of the narrative of the great Irish traveller St. Brendan."[2] The vision of heavenly Jerusalem fired the imagination of many who in other circumstances might have found their inspiration in the hope for a better society on earth. This orientation toward the celestial homeland found expression in both the poetry and prose of the era. Fulbert of Chartres, St. Peter Damian, Abelard, and à Kempis all wrote Latin poems in praise of the Jerusalem on high, and the age's literary masterpiece reaches its climax and goal in the *Paradiso*. Thomas Aquinas divided man's ethical life into the two arenas of earthly and heavenly virtue when he distinguished between the acquired moral virtues "by which we behave properly in the human community" and the infused moral virtues "by which we comport ourselves as *fellow citizens with the saints and familiars of God*," as members *in via* of the heavenly community.[3]

Among those living on earth, the citizen par excellence of the city above was, according to St. Bernard, the cloistered monk whose monastery was "a Jerusalem associated with the heavenly one through the heart's complete devotion, through the imitation of its life, and through real spiritual kinship."[4] The medieval religious house, therefore, constituted the supreme expression of the age's otherworldly habit of mind. Surely one would hardly have expected such a place to influence utopian literature when it finally reemerged in the Renaissance. It turned out, however, that the monastic presence made itself felt in More's *Utopia*, Rabelais's Abbey of Thélème, and Campanella's *City of the Sun*, three Renaissance attempts to depict new worlds and ways of living.[5] The effect of the monks upon the utopian imagination illustrates the part which historical fact plays in the evolution of an idea, and the monastic achievement that was realized between Plato and More sheds much light on the differences between their ideal states. So to understand better what happened to utopian thought when Thomas More picked up his pen in the early days of the English Renaissance, we will examine the monastic antecedents to his *Utopia*. By relating this medieval phenomenon to the book, we also hope to uncover the spiritual tie between the two that brings out the singular attitude distinguishing More's classic from later Renaissance utopias.

At the very beginning of the history of western monasticism, we can discern both a contempt of and flight from the world of purely material and temporal pursuit. The golden years of the Thebaid, which witnessed the first great Christian migration into the desert, coincide with the church's earliest days of officially recognized establishment within the Roman Empire.[6] For the first time, being a Christian could win social and political preferment. Martyrdom became a thing of the past, but the will to sacrifice still remained active in some zealous spirits who abandoned the allurements of the city for the broad, desolate stretches of Egypt. Over two centuries of cenobite experiment passed before the great designer of community life wrote his famous rule, and Benedict of Nursia there regularized the already established antagonism between the monk and the world about him. As Benedict conceived the religious life, the monastery was meant to set her inmates to school in the correct manner of serving God and to exclude in the process all contact with the surrounding populace that could not be reconciled with the monk's first obligation to the *opus Dei*. The primary concern of the place lay within the cloister precincts. The monastery looked to its own good, not to its neighbors; it minded the things above, not below.[7] Such was the ideal as formulated by the gospels and the desert fathers and implemented by St. Benedict.

An ideal, however, is not reality, and the world of action works its own kind of wonders upon the highest flights and richest returns of contemplation. Paradoxically, the men of this disengaged, uninvolved, otherworldly habit of intellect and will eventually arrived at shaping anew the views of men concerning the pattern that life here on earth should take. Although not intended as such, the Benedictine motto, "laborare est orare," had revolutionary effects upon society at large. By allotting a period for manual labor in the contemplative's order of the day, Benedict joined in one life what the ancient world had preferred to keep apart: manual and intellectual activity.[8] The monks gave to physical work a new dignity and delivered it from its previous association with slavery. Once liberated, the craftsmanship of the artisan took on new dexterity as is evidenced by the medieval stonework of the freemasons. This monastic respect for labor at times stretched far beyond the limit originally placed on work by Benedict. The first Cistercians in England attracted a large labor force of *conversi* who, by means of their grange system, became the country's first producers of wool on a large scale.[9] For a period, these monks were instrumental in improving the agricultural techniques of Britain. In the higher endeavors of the spirit, the monastery could prove itself a revitalizing source to the world around it. The Norman abbey of Bec was an intellectual center for northern Europe in the days of Lanfranc and Anselm. Cluny, in the eleventh century, and Clairvaux, in the twelfth, effected a spiritual rejuvenation that was felt throughout western Christendom.[10] The greater abbeys of England, France, and Italy "exercised a command over urban life, even over its architectural forms, out of all proportion to their numbers."[11] Within the monastery "the ideal purposes of the city were sorted out, kept alive, and eventually renewed. It was here, too, that the practical value of restraint, order, regularity, honesty, inner discipline was established, before these qualities were passed over to the medieval town and post-medieval capitalism, in the form of inventions and business practices: the clock, the account book, the ordered day."[12] In so many ways these otherworldlings had given the lead for improving and enriching life on this earth.

In addition to its leadership in many areas of secular endeavor, the medieval religious house that maintained its original fervor concretely embedded for its neighbors the Christian spirit and ideology. Like a little city within itself, the monastery recalled to the entire church's memory the selfless, communal life of her earliest days. Such a witness drew praise from the usually critical voice of William Langland:

> But alle is buxumnesse there and bokes · to rede and to lerne.
> For if heuene be on this erthe · and ese to any soule,
> It is in cloistere or in scole · be many skilles I fynde;
> For in cloistre cometh no man · to chide ne to fiȝte,
> (*Piers the Plowman*, B. X. 300–03)

This image of heaven on earth shows the idyllic hold that the monastery could sustain over the medieval imagination, and that hold was to endure into the Renaissance, for the utopian writers of the latter period could not quite wash the monastic patterns out of their minds with the result that the community of men whose lives were directed toward heaven paradoxically contributed to the models for a better society on earth.

The monastic achievement, I believe, helps to explain the difference when one turns from Plato's *Republic* to the *Utopia*. More's commonwealth is easily distinguished from Plato's in that it is pictured as existent and operating, and many details of the picture are borrowed from the monks: the uniform clothing of the citizenry, their communal meals, their reading at table, and the layout of their houses with an interior spaciousness provided by the cloistral setting of their enclosed gardens. The utopian day follows the monastic *horarium* in the balance it achieves between physical and mental exercise, between work and contemplation.

As in religious houses, obedience of mind and docility of spirit are fostered, and, most basically of all, the Utopians follow that "common way of life . . . still in use among the truest societies of Christians."[13] The historical fact and experience of monasticism buttresses More's imagination as he creates his fable. And so, with no small thanks to the religious orders, utopian literature as it enters the Renaissance is completely outfitted: naked Platonic thought is given full dress and edges its way toward reality.[14] Here we happen upon the most significant aspect of the influence that the monastic experience exercised on More's fantasy. Although his account must be defined as imaginative fiction, its relationship to elements of actual history makes the book susceptible of a serious interpretation. The depiction, which to an extent follows a monastic pattern, brings the *Utopia* much closer to reality than the *Republic* ever comes. And so the question naturally arises as to just how earnestly More himself took that depiction.

Although Utopia is "No-place," the book's introductory verses say that it ought to be called Eutopia or "Nice-place." An intentional ambiguity seems to be established and maintained regarding the way the fable is to be understood. The title page announces that the work is both entertaining and beneficial. How beneficial? Enough to be put into practice? Or does its value as entertainment forewarn us against thinking that any of this is meant to be realized? I think it is difficult to answer these questions satisfactorily and maintain at the same time the delicate balance established by More's ambivalent utterance. Because the tone of *Utopia's* entire statement is consistently ironic and nonexplicit, those critics who wish to extract a flat answer from it must go, not to the text, but to a source. T. S. Dorsch would have us see *Utopia* as an enormous, satirical joke, but, failing to find an open avowal of this in the book, he is forced to a source, the *True History*, where Lucian tells us not to believe a word he is saying, that his story is, in fact, false and not meant to be taken seriously.[15] *Utopia*, however, is not Lucianic in this sense. It never states explicitly that it is just a joke. Similarly, when Northrop Frye suggests that *Utopia* is meant to inhabit the mind alone, his best piece of supporting evidence does not come from More but from the "principle of *paradeigma* which Plato sets forth in his Ninth Book" of the *Republic* where the beautiful city exists here below as an idea only.[16] Once more we are given a key to More's kingdom that fits another's gate. But does it fit his? There is nothing in *Utopia* that states so plainly as does the *Republic* that this place is intended for the mind only. My point is not to prove either of these men wrong. One or the other could be right, but *Utopia* begrudges them a clinching argument. From it they can only glean hints, and, in going to its sources for a clear statement, they illustrate a unique and original facet about the book: where Plato and Lucian are direct, More is oblique.

The author's tantalizing reluctance to state clearly how he means us to understand *Utopia* constitutes the truly volatile quality of the work. It is dangerous reading because it permits many differing interpretations, and the reading which threatens most is the literal one where the book is accepted as a solution to the problems of mankind. For the moment, I would like to concentrate on this aspect, realizing that a one-sided approach to the work has to leave out its dialectical tension, make-believe, word-play, and irony. But *Utopia* undeniably has a serious side, and any reading that ignores this will ultimately disappoint us because of its partial criticism. To allow pure joke to swallow More's gravity is to reduce the fullness of his irony by half, and, although his fiction does not necessarily insist upon translation into fact, it opens itself to that possibility.

Insofar as Utopia follows a monastic pattern, its feasibility has already been proven by history. Of course, one considerable difference can be observed between the monastic arrangement and More's. The founders of the cenobite rule, operating from a premise similar to Plato's aristocratic bias, took it for granted that the communal, religious life was ordained only for an elite group. *Utopia*, on the other hand, puts forward the novel suggestion that the wealth of an entire nation be shared by all of its citizens. Could More have taken this staggering leap in earnest? Some one-sided interpretations of *Utopia* answer in the affirmative, but, more to the point, we know from the author's other writing that he felt strongly about the corrosive effect that private interest has upon society at large. Even if we grant that he does no more than entertain the notion of a communistic state in *Utopia*, we have proof that he took social possessiveness very seriously. See how he writes to a monk concerning the exclusivism of the religious orders:

Everyone loves his own premises, his own money; everyone is interested only in his own profession, or his own corporation; anything at all which we can call our own attracts our attentions to itself and away from common interests. . . . The more personal a thing is, in the eyes of many of you, the more valuable it is. As a result, many treasure their own private devotions more highly than those of the monastery; those of the monastery more highly than those of the order; those peculiar to their own order more highly than those common to all orders; and those which belong to all religious they regard much more highly than the lowly, humble things, not exclusively their own, but possessed in common with absolutely all Christians, such as the ordinary virtues of faith, hope, and charity, fear of God, humility, and the like.[17]

The thrust of this passage obviously leads away from private to communal interest; it indicates how seriously More takes the problem which *Utopia* playfully solves. In this letter, he is attacking the very people whose ideals he employs in answering the social evils adhering to possessiveness. More faults the monks for their lack of universal concern. Because of their myopic failure to see beyond the limits of the monastery garden, the life sworn to brotherhood degenerates into mere corporate self-interest.

Abbots are listed among the wool-market monopolists in the first book of *Utopia*. More's impatience with the monks results from the abbey's selfish habit of sharing its wealth only within its own precincts; the monastery's social concern seemed to stop at the gatehouse. *Utopia* replies to this deficiency by allowing the cenobite ideal to break cloister until an entire nation is permeated with it.

This notion of otherworldly detachment escaping its monastic confines does not originate with *Utopia*. Herbert B. Workman has traced the development of the monastic ideal from the totally solitary life into the cenobitic community and, thence, with the coming of the friars, beyond the cloister into the world at large.[18] The Franciscans, in their earliest days, took an adventurous step away from the enclosed security of the monastery that had begun to give in to a debilitating sense of elitism destructive to its original genius. Saint Benedict's concept of communal living provided that, apart from the deference paid to offices and seniority, all monks should live on equal footing and share the ordinary domestic duties together. With the passing of time, however, this homogeneity broke down under the weight of distinctions between choir monk and lay brother, scholar and field hand.[19] By the thirteenth century, this exclusivism, which had come to shape the interior of the monastery, also affected its attitude toward the outside world. The monk who belonged to a vast religious confederation like that of Citeaux was a member of a powerful, landed chain of communities that corporately constituted a real economic force and tended to preserve its own preferential rank at the higher levels of the medieval establishment. Nothing could have been further from the new and disturbing Franciscan vision. The friars, at their inception, were given to the most menial tasks: the care of lepers, the rebuilding of ruined shrines, the gathering of crops, the stripping of vines, and other manual chores. They found the "highest joy of life in the meanest drudgery that only love would undertake."[20] Hand in hand with this love of lowly tasks went a disdain of learning and the honor to which it could lead. Their very name, the Friars Minor, meant the brothers "guildless" or "classless." They cut across every kind of social distinction, mixed kings with beggars in their tales, and provided room for the married laity within the framework of their order.

There is a striking similarity between the early Franciscans and the Buthrescae or the people whose lives are dedicated to religion in *Utopia*. These, too, disdain leisure and learning and undertake the hard labor of tending the sick, repairing roads, and cleaning out ditches. "If anywhere there is a task so rough, hard, and filthy that most are deterred from it by the toil, disgust, and despair involved, they gladly and cheerfully claim it all for themselves."[21] These Buthrescae follow the friars as well in their democratic conception of a spiritual calling meant for all walks of life. Like the Franciscans, they find place for the married laity within their ranks. If we add to this the burning desire for a society based upon the poverty of spirit that the first friars and all Utopians represent, we begin to appreciate the affinity of soul between Francis of Assisi and Thomas More. No wonder the latter, in the description of his utopian daydream, sees himself, the King of all Utopia, dressed in a Franciscan robe.[22]

Once again, *Utopia* corresponds to a history that has preceded it and that enhances its credibility. Some dreams do come true, and More's definitely hovers at the threshold of realization. Surely, in regard to its possibility of enactment, it is more positive than Plato's *Republic*. Perhaps it is no more than a thing to be desired or wished for, but the wish is there nonetheless. Its very location in the regions of recent discovery lends it just a touch of hopeful prophecy. Columbus believed that he had sailed near the Earthly Paradise and was convinced that God had chosen him as the apocalyptic herald of the new world promised by Saint John in the twentieth chapter of *Revelation*. Mircea Eliade has pointed out that the "colonization of the two Americas began under an eschatological sign" and that the Europeans of the period "believed that the time had come to renew the Christian world, and the true renewal was a return to the Earthly Paradise."[23] By its geographical site in newly found waters, was *Utopia* suggesting that it had a place in the world to come and projecting itself into a redeeming future?

As a matter of fact, *Utopia* did become part of the New World and found an actual habitat among the natives of Mexico. Within two decades of the book's first appearance, Vasco de Quiroga had established two settlements – one near Mexico City and the other in Michoacán – in which the life of the Indian community was largely patterned on the model that Quiroga had discovered in *Utopia*. This debt he openly acknowledged, and his experiment flourished and continued into the seventeenth century when the natives of one of these pueblos were described as "imitating the monks, living together in communities and devoting themselves to prayer and the pursuit of a more perfect life."[24] Here we see the monastic idea, which helped More to elaborate his dream society, finding its way, through the work of Quiroga, back to the real world. What More had imagined, Quiroga enacted, and this difference between the two men also marks the difference between *Utopia* and the utopian thought which comes after More.

A brief look at the utopian tradition as it evolves from the sixteenth century into the seventeenth will serve, by way of contrast, to define the limits of the seriousness we can attribute to *Utopia* and also to illustrate the way the book adheres to a world that was dying while it was being written. The desire, which we notice in Quiroga, to realize an ideal community on earth gathered momentum from non-humanist sources in the years that followed the publication of *Utopia*. Within a decade of its appearance, the millenarian hysteria, which had flared up on occasion during the last centuries of the Middle Ages, broke out once more under the inspiration of Thomas Müntzer whose new gospel found ready listeners among the German peasants. Müntzer preached that the day of reckoning was at hand when the proud nobility would be struck down, the poor raised up, and the egalitarian, messianic kingdom established on earth. Only nine years after Müntzer and 5,000 of his peasant followers had been slaughtered by Philip of Hesse's army, the Anabaptists inaugurated at Münster a regime that sought to erect the New Jerusalem on German soil.[25] This millenarian trend was to affect both Catholic and Protestant extremists in the years to come and ultimately to lend its own earnestness to the utopian thought of the seventeenth century. For the Spanish conquistadors, in their ambitious explorations, the tendency became a search for the paradisiac Seven Cities of Antilla; for the Spanish friars, it took the shape of a desire to regain by means of the docile aborigines the communal religious society that existed in the primitive church.[26] Some of the same characteristics appear in the thought and activity of the Reformation leaders. At Geneva, Calvin attempted to concretize the Holy City here below,[27] and one branch of the tradition that originates with him became that of the zealous Puritans who strove to establish the New Jerusalem, first in England, then in America.

Now, although *Utopia* partakes of and presages some of this, especially in the suggestion of diffusing monastic structure and industry throughout an entire country, its urgency, balanced as it is by More's humor, is of an order other than that found in the utopian authors of the seventeenth century among whom we find religious enthusiasm assuming the form of millenarian fantasy. Tommaso Campanella, the Italian Dominican, wrote his *City of the Sun* while possessed by a "strange and powerful dream . . . that the moment had come for the creation of an Universal Republic."[28] Campanella's visionary excitement necessitated the introduction into his book of two new elements that would became common in seventeenth-century utopian literature: an intense seriousness and a diminishing of the distance between the site of the ideal state and the real world. It can be argued that Campanella composed his *City of the Sun* in order "to explain what would have been carried out had he been successful" in his attempt to take control of Calabria.[29] Valentin Andreae's *Christianopolis*, published in 1619, is partly inspired by the Christian witness of Calvin's Geneva and partly based on the author's sociological experiments at Calw.[30] Andreae's utopia enjoys a greater concreteness than either More's or Campanella's because more of its details are drawn from a lived experience. The line demarcating Nowhere from Somewhere has all but vanished. *Christianopolis* influenced the *Nova Solyma* of the Englishman Samuel Gott that first appeared in 1648. In this work, the founding at Jerusalem of an ideal Christian society results from a sudden, universal illumination of the people by God, a clear indication of the chiliastic nature of the book. Another English utopia of the same period typifies the new trends which now dominate the genre. Samuel Hartlib offered his very practical *Description of the Famous Kingdom of Macaria* to Parliament for the enactment of any part which stood "with their pleasures."[31] In his preface, the author states that he chose both More and Bacon as his patterns, but, save for the title of the work, *Macaria* owes nothing to *Utopia*. If anyone, Bacon must suffer the charge of influence here. As well as being tinged with millennial fever, Hartlib's sanguine hope for the immediate realization of a grand new society on earth was also encouraged by his Baconian progressivism. The waters of utopia had now mingled with the streams of religious enthusiasm and scientific thought, two forces supportive of the optimistic belief in the imminent descent of the heavenly Jerusalem. Hartlib's *Macaria* speaks out with conviction and unwinking gravity. Gone now is the satirical criticism that distinguished More's work; the comic muse had abandoned utopia and the precedent had been established for the grave utterances of the modern social tract.

Of course, it may be objected that *Utopia* contains the same kind of serious speech as is found in Campanella or Hartlib. Indeed, Hythlodaeus, in his impassioned pleading for social justice, reminds one critic of the stern gospel preached by Savanarola in Florence. In J. H. Hexter's reading of the character, Hythlodaeus rises like a prophet to condemn Christendom, and his vision of Utopia bears a striking resemblance to the theocratic commonwealth realized by Calvin at Geneva.[32] Although there can be no doubt that Hythlodaeus declares his mind with great earnestness, we still can debate whether the reader is meant to understand him in the same grave and rigid temper of mind with which he declares himself. "He learns who takes a meaning in the spirit of its utterance."[33] Even if Hythlodaeus's attitude strikes us with a transparency we cannot question, we are not equally certain of the spirit in which his author has created him. Because he is, after all, a dramatis persona, a creation of More's imagination to serve as the spokesman for Utopia, our understanding of the island and the book intrinsically depends on our assessment of Hythlodaeus and what we judge to be Thomas More's view of him.

In one sense, Hythlodaeus is a paradigm of the Utopian character: remote as the island itself, detached from family ties as are the islanders, zealous, principled, and, like those plainly clad followers of communal life, monkish in his simple tastes and predisposition for the contemplative life. We are told by Thomas Morus,[34] the persona, that Hythlodaeus might not "brook any opposition to his views," a trait in keeping with one of unswerving opinion.[35] This aspect of the man leaves the impression that Hythlodaeus may not only be narrow of mind but actually "blinded by his own Utopian vision,"[36] and this is indicated by his failure to see the obvious defects in the commonwealth he describes. Raphael mentions without a hint of criticism a Utopian penal code as oppressive as the

English system which he decries and a foreign policy that appropriates the right to invade countries when the Utopians judge them to be backward in the exploitation of their natural resources. These and other instances of dubious justice pass unnoticed in Hythlodaeus's description of the island and probably account for Morus's guarded reaction to the story. The circumspect politician warily maintains a certain distance from the enthusiastic man of bright ideals when, at the end of the mariner's tale, he leads him by the hand into supper. This final gesture of the book has been read as the act of "a father watching over his child. . . . Hythlodaeus, once so proudly independent, so all-knowing and all-seeing, now needs a helping hand quite desperately. Blinded by his absorption in his own vision, cut off from his auditors by being hypnotized with himself, he can no longer find his way back to reality."[37]

The negative assessment of Raphael squares with the surname which the author fastens on him: "Hythlodaeus" can claim to be only "learned in nonsense." This passionate spokesman not only for Utopia but also, in some sense, for the author himself cannot cleanly escape the suspicion that his role involves him in comedy. Morus suggests this when he compares the serious rhetoric of Hythlodaeus to a tragic monologue delivered on a comic stage. Even his dream island partakes of a festively comic spirit when it serves to satirize the false ideals of European society as the procession of the Anemolian ambassadors illustrates. Whatever else we may say of Hythlodaeus, we cannot deny that he exemplifies, as perhaps no other character created by More, the author's power to create serio-comic art. Socially awkward, with a poor sense of timing and situation, Hythlodaeus makes of his world a hodgepodge of comedy and tragedy. *Utopia*, therefore, can most readily be distinguished from the later Renaissance writings in the same genre by the mockery it directs at its main character and central voice, and the raison d'être of this comedy, I feel, illuminates for us the wisdom in More's vision.

Raphael Hythlodaeus, the mouthpiece for the brave new world of his creator's imagination, is "learned in nonsense," a blind contemplative, a self-deluded visionary with monkish tendencies. Why? Let us first recall that Hythlodaeus, in his fiery, moral enthusiasm, fills the role of a prophet justifying the comparison between him and Savanarola. As well as looking back toward the reformer of Florence, he anticipates the holy revolutionaries who were to rise up within a little more than a decade after the publication of *Utopia*. Thomas Müntzer of Thuringia, his disciple Hans Hut, and the Münster Anabaptists Jan Matthys and Jan Bockelson all burned with a zeal to overthrow society and renew their worlds.[38] Like Hythlodaeus, these stern devotees were possessed of a social vision intimately connected with their religious beliefs, and they were willing to seize their new earthly kingdoms by force. The wrath discernible in these prophets would seem to maintain only the most tenuous link with what the scriptures call "holy anger." The violence in their histories has also been suggested as a facet of Hythlodaeus's makeup: "uprooted himself and an uprooter of others," his "most urgent pleas for reform bristle with metaphors of deracination and eradication."[39] Raphael would readily pluck out vice just as his Utopians punish adultery with death.

Why has More inserted this note of violence into the character? Is it not possible that he is exploring the nature of the idealist, the reformer possessed not only by a glaring vision but also by a demon unknown to him? Violence, either of spirit or action, seems to beset the inspired rebel even in the most religious of causes, and, in exploring Hythlodaeus, More may quite possibly be examining himself on the eve of assuming a responsible position in government. I do not think it wise in this case to divorce the character completely from his creator. A man of More's dedication had to cherish high ideals, to be firm of grip, unyielding in his most basic commitments. Like his Hythlodaeus, he carried with him all through life a desire for solitude and a feeling at court of being "an unaccustomed rider in his saddle."[40] Before launching his public career, he lived with the Carthusians, and, at the end of it, confessed to his daughter that, were it not for his family, he would have contented himself in the seclusion of a room narrower than his prison cell.[41] The idealist, the monk, the contemplative – these are sides not only of Hythlodaeus but of the author as well.

Now in exposing his Raphael to mockery, in undermining his credentials, in appending nonsense to his name, might not More be exorcising the demon violence indigenous to political ideals and political idealists, even including his own, himself? As in Koestler's theory of laughter, where the "function of the reflex is to dissipate harmlessly certain 'self-assertive or aggressive' emotions,"[42] Utopian comedy discloses and ridicules the aggression latent in the zealous eyes of the reformer. The eyes in question here are not only those of Hythlodaeus but the author's as well. To the extent that the creator is identifiable with the character, More has parodied himself. The prospect of a Europe modeled after that community of the early church probably shone in this saint's mind as it did in the other reformers of that age, but he was also shrewd enough to see the temptation disguised in that ideal. Hence, he could fashion a character as a projection of his own dream and, at the same time, hold that character up to ridicule.[43]

Having noted already the identical features shared by the author and his brainchild, we can complete this inquiry into character by recalling one obvious difference of outlook between the two. Hythlodaeus sees Utopia, the "place": an ideal society, a pattern absorbing all his enthusiasm, while More sees *Utopia*, the work of art: an island in its proper setting, objectified, laughed at, a mirage. What Hythlodaeus takes with the utmost seriousness, More presents with something less than total gravity. In the mind of the dramatis persona, the island is rational, Apollonian, chaste; in the mind of the dramatist, the island is placed in a comic perspective suggesting the half-world that Utopia is and the Dionysian forces that it represses and ignores. In the premarital inspection of bodies, the sexual union is deromanticized and the look of love is compared to a merchant's eye at a horse auction. The humor here is intentional as is the juxtaposition of the treatment of marriage with that of slavery and the stern laws against adultery. Indigenous to most utopias is a fear of sex, the force that threatens the group and tribal order because it reaches over boundaries. The *New Atlantis* celebrates the Feast of the Family by heaping honor on the solemn paterfamilias and by encasing his spouse in a loft where "she sitteth but is not seen," quarantined as it were from the Baconian festivities.[44] In Campanella's *City of the Sun,* "the breeding of children has reference to the commonwealth and not to individuals."[45] What redeems More's work from the unrelenting purposefulness of the last two Renaissance utopias is precisely the distance and balance that the satirical representation of its visionary narrator achieves.

Now the presence of comedy and especially the author's parody of himself suggest a detachment on More's part both from his subject matter and his own opinion about it: while holding to the world, he can let it pass. The serio-comic tone of the work gauges the balance between involvement and non-involvement. Insofar as its author rejects a heavy-handed, pragmatic approach so typical of the seventeenth-century utopias, he betrays the fact that his book has not completely escaped the spirit of those monastic ages when religious thinkers tried to maintain a distance between themselves and the world of affairs. The heaven-bent vision of the medieval period led to the erection of immense houses of prayer whose ultimate meaning lay beyond this life and whose construction depended in part on gifts from which the donors could expect no return as one might on an investment. In this sense, the cathedrals were profitless undertakings. Aquinas likened contemplation to play because neither admits of a purpose beyond itself.[46] It was natural, therefore, that the house of contemplation should also provide the birthplace for medieval religious drama. After all, neither playing nor contemplative praying is of any earthly use. Likewise, to the extent that *Utopia* is mere entertainment and a comic fable, it intimidates the serious, purpose-filled interpretation of what it is saying. Like contemplation and play, it may be of no earthly use at all.

The very cornerstone of Utopian government, its "common life and subsistence – without any exchange of money," is written off as nonsensical because it "utterly overthrows all the nobility, magnificence, splendor, and majesty . . . the true glories and ornaments of the commonwealth," the very things that Book Two has satirized.[47] At the core of *Utopia*, then, lies this magnificent absurdity which points to the folly of mankind in its political endeavors, and exposes "the great emptiness lying concealed at the heart of things," as the introductory verses put it.[48] The Utopian void points, however, to more than the vain strivings of men; it also suggests that still point of self-possession where play and contemplation meet, that state of activity where movement has no purpose other than that contained within itself, an emptiness, in other words, implying fulfillment. Here we reach the deep spiritual relationship between Utopian comedy and the monastic ideal.

We began by noting how the monastery's social structure aided More in organizing his Utopian world. We were then treating what must be called an external similarity resulting from one outer form, one shell, guiding the edification of another. Now the resemblance is seen in the intrinsic makeup of each. As contemplation constitutes the very soul of monastic life, so a comic state of mind inheres to the essence of the Utopian vision: both ignore a secular purpose, both aim at disengaging the heart from attachment to created things. So the outward resemblance between Utopia and the monastery inclines the reader to take More's fiction literally as a model or pattern for life on earth while the inner resemblance between the two encourages us to interpret the book as an invitation to strive after an interior disposition of soul, that same detachment we find in both the Utopian disregard for gold and the author's own freedom from the despotic imperatives linked to his ideal. Those who understand *Utopia* as a social blueprint will favor the former interpretation; those who eschew what they call a one-sided reading and stress the presence of comedy can salvage the serious content of the work by opting for the latter position. This reading sees the bias of More's intention leaning toward "detachment within involvement"[49] and fostering a state of soul rather than a political constitution. This condition would be realized when the remote, monastic heart, delivered not only from the hold of selfish desire but also from the captivity of self-delusion, engages in the world of affairs.

NOTES

1. Marie Louise Berneri in *Journey through Utopia* (London, 1950), Joyce O. Hertzler in *The History of Utopian Thought* (New York, 1923), and Lewis Mumford in *The Story of Utopias* (New York, 1922), all omit the Middle Ages.
2. Berneri, p. 52.
3. *Summa Theologiae*, 1a–2ae.63.4. Translation by Thomas Gilby in St. Thomas Aquinas, *Theological Texts* (London, 1955), p. 224.
4. Epistola 64, "Ad Alexandrum Lincolniensem Episcopum," *PL* 182:169–70. Translated by Catherine Misrahi in Jean Leclercq, *The Love of Learning and the Desire of God* (New York, 1961), pp. 68–9.

5. Northrop Frye ("Varieties of Literary Utopias" in *Utopias and Utopian Thought*, ed. Frank E. Manuel [Boston, 1966], pp. 25–49) estimates that the "influence of the monastic community on utopian thought has been enormous. It is strong in More's *Utopia*, and much stronger in Campanella's *City of the Sun.* . . ." He adds that the "conception of the ideal society as a secularized reversal of the monastery . . . appears in Rabelais' scheme for the Abbey of Thélème" (p. 35).

6. David Knowles, *Christian Monasticism* (New York, 1969), pp. 12–15.

7. David Knowles, *The Monastic Order in England* (Cambridge, 1949). "No work done within it [the monastery], whether manual, intellectual or charitable, is directed to an end outside its walls." The monastery's "primary concern is with itself" (p. 4).

8. Lynn White, Jr., *Machina ex Deo: Essays in the Dynamism of Western Culture* (Cambridge, Mass., 1968), pp. 64–5.

9. Knowles, *The Monastic Order in England*, pp. 352–3.

10. *Ibid.*, pp. 88–99 (for Bec, Lanfranc, and Anselm), pp. 145–50 (Cluny), and pp. 208–26 (Clairvaux).

11. Lewis Mumford, *The City in History: Its Origins, Its Transformations, and Its Prospects* (New York, 1961), p. 247. An example of the monastic influence on architecture can be read in Alan Temko's account of Suger, abbot of Saint-Denis, who contributed significantly to the flowering of the gothic style in northern France (*Notre-Dame of Paris* [New York, 1959], pp. 73–82).

12. Mumford, *The City in History*, pp. 246–7.

13. St. Thomas More, *Utopia*, ed. Edward Surtz and J. H. Hexter (New Haven, 1965), p. 219. For reflections upon the likeness between the monastic life and Utopia, see J. H. Hexter, *More's Utopia: The Biography of an Idea* (Princeton, 1952), pp. 85–90; P. Albert Duhamel, "Medievalism of More's *Utopia*," *SP*, vol. 52, 1955, pp. 119–20; D. B. Fenlon, "England and Europe: *Utopia* and Its Aftermath," *Transactions of the Royal Historical Society*, 5th series, vol. 25, 1975, pp. 115–36.

14. Although the *Republic* does not show us the ideal city in the concrete, Plato apparently planned to do just that in his myth of the war between Atlantis and the primeval Athens. With this in mind, he began the *Critias*, which, alas, he abandoned after writing the introduction. So it was left to More to create the first great utopian fable.

15. "Sir Thomas More and Lucian: An Interpretation of *Utopia*," *Archiv für das Studium der neueren Sprachen und Literaturen*, vol. 103, 1967, pp. 349–50.

16. Frye, p. 37.

17. *St. Thomas More: Selected Letters*, ed. Elizabeth Frances Rogers (New Haven, 1961), p. 130.

18. *The Evolution of the Monastic Ideal* (1931; reprint ed., Boston, 1962).

19. David Knowles, *From Pachomius to Ignatius* (Oxford, 1966), pp. 19 and 29–30.

20. *Evolution of the Monastic Ideal*, p. 286.

21. *Utopia*, p. 225.

22. *Selected Letters*, p. 85.

23. "Paradise and Utopia: Mythical Geography and Eschatology," in *Utopias and Utopian Thought*, pp. 262–3.

24. Silvio Zavala, *Sir Thomas More in New Spain: A Utopian Adventure of the Renaissance* (London, 1955), p. 19.

25. For an account of the millennial hysteria in Germany during the early

Reformation, see Norman Cohn, *The Pursuit of the Millennium*, rev. ed. (New York, 1970). Cohn treats both Müntzer (pp. 234–51) and the Münster Anabaptists (pp. 261–80).

26. The story of the millenarian visionaries in the Catholic lands of the Americas is told by John Leddy Phelan in *The Millennial Kingdom of the Franciscans in the New World*, 2nd ed., rev. (Berkeley, 1970).

27. J. H. Hexter, *The Vision of Politics on the Eve of the Reformation: More, Machiavelli, and Seyssel* (New York, 1973). On pages 107–17, Hexter examines Calvin's New Jerusalem and compares it to Utopia.

28. Berneri, p. 90.

29. *Ibid.*, p. 92.

30. For the background to Andreae's creation of his utopia, see Felix Emil Held's introduction to his translation of *Johann Valentin Andreae's Christianopolis: An Ideal State of the Seventeenth Century* (New York, 1916).

31. *Samuel Hartlib and the Advancement of Learning*, ed. Charles Webster (Cambridge, 1970), p. 80. This collection of writings by Hartlib and John Dury includes the complete text of *Macaria* (pp. 79–90).

32. Hexter, in *The Vision of Politics*, situates *Utopia* within the general context of a "Christian Revival" that includes the work of Savanarola at Florence (pp. 94–107). For his comparison between Geneva and Utopia, see note 27.

33. Aquinas, *In Joannem*, 6, *lectio* 5. Translation by Thomas Gilby in *St. Thomas Aquinas: Philosophical Texts* (London, 1951), p. 34.

34. I have retained the Latin spelling of *Morus*, the character in *Utopia*, in order to distinguish him from More, the author.

35. *Utopia*, p. 245.

36. Robbin S. Johnson, *More's Utopia: Ideal and Illusion* (New Haven, 1969), p. 66.

37. Richard S. Sylvester, "'Si Hythlodaeo Credimus': Vision and Revision in Thomas More's *Utopia*," *Soundings*, vol. 51, 1968, pp. 288–9.

38. Cohn, pp. 234–80.

39. Sylvester, p. 284.

40. *Selected Letters*, p. 94.

41. "Furthermore, being prisoner in the tower, he [More] told his said daughter that his short penning and shutting up did little grieve him; for, if it had not been for respect of his wife and children, he had voluntarily long ere that time shut himself in as narrow or narrower a room than that was" (Nicholas Harpsfield, *The Life and Death of Sʳ Thomas Moore, Knight*, ed. Elsie Vaughan Hitchcock, EETS OS 186 [London, 1932], pp. 17–18). I have modernized the spelling and punctuation.

42. Edward L. Galligan, "The Usefulness of Arthur Koestler's Theory of Jokes," *The South Atlantic Quarterly*, vol. 75, 1976, p. 146.

43. In a letter to Erasmus, More writes playfully of his Utopian daydream. See *Selected Letters*, p. 85.

44. *Francis Bacon: A Selection of His Works*, ed. Sidney Warhaft (New York, 1965), p. 439.

45. *Peaceable Kingdoms: An Anthology of Utopian Writings*, ed. Robert L. Chianese (New York, 1971), p. 21. The translation of Campanella's *Civitas Solis* in this volume is by T. W. Halliday.

46. "Notice how aptly contemplating is compared with playing, and because of two characteristics. First, play is delightful, and the contemplation of wisdom brings the greatest joy; *my spirit is sweet above honey*. Second, sports are not means to ends but are sought for their own sake, so also are the

delights of wisdom" (Opusculum IX, *De Hebdomadibus*, Prologue). Translated by Gilby in *Philosophical Texts*, pp. 1–2. See also *Summa Contra Gentes*, 3.2.

47. *Utopia*, p. 245. Edward Surtz (*The Praise of Pleasure* [Cambridge, Mass., 1957], p. 183) claims that this passage "embodies the most skilled and subtle irony."

48. *Ibid.*, p. 31.

49. Johnson, p. 31.

The Renaissance Conventions of Envy

R. B. GILL

In the admirable and high-minded *Musophilus,* Samuel Daniel defends poets against the "viperous Creticke" and the wounding "reproches and despight" of Envy. His defense is one of many Renaissance complaints against slanderous detractors of poets and poetry. Thomas Campion, who differed sharply with Daniel about the nature of English verse, agreed about the writer's plight; in a Latin epigram less high-minded than Daniel's poem but equally typical of the age, he urges Thomas Nashe to slay with his critical teeth a disgusting "dog" who has shamelessly attacked the sacred poets.[1] Of course, there have always been protests that critics are motivated by envy, but the complaints are especially frequent in the last years of Queen Elizabeth's reign, when they appear not only in critical treatises but also in addresses to the reader before all types of books, in separate poems, in satires, and in plays. A climax of sorts is reached in the late-century satires of Joseph Hall and John Marston and in related plays like Ben Jonson's *Poetaster.*

There are reasons for this contentiousness. The 1590s were a difficult time for writers. The economic monopoly of the Stationers, the bickering between academic and professional writers, the frequent personal quarrels of the age, the normal contentiousness of the many student writers, the rivalries between members of the Inns of Court, moral objections to the contents of satires and epigrams, and, of course, peculiarities of personality in writers like John Marston are all sources of faction. But protests against critics' envious detraction occur so often that they become conventional and lose the feel of sincerity. Again and again we hear of carping envy, despite, vipers, dogs, wounding teeth, and the poet's contempt for them all. Disdain of envy provides the basic tone and manner of many satires of the period, giving satirists an excuse for exaggerated scorn of the vulgar and assertions of their own virtues and poetic abilities. Many of the complaints are imitations of classical protests; many are the occasion for ostentatious epigrammatic wit. Sir John Harington, for instance, ends his prologue to *The Metamorphosis of Ajax* wittily urging Zoilus and Momus, two classical carpers, to bite away at his scatological matter.

Scholars have wondered whether attacks on writers were frequent enough to justify this outpouring of complaints, but their conclusions have been understandably hesitant.[2] On the one hand, there were indeed frequent attacks. Campion, for example, attacks critics in his epigram but then turns critic himself in another epigram attacking Nicholas Breton. And, no doubt, in a climate of contention most attacks were oral and, consequently, have not survived. On the other hand, the insistent repetition and conventional nature of the complaints cause doubt about their sincerity. Although it is difficult to assess the matter with certainty, it is clear that writers drew their complaints from a tradition of protests against envy that stretches back through the Middle Ages to antiquity and that they used them as sources for their own material much as they used other ancient conventions.

Critical envy, then, is a *topos*, a rhetorical convention, but it has not been recognized as such because it seems personal and part of the contentious literary environment of late Elizabethan England. In order to establish its conventionality, let us trace its occurrences from Martial to Shakespeare and examine its effect on some Elizabethan satires, where it figures most prominently. We shall gain insight into the choice of terminology used by writers like Spenser and Shakespeare, and we shall see that attacks on envy shape the very mode of many Elizabethan satires. They are an important component in the intense self-consciousness of the satirists, their belligerent assertiveness, and their strange relationship with their audience. We shall find that the atmosphere of critical envy reinforces whatever defensiveness an author might normally feel by giving him a fashionable and ready-made means of anticipating criticism. We are never quite certain, then, whether these attacks on envy initiate quarrels, reply to other attacks, or just engage in fashionable swagger. Protest against envy is complex because it is a convention that pretends to be personal; it both reflects the realities of Elizabethan literary life and, most interestingly, shapes those realities as well.

Greek and Latin use of envy sets important precedents for the Elizabethan conventions. First, Diogenes, the Cynic philosopher and railing critic, lends to Elizabethan satire not only his name but also his oddly mixed reputation for questionable actions and austere virtue, for peevish railing and incorruptible censure of wrongdoing. His cankered character sets him apart from the common mass, his scurrilous actions serve as ironic comments on the indecent decorousness of a hypocritical society. He is, in short, remarkably similar to the ill-tempered Elizabethan satiric persona. Secondly, Elizabethan satirists could find in Diogenes' railing a method of attack rather than a defensive reaction to critics' envy. Likewise, complaints against Momus and Zoilus, the envious critics who appear in a number of classical works including the satiric epigrams of Martial and the Greek Anthology, are often not so much defenses against actual criticism as means of attack. For instance, in Martial's epigrams the specific identity of Zoilus matters little; he, therefore, serves as a convenient catch-all of faults for Martial to criticize.[3] Elizabethan satirists, then, could find ample classical precedent for using complaints against envy as satiric devices rather than as heartfelt replies to real calumny. Thirdly, Elizabethan use of barking, snarling, and biting as metaphors for envious criticism is also due to classical influence, for the Cynics were associated with dogs in name and in currish habits as well. References to Cynics in titles and within satires abound. As Edward Topsell notes in his *Historie of Fovre-Footed Beastes* (1607), "the voice of a Dogge, is by the learned, interpreted a rayling and angry speech: wherof commeth that *Canina facundia* among Authors, for rayling eloquence" (p. 139).[4] "Biting," however, is a natural metaphor for criticism and does not belong to the Cynics alone. Snakes, for instance, account for some of its use. Ovid paints a pale Envy who eats snakes and drips venom from her teeth (*Metamorphoses* 2.775).

In the Middle Ages the status of envy as a Deadly Sin reinforces its conventional nature and, at the same time, makes it a matter more serious than the ignorant carping of Greek and Roman critics. But medieval use of envy also owes much to classical examples. Even Diogenes and Zoilus appear in medieval satire. Because of classical and biblical influence and, no doubt, because of the naturalness of the association, envy is connected with dogs and especially with serpents. *The Ancren Riwle* notes that the serpent in the Garden was motivated by envy, and it speaks of sins as the dogs of Hell. *The Book of Vices and Virtues*, one of the better known divisions of the sins, compares the envious man to a "basiliske," calls backbiters venomous, and "mysseyers" biting hyenas. *Piers the Plowman* mentions Envy's "Addres tonge" and his loveless life "lyke a luther dogge." Chaucer's Parson warns us of the "venym of Envye." Such examples are numerous.[5] Envy, then, enters the sixteenth century as a serious matter yet, at the same time, as a well-established and somewhat worn convention.

Much of the literary disputatiousness in which Renaissance envy flourishes is a continuation of medieval practices. Renaissance schoolboys, like their medieval counterparts, wrote invectives as exercises. Contention among scholars and wits, an important source of sixteenth-century disputation, finds precedent in the "capcyous and subtyl" wits in fifteenth-century English universities; and the use of invectives, satires, and epigrams by early Tudor court orators and poets like John Skelton is similar to medieval sirventes and political satires.[6] Many sixteenth-century attacks on envy use alliterative abuse, another medieval form. Examples are numerous in poems by writers like Robert Sempill, Gavin Douglas, and Skelton. But most interesting of all is "Rede me and be nott wrothe" (1528) by William Roy and Jerome Barlowe, a commentary on corruptions in the English Catholic church. At one point the speaker says that he will "rehearce a brefe oracion" dedicated to Cardinal Wolsey; he then launches into eight stanzas of rhyme royal alliterative criticism, beginning with "O miserable monster / most malicious." "Thou raylest nowe of a fassion," replies his comrade, and the first speaker notes that "popisshe curres" may bark at his words.[7] This is a set piece of invective, given the title "oracion" and marked off from the main text by its formal nature, its alliteration, and its rhyme royal. In short, it tells us that by the early 1500s the classical and medieval conventions of envy like dogs, barking, railing, and alliterative abuse were coalescing into a recognized, fashionable type of rhetoric well adapted to Renaissance invective.

Flytings are another important influence on this fashionable rhetoric of envy, especially on its authorial ostentatiousness. These contests of abuse are frequent in the earlier 1500s but continue throughout the century. They are cockfights between writers, often sanctioned and urged on by the king seemingly as a type of barbaric amusement. Thus, in spite of their viciousness, it is arguable that they are more like command performances than heartfelt disputes. Certainly, they are highly conventional. Dunbar's flyting with Kennedy (1508) seems to rely on vigor and excess more than on seriousness. Each section of Skelton's flyting with Garnesche (1513–14) ends with the explanation "By the kynges most noble commaundment." James V of Scotland with "wennemous wryting" commanded Sir David Lindsay's "Answer to the Kingis Flyting" (1536).[8] Thomas Churchyard's "Contention" (1560) with a critic named Thomas Camell claims that Camell barks "lyke a curre dogge, at euery good worke" (sig. Aiii^r); in like terms Camell replies by calling Churchyard "Master Mome" (sig. Bi^r). Later in the century (c. 1582) Alexander Montgomerie flytes with Sir Patrick Hume of Polwarth. A preface to the printed edition (Edinburgh, 1629) stresses the bravado of the flyters and denies that any bitterness exists between them; there is "No cankring Envy," for they are "Curres" who bark but "neuer seeke to bite" (sig. [ ] 1^v). Thus, each of these flytings focuses interest on the author's poetic vigor. There are other examples of flytings and, as we shall see, numerous similar sixteenth-century invectives. For our purposes their importance lies in the fact that they are an influential body of highly conventional invectives that call attention to the author as much as to his subject matter.

Another form of early sixteenth-century contentiousness in which the author seeks to display himself by rebuking an opponent is the debate between rival scholars. One of the earliest disputes to seek the publicity of the English printing press was the Grammarians' War (c. 1520), which embroiled, among others, Robert Whittinton, William Horman, William Lily, and John Skelton in acrimonious contention. The details of their quarrel, which seems to have centered on competing Latin textbooks, do not matter as much as the form it took. In scholarly Latin they accuse each other of belching out envy, of snarling in drunken cups, of viper's venom, of biting, and so on. The main effect lies not in the truth of what they say so much as in the vigor of the attack. Like flytings the Grammarians' War establishes early in the sixteenth century a pattern of vigorous and ostentatious abuse. In it we find Momus, Zoilus, biting dogs, venomous snakes, accusations of envy, and authorial ostentation. Each of these becomes commonplace in sixteenth-century literary quarrels.[9]

The conventions of envy that give body to the humanists' rivalries in the Grammarians' War continue as a standard part of scholarly publishing.[10] Ostentatious abuse appears in a group of prefatory attacks on envy by Jasper Heywood, Barnabe Googe, Alexander Neville, George Turbervile, and Edward Hake in the 1560s.[11] These writers apply the techniques of flytings and quarrels specifically to envy and develop for their use an energetic vocabulary, which they pass on to later sixteenth-century writers. They speak of "surgyng seas of depe disdayn," "boylyng Rancour," "curious, canckard, carping mouthes," "cankerd caytifes," as well as the standard vipers and curs. By treating the envy figure in a dramatic manner, often in terms of military conceits ("No, no, I martch gainst *Momus* once againe"), they turn him from a mere name into a figure of active guile, sometimes the leader of an energetic crew of "ragyng feends." These poems have the forceful vituperation of flytings. Neville's curse on "Momus monstrous broode" is as vigorous as any of Skelton's invectives; Hake even refers to his "flytting Muse." As in flytings, their main effect lies in the vigor of the author's attacks rather than in the truth of his charges; and even more so, for the flytings attack specific men, but these prefaces have only unspecified adversaries. It is, therefore, difficult to see that they attack anything other than false criticism in general, with the result that they, like flytings and later satires, often seem less interested in their ostensible subject than in their own rhetoric. Even when specific attacks are mentioned, as in Turbervile's "To the rayling Route of Sycophants" (ll. 37ff.), the focus still lies squarely on the poet himself. Turbervile's poem is a little showpiece of invective wit, a fitting bit of swagger before a young man's book of sonnets. These prefatory attacks on envy justify the author's book; they explain the plea for a patron's protection; and they imply by their disdain of unskillful critics that the author is skillful and desires only an audience with the very best judgment. In short, these prefaces are author-oriented and have less to do with envious criticism than with fashionable, conventional, and rhetorically effective introductions to the authors' literary abilities.

After the outcropping of attacks in the 1560s lies a quarter century of prefaces that worry about envy in the familiar ways. But in the 1590s envy begins to assume real literary importance, in satire especially but also in the works of Shakespeare and Spenser, where its influence, though unmistakable, has been overlooked. In Shakespeare's plays the conventions of envy are unobtrusive but numerous. Shakespeare turns them to his own purposes, tightly integrating them with the dramatic context. They often

explain his choice of terms: the "envious barking of your saucy tongue,"
"with envious carping tongue," and "rancorous spite" in *1 Henry VI;*
"lean-faced Envy" with "deadly hate," "fell serpents" with "envenomed
and fatal sting" in *2 Henry VI;* "carping censures" in *Richard III;* and the
"fangs of malice" in *Twelfth Night*. Similar references occur frequently.
More importantly, envy adds depth to characterization. At the end of
3 Henry VI, Richard notes that he was born with teeth and "should snarl
and bite and play the dog" (5.6.75–7). At the beginning of *Richard III,*
Richard tells us that his figure causes dogs to bark as he halts by them
(1.1.23). In each case the reference to dogs is justified by the context,
but each reference is made more complex by its unmistakable dependence
on conventional association of dogs with criticism. The convention likewise adds depth to Gloucester's description of Buckingham and York in
2 Henry VI:

> Sharp Buckingham unburthens with his tongue
> The envious load that lies upon his heart;
> And dogged York, that reaches at the moon,
>   . . .
> By false accuse doth level at my life.
>   (3.1.156–60)

"Dogged York" might pass as merely an appropriate epithet for a man
who "reaches at the moon" if it did not occur in the context of envy and
false accusation. Here the convention is clear, unobtrusive, and perfectly
integrated with the context. In *Titus Andronicus* Aaron wishes to "utter
forth / The venomous malice of my swelling heart," to which Lucius replies, "Away, inhuman dog!" (5.3.12–14). The quick switch from venom
to dogs is explained by their close association in the conventions of envy.
Although examples of the conventions occur throughout Shakespeare's
work, interestingly the most explicit and frequent use of them is found
in the *Henry VI* plays. Perhaps this fact can be explained by the younger
Shakespeare's greater dependence on fashionable material. In any case, it
testifies to the recognizability of the conventions early in the 1590s, well
before the rash of envy in the satires that soon followed.

Without doubt the most illustrious literary use of the conventions of
envy is Spenser's. In Book V of *The Faerie Queene,* Spenser describes the
"ill fauour'd Hags" Envy and Detraction in terms drawn from Ovid;
Envy, for instance, eats a snake. The other strains of envy are also present
in their reviling and railing, their "cancred kynd," and their barking like
curs (5.12.28–43). Their accompanying monster, the alliterative Blatant
Beast, was begotten of dogs and serpent-like creatures. In the fifth canto
of Book VI, Despetto (Malice), Decetto (Deceit), and Defetto (Detraction) send the Beast against Timias. There we find him a hound or barking
cur-dog with "tooth impure" and "inward rancour and despight." Similar
descriptions occur in the sixth and twelfth cantos of Book VI; there we

have the "poysnous sting," the "hellish Dog," "venemous despite," bark-ing, raging, railing, reproach, backbiting, and so on (6.6.1, 9, 12; 12.22–41). Spenser's vocabulary is clearly indebted to the prefaces of the 1560s, and he follows them in dramatizing envy as a monster. Although the Bla-tant Beast is certainly conceived on a grander scale than the "spiteful Beast" of the prefaces, he is of essentially the same nature. Like Turber-vile's narrator, Sir Calidore marches against the Beast, but his victory is only temporary for the Beast later breaks loose. Like Googe and Neville, Spenser must accept the backbiting that the venomous monster still directs at the "gentle Poets rime." The result is that Book VI ends with off-handed irony or sarcasm uncharacteristic of Spenser:

> Therfore do you my rimes keep better measure,
> And seeke to please, that now is counted wisemens threasure.

Spenser has certainly not lowered his poetic ideals to the more moderate goal of merely "pleasing." He, like many of his predecessors and espe-cially like the satirists who write immediately after him, is using sarcastic self-abasement to show the inevitable result of continued slander on true poetry.

Spenser knew that his sixteenth-century audience would recognize the conventions of envy in Books V and VI of *The Faerie Queene*. And if we too recognize in the Blatant Beast a kinship with that long series of sixteenth-century attacks on envy, we shall find him less puzzling. Cer-tainly, seen in this light his escape into the historical world is not in-explicable, as one critic has complained. What was essentially a conven-tion of prefaces and commendatory poems Spenser expands into some of the most vivid episodes in *The Faerie Queene*, which becomes an impor-tant source of envy for the late-century satirists.[12] His skill gave authority to the vigorous language of envy. Most importantly, his major emphasis on the envious Blatant Beast reinforced and added respectability to the tendency of Elizabethan authors to pose as bastions of virtue beset by vul-gar readers.

The conventional uses of envy are also evident in a host of other late Elizabethan writers. Like Spenser, Thomas Lodge adopts a defensive pose of virtue in an address to the gentlemen readers of *A Fig for Momus* (1595), the volume that contains his satires. Referring to dogs, biting, Momus, and railing, he expresses contempt for the unlearned, responds to critics, and includes a defense of his satires. Whatever his true attitude to-ward critics may have been, he clearly uses the conventions of envy as pretext for exhibition of his own aloof integrity. No doubt he considered the pose decorous for a satirist. Of course, it is easy to find in Nashe's mettlesome prose evidence of quarrels used to show off the author's skill-ful rhetoric. R. B. McKerrow cites the ending of the preface to *Strange Newes* (1592): "Saint Fame for mee, and thus I runne vpon him." After assaulting Harvey in *Pierce Penilesse,* Nashe turns to the reader for judgment: "haue I not an indifferent prittye vayne in Spurgalling an Asse?" This is like Everard Guilpin's later *Whipper of the Satyre his Pennance* (1601), which, after blasting Breton, asks the readers, "Now censure (gentle spirits) i'st not faire? / Haue I not cast him clenly? Iudgement hoe?"[13] Guilpin's *Skialetheia* (1598) contains both the vocabulary of envy and the contorted tone of belligerence and self-criticism; his nonchalant dismissal of his work is a disarming technique of the sort that we found at the end of Book VI of *The Faerie Queene* and shall find again in the satires of Hall and Marston.[14]

Envy is used in conventional ways by a long list of other late Elizabethan satirists and epigrammatists, including John Weever, Sir John Harington, Thomas Bastard, William Rankins, Thomas Middleton, Samuel Rowlands, Nicholas Breton, and the authors of the Parnassus plays, to cite only writers active in the four-year period at the turn of the century. The preface of *A Pleasant Satyre,* translated from the French in 1595, speaks of "Cyniquized" satires.[15] Of Jonson's non-dramatic works, "To Censorious Courtling" (*Epigrammes* LII) mentions critical spite; the first line of his poem to the memory of Shakespeare disavows envy; and "To My Detractor" refers to the Blatant Beast and hurls dog epithets with vigor. Drayton's ode, "His Defence Against the Idle Critick," calls his envious critic a "Beast" with "vilenesse" and "resolved Hate." Even Donne uses "railing" to designate the function of the satirist at the beginning of "Satyre III" and refers to reprehenders and "my bitings" in the Epistle to "The Progresse of the Soule."

This repeated use of envy makes understandable the great effect it has on tone and author figures in satires. Years of prefaces like those in the 1560s make a defense of one's work an expected topic. The result is contention and ostentation. Contentious references to their own propriety and to the failings of their rivals fill many late Elizabethan satires. There is a feeling of competition, a sense that the satirist expects his work to be compared critically with other satires. These works develop a curious tone composed of defensiveness mixed with self-assertion and attacks on other writers. Weever's "Prophesie of this present yeare, 1600" attempts an ironic defense of satire that soon turns to the familiar attacks on other satirists. Cyril Tourneur's strange *Transformed Metamorphosis* (1600) begins with swaggering disdain of critical "flowts" and malice, but at the same time insists on his "Tyrocinie," "weak ioynted rime," "infant eie," and "youths obscuritie." His tone, then, is a self-conscious mixture of contention and pretentious humility, all directed at the potentially envious reader, whom Tourneur addresses with the conventional "Thine as I see thy affection" (see Lodge's "To the Reader" in *A Fig for Momus*).[16] In this context many of the puzzling aspects of late Elizabethan satire become much clearer. Hall's satires, we shall see, show the effects of envy;

so do Marston's, but, interestingly, they show a better understanding of those effects and use them for satirical purposes.

Cynicism gives Hall his terminology and colors his conception of the satirist. Although he does not go as far as Marston in creating a Diogenes-like persona who has the biting characteristics he criticizes in others, he does see the two-faced aspect of cynicism as part of the satirist's character. In *Virgidemiae* (1597) Hall uses cynicism in slighting remarks about bad poets and carping critics but also finds it useful to describe his own work. He calls the last three books "byting Satyres," as opposed to the "Tooth-lesse" first three. He addresses Juvenal as "carping" Aquine.[17] Other references to envy stud *Virgidemiae*. As Lodge had done, Hall begins with a "Defiance to Enuie"; he makes envy an important theme in the prologues to Books I, II, the "Authors charge" before Book IV, and the "Post-script to the Reader." And, in addition to the cynicism, he uses envy in four other satires (1.9.1, 4.1.1, 4.6.88, and 6.1.1).

The intensity of Hall's self-consciousness is unusual even for an Elizabethan poet. He is young and wishes his "tender" muse to make a good show. As an academic author still at Cambridge, he is concerned that he not violate proper decorum. In fact, he so repeatedly defends his decorum that he seems to expect readers to approach his satire with the same academic scrutiny that they would bring to Juvenal and Persius. But academic fastidiousness is not the only source of Hall's self-consciousness, for the shape of his defense is dictated by the conventions of envy. He begins *Virgidemiae* defying "dread Enuy and ill tongues" and ends it still worrying about being "set vpon the racke of many mercilesse and peremptorie censures." His "Defiance to Enuie" sets the tone of his satires. He knows that his work must face hostility, so he adopts that common response to envy, a swaggering humility. Let others be proud; his lowly satires are "not worth their enuying." The pose allows him to attack his fellow writers and to dismiss his own work as "refuse rimes" written "withouten second care," in "carelesse pride." This nonchalance is meant to defend his satires against accusations of envious ambition and to set him up as a disinterested, objective critic. But the peculiarity of Hall's tone and persona, as of Marston's, lies in their combination of "humility" with belligerence. Just after the remarks on "refuse rimes," Hall boasts in the Prologue to Book I, "I First aduenture . . . To tread the steps of perilous despight: / I first aduenture: follow me who list" (ll. 1–3). Hall assumes from the beginning that he must fight envy.

Though he cites good reasons why English satire must differ from its Latin precedents, Hall feels compelled to defend his work against accusations that he has not "any whit kindly raught my ancient Roman predecessors" ("A Post-script to the Reader"). He notes that he has made the first satire of Book IV "somewhat resemble the soure and crabbed face of

Iuuenals," as a sop to critics lest they think him ignorant of proper satiric decorum. Yet, when we look at that satire, which his fear of criticism led him to include, we see that the climate of envy has warped his imitation of Juvenal in quite unclassical ways. His repeated references to himself and his poem lack the nonchalance of Horace and the calculated personal anger of Juvenal. His attempt to incorporate into his theme a comparison of his poem with other satires amounts to little more than name-dropping (see ll. 1–4). In a way characteristic of his time, Hall thinks that Juvenal's "soure and crabbed style" results from obscure allusions, a belief that gives him license to run riot with learned references, concocted Latin names, and condescending treatment of contemporary works. The result is ostentatious obscurity rather than what Hall takes to be the functional obliquity of Juvenal's style. In fact, this satire is as much about itself as about its ostensible subject matter. Hall's desire to forestall envious criticism leads him into a self-conscious display of decorum that is alien to his models. How much of his fear of criticism is justified by contemporary conditions and how much is merely excuse for his learned pose is hard to say. Marston called him a pedant and Hall himself notes that his rhymes were said to "relish of the Ferule still" (4.1.170). Hall claims that the academic flavor of his work stems from youthful "hote-bloodes rage," but we can see in that youthfulness a predisposition to show off aggravated by the contemporary climate of envy. Ironically, an atmosphere that provokes showy learnedness, belligerent responses, and self-excusing humility before the attacks have even been made prevents Hall from developing the sophisticated, low-keyed "chats" of Horace and the well-controlled, righteous indignation of Juvenal.

Marston, like Hall, lets the conventions of envy shape his satires, but he shows a greater awareness of envy and attempts to explore its possibilities in satirical ways. Like Hall and many of his contemporaries, Marston writes as if he were entering a competition before hostile judges. His works thus read like a combat with critics, for Marston attempts to answer the envious, forestall attacks, show off his decorum, distinguish his work from "base ballad stuffe," and scorn the "barmy-froth" of shallow brains. He begins *The Metamorphosis of Pigmalions Image and Certaine Satyres* (1598) with an ironic dedication to "Good Opinion" and self-consciously alludes to his "young new-borne Inuention."[18] He follows *Pigmalion* with a disavowal of its seriousness; begins his first four satires with references to himself; and includes "Reactio," an attack on the "curre dogge" critic Hall. *The Scourge of Villanie* (1598) he dedicates to himself and presents to Detraction. He laments that his "Cynick worke" will be railed at by "each lewd Censurer" and desires only readers whom "no kennel thought controules" ("In Lectores"). He then includes a preface explaining his work to "iudiciall perusers" (there is a similar postscript). Next comes a series of the most self-conscious, swaggering satires in English, interspersed with other belligerent explanations of his intentions (the Proemia to Books II and III, "Ad Rithmum," and "Satyra Nova"). References to Cynics, Diogenes, envy, and detraction occur repeatedly. In short, much of the strange tone of Marston's satires results from the fact that they read like a compendium of the conventions of envy.

"To Detraction," which begins *The Scourge of Villanie*, is a hallmark of late Elizabethan literary self-consciousness. Both Lodge and Hall had begun volumes of satires with a defiance of envy, but Marston is more intensely defiant than they were. Calling Detraction the child of Envy, Marston scorns its spite and the critics' rage. He uses the familiar vocabulary of envy: detraction, spite, despite, disdain, "foule canker," "vile blaster," "raging hate," "malignant Hate," "rancors villanie." In essence, "To Detraction" is one of those self-conscious prefaces that show off the author's skill and answer criticism before it can even be made. "To Detraction" gives Marston opportunity to establish a persona that disdains the "dungie muddy scum / Of abiect thoughts" and insists on his own "powers intellectuall." This pose allows him to characterize his persona as scornful of shallow detraction but knowledgeable and honest about his faults. It allows him at once the Cynic pose of aloof self-sufficiency and the belligerent self-display that was traditionally associated with envy.

Marston's use of the conventions of envy is nowhere more puzzling than in his censure of *Pigmalion*. At the beginning of *Certaine Satyres*, he lashes out at readers who took his *Pigmalion* seriously. His lines are froth, he claims, so he censures himself before others can: "hauing rail'd against my selfe a while, / Ile snarle at those." Although some recent critics have been willing to grant Marston his "dissembling shifts," most readers have thought that there is more posture than irony in his claim. His contemporaries considered him the roaring boy of cynicism, absurdly caught up in his dogged pose.[19] The self-conscious pretense of humility with which Marston excuses his *Pigmalion* is repeated throughout his satires. Because he is himself not immaculate, Marston tells us in "Satire II" of *Certaine Satyres*, he will leave "biting rimes" to the "hungry fangs" of our modern Satyre – Hall, no doubt. In his address to the "iudiciall perusers" of *The Scourge of Villanie*, he defends his work by asserting that "Hee that thinks worse of my rimes then my selfe, I scorne him, for he cannot, he that thinks better, is a foole" (p. 101). Of course, this defense against envious censure does not convince us that Marston thinks ill of his rhymes. Should we believe his disclaimer of *Pigmalion* any more? Perhaps, but there is room for doubt. The language of his self-censure is dictated by the conventions of envy; his pretense of humility has precedents in Hall's attempts to disarm the envious and Spenser's sarcastic self-abasement; and we have seen that in the same year Guilpin also self-consciously dismisses his work, though with considerably more nonchalance than Marston, and that Tourneur later poses with a swaggering humility similar to Marston's.

Clearly, Marston is influenced by conventional envy, but he goes further than Hall in making it part of his satirical manner. Perhaps it was because his intense personality was especially responsive to envy that he came to realize its possibilities. Belligerent posing had been present since the flytings and cankered debates between early humanists. Marston has the perception and the gall to explore fully the consequences of that absurd pose. Thus, he makes envy an integral part of his satires as well as his prefaces; he includes a greater number of references to envy than his predecessors had; he intensifies those references; and he often explicitly identifies satire with cynicism. In "Reactio" Marston exposes some of the qualities in Hall's satires that conventional envy promotes – ostentation (l. 131), academic pedantry (ll. 72, 101), detraction (ll. 5, 169, passim) – and attributes them to cynic envy. Here Marston plainly associates contemporary satire with cynicism, but he does not approve. Yet, in keeping with the two-faced character of cynicism, Marston refers to himself in "The Authour in prayse of his precedent Poem" as a "barking Satyrist," as if his exasperation with the critics of *Pigmalion* had driven him to adopt their tactics. In *The Scourge of Villanie* Marston becomes a cynic satirist: he "cannot choose but bite" (8.50); he promises Juvenal that he will not be muzzled nor his "tearing paw" restrained (3.191–5), thus associating both himself and Juvenal with cynicism; and he titles "Satyre VII" "A Cynicke Satyre."

Marston employs envy more profitably than his contemporaries do because he understands its effects on satires like Hall's and does not hesitate to use it himself even in its most exaggerated forms. His most vigorous satires use *canina facundia* to respond to envious criticism or accuse others of it. "Satyra Nova" recounts his quarrel with Hall in an unusually open way by quoting the epigram that Hall had pasted in copies of *Pigmalion* at Cambridge. Actually, the epigram makes a telling jibe at Marston's "mad dog" behavior, but Marston no doubt thought that he could turn Hall's cynic jest against him. Because Marston knows that his readers have often been warned against envious critics, he feels that he can easily cast Hall in that role, as he had already done in "Reactio." The epigram, then, is evidence of envy and a target for Marston's retorts. Hall's jest rises from a "schoole-boyes childish braine" (l. 60); Hall, the poet and critic of poets, is a hypocrite, a "nittie pedant," applauded by the "pure fraternitie" of his cronies at Emmanuel College (ll. 39–40). "How wittily," Marston notes sarcastically, "a Maisters-Hoode can scold" (l. 46). This insistence on Hall's academic pride hits home. Finally, the epigram gives Marston occasion to dissociate himself from the "scurrill iests, light gewgawes, fruitlesse, vaine" (l. 22), and to advance his favorite pose of scorning "Iugling Opinion" (l. 65). "Satyra Nova," then, like "Reactio," is one of Marston's most interesting works because it turns Elizabethan attitudes toward critical envy to vigorous satiric purposes.

The intriguing question about "Satyra Nova," and indeed about all of

Marston's satires, concerns the character of the author or his persona. When a satirist passes moral judgment, we want to feel that his opinion is mature and well considered. But what can we say about the accusations hurled between Marston and his fellow satirists? Although it is clear that Marston tries to use his personal quarrels as a means of expressing general moral judgments, his swaggering makes us doubt whether the moral or the pose is his chief aim. "Nor shall the kennell route of muddy braines," he exclaims in "Satyra Nova," "Rauish my Muses heyre" (ll. 77–8). Here, as so often elsewhere, the conventions of envy lead him into displaying himself rather than convincing his readers. It would be satisfying if we could wholly attribute his strangely vehement tone to a purposeful use of the conventions of envy, but there is a certain naiveté in Marston's work that stems from overinsistence on integrity and ability, a certain youthful love of swagger and Inns-of-Court combativeness, that makes readers hesitate to say that he is in control of his conventions. The truth seems to be that he is well aware of his vehement use of the conventions but allows them to exaggerate his self-display rather than to give him a controlled means of expression. Marston, however, has greater depth and interest than his fellow satirists precisely because of his peculiar excessive intensity. Envy brought out the snarling critic in Marston and gave form to his own darkly cynic nature.

A long tradition of envious complaints culminates in late Elizabethan satire, influencing its basic tone and manner in several important ways. First, it is an important contributor to the moral ambiguity that Alvin Kernan finds in the satiric persona.[20] As Kernan points out, the satyr supplies the supposed etymology of "satire," but we can now add that the roughness, lasciviousness, and delight in reprehending vice that he attributes to satyrs are also associated in the Renaissance mind with Diogenes. And the ubiquitous biting, railing, vipers, dogs, and cynicism belong to the conventions of envy rather than to the satyr. In short, though the satyr provided Elizabethan satire with its prototype, envy determined which of the satyr's characteristics were thought appropriate to satire, for satyrs need not be cankered.

Secondly, envy influences the unity of Elizabethan satire. Never a tightly structured genre, verse satire is further loosened by the fact that envy encourages personal belligerence and swagger. It promotes conflicting attitudes of defense and aggression, humility and pride. The satirists are as often concerned with a defense or display of themselves as with a consistent, well-constructed explanation of their subject. We are reminded that not every generation of poets has the impersonal, well-made poem as its ideal, and we find ourselves less confident about recent attempts to impose unity on Elizabethan satire. Envy gives these works a farrago of both personal and conventional material.

Finally, envy influences satire by giving form and thus a literary outlet to the youthful combativeness of the late Elizabethan satirists. Indeed, much of the questionable character of their personae is just this youthful combativeness in the guise of reprehending envy. As their frequent references to "Tyrocinie" and "the first bloomes of my Poesie" testify, these were new authors, usually students as much interested in making a show on the London literary scene as in creating mature, well-considered work. It was in fact to the cankered conventions of envy rather than to the controlled indignation of Juvenal that they went for their satiric style. Their very conception of Juvenal was colored by envy; as we have seen, he was carping Aquine to them. These young authors, who so value their knowledge of decorum, were fortunate to inherit conventions of envy that allowed them to interpret decorum in ways congenial to their own predilections. The results may lack tight form, but they pass on the appealing exuberance of Elizabethan personalities. An understanding of envy, then, lets us know some of the most important Elizabethan satiric conventions, but it also opens up our concept of this satire by showing us how these conventions encourage personal belligerence and swagger. "Snarle, raile, barke, bite," cries Marston, giving voice to a convention ancient in its origins but absolutely contemporary with his young Elizabethan sensibility.

NOTES

1. See *Musophilus*, lines 54, 117, 208, 263, 458–63, and 526, in *Poems and A Defence of Rhyme*, Arthur Colby Sprague, ed. (1930; reprint ed. Chicago, 1965), and *The Works of Thomas Campion*, Walter R. Davis, ed. (New York, 1967), pp. 432–5.

2. For discussions of envy in literary quarrels, see Charles Read Baskervill, *English Elements in Jonson's Early Comedy* (1911; reprint ed. New York, 1967), pp. 155–63, 170–2, 286–9; C. H. Conley, *The First English Translators of the Classics* (New Haven, 1927), pp. 84–101; H. S. Bennett, *English Books and Readers* (Cambridge, 1952–70), I, 50–3, II, 5–10, III, 231–2; and Frederick Tupper, "The Envy Theme in Prologues and Epilogues," *JEGP*, vol. 16, 1917, pp. 551–72.

3. For examples see 2.16, 19, 42, 58; 3.29, 82; 11.12, 30, 37, 54. For the life of Diogenes, see Diogenes Laertius, *Lives of Eminent Philosophers*, R. D. Hicks, trans., Loeb Classical Library (Cambridge, Mass., 1925), II, 22–85.

4. The place of publication of Renaissance editions is London, unless otherwise noted.

5. For medieval references to Diogenes and Zoilus, see F. J. E. Raby, *A History of Secular Latin Poetry in the Middle Ages* (Oxford, 1957), II, 51, 306. Morton W. Bloomfield, *The Seven Deadly Sins* (East Lansing, Mich., 1952), contains information on envy in the Middle Ages, including a reference to *The Ancren Riwle* (p. 149). See also G. R. Owst, *Literature and Pulpit in Medieval England* (Oxford, 1961), pp. 450–8; *The Book of Vices and Virtues*, W. Nelson Francis, ed., EETS (London, 1942), pp. 22–5 and 58–60; and William Langland, *Piers the Plowman*, Walter W. Skeat, ed. (Oxford, 1965), pp. 45–7 (Passus V, 11.76–133).

6. For references to contention, see Bennett, *English Books and Readers,* II, 5; Raby, II, 45; H. S. Bennett, *Chaucer and the Fifteenth Century* (New York, 1947), p. 151; and William Nelson, *John Skelton: Laureate,* Columbia University Studies in English and Comparative Literature, No. 139 (1939; reprint ed. New York, 1964), p. 26. For Skelton and sirventes, see *The Poetical Works of John Skelton,* Alexander Dyce, ed. (London, 1843), I, 182–94; and "Batayl of Banocburn" in *Political Poems and Songs Relating to English History,* Thomas Wright, ed. (London, 1859), I, 61–2.

7. "Rede me and be nott wrothe" in *English Reprints,* Edward Arber, ed. (London, 1871), VIII, 114–16.

8. *Sir David Lyndesay's Works: The Minor Poems,* J. Small and F. Hall, eds., EETS (London, 1871), pp. 563–5. See also "The Flyting of Dunbar and Kennedie" in *The Poems of William Dunbar,* W. Mackay Mackenzie, ed. (London, 1932), pp. 5–20. Another flyting-like poem by Dunbar is "Of James Dog," pp. 61–2. Skelton's flyting is reprinted in *The Poetical Works,* I, 116–31; see also "Against a Comely Coystrowne," I, 15–17, and "The Douty Duke of Albany," II, 68–84.

9. For an account of the Grammarians' War, see the Introduction to *The Vulgaria of John Stanbridge and the Vulgaria of Robert Whittinton,* Beatrice White, ed., EETS (London, 1932). A discussion of quarrels between continental humanists like Poggio Bracciolini, Francesco Filelfo, and Laurentius Valla can be found in Jean Maloney, "Flyting: Some Aspects of Poetic Invective Debate," Dissertation, Ohio State University, 1964, p. 14; and Jeffery W. Kurz, "The Flyting," Dissertation, Columbia University, 1964, pp. 9, 37–8.

10. For examples see *The Poems of Desiderius Erasmus,* C. Reedijk, ed. (Leiden, 1956), p. 402; Theodore Beza, *Poemata Varia* (Geneva, 1597), sig. ¶¶iiii^v; *The Poetical Works of Gavin Douglas,* John Small, ed. (1874; reprint ed. New York, 1970), II, 116–17; Thomas Drant, "To the Reader" in Otto L. Jiriczek, "Der Elisabethanische Horaz," *Jahrbuch der deutschen Shakespeare-Gesellschaft,* vol. 47, 1911, p. 54; *The Complete Works of George Gascoigne,* John W. Cunliffe, ed. (Cambridge, 1910), II, 135–43; Skelton, I, 132–6; George Buchanan, *Opera Omnia* (Leiden, 1725), II, 362; Timothe Kendall, *Flovvers of Epigrammes,* The Spenser Society, No. 15 (Manchester, 1874), pp. 7, 13, 21, 22, 27, 29, 57, 59, 70, 264, 265, 268, 285; *The Proverbs, Epigrams, and Miscellanies of John Heywood,* John S. Farmer, ed. (1906; reprint ed. New York, 1966), pp. 305–9; *Tottel's Miscellany,* Hyder Rollins, ed., rev. ed. (Cambridge, Mass., 1965), I, 130, 193–4; and John Parkhurst, *Ludicra* (London, 1573), sigs. Oiii^r, Pii^v, Rii^r, Siiii^r, Xiiii^v.

11. See the prefatory epistle in Alexander Neville's translation of *Oedipus* (London, 1563); Thomas de la Peend's "To the Reader" in John Studley's translation of *Agamemnon* (London, 1566); Marcellus Palingenius, *The Zodiake of Life,* Barnabe Googe, trans. (New York, 1947), sig. *viii^r; Barnabe Googe, *Eglogs, Epytaphes, and Sonettes* in *English Reprints,* Edward Arber, ed. (London, 1871), VIII, 21–3; *The Heroycall Epistles of . . . Publius Ovidius Naso,* George Turbervile, trans., Frederick Boas, ed. (London, 1928), pp. 341–3; George Turbervile, *Epitaphes, Epigrams, Songs and Sonets* (London, 1567), sig. *viii^v; and Edward Hake, *Newes out of Powles Churchyarde,* Charles Edmonds, ed., Isham Reprints, No. 2 (London, 1872), sigs. Avi^r–Avii^r.

12. For examples see *The Second Part of The Return from Parnassus,* lines 2110–14, in *The Three Parnassus Plays,* J. B. Leishman, ed. (London, 1949), and *Ben Jonson,* C. H. Herford, *et al.,* eds. (Oxford, 1947), VIII,

408. Other references are noted in Leslie Hotson, "The Blatant Beast," in *Studies in Honor of T. W. Baldwin,* Don Cameron Allen, ed. (Urbana, Ill., 1958), pp. 34–7; and Merritt Y. Hughes, "Spenser's 'Blatant Beast,'" *MLR,* vol. 13, 1918, pp. 267–75. Humphrey Tonkin, *Spenser's Courteous Pastoral* (Oxford, 1972), p. 52, briefly discusses similarities between the Blatant Beast and earlier prefaces.

13. See *The Works of Thomas Nashe,* Ronald B. McKerrow and F. P. Wilson, eds. (Oxford, 1958), I, 190–1, 199, 263, and V, 88; and *The Whipper Pamphlets,* Part II, A. Davenport, ed., Liverpool Reprints, No. 6 (Liverpool, 1951), p. 46.

14. See the closings of Guilpin's Epigram 70 and Satire V in *Skialetheia,* D. Allen Carroll, ed. (Chapel Hill, 1974). See also Epigrams 1, 2, and 7.

15. See John Weever, *Epigrammes in the Oldest Cut and Newest Fashion,* R. B. McKerrow, ed. (London, 1911), pp. 5, 6, 11, 12, 17, 23, and 98; John Weever, *Faunus and Melliflora,* A. Davenport, ed., Liverpool Reprints, No. 2 (Liverpool, 1948), lines 1073–86, 1600–7, 1677, and "A Prophesie," line 4; John Weever, *The Whipper of the Satyre,* p. 4 and lines 157–62, 337–42, 358, and 448 in *The Whipping Pamphlets,* Part I, A. Davenport, ed., Liverpool Reprints, No. 5 (Liverpool, 1951); *The Letters and Epigrams of Sir John Harington,* Norman Egbert McClure, ed. (Philadelphia, 1930), pp. 149 and 174; Thomas Bastard, *Chrestoleros,* The Spenser Society, No. 47 (Manchester, 1888), pp. 11, 34, 39, and 123; William Rankins, "To . . . Iohn Salisbury," and "Satyr tertius" in *Seven Satires,* A. Davenport, ed., Liverpool Reprints, No. 1 (Liverpool, 1948); *Microcynicon* in *The Works of Thomas Middleton,* A. H. Bullen, ed. (1886; reprint ed. New York, 1964), VIII, 114–16; *The Letting of Humours Blood* in *The Complete Works of Samuel Rowlands,* Hunterian Club (Glasgow, 1880), I, 84; Nicholas Breton, *No Whippinge,* lines 23, 34, and 129 in *The Whipper Pamphlets,* Part II; *The Second Part of The Return from Parnassus,* lines 7–55, 266–8, 1155–9, 1616–17, 1718–19, 2108–18, and 2141–52; and *A Pleasant Satyre* (London, 1595), sig. Bh1r.

16. See "A Prophesie of this present yeare, 1600" in *Faunus and Melliflora,* pp. 66–70; and *The Transformed Metamorphosis* in *The Works of Cyril Tourneur,* Allardyce Nicoll, ed. (London, 1930), pp. 53–6.

17. 4.7.9 in *The Poems of Joseph Hall,* Arnold Davenport, ed. (Liverpool, 1949), p. 72.

18. *The Poems of John Marston,* Arnold Davenport, ed. (Liverpool, 1961), p. 49.

19. For three of the many contemporary comments, see Hall's epigram in *The Poems of John Marston,* pp. 164–5; *The Second Part of The Return from Parnassus,* lines 267–78; and the character of Crispinus in Jonson's *The Poetaster.* Recent critics who see irony in Marston's work are Louis Lecocq, *La Satire en Angleterre de 1588 à 1603,* Etudes Anglaises, 32 (Paris, 1969), pp. 303–15, 428–502, and Adrian Weiss, "Rhetoric and Satire: New Light on John Marston's *Pigmalion* and the Satires," *JEGP,* vol. 71, 1972, pp. 22–35. Lecocq's work contains important comments on envy in Renaissance satire.

20. *The Cankered Muse* (New Haven, 1959), chs. 1 and 3.

Review Notices

Christopher N. L. **Brooke** assisted by Gillian Keir. *London 800–1216: the Shaping of a City*. Berkeley and Los Angeles: University of California Press, 1975. Pp. xxii, 424; 53 illustrations, 5 maps, 4 appendices. $21.00.

This treatment of the origins and early development of London will be a standard work. Ninth-century London was a small settlement within the Roman wall, a frontier position between the Anglo-Saxon kingdoms and later between Wessex and the Danelaw. By the thirteenth century it was a great city, "the commercial capital of a large area of north-western Europe" (p. xiii). While other works, notably Gwyn Williams' *Medieval London: from Commune to Capital* (London, 1963), have portrayed the thirteenth century as the great age of expansion, Brooke and Keir maintain that this is an illusion created by the survival of a greater volume of documentation, and that London assumed its essential form in the eleventh and twelfth centuries.

There are few documents and a substantial previous literature. Hence it is hardly surprising that the best and most original parts of this book are those based on recent findings in archaeology, toponymy, and onomastics. To their credit, the authors reject a narrowly legal approach to urban origins. Their central thesis is based on an analysis of parish establishments. London had over one hundred parishes, or one for every 3½ acres, by 1200, and the number did not increase appreciably thereafter. Most were small oratories or proprietary churches, maintained by voluntary offerings with such tiny endowments that many which continued to function into the modern period were too poor to tithe by 1254. This is a striking contrast with parish growth in most cities on the continent. Brooke and Keir find that most parishes within the Roman wall, which London never extended, were founded by private charity before 1100, with the vast majority in the eleventh century. They were joined by a few suburban parishes in the less densely settled north and east in the twelfth century. Parish boundaries remained essentially unchanged thereafter, a fact suggesting considerable density of settlement in west London within a generation of the Norman conquest.

The ward was the urban equivalent of the hundred. Twenty-four of the present twenty-six wards existed by 1200. While parish boundaries generally followed the city wall, ward demarcations often did not, for with one exception the wards at the edge of the city were established to defend the gates. Most are found in the first half of the eleventh century, slightly earlier than most parishes, in an age when settlement was less evenly distributed, but their borders underwent more change in the late Middle Ages than did those of the parishes.

Brooke and Keir emphasize the continuation of London's primeval bonds with its rural hinterland. Settlement was most dense in the northwest, which had easy access to the interior and where the victual markets were located. Enclaves of seigniorial jurisdiction within the walls, particularly in east London, gradually weakened during the twelfth century. Edward the Confessor's move to Westminster was a crucial development, for it created a western pull, and the fiscal needs of the court gave rise to settlements of foreigners, particularly along the Thames and the roads leading to Westminster. The city rich of the twelfth century were landlords and grain merchants, while their successors of the thirteenth tended to be in long-distance trade. Still, there was no strict occupational differentiation, and most powerful persons had economic and social links with both the city and the rural areas. Foreigners, particularly Flemings, did tend to be more active in international trade than did London merchants. Yet while the English were selling wool to the Flemings and purchasing finished textiles from them, the absence of substantial hoards of English coins in Flanders suggests that at least through the twelfth century, the balance of trade was in England's favor.

The authors are necessarily less original on institutional and social developments. London had grown so powerful by the 1130s that princes had to court it during the "Anarchy." By mid-century most sheriffs were Londoners, although men who also owned property in the countryside did turns as sheriff in London and various eastern counties. The grant of a "commune" and the reduction of the farm, formal recognition of the right to elect sheriffs, and the mayoralty all appeared in the 1190s. The first mayor, Henry fitzAilwin, served nearly two decades, and the early part of his tenure was marked by the violence of persons seeking greater participation in local affairs. Henry evidently came to power with the assistance of Richard I's representatives. These facts, together with the agitation around 1200 to suppress the weavers' guild and the comparative instability in city administration after 1212, suggest that the establishment of the London commune, far from being a revolutionary act directed against outside authority, was actually the work of an oligarchy of king's men acting on behalf of a monarch who wanted stability in his largest city.

The volume does have weaknesses. Brooke's claim that the supposed charter of Henry I for London is a genuine reflection of city customs save in its reduction of the farm to £300 is more convenient than logical. The authors are to be commended for adopting a comparative approach with continental towns; but while this unquestionably enriches their treatment, they overlook some analogies which a deeper knowledge of the cities of northwestern Europe would have provided. Contrary to the impression given on the title page, most original research for the book was done by Mrs. Keir (p. xvii). Professor Brooke's contributions were generally in areas of his previous research and in synthesizing material quite well known. He ties his treatment of monks and monasteries to the royal court rather than to the city, but follows it with an extremely suggestive description of the prebendary system of St. Paul's cathedral. Provision to the canonries was an important source of royal influence in London, and the endowments of the stalls contributed substantially to the city's food supply.

Finally, there is an annoying amount of thematic and factual repetition. The introductory chapters often seem a travelogue rather than an analysis of urban growth, and the contents of Brooke's chapter on the political history of London reappear later in the book. A more tightly organized treatment would have shortened this volume considerably, but might have detracted from its readability, which is always a strong point of Christopher Brooke's work. The fact remains, however, that the authors have written a clear, authoritative, penetrating, imaginative, and at times extremely provocative history of London through the reign of John.

David Nicholas
University of Nebraska

David C. Douglas. *The Norman Fate, 1100–1154*. Berkeley and Los Angeles: University of California Press, 1976. Pp. xv, 258; 8 plates. $22.50.

David Douglas, emeritus professor of the University of Bristol, is one of the great luminaries of contemporary medieval scholarship. For the past fifty years grace and insight have marked his passage from editions of local records in East Anglia, Bury Saint Edmund's, and Christ Church, through Domesday Book and British historiography, to the glowing magisterial account, *William the Conqueror* (1964). Then, believing there was an inherent unity to all the Normans wrought, in 1969 he undertook an imaginative comparison of their volatile constructive world, England, Normandy, southern Italy and Sicily, and the crusader principalities, and analyzed their heroic conquests in a distinguished, widely praised book, *The Norman Achievement, 1066–1100*. The present somewhat ambiguously named sequel treats the following five decades of consolidation. It is a measure of our own times that this equally fine and similarly sized volume costs $22.50, while its recent predecessor originally sold for $8.50.

Although the two monarchs never met, Professor Douglas finds many parallels in the careers of Henry I of England (1100–1135) and Roger the Great, Count of Sicily from 1103, Duke of Apulia from 1127, and King of Sicily and Apulia from 1130 to 1154. Both men were sons of powerful mothers and conquering fathers. Each struggled to an exceptionally wealthy throne and then long ruled a diverse realm divided by water. Both were cruel unloveable men lacking such "fashionable feudal virtues" as martial ardor and openhanded generosity, but possessing extraordinary administrative talent. Each opposed papal aggrandizement, but yet enjoyed Christ centered liturgical kingly veneration. Both ruled strongly feudalized countries, but also presided over local cultural renaissances. Each brought Norman power and influence to an apex which was unsustained by his successors.

Innumerable important judgments enhance the examination of these and other fascinating personalities. For example, Douglas maintains that the development of the two Norman kingdoms helped diminish the preponderance of Germanic empire. Although almost entirely neglecting England between 1135 and 1154, he observes that the conflict of Stephen and Matilda was really a crisis in the power politics of all Western Europe, a struggle between Anjou and Blois. The First Crusade became an attempted third Norman conquest for unfulfilled families and individuals; five of its eight principal leaders had Norman connections. Disaster in the Second Crusade is blamed squarely upon King Roger's ambition, rapacity, and territorial aggression. In fact, the last quarter of the book, which reviews the Norman Levantine adventures, includes the most sparkling pages, proving again that Douglas' heart is with the heroic conquerors. His contention that crusader problems deserve re-examination in light of Norman personnel and political action is entirely valid as are his links between Robert Guiscard's earlier Holy War and the subsequent international papal-sponsored crusader ethos.

The task of unenthusiastic stay-at-homes, like Henry and Roger, was to strengthen the machinery of central government so that its influence and authority could pervade local administration. At this point Douglas strains his comparisons a bit. It is true that the English ruling class consisted of only fifty or sixty baronial families, that royal patronage was important in both countries, that few great earldoms were created, that fiefs were rarely compact units, and that undertenants swore liege homage to kings, but in England a young generation of immigrant bureaucrats led by Roger of Salisbury enlarged Saxon precedents and created new governmental institutions, while in Sicily, Arabs, Greeks, and Normans shared administrative, especially fiscal, responsibilities and utilized Saracen procedures. Moreover, the early connections between the two island kingdoms are not very persuasive. Even if a certain correspondence in chancery style can be detected, the familiar English title, justiciar, evidently did not reach Sicily for three decades. The spirit of Charles Homer Haskins enlivens much of Douglas' thought, by the way, and it is pleasing to note the compliments paid to the master and interesting to observe how little scholarship has changed in some areas he first investigated.

In a few particulars Douglas' own emphasis can be debated. For example, one might modify the repulsive characterization of Henry I, or interpret Stephen's ecclesiastical policy somewhat differently. That England and parts of France constituted a natural realm or inevitable empire can surely be disputed. A tendency to attribute all effective action to monarchs underestimates the fact that Henry spent fully one-half his reign outside England. Indeed, other current scholarship reveals what rich, creative, satisfying lives individuals could enjoy quite apart from any royal impetus or direction. Most controversial is Professor Douglas' repeated assertion that Kings Henry and Roger established a type of secular state government. One can hardly quarrel with a demonstration that administration became more pragmatic, profitable, efficient, effective, and even business-like, but, certainly in England, those few men who reflected on government saw civic activity as meritorious service. Law, order, and justice, all sought a divine plan and guidance. Moreover, many administrators, such as Roger Bishop of Salisbury, the viceroy and regent of the king, were themselves active clergymen and occasionally quite devout in their own ways. Indirectly, through royal charity, government recognized authentic social responsibilities for communal worship, but increasingly Henry and his able officials also turned attention to health and hospital care, to education, and to public convenience and safety.

There is, however, no doubt that the Norman experience did raise issues about the relationship of mind and power, of politics and ethics which were to endure for centuries. In painting this canvas Professor Douglas has created a brilliant work of art. He offers great knowledge, mature wisdom, and genuine pleasure. His latest book enriches our history and repays successive readings. Once more we are all in his debt.

Edward J. Kealey
Holy Cross College

Frederick H. Russell. *The Just War in the Middle Ages,* Cambridge Studies in Medieval Life and Thought, Third Series, 8. New York: Cambridge University Press, 1975. Pp. xi, 332. $32.50.

As Russell himself points out in his introduction, most histories of the medieval theories concerning the just war have been written from particular modern standpoints that are closer to international law and modern pacifism than to historical scholarship. As a consequence such histories as those of Regout, Vanderpol, and Bainton either skim the work of the best-known medieval thinkers or simply assume that "medieval thought" was a seamless web and that one thinker could be taken to represent it as well as another. In fact, there was never any "medieval thought" about any subject; there were only, as Russell's title indicates, medieval theories. Those theories depended upon the intellectual vigor and the professional capacity of writers who enunciated them. The first virtue of Russell's fine and learned study is his explicit recognition that Roman lawyers, theologians, decretists, and decretalists all started from different points, considered different questions, and turned up different answers. Russell's taxonomy of medieval theories of the just war is not the least attractive feature of his orderly and intelligent study.

This book consists of an Introduction followed by seven chapters that deal with medieval theories of the just war from St. Augustine to the successors of Thomas Aquinas in the early fourteenth century. The chapters, however, are topically rather than chronologically arranged. After the first chapter surveys a variety of source materials between the fifth and the twelfth centuries, the second deals with the ideas of medieval Roman lawyers. The third, fourth, and fifth chapters deal with the general field of canon law, treating respectively Gratian's *Decretum*, the commentaries of the decretists, and the commentaries of the decretalists, the last focusing upon the thought of Innocent IV and Hostiensis. These chapters on canon law occupy 158 pages, exactly half the length of the book, and they constitute Russell's most important contribution. Chapters 6 and 7 deal with medieval theologians' treatment of the topic and with St. Thomas Aquinas and his circle. The seven chapters are followed by a short concluding essay and an appendix, Russell's transcription of "A Judgement of a War between Two Princes," written around 1290 by Gervais du Mont-Saint-Eloi, a text that illustrates just how complex and contradictory the application of some just war theories could be. The text printed in the Appendix is discussed by Russell on pages 248–50. The bibliography is extensive and useful, and Russell's manuscript citations are generous. The Index is clear and easy to use. Although the book is attractively printed, there are many typographical and copy errors; e.g., page 290, note 1, page 18, page 27, and elsewhere. The printing is not as carefully done as it should be. Regrettably, there are also several errors in the citations, the most unfortunate of which is the consistent misspelling of Stanley Chodorow's last name. Overall, however, Russell has managed his citations and his voluminous materials very skillfully.

Russell's short treatment of medieval Roman lawyers' theories of the just war is justified by the unique character of their work. The chief problems the Roman lawyers faced were those of reconciling the texts of the *Corpus Iuris Civilis* with the fragmentation of military authority in the medieval world, in the *Libri Feudorum*, and in the constitutions of medieval Roman emperors. The meager technical contributions of the Romanists were used much more vigorously by twelfth- and thirteenth-century canon lawyers. Gratian's *Decretum* assembled a "conscientious montage" of texts that covered much wider moral and legal ground than had the Romanists. In particular, Gratian added to the Romanists' views the problem of offenses against the Church and the juridical problems of penitence. The variety of decretist commentaries on the texts of Gratian's *Decretum* was considerable. In general, they were concerned to define precisely the Church's role in authorizing and conducting wars and in constructing legal justification for wars that avenged injustices done to God, the Church, and all Christians, rather than purely secular conflicts.

Russell's greatest interest, however, is in the work of the decretalists. The first paragraph of page 127, which emphasizes the legal training of such popes as Alexander III and Innocent III, must now be modified somewhat in the light of recent work on these problems by Kenneth Pennington and John Noonan. Russell's analysis of Hostiensis' sevenfold typology of the just war is masterly, and he concludes that "the Decretalists sought to limit [warfare] to purposes useful to obedient princes and Church prelates." Having defined the just war, decretalists "sought to endow the champions of the just cause with abundant spiritual and material advantages and to deprive the unjust warrior of the manpower and resources necessary to render attractive his pursuit of injustice and sin."

Medieval canon lawyers could and did build upon earlier Roman law, theology, and temporal circumstances, and their contribution to the subject was necessarily the most sophisticated and complete. Medieval theologians had no such variety of texts and circumstances to discuss, nor were they primarily concerned with legal problems. The theologians were far more concerned with the moral condition of military participants, just or unjust, and with the somewhat abstract and general moral ideals that their scriptural, Augustinian, and other doctrinal sources praised. Aquinas' philosophical speculation contrasts sharply, for all of its use of Aristotle, with the hard legal analysis of Hostiensis.

Russell's most significant contribution in his analysis of different kinds of medieval thought about the just war is his insistence upon the limits of each approach. The Romanists had little moral concern; the theologians little legal concern, and both groups offered only limited theories. Of them all, the canonists were certainly the most comprehensive and ambitious, but even the greatest canonists, such as Hostiensis, pursued an exclusively juridical track. But they failed to find a judicial process that could make their doctrines effective. Within his fine discussion of the canonists, Russell properly emphasizes the variety and complexity of their ideas. In this respect his book is an important contribution to the study of the importance of medieval canon law that has been represented in recent years by the work of Kuttner, Le Bras, Stickler, Tierney, and Ullmann. To say that it is unlikely that other scholars working with the same sources in Roman, canon, and feudal law and theology will come up with significantly different conclusions from those of Russell is to underline the genuine importance of this study, not only for medieval history, but for other disciplines which have hitherto hunted so cavalierly among medieval sources to provide some shallow background to modern problems. The problems of war and peace are still sufficiently pressing to require that the scholarship in their history be at least as detailed, conscientious, and expertly displayed as they are here in Russell's book.

There are a number of problems which this book presents and illustrates, rather than solves. The Introduction, which compresses Aristotle, Cicero, Roman Law, the Old Testament, Origen, St. Ambrose, and the *Codex Theodosianus* is far too short. So is the treatment of Carolingian writers after St. Augustine and before the systematization of different branches of knowledge in the twelfth century. Liturgical texts are hardly used at all. Nor is there, outside of brief passages on pages 45, 52, and 65 to 68, much discussion of the important historical semantics of theorists' terminology. Finally, the treatment of the Crusade, discussed too briefly on page 2 and then on several occasions later in the book, is intermittent and sketchy, although Russell has some very important things to say about it. His description of canonists' concerns for separating ecclesiastical authorization for a crusade from the dirty business of running one, and the theologians' failure to give unreserved approval to the crusade possess considerable implications for the decline of the Crusade idea in the thirteenth century. Here, Russell's remarks deserve a place beside the old work of Palmer Throop, and perhaps (*pace*, Russell!) a separate study of the Crusade in the light of this first work.

As Russell sees it, just war theories were most helpful in combatting private violence, strengthening the legal context of the most influential discussions, and strengthening the hands of territorial monarchies and city-states in the new world of early international law. As Russell puts it, "The just war is really an ethical and religious doctrine surfaced with an often thick veneer of legality." And, as he also says, medieval theories of the just war failed. Later theorists of international law succeeded in developing the legal problems of warfare to a fine and delicious science. In doing so, however, they failed even to come to terms with what was one of the most heroic of medieval achievements, the stubborn refusal to avoid the ethical and moral questions inherent in their culture and their approach to war. That task has been left absentmindedly to modern propagandists for the sovereign state, and their ghastly work is a parody of medieval thought. It is Russell's great virtue to have laid this thought bare in its most complex, contradictory, inadequate, and time-bound circumstances. He has done justice to his sources and to his readers.

Edward Peters
University of Pennsylvania

Theodore Evergates. *Feudal Society in the Baillage of Troyes under the Counts of Champagne, 1152–1284.* Baltimore, Md.: The Johns Hopkins University Press, 1975. Pp. xii, 273; 7 maps, 9 figures, 17 tables. $14.00.

Here is a fine regional monograph in medieval French social history. In it Theodore Evergates, expanding on a doctoral dissertation written at Johns Hopkins, studies peasant and aristocratic society in the Baillage of Troyes from the mid-twelfth to the end of the thirteenth century. During this period the Baillage of Troyes was an administrative subdivision of the county of Champagne, roughly square in shape and about 50 miles on a side, which contained ten castellanies. Dictating his choice of terminal dates is the survival of a uniquely detailed series of countal administrative documents from the years 1172, 1252, 1265, and 1274–75. These are the long known but little studied fief roles of the Counts of Champagne listing the names of fief holders, the composition and value of their holdings, their rear vassals, etc. All in all, a veritable mine of information on the local aristocracy.

With regard to the peasantry, Evergates is concerned almost exclusively with the question of personal status. Were the peasants of the Troyes region serfs or freemen, and what was the importance of the charters of franchise increasingly accorded to village communities in the thirteenth century? By means of a careful analysis of the critical Latin terms used in contemporary charters he concludes that by 1120 the older Carolingian distinction between free and unfree peasants had already lost its meaning and that all were dependents of lords though their submission to the latter's justice and through their payment of the *taille*, *mainmorte*, and *formariage*. Furthermore these obligations came with the land by virtue of tenancy, not personal status, and they did not constitute serfdom. Then in the later twelfth century increasing peasant mobility resulted in the modification or elimination of dependency for a growing number of peasants. In order to attract and keep peasants on their lands, successive counts of Champagne issued charters of franchises exempting all inhabitants of a village from some or all of these exactions. From this time on the freedom of the franchised from taxes paid by the less fortunate indeed justifies speaking of a clear distinction between the two groups of peasants but even then Evergates is reluctant to call the latter serfs since contemporaries did not employ the term. It should be pointed out that Evergates studies the peasantry exclusively from the viewpoint of tenurial obligations and makes no attempt to classify peasants by wealth, occupation, or standard of living. In this respect his treatment of the Troyes peasantry is more limited in scope than that of a number of other comparable regional monographs.

The most important part of this book deals with the aristocracy. Evergates seeks to determine the criteria for membership in the aristocracy, how many such families there were, their ability to preserve their status during the period in question, and the relationship between knights and the greater families. The richness and comparability of the various fief roles enabled him to computerize his data and correlate a number of variables including title (hence status); sex (the number of female fief holders increased to 20 percent in the thirteenth century); size, makeup, and value of fiefs; castle guard duty; liege homage to the Count of Champagne, and number of rear fief holders. From this emerged several chronological trends regarding the size of the group of fief holders (it declined strikingly), the men-to-women ratio, the size and makeup of differing status groups within the fief holders as a whole, the number of those owing liege homage to the Count, the number of those owing castle guard duty, and so forth. Following the terminology of the roles, he separates the fief holders into counts, lords (i.e., castellans), and knights, and studies the traits of each group. To accomplish this he identifies individual families, establishes genealogies where possible, and then follows their histories over this period. The results are summarized in the text, the family histories and genealogical charts are arranged in alphabetical order in an appendix, which provides a useful dictionary for looking up a given individual or family.

What are Evergates' findings and what is their importance? To begin with, it is one of the strongpoints of this book that the author concludes his work with a chapter describing the current state of studies on medieval peasantries and aristocracies and then attempts to see where his own work fits. Aligning himself with Genicot and Werner, he disputes Marc Bloch's contention that the aristocracy of the eleventh and twelfth centuries was essentially a new group of men who replaced older Carolingian families on the basis of their military power. Rather, they were an aristocracy of birth and wealth whose authority was independent of fief holding from the Count. In his region twelve families made up this group which he calls the old aristocracy – the counts (three families in all) and the lords of the fief roles. The great majority of fief holders listed in the rolls fall into the category of knights but through the twelfth century these people were armed retainers not nobles. Only in the thirteenth century did they begin to work thir way into the aristocracy. The author finds that the survival rate of aristocratic families in his baillage approximates that in other regions where it has already been measured, notably the county of Forez. Likewise the demilitarization of the aristocracy in the thirteenth century as marked by the declining numbers of nobles to be knighted parallels trends seen elsewhere.

In sum, rather than offering new and startling hypotheses about the history of the aristocracy of the eleventh to thirteenth century, this study confirms recent findings of other scholars. Yet to say no more than this hardly does the book justice. The wealth of detail available from the uniquely rich Champagne fief roles enables Evergates to document his conclusions with a precision not possible elsewhere and thereby to draw a picture of a regional aristocracy unrivaled in its concreteness and wealth of detail. But richness of documentation would have been of little value had it not been for Evergates' exemplary methodology. Taking nothing for granted and bringing to his research as few preconceptions as possible, he bases his conclusions on a rigorous analysis of crucial Latin terms and on a correlation of data aided by the computer. To my knowledge this is the first application of computer techniques to the study of medieval aristocracies; the study is so well carried out that future historians of this topic will have to compare their findings with those of this book.

George T. Beech
Western Michigan University

Gordon Leff. *William of Ockham. The Metamorphosis of Scholastic Discourse*. Manchester: Manchester University Press, 1975. Pp. xxiv, 666. $47.50.

William of Ockham was a many-sided thinker and a prolific writer. Accordingly, most of the monographs written about him treat one aspect of his teaching. Leff in this massive volume attempts to bring to his readers the whole Ockham: the philosopher, the theologian and the social theorist.

In his presentation, the author follows the text of Ockham closely and paraphrases his reasoning, sometimes in great detail. The advantage of this method is that it gives the modern reader a taste of the medieval classroom.

It is to the author's credit that he approaches Ockham without prejudice and preconceptions and tries to present him as he appears in his own writings. I agree with Leff that Ockham should not be judged in the light of Ockhamism or of what developed after him. But I think that Leff should have paid more attention to Ockham's philosophical predecessors because even the authors he criticized contributed to the formation of Ockham's views.

The value of the book, however, is seriously impaired by a large number of errors, both of scholarship and interpretation, apparently resulting from the author's haste in preparing so long a book on so difficult a topic. It is regrettable that the author did not spend more time in rethinking, revising and correcting his manuscript. There are numerous misreadings and misunderstandings, not to speak of vague and ambiguous renderings of Ockham's arguments. Space permits mention of only a few.

On intuitive knowledge, Leff says that contrary to Boehner, Ockham held that "some things known intuitively can be doubted" (p. 28). But if this is true Ockham contradicted his own definition of intuitive knowledge: intuitive knowledge is evident knowledge, and evident knowledge excludes any doubt. When we examine the passage Leff cites, we find: "nulla res est . . . quin illā cognitā ab intellectu." This use of the ablative absolute means that according to Ockham, we can doubt the existence of a thing *after having once* known it intuitively; it does not justify Leff's interpretation.

Leff also writes that according to Ockham, it is possible for intuitive knowledge to err "only supernaturally" (p. 38). Leff cites "Ockham's reply to the second doubt," but the reply is not Ockham's. It is considered only to be categorically rejected a few lines later: "Ideo dico quod cognitio intuitiva est illa qua existente iudico rem esse quando est et non esse quando non est . . . sive causetur naturaliter sive supernaturaliter . . . et sic nullo modo ponit intellectum in errore" (*Reportatio* II, q. XV, DD–EE).

In general, Leff's treatment of the text is not careful, as the errors found on just two pages will illustrate. On page 61, we read, as Ockham's statement of common opinion: "Similarly it is generally held that many angels do not know of the incarnation and yet freely assent to its truth." But this is not the view Ockham cited. Here and in other instances, the reader should refer to the original text to understand what is meant. Leff translates Ockham's "contactus situalis et virtualis" as "spiritual and virtual contiguity" (p. 62). In the next lines we read: "Like the human soul, however, the angelic soul does not have the same powers which it has in conjunction with a body (in its case spiritual)." "Angelic soul," "spiritual body"? Ockham is the most unlikely author to revive such an outdated opinion. The body (corpus) he speaks of is any material substance which may act upon the human soul or upon an angel as an object of intellect or will.

In a few pages towards the end of the book, "pena" becomes "sin" in "as sin both voluntarily sustained and naturally inflicted" (p. 513). "[S]ine expulsione culpae" is translated on page 515 as "before the expulsion of sin," with reference to Adam and the angels before the fall, the Blessed Virgin and even Christ himself. On page 516, we hear of "natural affinities between grace and sin." Affinities between grace and sin? Why not between light and darkness, Christ and Belial?

To return to more substantive issues, Leff says that God's absolute power (p. 17) represents "God's direct intervention in actions ordinarily performed by creatures." But God's absolute power has nothing to do with miraculous intervention. For the distinction between absolute and ordinary power is not to be confused with the distinction between God's actions praeter consuetum cursum naturae and secundum consuetum cursum naturae. Absolute power is an abstraction which enables us to discuss God's power apart from his foreknowledge and preordination. While it is true that, according to Ockham, God can do anything which does not involve contradiction de potentia absoluta, it would be false to say that God actually ever does anything except de potentia ordinata. (Cf. *Opera Politica*, II, 719–22, 230–34.)

According to Leff's interpretation of Ockham's views: "everything which exists outside the mind comes under the category of substance and as such is capable of admitting contrary qualities" (p. 108). If this is true, Ockham denied the extramental reality of all accidents. Not a razor, but an ax, would be required to chop off such an integral part of scholastic philosophy and theology. What Ockham really says is: Everything outside the mind which is in the category of substance is susceptible of contrary properties. He does not deny the reality of accidents.

Neither is it true, as Leff writes, that Ockham upholds "in Aristotle's, rather than his own, name" that quality is an absolute category (p. 203). That qualities of the third species are real accidents outside the mind is a view that Ockham held in his own name and would have held even if Aristotle had denied it. For Ockham maintained the separability of accidents from substance, knowing full well that Aristotle would have denied it. (Cf. Boehner's reply to De Wulf, *Collected Articles*, pp. 141–43.)

Finally, one wonders if anyone took the trouble to read the proofs of this book. On page 65, l. 34, "distinct" is written for "indistinct"; on page 95, l. 21, "predictable" for "predicable'; on p. 216, l. 33, "could not exist for "could exist'; on page 514, l. 18, "does" for "does not." (Perhaps the addition or deletion of such a short word as "not" makes little difference.)

Gedeon Gál, O.F.M.
St. Bonaventure University

David O. McNeil. *Guillaume Budé and Humanism in the Reign of Francis I* (Travaux d'Humanisme et Renaissance, No. CXLII). Geneva: Droz, 1975. Pp. vi, 156.

The last biography of Guillaume Budé appeared some ninety years ago; in the meantime the most influential study was that of L. Delaruelle, whose thesis was however confined to the earlier years and writings and was never followed up by the promised second volume. This monograph, the revised version of a 1972 thesis, claims to be a general survey, with the main emphasis on the last twenty-five years of the scholar's life. One gasps with astonishment that a young graduate, however promising, should have been set to work on a subject of such magnitude and complexity as to daunt colleagues of greater seniority and experience; and one has to ask oneself whether this was the most opportune moment to publish such a survey when much new research on various aspects of Budé's career is on the stocks.

After an initial chapter dealing with the early life and milieu (though oddly the date of birth is omitted), we pass on to more substantial matters: Budé's legal studies, attacking scholastic jurisprudence and the contemporary validity of the corpus juris, but showing high sensitivity to issues of the day – a feature also prominent in the *De Asse*; the political thinker whose work is closely connected with his political involvement and advancement at court; relations with Erasmus and other humanists; Budé's concept of *philologia*; a final chapter on the scholar's religious views.

The leitmotiv running through the book is Budé's passionate loyalty to France and to the Crown; and McNeil shows a wide acquaintance with secondary as well as with primary material. He is eager to show that Budé was not cast simply in the mold of the Italian humanist, as Delaruelle tended to suggest. In this he is surely right, but the chauvinistic temper of French humanists has been recognized for some considerable time; on the other hand, more might have been made of Budé's comparison of the royal readerships in 1529 with a *musaion*, a term which shows that he distinguished their prospective establishment from what had been going on in Florentine circles. Whether the evidence submitted to substantiate claims of greater political involvement on Budé's part proves the case is not certain; a good deal of obscurity still lurks around his actual standing at court, and it might be added that the *maîtres des requêtes* were not all in attendance on the King's journeys – there was a roster which ensured that two were on duty. Nevertheless, the stress on Budé's political orientation has its merits and certainly gives a clear-cut unity to aspects of his career; at the same time, it may have led McNeil to play down other matters somewhat. For instance, though on page 97 he recognizes that there was in Budé a perpetual struggle between the contemplative and the active existence, in practice the *vita activa* has the lion's share in the general portrait. Secondly, this view, perhaps unconsciously, tends to bring out the less admirable qualities of Budé's character: he emerges as a touchy little man, time-serving at court, ungenerous to others, unable to forget a slight. These traits are undeniable, of course, but the man had also more generous characteristics and a charisma which many contemporaries were quick to recognize. Finally, I suspect that this also leads to an underplaying of Budé'e involvement with evangelical currents (though an escape route is allowed for, p. 130). Of course, McNeil also links Budé's outlook with his bourgeois, conservative Gallicanism (p. 112), in other words with the attitudes of his social class. Nevertheless, there are still a lot of questions to be solved in this area: McNeil inclines to the view that Budé's religious views were essentially formed during the years 1508–15 (p. 110), but we do really need to know much more about Budé's early years, his possible familiarity with Florentine Neoplatonism, his acquaintance with the Church Fathers, his friendships with humanists, especially those with Greek interests (Bérault, Salmon Macrin, Germain de Brie). McNeil is aware that these matters are at present under investigation, but it does seem a bit cavalier to mention this research and then build up a portrait of Budé which must surely be modified by the results of this work, to which frankly the author has not contributed.

Though a fairly thorough description is given of Budé's conception of and contribution (especially political) to *philologia*, there is really nothing on the quality of his classical scholarship or his lexicography or for that matter on the nature of his impact on later scholars. This is partly deliberate (p. 130), as McNeil takes these achievements as "classés" and believes that Budé's greater importance lies in "his *advocacy* of philology" (*ibid.*): he goes so far as to say that "others in his century could have accomplished all this without him." It may be asked, however, to what extent we do have detailed and up-to-date analyses of Budé's scholarly achievements; and whether Budé was not also important because he was the man of the *moment;* without him surely the course of French humanism would have been more halting, and lesser, though not insignificant, figures might not have made the contributions that helped to form the indispensable prelude to the flowering of French scholarship in the middle of the sixteenth century, and indeed to the emergence of the Pléiade. The traditional views of Budé's style(s) are taken for granted, but there are scholars in France today who think well of certain aspects of his writing, and here too, up-to-date reassessment would be welcome. The division of material into the nine chapters works generally well, but this does not prevent fragmentation in the discussion of certain topics (Erasmus' consideration of a possible post in France, pp. 87 and 117, Dreux Budé, ch. I and p. 59, n. 35, with a different date of birth, More, pp. 56 and 61, *disciplinae humanae*, pp. 80 and 82, etc.); and this may lead to unnecessary repetition, sometimes even of phraseology.

The Bibliography is set out under sensible subsections. The list of secondary works is quite copious for the size of the monograph: I would add J. Paquot's thesis on Jérôme Aléandre, M. A. Screech's complementary article to that of Duncan Derrett mentioned on p. 145 (also *BHR*), Mme. de la Garanderie's article on Budé in Franco Simone's *Dizionario critico*, D. Maffei, *Gli inizi dell'Umanesimo giuridico*, Milan, 1955; Professor Simone's introduction to *Politique et culture à l'époque de la Renaissance* (Acta of the Turin-Venice Congress 1971) no doubt appeared too late to be taken into account. The listing of the primary material is less satisfactory. There is no clear order in the setting out of the manuscripts, which appear to be incomplete; sources or copies in the Institut, Rouen, the Arsenal, Bremen, or Geneva are omitted, though Bremen and the Arsenal are mentioned in the main text. The list of published primary sources (p. 134) is not displayed in any comprehensible order, and to mention editions simply by date and place is not really enough (e.g., the *Institution du Prince*). And in Section B (*Other Contemporary Imprints*), p. 135, there appears the 1783 edition of Vives.

As a provisional monograph, this book may have its uses; but what is more urgently needed now are, first, more studies of individual texts; second, further explorations into Budé's links with humanists, especially those whose appearance in the correspondence is nugatory or nonexistent; third, and most important, closer inquiry into Budé's early intellectual and religious formation. It is often claimed that Budé's real merits have been obscured by his own indigestible style and apparently formless treatises, not to speak of his predilection for writing in Latin. But it is also because his range is so great that it is very difficult for one man to cover the field; this is no doubt one reason why Henri II Estienne has never been the subject of an adequate general study. Of humanists such as this, *veritas filia temporis.*

I. D. McFarlane
University of Oxford

Mark U. Edwards. *Luther and the False Brethren*. Stanford: Stanford University Press, 1975. Pp. 242. $10.00.

The subject of this book is Luther's polemics with his fellow evangelicals between 1522–1546. During this period Luther had the most bitter quarrels with Karlstadt, Müntzer, Zwingli, Oecolampadius, Bucer, Agricola, and Schwenckfeld. Among the issues over which they disagreed were the nature of Christ's presence in the Lord's Supper, the liturgy, the relation of law and gospel, and the separation of secular and spiritual authority. Edwards finds that Luther progressively made unique claims about himself after the confrontation with Karlstadt and the Wittenberg radicals in 1522. Thereafter he became hypersensitive to disagreement, perceiving it as competitive with his authority and even a danger and disgrace to the Reformation. Forced to separate his Reformation from Karlstadt and the Wittenberg radicals in order to save it from political suppression, Luther denounced them as false prophets led by Satan. A pattern of *ad hominem* argument was here established and continued thereafter whenever Luther found himself challenged by evangelical opponents. He became convinced that Karlstadt was an atheist and even believed a story that the Devil took him away at his death. He described Zwingli as "unChristian" and despaired of his salvation.

Edwards believes that Luther might have been less aggressive and self-assertive had Melanchthon been stronger. But he also suspects that Luther found himself in a situation that could not be controlled by theological arguments alone and rather required the strongest possible personal assertions of authority. Whatever the exact reasons for it, by the 1530s Luther saw himself as far more than the humble Wittenberg Doctor of Theology who began the Reformation in 1517. He came to identify himself closely with St. Paul, believing that he was in the same embattled position against his opponents as true prophets and apostles in the Bible had been, and he considered himself possessed with unique spiritual insight into true doctrine.

Most of Luther's evangelical opponents were shocked by his aggressive behavior and uncompromising claims to authority. Many believed that the issues at state were not so important. Whenever they capitulated, even under force, as in the Wittenberg Concord, Luther took it as further confirmation of his rightness. He also tended to be absolutely unforgiving of his opponents. Edwards gives the impression that had his opponents been less deferential and charitable to Luther, the divisions within the ranks of Protestants would have become irreparable. Edwards also suggests that a "humanist concern for modesty and temperance" (whatever that is!) may have been a moderating factor among Luther's opponents.

Edwards may miss the rhetorical dimension in these polemics. Müntzer said equally uncomplimentary things about Luther and also considered himself a true prophet. Zwingli, whose sense of self was every bit as large as Luther's, thought Luther mad and lumped him with the pope. Is the attribution of a Satanic spirit to one's opponent the sixteenth-century version of calling someone an "S.O.B."? And who among the reformers, Protestant or Catholic, did not seen himself in the succession of the prophets and apostles?

There is little new in Edwards' study, but he does assess these well-known confrontations from the novel viewpoint of Luther's psychological reaction to competition from fellow Protestants. Edwards' present research, a study of "old man Luther," promises to deepen and complete what is here begun.

Steven Ozment
Yale University

Stephen Gardiner. *A Machiavellian Treatise,* edited and translated by Peter Samuel Donaldson. Cambridge Studies in the History and Theory of Politics. New York: Cambridge University Press, 1975. Pp. x, 173. $22.50.

And therefore the form of writing which of all others is fittest for this variable argument of negotiation and occasions is that which Machiavel chose wisely and aptly for government; namely, discourse upon histories or examples.

So Bacon in 1605; and even by that date, he knew of no works by Englishmen that could be put beside the Italian's *Discorsi.* Thus the manuscript edited by Professor Donaldson is of astonishing interest: written in the mid-1550s, using historical examples with a very precise political purpose, the work here called *A Machiavellian Treatise* exactly fits Bacon's definition.

Bishop Stephen Gardiner, to whom the *Treatise* is attributed, had spent the reign of Edward VI in prison. Then, when Mary succeeded her piously Protestant brother, Gardiner was once more in a position to be at the center of counsel. Almost at once, he ran into danger: Mary, anxiously seeking a husband, turned toward Philip of Spain, while Gardiner recommended the Earl of Devon. No doubt, Gardiner's recommendation had in it something of personal ambition – he and Devon had become friends in prison – but there was in it too an appreciation of that lightly covered English xenophobia which the importation of a foreign king would surely reveal. For all that, once Mary's mind was made up, Gardiner changed his position, and from an enemy of the Spanish match became an enthusiastic supporter. But the marriage was a failure: it led to Wyatt's revolt; it did not produce a Catholic heir; in the end, it did not even provide Mary with the helpmeet she had dreamed of, for Philip stayed away from England as much as he could. Against this backdrop, we are told, Bishop Stephen Gardiner prepared for Philip a treatise on how a new prince should behave in order to establish himself and his dynasty permanently. The theoretical foundations of the treatise were Machiavellian, the history from which it drew was British.

Two gentlemen – Stephano the Englishman and Alphonso the Spaniard – while away an afternoon by discussing the invasions of England. For much of their time they analyzed the coming of the Saxons: how Vortigern, the last British king, invited in Hengist to help fight the Scots and Picts, how Hengist and his Saxons gradually seized the kingdom from the too-trusting Vortigern. The facts, such as they are, Gardiner took from Polydore Vergil's *Anglica Historia;* the discussion of the value of mercenaries, to which Vortigern's sad story gave rise, came from Machiavelli. Polydore had a few words on how Vortigern alienated his nobility; with the aid of Machiavelli, Gardiner expanded the hint into an analysis of the relationship between prince and barons. Canute's invasion and the Norman Conquest were treated in much the same way. The novelty of Gardiner's approach may be seen in this: the earliest previously known example of treating William I as a Machiavellian new prince was, I believe, John Hayward's book on the three Norman kings (1613).

Plainly this sudden early Machiavellianism needs to be explained. That Machiavelli was known and read in England by 1553 does not require further proof; the puzzle here is that most of the known "Machiavellians" – Thomas Cromwell, Richard Morison, William Thomas – might be listed among Gardiner's political enemies. There is, of course, no reason why Gardiner could not have learned something from his opponents. Moreover, we know that Gardiner was in that band of Englishmen who had an interest in things Italian. Nonetheless, it must be admitted that those of Gardiner's works previously known do little to prepare one for accepting him as a disciple of Machiavelli. One can imagine him quoting some dictum from *The Prince*, but it is rather more difficult to see him writing a historical discourse Historical examples are scarce in Gardiner's treatises and in his correspondence, and his only extended comment on the nature of history (in a letter to Cranmer, 1547) points out how difficult it is to validate the truth of historical stories. Perhaps Gardiner spent the Edwardian years in the Tower reading history and political theory, and made use of his reading to influence the confused politics of Mary's reign. Or perhaps someone found it expedient to put Gardiner's name to the treatise: the two manuscripts were made, and sent, after the bishop's death. Gardiner's or not, the book remains extraordinarily interesting.

Professor Donaldson has used the two known MSS. of the treatise to produce his text; he has provided a translation of the original Italian (made from a lost English draft by one George Rainsford); and the notes, which print the appropriate passages from Machiavelli and Polydore Vergil (among others), indicate the debts Gardiner incurred. Professor Donaldson has promised us as well an edition of Rainsford's own description of England, appended to the original MS. by its translator, as well as a new study of Gardiner. Between them, these two additional works will, I hope, remove the nagging doubts raised by the attribution of the dialogue to Bishop Gardiner. Professor Donaldson has already put us in his debt by publishing this *Treatise*, so sophisticated for its date as to appear almost anachronistic; the task now remains to rewrite the history of Machiavellianism in Tudor England so as to take account of this discovery.

F. J. Levy
University of Washington

Wolfram Setz. *Lorenzo Vallas Schrift gegen die Konstantinische Schenkung*. Bibliothek des Deutschen Historischen Instituts in Rom, vol. XLIV. Tübingen: Max Niemeyer Verlag, 1975. Pp.xix, 247. DM 62.

Lorenzo Valla's work *De falso credita et ementita Constantini donatione* is not only the most widely known text by that celebrated humanist, but also one of the most famous examples of Italian Renaissance thought. In the pages of Setz's careful new edition, Valla reveals the rhetorical and forensic talents that are his special hallmark. No humanist, not even Poggio, can gnaw more ferociously, or with greater satisfaction, on the hide of an opponent, having first riddled it with the arrows of philological and historical argument, personal invective, and self-serving moral outrage. Though Valla was far from the first writer to challenge the genuineness of the Donation of Constantine, or even to demonstrate its spuriousness, the felicitous combination of talents and skills to which I have alluded made it, in a very real sense, *his* issue. Generations of scholars, pamphleteers, political theorists, and reformers beginning with his own contemporaries used his treatise. It circulated widely in manuscript, and then soon in print, with many vernacular translations. Indeed, as Setz shows, the text seems to function almost as a litmus test of the ecclesiologies of important fifteenth- and sixteenth-century thinkers, ranging from St. Antoninus to Ulrich von Hutten, from Antonio Cortese to Martin Luther.

This book, which grows out of the author's dissertation under Professor H. Fuhrmann at Tübingen in 1971, accomplishes more than its modest title would suggest. Setz undertakes an interpretation and analysis of Valla's treatise and an assessment of it in the context of his career and his other writings. His goal is to understand its role in the tradition of humanist criticism and in the history of the running debate on the Donation; and to identify and explain some of the many responses to Valla's work, responses produced by those involved in the substantive elements of the controversy and by later generations of historians who, in Setz's opinion, mistakenly regarded Valla as a forerunner of the *Risorgimento*.

The book retains both the virtues and defects of its original genre. It is organized with a kind of artless rigidity, and one reads it as one would read an outline. It is as easy to consult as a reference book, but it suffers from a pace that is dutifully plodding. There are two major sections, preceded by a bio-bibliographical essay. The first has to do with Valla's critique of the Donation, and consists of three chapters. The initial chapter is a brief synopsis of the interpretation of the *Donation* in the Middle Ages, admittedly a résumé of the findings of Maffei and others. The second discusses the relevant writings of Valla's contemporaries, Nicholas of Cusa and Reginald Peacock, reviewing the well-worn issue of their relationship to Valla's work. The third, and major chapter, concerns the treatise itself, and is in its turn divided into five numbered sections, each of which is further divided into a series of subtopics. This is the central core of Setz's book, for it is here that he develops his own interpretation of Valla as philologian and polemicist, suggests humanist precedents for Valla's approach, and tries to place the work in the context of contemporary events, notably the Council of Ferrara-Florence and the territorial controversies between Pope Eugenius IV and Alphonso, King of Naples. The discussion is cautious, stays close to the texts, and is scrupulous and fair in representing and criticizing other opinions.

Setz aligns himself with a group of scholars (represented in Germany by Peter Herde, and in the United States by Hannah Gray, Jerrold Seigel, and Ronald Witt) which sees much humanist writing, and especially panegyrical, patriotic, and controversial writing, as essentially rhetorical exercise modeled upon Cicero or Quintilian. He claims that Valla has been systematically misinterpreted as a political theorist, whereas he can only be properly understood as a humanist rhetorician, using the eloquence of classical debating style to clarify several juridico-theological issues of long standing. Various bits of evidence are introduced, some of them from Valla's letters, to firm up Setz's argument that ". . . Valla seine Schrift in erster Linie als rhetorisch-literarisches Werk verstanden wissen wollte." Valla's relations with Eugenius and Alphonso are also combed, to show that the humanist intended no disruptive attack on the papacy or its incumbent.

While earlier generations of historians were perhaps overly insistent in arguing that much humanist writing is in some sense a direct product of specific political events, I am inclined to think that the pendulum has swung too far in the opposite direction. To have discovered the formal prototypes of humanist writing and noticed the centrality of eloquence to their self-perception as men of knowledge is not, as some have assumed, to understand their entire motivation. I must take issue with this central aspect of Setz's interpretation, because I think that Valla's treatise, like Bruni's *Laudatio* and *Historia*, must be seen not merely as the literary exercise of a kind of secular monk using Cicero as the Bible, but as a seminal document in the expanding historical and political awareness of Western man. To deny this on the grounds that it is written within a conventional rhetorical mode, or that it utilizes traditional arguments or does not dwell on current issues is like claiming, for example, that *Common Sense* is merely an exercise in Lockean rhetoric.

The second section is a long and very conscientious discussion of the influence of Valla's critique on the ongoing discussion of the *Donation* in early modern Europe. Here again we have six chapters, each broken down into a number of subsections. Most of these are devoted to individual supporters or antagonists of Valla's, including (*contra*) Lauro Quirini, Bartolomeo Pincerno, *Il Galateo*, Lodovico Bolognini, Giov. Ant. Sangiorgio, and Pietro Edo; and (*pro*) Ulrich von Hutten and Martin Luther, who thought Valla was "ein frommer man . . . purus, simplex, dexter, candidus . . . is coniunxit pietatem cum literis." The treatise stirred up a storm of controversy, as churchmen, jurists, and theologians sprang to the defense of the *Donation*. During the Reformation (which Setz calls "Der politischen und religiosen Auseinandersetzung mit Rom") Valla became a kind of cultural hero in the circles of the German humanists and Lutherans. Setz provides useful synopses of all the major works in this long controversy, and gives needed attention to the printed editions of the treatise. Though specific points of interpretation may be open to question, it will be difficult to add significantly to the body of material that Setz has brought together here. Students of both northern and Italian humanism, church history, jurisprudence, the Reformation, and other specialties will consult this section with profit.

An index of names and a bibliography complete the work which, it should be noted, is written in exceptionally clear and serviceable German.

Werner L. Gundersheimer
University of Pennsylvania

Books Received

This list was compiled from books received between 9 February 1977 and 20 January 1978. The publishers and the editorial board would appreciate your mentioning *Medievalia et Humanistica* when ordering.

Abulafia, David. *The Two Italies: Economic Relations Between the Norman Kingdom of Sicily and the Northern Communes*. Cambridge: Cambridge Univ. Press, 1977. Pp. xvii, 310. $32.50.

Ackerman, James S. *Palladio*. New York: Penguin Books, 2nd ed. 1977. Pp. 200, 96 plates. $4.95 paper.

Acta Universitatis Nicolai Copernici: Historia, IX. Torun, 1973. Pp. 314.

Barroll, J. L., ed. *Shakespeare Studies: An Annual Gathering of Research, Criticism, and Reviews*, IX. New York: Burt Franklin & Co., Inc., 1976. Pp. xi, 420.

Beame, Edmond M., and L. G. Sbrocchi, trans. *The Comedies of Ariosto*. Chicago: Univ. of Chicago Press, 1975. Pp. xlv, 322. $17.50.

Bergin, Thomas G., and A. S. Wilson, trans. *Petrarch's Africa*. New Haven: Yale Univ. Press, 1977. Pp. xix, 289. $17.50.

Blaisdell, Jr., F. W., and M. E. Kalinke, trans. *Erex Saga and Ivens Saga: The Old Norse Versions of Chrétien de Troyes's Erec and Yvain*. Lincoln: Univ. of Nebraska Press, 1977. Pp. xxiii, 88.

Bloch, R. Howard. *Medieval French Literature and Law*. Berkeley: Univ. of California Press, 1977. Pp. xii, 267. $14.50.

Bonner, Stanley F. *Education in Ancient Rome: From the Elder Cato to the Younger Pliny*. Berkeley: Univ. of California Press, 1977. Pp. 404. $18.50.

Boswell, John. *The Royal Treasure: Muslim Communities under the Crown of Aragon in the Fourteenth Century*. New Haven: Yale Univ. Press, 1977. Pp. 526. $25.

Branner, Robert. *Manuscript Painting in Paris during the Reign of Saint Louis*. Berkeley: Univ. of California Press, 1977. Pp. xxiv, 270, 412. $48.50.

Brinner, William M., trans. *An Elegant Composition Concerning Relief after Adversity* (Yale Judaica Studies, Vol. XX). New Haven: Yale Univ. Press, 1977. Pp. xxxiii, 196.

Bronson, Bertrand H., ed. *The Singing Tradition of Child's Popular Ballads*. Princeton: Princeton Univ. Press, 1976. Pp. xlvi, 526. Cloth $25.00, paper $12.50.

Brucker, Gene. *The Civic World of Early Renaissance Florence*. Princeton: Princeton Univ. Press, 1977. Pp. xii, 526. $25.

Bulletin de Philosophie Médiévale, Vol. 18. Louvain, 1976. Pp. 140.

Burlin, Robert B. *Chaucerian Fiction*. Princeton: Princeton Univ. Press, 1977. Pp. 292, $14.50.

Burrow, John, ed. *English Verse 1300–1500*. London: Longman, 1977. Pp. xxvii, 397.

Burton, Elizabeth, and F. Kelly. *The Pageant of Early Tudor England 1485–1558*. New York: Charles Scribner's Sons, 1977. Pp. xi, 305. $8.95.

Butterworth, Charles E., trans. *Averoës' Three Short Commentaries on Aristotle's "Topics," "Rhetoric," and "Poetics."* Albany: State Univ. of New York Press, 1977. Pp. 206. $30.

Carmilly-Weinberger, Moshe. *Censorship and Freedom of Expression in Jewish History*. New York: Sepher-Hermon Press, Inc., 1977. Pp. 295. $12.50.

Chaucer, Geoffrey. *Troilus and Criseyde (Abridged)*. Eds. D. S. and L. E. Brewer. London: Routledge & Kegan Paul, Ltd., 1969. Pp. liii, 161. $2.70 paper.

Clark, John P. *The Philosophical Anarchism of William Godwin*. Princeton: Princeton Univ. Press, 1977. Pp. 343. $16.50.

Clemoes, Peter, ed. *Anglo-Saxon England 6*. Cambridge: Cambridge Univ. Press, 1977. Pp. 316. $27.50.

Cooke, Thomas D. *The Old French and Chaucerian Fabliaux: A Study of their Comic Climax*. Columbia: Univ. of Missouri Press, 1978. Pp. 220. $15.

Cottino-James, M., and E. F. Tuttle, eds. *Boccaccio: Secoli di vita, Atti del Congresso Internazionale Boccaccio 1975 Università di California, Los Angeles*. Revenna: Longo Editore, 1977. Pp. 310. Lire 10,000.

Crocker, Richard L. *The Early Medieval Sequence*. Berkeley: Univ. of California Press, 1977. Pp. x, 470; 5 plates, 1 table. $30.

Darby, H. C. *Domesday England*. Cambridge: Cambridge Univ. Press, 1977. Pp. xiii, 416. $45.

David, Alfred. *The Strumpet Muse: Art and Morals in Chaucer's Poetry*. Bloomington: Indiana Univ. Press, 1976. Pp. 280. $15.

Davis, Michael. *William Blake: A New Kind of Man*. Berkeley: Univ. of California Press, 1977. Pp. 181. $12.95.

Edwards, Robert. *The Montecassino Passion and the Poetics of Medieval Drama*. Berkeley: Univ. of California Press, 1977. Pp. 204. $12.50.

Ensor, A. R., and T. J. Heffernan, eds. *Tennessee Studies in Literature*, Vol. xxii. Knoxville: Univ. of Tennessee Press, 1977. Pp. 184. $4 paper.

Erdmann, Carl. *The Origin of the Idea of Crusade*. Princeton: Princeton Univ. Press, 1977. Pp. xxxvi, 446. $28.50.

Finucane, Ronald C. *Miracles and Pilgrims: Popular Beliefs in Medieval England*. Totowa, New Jersey: Rowman and Littlefield, 1978. Pp. 248. $13.50.

Fleming, John V. *An Introduction to the Franciscan Literature of the Middle Ages*. Chicago: Franciscan Herald Press, 1977. Pp. xiv, 274. $10.95.

Ford, Patrick K., trans. *The Mabinogi and Other Medieval Welsh Tales*. Berkeley: Univ. of California Press, 1977. Pp. xii, 205. $11.75.

Forti, Fiorenzo. *Magnanimitade: Studi su un tema Dantesco*. Bologna: Pàtron Editore, 1977. Pp. 238. Lire 7400 paper.

Fraser, Russell. *The Language of Adam: On the Limits and Systems of Discourse*. New York: Columbia Univ. Press, 1977. Pp. 288. $15.

Fussell, Paul. *The Great War and Modern Memory*. London: Oxford Univ. Press, 1975, rpt. 1977. Pp. 363. $3.50 paper.

Gatch, Milton M. *Preaching and Theology in Anglo-Saxon England: Ælfric and Wulfstan*. Toronto: Univ. of Toronto Press, 1977. Pp. xiii, 256. $15.

Gilbert, Martin. *Jerusalem History Atlas*. New York: Macmillan Publishing Co., 1977. Pp. 136. $8.95.

————. *Jewish History Atlas.* New York: Macmillan Publishing Co., 1969, rev. 1976. Pp. 125. $8.95.

Gimpel, Jean. *The Medieval Machine: The Industrial Revolution of the Middle Ages.* Harmondsworth: Penguin Books, 1976. Pp. 274. $2.95.

Given, James B. *Society and Homicide in Thirteenth-Century England.* Stanford: Stanford Univ. Press, 1977. Pp. 262. $12.50.

Grafenberg, Wirnt Von. *Wigalois: The Knight of Fortune's Wheel.* Trans. J. W. Thomas. Lincoln: Univ. of Nebraska Press, 1977. Pp. 236. $10.95.

Grendler, Paul F. *The Roman Inquisition and the Venetian Press, 1540–1650.* Princeton: Princeton Univ. Press, 1977. Pp. 374. $21.50.

Hanning, Robert W. *The Individual in Twelfth-Century Romance.* New Haven: Yale Univ. Press, 1977. Pp. 303. $17.50.

Hawkes, Terence. *Structuralism and Semiotics.* Berkeley: Univ. of California Press, 1977. Pp. 192. $3.95 paper.

Head, Constance. *Imperial Twilight: The Palaiologos Dynasty and the Decline of Byzantium.* Chicago: Nelson-Hall, 1977. Pp. 197. $11.

Heiserman, Arthur. *The Novel before the Novel: Essays and Discussions about the Beginning of Prose Fiction in the West.* Chicago: Univ. of Chicago Press, 1977. Pp. ix, 238. $15.

Hinton, David A. *Alfred's Kingdom: Wessex and the South 800–1500.* London: J. M. Dent & Sons, 1977. Pp. 228. $10.75.

Hollander, Robert. *Boccaccio's Two Venuses.* New York: Columbia Univ. Press, 1977. Pp. xi, 246. $17.50.

Hughes, Kathleen. *The Early Celtic Idea of History and the Modern Historian:* An *Inaugural Lecture.* Cambridge: Cambridge Univ. Press, 1977. Pp. 24. $1.25 paper.

International Medieval Bibliography, July–December 1976. Ed. R. J. Walsh. Leeds: Univ. of Leeds, 1976. Pp. xlvi, 246. $75 paper.

Jahrbuch des italienisch-deutschen historischen Instituts in Trent. Vol. 1, 1975. Bologna: Società editrice il Mulino, 1976. Pp. 289. Lire 12,000 paper.

Jones, J. W., and E. F. Jones, eds. *The Commentary on the First Six Books of the Aeneid of Vergil Commonly Attributed to Bernardus Silvestris.* Lincoln: Univ. of Nebraska Press, 1977. Pp. xxxi, 163. $25.

Kantrowitz, Joanne S. *Dramatic Allegory: Lindsay's Ane Satyre of the Thrie Estaitis.* Lincoln: Univ. of Nebraska Press, 1975. Pp. 166. $10.

Ker, N. R. *Medieval Manuscripts in British Libraries.* Vol. II: *Abbotsford – Keele.* Oxford: Clarendon Press, 1977. Pp. xliii, 999. $66.

Kessler, Herbert L. *The Illustrated Bibles from Tours.* Princeton: Princeton Univ. Press, 1977. Pp. xvii, 157; 213 illustrations. $42.50.

Korzeniewski, Dietmar. *Hirtengedichte aus Spatromischer und Karolingischer Zeit.* Darmstadt: Wissenschaftliche Buchgesellschaft, 1976. Pp. xiv, 148.

Laiou-Thomasakis, Angeliki E. *Peasant Society in the Late Byzantine Empire: A Social and Demographic Study.* Princeton: Princeton Univ. Press, 1977. Pp. xiv, 332. $20.

Lambert, Malcolm. *Medieval Heresy: Popular Movements from Bogomil to Hus.* New York: Holmes & Meier, 1976. Pp. xvi, 430; 12 maps, 8 illustrations. $29.50.

Lansing, Richard H. *From Image to Idea: A Study of the Simile in Dante's Commedia.* Revenna: Longo Editore, 1977. Pp. 173. Lire 7500.

Lutz, Cora E. *Schoolmasters of the Tenth Century.* Hamden: The Shoe String Press, 1977. Pp. 202. $12.50.

McGrath, Daniel F. *Bookman's Price Index: A Guide to the Values of Rare and Other Out-of-Print Books,* Vol. 12. Detroit: Gale Research Co., 1977. Pp. ix, 653. $58.

McGuire, Martin R. P., and H. Dressler. *Introduction to Medieval Latin Studies: A Syllabus and Bibliographical Guide*. Washington, D.C.: Catholic Univ. of America Press, 2nd ed., 1977. Pp. 406. $16.95.

Mahl, Mary R., and H. Koon, eds. *The Female Spectator: English Women Writers Before 1800*. Bloomington: Indiana Univ. Press, 1977. Pp. vi, 310. $15.

Margolin, Jean-Claude. *Neuf années de bibliographie Erasmienne (1962–1970)*. Paris: Librairie J. Vrin, 1977. Pp. xi, 850. $75.

———, et al. *L'Avènement des temps modernes*. Paris: Presses Universitaires de France, 1977. Pp. 771.

Marrocco, W. T., and N. Sandon, eds. *The Oxford Anthology of Music: Medieval Music*. New York: Oxford Univ. Press, 1977. Pp. 240. $15.50 paper.

Matthews, Jack. *Collecting Rare Books: For Pleasure and Profit*. New York: G. P. Putnam's Sons, 1977. Pp. 317. $12.95.

Miner, Earl, ed. *Literary Uses of Typology: From the Late Middle Ages to the Present*. Princeton: Princeton Univ. Press, 1977. Pp. xxi, 403. $25.

Moorman, Charles, ed. *The Works of the Gawain-Poet*. Jackson: University Press of Mississippi, 1977. Pp. xii, 452. $25.

Morton, A. L., ed. *Freedom in Arms: A Selection of Leveller Writings*. New York: International Publishers, 1974. Pp. 354. $2.25.

Nolan, Barbara. *The Gothic Visionary Perspective*. Princeton: Princeton Univ. Press, 1977. Pp. xviii, 268. $16.50.

Ong, Walter J. *Interfaces of the Word: Studies in the Evolution of Consciousness and Culture*. Ithaca: Cornell Univ. Press, 1977. Pp. 352. $17.50.

Osheim, Duane J. *An Italian Lordship: The Bishopric of Lucca in the Late Middle Ages*. Berkeley: Univ. of California Press, 1977. Pp. xvi, 211. $9.

Owen, Charles A. *Pilgrimage and Storytelling in the Canterbury Tales: The Dialectic of "Ernest" and "Game."* Norman: Univ. of Oklahoma Press, 1977. Pp. 253. $12.95.

Papuli, G., ed. *Bollettino di Storia della Filosofia*. Universita degli Studi di Lecce, Italia. Vol. 2, 1974. Pp. 421.

Parker, Geoffrey. *The Dutch Revolt*. Ithaca: Cornell Univ. Press, 1977. Pp. 327. $17.50.

Partner, Nancy F. *Serious Entertainments: The Writings of History in Twelfth-Century England*. Chicago: Univ. of Chicago Press, 1977. Pp. 289. $18.

Pearsall, Derek, ed. *Old English and Middle English Poetry*. London: Routledge & Kegan Paul, Ltd., 1977. Pp. xiv, 352. $17.75.

Pedretti, Carlo. *The Literary Works of Leonardo Da Vinci: A Commentary to Jean Paul Richter's Edition*. Vols. 1 and 2. Berkeley: Univ. of California Press, 1977. Pp. 871; 350 figures, 48 plates. $60.

Peterson, Clifford, ed. *Saint Erkenwald*. Philadelphia: Univ. of Pennsylvania Press, 1977. Pp. ix, 147; 1 plate. $22.

Petti, Anthony G. *English Literary Hands from Chaucer to Dryden*. Cambridge, Mass.: Harvard Univ. Press, 1977. Pp. 133, 67 plates. $22.50.

Phillips, Mark. *Francesco Guicciardini: The Historian's Craft*. Toronto: Univ. of Toronto Press, 1977. Pp. xi, 195. $17.50.

Planchart, Alejandro E. *The Repertory of Tropes at Winchester*. Vols. 1 and 2. Princeton: Princeton Univ. Press, 1977. Vol. 1: pp. ix, 392; Vol. 2: pp. viii, 395. $22.50.

Rawcliffe, Carole. *The Staffords, Earls of Stafford and Dukes of Buckingham 1394–1521*. (Cambridge Studies in Medieval Life and Thought, Third

Series, Vol. 11). Cambridge: Cambridge Univ. Press, 1978. Pp. xiii, 279. $22.50.

Reeves, Marjorie. *Joachim of Fiore: And the Prophetic Future.* New York: Harper & Row, 1976. Pp. vii, 212; 7 plates, 6 diagrams.

Reynolds, Susan. *An Introduction to the History of English Medieval Towns.* Oxford: Clarendon Press, 1977. Pp. x, 234. $17.75.

Richards, Peter. *The Medieval Leper and His Northern Heirs.* Totowa, New Jersey: Rowman and Littlefield, 1977. Pp. xiii, 178; 46 plates, 2 maps. $12.50.

Ridgway, Brunilde S. *The Archaic Style in Greek Sculpture.* Princeton: Princeton Univ. Press, 1977. Pp. xix, 336; 69 illustrations. $40.

Riley-Smith, Jonathan. *What Were the Crusades?* Totowa, New Jersey: Rowman and Littlefield, 1977. Pp. 92. $9.50.

Ruggiers, Paul G., ed. *Versions of Medieval Comedy.* Norman: Univ. of Oklahoma Press, 1977. Pp. 252. $12.50.

Russell, Frederick H. *The Just War in the Middle Ages.* Cambridge: Cambridge Univ. Press, 1975. Pp. xi, 332. $9.95 paper.

Rustaveli, Shota. *The Lord of the Panther-Skin.* Trans. R. H. Stevenson. Albany: State Univ. of New York Press, 1977. Pp. xxix, 240. $15.

Sawyer, P. H., ed. *Medieval Settlement: Continuity and Change.* London: Edward Arnold. Pp. 352. $39.50.

Shelby, Lon R., ed. and trans. *Gothic Design Techniques: The Fifteenth-Century Design Booklets of Mathes Roriczer and Hanns Schmuttermayer.* Carbondale: Southern Illinois Univ. Press, 1977. Pp. xiii, 207; 8 plates. $15.

Smith, R. E. F. *Peasant Farming in Muscovy.* Cambridge: Cambridge Univ. Press, 1977. Pp. xii, 289. $22.50.

Smither, Howard E. *A History of the Oratorio.* Vol. 1: *The Oratorio in the Baroque Era: Italy, Vienna, Paris.* Vol. 2: *Protestant Germany and England.* Chapel Hill: Univ. of North Carolina Press, 1977. Vol. 1: pp. 480, $24.95; Vol. 2: pp. 393, $21.95.

Somogyi and Somogyi. *Faith and Faith: A Short Cultural History of the Hungarian People Through a Millennium.* Cleveland: Karpat Publishing Co., 1976. Pp. 208. $5.95 paper.

Stinger, Charles L. *Humanism and the Church Fathers: Ambrogio Traversari (1386–1439) and the Revival of Patristic Theology in the Early Italian Renaissance.* New York: State Univ. of New York Press, 1977. Pp. 328. $30.

Tentler, Thomas N. *Sin and Confession on the Eve of the Reformation.* Princeton: Princeton Univ. Press, 1977. Pp. xxiv, 395. $25.

Thrupp, Sylvia L. *Society and History.* Eds. R. Grew and N. H. Steneck. Ann Arbor: Univ. of Michigan Press, 1977. Pp. 363. $18.50.

Tolkien, J. R. R., ed. *The Father Christmas Letters.* Boston: Houghton Mifflin Co., 1976. $8.95.

Tuve, Rosemond. *Allegorical Imagery: Some Mediæval Books and Their Posterity.* Princeton: Princeton Univ. Press, 1966, rpt. 1977. Pp. 461. $5.95 paper.

Ullmann, Walter. *Medieval Foundations of Renaissance Humanism.* Ithaca: Cornell Univ. Press, 1977. Pp. xii, 212. $12.50.

Viator: Medieval and Renaissance Studies. Vol. 8. Berkeley: Univ. of California Press, 1977. Pp. 468. $16.

von Gradenberg, Wirnt. *Wigalois: The Knight of Fortune's Wheel.* Lincoln: Univ. of Nebraska Press, 1977. Pp. 236. $10.25.

Wade, Ira O. *The Structure and Form of the French Enlightment.* Vol. 1:

Esprit Philosophique. Vol. 2: *Esprit Révolutionnaire*. Princeton: Princeton Univ. Press, 1977. Vol. 1: pp. xxiii, 690, $40; Vol. 2: pp. 456, $25.

Warren, W. L. *Henry II*. Berkeley: Univ. of California Press, 1973, rpt. 1977. Pp. 693. $8.95 paper.

Wenzel, Siegfried, ed. *Medieval and Renaissance Studies*. No. 8. Chapel Hill: Univ. of North Carolina Press, 1978. Pp. viii, 133. $10.95.

West, Larry E., trans. *The Saint Gall Passion Play*. (Medieval Classics: Texts and Studies, No. 6). Leiden: E. J. Brill, 1976. Pp. 126. $11.50.

Whitlock, Ralph. *The Warrior Kings of Saxon England*. Atlantic Highlands, New Jersey: Humanities Press, 1977. Pp. 160. $8.50.

Williamson, Craig, ed. *The Old English Riddles of the Exeter Book*. Chapel Hill: Univ. of North Carolina Press, 1977. Pp. xx, 484. $30.

Ziolkowski, Theodore. *Disenchanted Images: A Literary Iconology*. Princeton: Princeton Univ. Press, 1977. Pp. ix, 273. $12.50.